To Juliet

The Theft of History

Jack Goody

CAMBRIDGE
UNIVERSITY PRESS

CAMBRIDGE
UNIVERSITY PRESS

University Printing House, Cambridge CB2 8BS, United Kingdom

One Liberty Plaza, 20th Floor, New York, NY 10006, USA

477 Williamstown Road, Port Melbourne, VIC 3207, Australia

314-321, 3rd Floor, Plot 3, Splendor Forum, Jasola District Centre, New Delhi - 110025, India

79 Anson Road, #06-04/06, Singapore 079906

Cambridge University Press is part of the University of Cambridge.

It furthers the University's mission by disseminating knowledge in the pursuit of education, learning and research at the highest international levels of excellence.

www.cambridge.org
Information on this title: www.cambridge.org/9781107683556

© Jack Goody 2006

First published 2006
Fifth printing 2010
Canto Classics edition 2012
4th printing 2018

A catalogue record for this publication is available from the British Library

ISBN 978-1-107-68355-6 Paperback

Too often the generalizations of social science – and this is as true in Asia as it is in the West – rest on the belief that the West occupies the normative starting position for constructing general knowledge. Almost all our categories – politics and economy, state and society, feudalism and capitalism – have been conceptualized primarily on the basis of Western historical experience.　(Blue and Brook 1999)

The Euro-American domination of world scholarship has to be accepted, for the moment, as an unfortunate but ineluctable counterpart of the parallel development of the material power and intellectual resources of the western world. But its dangers need to be recognized and constant attempts made to transcend them. Anthropology is a suitable vehicle for such an effect . . .　(Southall 1998)

Contents

Acknowledgements

I have presented versions of chapters of this book at conferences: on Norbert Elias in Mainz, in Montreal and in Berlin on Braudel (and Weber), on values at a UNESCO conference in Alexandria, more generally on the topic of world history at the Comparative History Seminar in London, on love to one organized by Luisa Passerini, to the Indian Section of the Johns Hopkins University in Washington, at the American University in Beirut, the Institute of Advanced Studies at Princeton, and extensively at the Cultural Studies Programme of Bilgi University in Istanbul.

In this enterprise, certainly one where angels might well fear to tread, a product of *la pensée sauvage* rather than *la pensée domestiquée*, but which touches upon many of my earlier interests, I have been much stimulated by the support and help of friends, especially Juliet Mitchell (not only for intellectual reasons but also for morale), Peter Burke, Chris Hann, Richard Fisher, Joe McDermott, Dick Whittaker, and many others including my son Lokamitra. I'm also most grateful for the assistance provided by Susan Mansfield (organizing), Melanie Hale (computing), Mark Offord (computing, editing), Manuela Wedgwood (editing), and Peter Hutton (library).

Introduction

The 'theft of history' of the title refers to the take-over of history by the west. That is, the past is conceptualized and presented according to what happened on the provincial scale of Europe, often western Europe, and then imposed upon the rest of the world. That continent makes many claims to having invented a range of value-laden institutions such as 'democracy', mercantile 'capitalism', freedom, individualism. However, these institutions are found over a much more widespread range of human societies. I argue that the same is true of certain emotions such as love (or romantic love) which have often been seen as having appeared in Europe alone in the twelfth century and as being intrinsic to the modernization of the west (the urban family, for example).

That is clear if we look at the account by the distinguished historian Trevor-Roper in his book, *The rise of Christian Europe*. He recognizes Europe's outstanding achievement since the Renaissance (though some comparative historians would put its advantage as dating only from the nineteenth century). But those achievements he regards as being produced uniquely by that continent. The advantage may be temporary but he argues:

The new rulers of the world, whoever they may be, will inherit a position that has been built up by Europe, and by Europe alone. It is European techniques, European examples, European ideas which have shaken the non-European world out of its past – out of barbarism in Africa, out of a far older, slower, more majestic civilisation in Asia; and the history of the world, for the last five centuries, in so far as it has significance, has been European history. I do not think that we need to make any apology if our study of history is European-centric.[1]

Yet he argues that the job of the historian is 'To test it [his philosophy], a historian must start to travel abroad, even in hostile country.' Trevor-Roper I suggest has not travelled far outside Europe either conceptually or empirically. Moreover, while accepting that concrete advantages began

---

[1] Trevor-Roper 1965: 11.

with the Renaissance, he adopts an essentialist approach that attributes its achievements to the fact that Christendom had 'in itself the springs of a new and enormous vitality'.[2] Some historians might regard Trevor-Roper as an extreme case, but as I intend to show there are many other more sensitive versions of similar tendencies which encumber the history of both continents, and of the world.

After several years' residence among African 'tribes' as well as in a simple kingdom in Ghana, I came to question a number of the claims Europeans make to have 'invented' forms of government (such as democracy), forms of kinship (such as the nuclear family), forms of exchange (such as the market), forms of justice, when embryonically at least these were widely present elsewhere. These claims are embodied in history, both as an academic discipline and in folk discourse. Obviously there have been many great European achievements in recent times, and these have to be accounted for. But they often owed much to other urban cultures such as China. Indeed the divergence of the west from the east, both economically and intellectually, has been shown to be relatively recent and may prove rather temporary. Yet at the hands of many European historians the trajectory of the Asian continent, and indeed that of the rest of the world, has been seen as marked by a very different process of development (characterized by 'Asiatic despotism' in the extreme view) which ran against my understanding of other cultures and of earlier archaeology (both before writing and after). One aim of this book is to face these apparent contradictions by re-examining the way that the basic shifts in society since the Bronze Age of *c*. 3000 BCE have been conceived by European historians. In this frame of mind I turned to read or re-read, among others, the works of historians whose work I much admire, Braudel, Anderson, Laslett, Finley.

The result is critical of the way that these writers, including Marx and Weber, have treated aspects of world history. I have therefore tried to introduce an element of a broader, comparative perspective into debates such as those about communal and individual features of human life, about market and non-market activities, about democracy and 'tyranny'. These areas are ones in which western scholars have defined the problem of cultural history in a rather limited frame. However when we are dealing with Antiquity and the early development of the west, it is one thing to neglect earlier ('small-scale'?) societies in which anthropologists specialize. But the neglect of the major civilizations of Asia, or alternatively their categorization as 'Asiatic states', is a much more serious issue which demands a rethink not only of Asian but of European history too.

[2] Trevor-Roper 1965: 21.

According to the historian Trevor-Roper, Ibn Khaldun saw civilization in the east as being more firmly established than in the west. The east had 'a settled civilisation which has thrown such deep roots that it could continue under successive conquerors'.[3] That was hardly the view of most European historians.

My argument, then, is the product of an anthropologist's (or comparative sociologist's) reaction to 'modern' history. One general problem I had was posed by my reading of the work of Gordon Childe and other pre-historians who described the development of Bronze Age civilizations in Asia and Europe as running along roughly parallel lines. How then did many European writers assume quite a different development in the two continents from 'Antiquity' onwards, leading eventually to the western 'invention' of 'capitalism'? The only discussion of this early divergence was framed in terms of the development of irrigation agriculture in parts of the east as contrasted with the rain-fed systems of the west.[4] It was an argument that neglected the many similarities deriving from the Bronze Age in terms of plough agriculture, animal traction, urban crafts and other specialisms, which included the development of writing and the resulting knowledge systems, as well as the many other uses of literacy that I have discussed in *The logic of writing and the organisation of society* (1986).

I suggest it is a mistake to look at the situation solely in terms of some relatively limited differences in the modes of production when there are so many similarities not only in the economy but in the modes of communication and in the modes of destruction including, eventually, the use of gunpowder. All these similarities, including ones in family structure and culture more generally, were set aside in favour of the 'oriental' hypothesis which stresses the different historical trajectories of east and west.

The many similarities between Europe and Asia in modes of production, communication, and destruction become more apparent when contrasted with Africa, and are often ignored when the notion of the Third World is applied indiscriminately. In particular, some writers tend to overlook the fact that Africa has been largely dependent on hoe agriculture rather than the plough and complex irrigation. It never experienced the urban revolution of the Bronze Age. Nevertheless, the continent was not isolated; the kingdoms of Asante and the Western Sudan produced gold which, with slaves, was transported across the Sahara to the Mediterranean. There it contributed to the exchange of oriental goods by Andalucian and Italian towns, for which Europe badly needed

---

[3] Trevor-Roper 1965: 27.   [4] Wittfogel 1957.

bullion.[5] In return Italy sent Venetian beads, silks, and Indian cottons. An active market loosely connected the hoe economies with the incipient mercantile 'capitalism' and rain-fed agriculture of southern Europe on the one hand, and with the urban, manufacturing economies and irrigated agriculture of the east on the other.

Apart from these links between Europe and Asia and the differences between the Eurasian model and the African one, I was struck by certain similarities in the family and kinship systems of the major societies of Europe and Asia. In contrast to the 'brideprice' (or better 'bridewealth') of Africa whereby the kin of the groom gave wealth or services to the kin of the bride, what one found in Asia and Europe was the allocation of parental property to daughters, either by inheritance at death or by the dowry at marriage. This similarity in Eurasia is part and parcel of a wider parallelism in institutions and attitudes that qualifies the efforts of colleagues in the history of the family and of demography, who were, and still are, trying hard to spell out the distinctiveness of the 'European' marriage pattern found in England since the sixteenth century, and to link this difference, often implicitly, to the unique development of 'capitalism' in the west. That link seems to me questionable and the insistence on the difference of the Occident and the Other appears ethnocentric.[6] My argument is that while most historians aim to avoid ethnocentricity (like teleology), they rarely succeed in doing so because of their limited knowledge of the other (including their own beginnings). That limitation often leads them to make unsustainable claims, implicitly or explicitly, about the uniqueness of the west.

The closer I looked at the other facets of the culture of Eurasia, and the more experience I gained of parts of India, China, and Japan, the more I felt that the sociology and history of the great states or 'civilizations' of Eurasia needed to be understood as variations one of another. That is just what notions of Asiatic despotism, of Asiatic exceptionalism, of distinct forms of rationality, of 'culture' more generally, make impossible to consider. They prevent 'rational' enquiry and comparison by means of the recourse to categorical distinctions; Europe had this (Antiquity, feudalism, capitalism), they (everyone else) did not. Differences certainly exist. But what is required is more careful comparison, not a crude contrast of east and west, which always finally turns in favour of the latter.[7]

There are a few analytical points that I want to make at the outset since their neglect seems to me partly responsible for our present discontents. Firstly, there is a natural tendency to organize experience by assuming the experiencer's centrality – be that an individual, a group, or

---

[5] Bovill 1933.   [6] Goody 1976.   [7] Finley 1981.

a community. One of the forms this attitude can take is what we term ethnocentricity, which was, unsurprisingly, characteristic of the Greeks and Romans too, as well as of any other community. All human societies display a certain measure of ethnocentricity which is partly a condition of the personal and social identity of their members. Ethnocentricity, of which Eurocentricity and Orientalism are two varieties, is not a purely European disease: the Navaho of the American south-west, who define themselves as 'the people', are equally prone to it. So too are the Jews, the Arabs, and the Chinese. And that is why, while I appreciate there are variations of its intensity, I am reluctant to accept arguments that locate such prejudices in the 1840s, as Bernal[8] does for Ancient Greece, or in the seventeenth and eighteenth centuries, as Hobson[9] does for Europe, since they seem to foreshorten history and to make a special case of something much more general. The Ancient Greeks were no great lovers of 'Asia'; the Romans discriminated against the Jews.[10] The rationale varies. The Jews ground theirs in religious arguments, the Romans prioritize in terms of proximity to the capital and to civilization, contemporary Europeans ground it in the success of the nineteenth century. So, a hidden ethnocentric risk is to be eurocentric about ethnocentricity, a trap post-colonialism and postmodernism frequently fall into. But if Europe didn't invent love, democracy, freedom, or market capitalism, as I will argue, it did not invent ethnocentricity either.

The problem of eurocentricity is, however, augmented by the fact that the particular view of the world in European Antiquity, which was reinforced by the authority derived from the extensively used system of Greek alphabetic writing, was appropriated and absorbed into European historiographical discourse, providing an apparently scientific overlay to one variant of the common phenomenon. The first part of the book concentrates on an analysis of these claims with regard to the sequencing and chronology of history.

Secondly, it is important to understand how this notion of a radical divergence between Europe and Asia emerged (this I will discuss mainly for Antiquity).[11] The initial eurocentricity was aggravated by later events on that continent, world-domination in various spheres which was often looked upon as almost primordial. Starting with the sixteenth century, Europe achieved a dominant position in the world partly through the Renaissance, through advances in guns and sails[12] which enabled it to

---

[8] Bernal 1987.   [9] Hobson 2004.   [10] Goodman 2004: 27.
[11] This point relates to Ernest Gellner's argument with Edward Said about Orientalism in Gellner 1994.
[12] Cipolla 1965.

explore and settle new territories and to develop its mercantile enterprise, just as the adoption of print provided for the extension of learning.[13] Towards the end of the eighteenth century, with the Industrial Revolution, it achieved virtually world-wide economic domination. In the context of domination, wherever it occurs, ethnocentricity begins to take on a more aggressive aspect. 'Other breeds' are automatically 'lesser breeds' and in Europe a sophisticated scholarship (sometimes racist in tone, although in many cases the superiority was considered to be cultural rather than natural) manufactured reasons why this should be so. Some thought that God, the Christian God or the Protestant religion, willed it that way. And many still do. As some authors have insisted, this domination needs to be explained. But explanations based on long-standing primordial factors, either racial or cultural, are unsatisfactory, not only theoretically, but empirically, since divergence was late. And we have to be wary of interpreting history in a teleological fashion, that is, interpreting the past from the standpoint of the present, projecting contemporary advantage back on to earlier times, and often in more 'spiritual' terms than seems warranted.

The neat linearity of the teleological models, which bracket together everything non-European as missing out on Antiquity and forces European history itself into a narrative of dubious progressive changes, has to be replaced by a historiography which takes a more flexible approach to periodization, which does not assume a unique European advantage in the pre-modern world, and which relates European history to the shared culture of the Urban Revolution of the Bronze Age. We have to see subsequent historical developments in Eurasia in terms of a dynamic set of features and relations in continuous and multiple interaction, especially associated with mercantile ('capitalist') activity which exchanged ideas as well as products. In this way we can comprehend societal development in a wider frame, as interactive and evolutionary in a social sense rather than in terms of an ideologically determined sequencing of purely European events.

Thirdly, world history has been dominated by categories like 'feudalism' and 'capitalism' that have been proposed by historians, professional and amateur, with Europe in mind. That is, a 'progressive' periodization has been elaborated for internal use against the background of Europe's particular trajectory.[14] There is therefore no difficulty in showing that

[13] This advantage has been queried by Hobson 2004, but we have to account for the success of the 'expansion of Europe' not only in the Americas but especially in the east where it came up against Indian and Chinese achievements in this area. See also Eisenstein 1979.

[14] See Marx and Engels 1969: 504.

feudalism is essentially European, even though some scholars such as Coulbourn have made stabs at a comparative approach, always starting from and returning to their western European base. That is not how comparison should work sociologically. As I have suggested, one should start with features such as dependent land tenure and construct a grid of the characteristics of various types.

Finley showed that it was more helpful to examine differences in historical situations by means of a grid which he does for slavery, defining the relationship between a number of servile statuses, including serfdom, tenancy, and employment, rather than using a categorical distinction, for example, between slave and freeman, since there are many possible gradations.[15] A similar difficulty arises with land-tenure, often crudely classified either as 'individual ownership' or as 'communal tenure'. Maine's notion of a 'hierarchy of rights' co-existing at the same time and distributed at different levels in the society (a form of grid) enables us to avoid such misleading oppositions. It enables one to examine human situations in a more subtle and dynamic manner. In this way one can analyse the similarities and differences between, say, western Europe and Turkey, without getting involved, prematurely, in gross and misleading statements of the kind, 'Europe had feudalism, Turkey did not'. As Mundy and others have shown, in a number of ways Turkey had something that resembled the European form.[16] Using a grid, one can then ask if the difference appears sufficient to have had the consequences for the future development of the world that many have supposed. One is no longer dealing in monolithic concepts formulated in a non-comparative, non-sociological way.[17]

The situation regarding global history has greatly changed since I first approached this theme. A number of authors, especially the geographer Blaut, have insisted upon the distortions contributed by eurocentric historians.[18] The economist Gunter Frank has radically changed his position on 'development' and has called on us to *Re-Orient*, to re-evaluate the east.[19] The sinologist Pomeranz has given a scholarly summary of what he has called *The Great Divergence*[20] between Europe and Asia, which

---

[15] See Bion 1970, frontispiece and p. 3. Also Bion 1963 where the notion of a grid has been used for understanding psychological phenomena.

[16] Mundy 2004.

[17] While I have spoken of this form of sociological comparison, there are few sociologists capable of carrying out one involving human institutions on a world-wide scale. Nor anthropologists, although in my view it is consistent with the work of A. R. Radcliffe Brown. Both professions are too frequently locked into east–west comparisons of a dubious kind. Probably the Durkheimian school of the *Année sociologique* came closest to achieving a satisfying programme.

[18] Blaut 1993, 2000.   [19] Frank 1998.   [20] Pomeranz 2000.

he sees as occurring only at the beginning of the nineteenth century; before that comparability existed between key areas. The political scientist, Hobson, has recently written a comprehensive account of what he calls *The Eastern Origins of Western Civilisation*, attempting to show the primacy of eastern contributions.[21] Then there is the fascinating discussion by Fernandez-Armesto of the major states of Eurasia, treated as equals, over the last one thousand years.[22] In addition, an increasing number of scholars of the Renaissance, such as the architectural historian Deborah Howard and the literary historian Jerry Brotton, have emphasized the significant part the Near East played in stimulating Europe,[23] just as a number of historians of science and technology have drawn attention to the enormous eastern contribution to the west's subsequent achievements.[24]

My own aim is to show how Europe has not simply neglected or underplayed the history of the rest of the world, as a consequence of which it has misinterpreted its own history, but also how it has imposed historical concepts and periods that have aggravated our understanding of Asia in a way that is significant for the future as well as for the past. I am not seeking to rewrite the history of the Eurasian landmass but I am interested in redressing the way we look at its development from so-called classical times, and at the same time to link Eurasia to the rest of the world, in an attempt to show that it would be fruitful to redirect discussion of world-history in general. I have confined my discussion to the Old World, and Africa. Others, especially Adams,[25] have compared the Old and New World with regard, for example, to urbanization. Such a comparison would raise other issues – their commerce and communication in the development of 'civilization', but it would clearly require greater emphasis on internal social evolution rather than mercantile or other diffusion, with important consequences for any theory of development.

My general goal has been similar to that of Peter Burke in his treatment of the Renaissance, except that I start from Antiquity. He writes: 'I seek to re-examine the Great Narrative of the rise of western civilisation' which he describes as 'a triumphant account of Western achievement from the Greeks onward in which the Renaissance is a link in the chain which includes the Reformation, the Scientific Revolution, the Enlightenment, the Industrial Revolution and so on'.[26] In Burke's review of recent research on the Renaissance he attempts 'to view the culture of Western Europe as one culture among others, co-existing and interacting with its

---

[21] Hobson 2004.   [22] Fernandez-Armesto 1995.   [23] Howard 2000, Brotton 2002.
[24] For details see Goody 2003.   [25] Adams 1966.   [26] Burke 1978: 3.

neighbours, notably Byzantium and Islam, both of which had their own "renaissances" of Greek and Roman Antiquity'.

The book can be divided into three parts. The first examines the validity of the European conception of a kind of equivalent of the Arabic *isnad*, a socio-cultural genealogy, arising from Antiquity, progressing to capitalism through feudalism, and setting aside Asia as 'exceptional', 'despotic', or backward. The second part examines three major historical scholars, all highly influential, who make an attempt to view Europe in relation to the world but who nevertheless privilege this supposedly exclusive line of development, namely, Needham, who showed the extraordinary quality of Chinese science, the sociologist Elias who discerned the origin of 'the civilizing process' in the European Renaissance, and the great historian of the Mediterranean, Braudel, who discussed the origins of capitalism. I do this to make the point that even the most distinguished historians, who would doubtless express a horror of teleological or eurocentric history, may fall into this trap. The concluding part of the book looks at the claim that many Europeans, both scholars and laymen, have made to be the guardians of certain prized institutions, such as a special version of the town, the university, and democracy itself, and of values such as individualism, as well as of certain emotions such as love (or romantic love).

Complaints are sometimes made that those critical of the eurocentric paradigm are often shrill in their comments. I have tried to avoid that tone of voice and to concentrate upon the factual treatment arising out of my earlier discussions. But the voices on the other side are often so dominant, so sure of themselves, that we can perhaps be forgiven for raising ours.

Part One

A socio-cultural genealogy

1   Who stole what? Time and space

Since the beginning of the nineteenth century, the construction of world history has been dominated by western Europe, following their presence in the rest of the world as the result of colonial conquest and the Industrial Revolution. There have been partial world histories (all are partial in some degree) in other civilizations, Arab, Indian, and Chinese; indeed few cultures lack a notion of their own past in relation to that of others, however simple, though many observers would place these accounts under the rubric of myth rather than of history. What has characterized European efforts, as in much simpler societies, has been the propensity to impose their own story on the wider world, following an ethnocentric tendency that emerges as an extension of the egocentric impulse at the basis of much human perception, and the capacity to do so is due to its *de facto* domination in many parts of the world. I necessarily see the world with my eyes, not with those of another. As I have already said in the introduction, I am well aware that contrary trends regarding world history have emerged in recent times.[1] But in my view that movement has not been pursued far enough in a theoretical direction, especially with regard to the broad phases in which world history is conceived.

A more critical stance is necessary to counter the inevitably ethnocentric character of any attempt to describe the world, past or present. That means firstly being sceptical about the west's claim, indeed about any claim coming from Europe (or indeed Asia), to have invented activities and values such as democracy or freedom. Secondly it means looking at history from the bottom up rather than from the top (or from the present) down. Thirdly it means giving adequate weight to the non-European past. Fourthly, it requires an awareness of the fact that even the backbone of historiography, the location of events in time and space, is variable, subject to social construction, and hence to change. It does therefore not

---

[1] See especially the initial discussion in C. A. Bayly's *The Birth of the Modern World 1780–1914*. Oxford, 2004.

consist of immutable categories that emanate from the world in the form in which they are present to western historiographical consciousness.

The current dimensions of both time and space were laid down by the west. That was because expansion throughout the world required time-keeping and maps which provided the frame of history, as well as of geography. Of course, all societies have had some concepts of space and time around which to organize their daily lives. These concepts became more elaborate (and more precise) with the advent of literacy which provided graphic markers for both dimensions. It is the earlier invention of writing in Eurasia that gave its major societies considerable advantages in the calculation of time, in creating and developing maps as compared with oral Africa, for example, rather than some inherent truth about the way the world is organized spatio-temporally.

Time

Time in oral cultures was reckoned according to natural occurrences, the diurnal progression of the sun through day and night, its position in the heavens, the phases of the moon, the passage of the seasons. What was absent was any numeral reckoning of the passing of the years, which would have required the notion of a fixed starting point, of an era. That came only with the use of writing.

The very calculation of time in the past, and in the present too, has been appropriated by the west. The dates on which history depends are measured before and after the birth of Christ (BC and AD, or BCE and CE to be more politically correct). The recognition of other eras, relating to the Hegira, to the Hebrew or to the Chinese New Year, is relegated to the margins of historical scholarship and of international usage. One aspect of this theft of time within these eras was of course the concepts of the century and of the millennium themselves, again concepts of written cultures. The author of a wide-ranging book on the latter,[2] Fernandez-Armesto, includes in his scope studies of the history of Islam, India, China, Africa, and the Americas. He has written a world history of 'our millennium', the latter half of which has been 'ours' in the sense of western dominated. Unlike many historians, he does not see this domination as being rooted in western culture; world leadership can easily pass again to Asia as earlier it had passed from Asia to the west. Nevertheless the framework for discussion is inevitably cast in terms of the decades, the centuries, and the millennia of the Christian calendar. The east as well as the centre often have other millennia in mind.

---

[2] Fernandez-Armesto 1995.

The monopolization of time takes place not only with the all-inclusive era, that defined by the birth of Christ, but also with the everyday reckoning of years, months, and weeks. The year itself is a partly arbitrary division. We use the sidereal cycle, others a sequence of twelve lunar periods. It is a choice of a more or less conventional kind. In both systems the beginning of the year, that is, the New Year, is quite arbitrary. There is, in fact, nothing more 'logical' about the sidereal year which Europeans use than about the lunar reckoning of Islamic and Buddhist countries. It is the same with the European division into months. The choice is between arbitrary years or arbitrary months. Our months have little to do with the moon, indeed the lunar months of Islam are definitely more 'logical'. There is a problem for every calendrical system of integrating star or seasonal years with lunar months. In Islam the year is adjusted to the months; in Christianity the reverse holds. In oral cultures both the seasonal count and the moon count can operate independently, but writing forces a kind of compromise.

The week of seven days is the most arbitrary unit of them all. In Africa one finds the equivalent of a 'week' of three, four, five, or six days, with markets to correspond. In China it was ten days. Societies felt the need for some regular division smaller than the month for frequent cyclical activities such as local markets, as distinct from annual fairs. The duration of these units is completely conventional. The notion of a day and a night clearly corresponds to our everyday experience but once again the further subdivision into hours and minutes exists only on our clocks and in our minds; they are quite arbitrary.[3]

The different ways of reckoning time in literate society all had an essentially religious framework, offering as their point of reference the life of the prophet, the redeemer, or the creation of the world. These points of reference have continued to be relevant, with those of Christianity becoming, as the result of conquests, colonization, and world domination not only the west's but the world's; the seven-day week, the Sunday day of repose, the yearly festivals of Christmas, Easter, Hallowe'en are now international. This has happened even though in many contexts in the west there has developed a widespread secular attitude – Weber's demystification of the world, Frazer's rejection of magic – which is now affecting much of the rest of the globe.

The continuing relevance of religion in everyday life is often misunderstood by observers and participants alike. Many Europeans see their societies as secular and their institutions as not discriminating between one creed and another. Muslim headscarves and Jewish headgear may be

[3] Goody 1968.

allowed (or not) in schools; non-denominational services may be the rule; religious studies make attempts to be comparative. In the sciences we think of freedom of enquiry about the world and all its contents as being a condition of their existence. Religions such as Islam on the other hand are often criticized for holding back the boundaries of knowledge, though Islam had a rationalist trend.[4] Yet the most advanced economy of the world, in economic and scientific terms, is marked by a strong measure of religious fundamentalism and a deep attachment to its religious calendar.

Religious models of constructing the world permeate every aspect of thought to such an extent that, even though they are abandoned, their traces continue to determine our conceptualization of the world. Spatial and temporal categories, originating in religious narratives, are such fundamental and pervasive determinations of our interaction with the world that we are prone to forget their conventional nature. However, at the societal level ambivalence about religion seems to be a general feature of human societies. Scepticism and even agnosticism about religion are a recurrent feature even of pre-literate societies.[5] In literate ones such attitudes occasionally resulted in periods of humanistic thought, as Zafrani describes for Hispano-Magrebian culture in the Golden Age of the twelfth century and others for Christianity in the medieval period. More radical changes of this kind occurred with the Italian Renaissance of the fifteenth century and the revival of classical learning (essentially pagan, though in many cases adapted to Christianity, as Petrarch envisaged). The associated humanism, both classical and secular, led on to the Reformation and to the abandonment of the authority of the existing church, although not of course to its replacement. But both developments encouraged the partial liberation of the frame of knowledge about the world and hence of scientific enquiry in the broad sense. Up to this point in time, China arguably had the greatest success in this field, in a context where there was no single dominant religious establishment, so that the development of secular knowledge, which permitted the testing or reassessment of existing information, was not impeded in the way that often happened with Christianity and Islam. However the ambivalence about religion, the co-existence of the scientific and the supernatural, remains a feature of contemporary societies, though today the mix is certainly different and societies are more divided between 'believers' and 'non-believers', and, since the Enlightenment, the latter have a more institutionalized status. Both however are still locked into specific religious concepts of time where the western notions have come to dominate a multi-cultural, multi-faith world.

[4] Makdisi 1981: 2.   [5] Goody 1998.

Returning to the measuring of time, clocks, which were unique to literate cultures, were obviously an important contribution to the measurement of time. They existed in the Ancient world in the form of the sundial and the clepsydra or water clock. Medieval monks used candles to record the passing of the hours. Complex mechanical devices were employed in early China. But the invention of the verge-and-foliot mechanism, which gave the tick-tock sound and controlled the unwinding of a spring, the clockwork, was a European discovery of the fourteenth century. Other escapement mechanisms had existed in China from 725 as well as mechanical clocks, but the latter were not as developed as they later became in the west.[6] Clockwork, which for some philosophers became the model for the organization of the universe, was eventually incorporated in portable watches that made it easy for individuals to 'keep time'. It also led to their utter contempt for people and cultures who could not, who followed 'African time', for example, and therefore could not conform to the demands of regular employment that not only factory work, but any large-scale organizations, demanded. They were not prepared for the 'tyranny', the 'wage slavery' of nine to five.

In a letter written in 1554, the Emperor Ferdinand's ambassador to the Turkish Sultan, Ghiselin de Busbecq, described his journey from Vienna to Istanbul. He comments on the annoyance of being woken up by his Turkish guides in the middle of the night because they did not 'know the time' (he also claims that they did not mark distances, but that too was incorrect). They did mark time, but by the call to prayer of the muezzin five times a day, which was of course of no use at night; there was the same problem with the sundial, while the water clock was delicate and hardly portable. The mechanical clock, we have seen, was largely but certainly not wholly a European invention, which travelled rather slowly, being taken to China by Jesuit priests in the process of Christianization, and becoming widespread in the Near East only by the sixteenth century. Even then it did not appear there in public places as its presence might seem to threaten the religious marking of time by the muezzin. Busbecq noted that this slowness to adapt was not due to a general unwillingness to innovate as some have posited: 'no nation has shown less reluctance to adopt the useful inventions of others; for example they have appropriated to their own use large and small cannons (in fact, arguably a Chinese discovery) and many other of our discoveries. They have, however, never

---

[6] Needham 2004: 14. He suggests that the insistence on the specificity of the invention of the verge-and-foliot mechanism is an aspect of European face-saving in this area, of redefining the problem of origins to their advantage, as in the case of the magnetic needle and the axial rudder (p. 73).

been able to bring themselves to print books and set up public clocks. They hold that their scriptures, that is, their sacred books, would no longer be scriptures if they were printed; and if they established public clocks, they think the authority of their muezzins and their ancient rites would suffer diminution.'[7] The first part of this quotation indicates that here we are very far from the static, non-innovating oriental culture posited by many Europeans and which we discuss at greater length in chapter 4. However, that rejection of print proved highly significant over the long term, both in respect of the measurement of time and of the circulation of written information. Both were central in the development of what was later called the Scientific Revolution or the birth of 'modern science' – their selective application of the technology of communication impeded advancement after a certain point in time, but this is a far cry from a complete inability to measure time, or ignorance as to its possibility and value. Still less does this reluctance (itself a relatively late phenomenon) justify the view that European ways of measuring time and European periodization are more 'correct', better than others.

There is another more general aspect to the appropriation of time and that is the characterization of western perception of time as linear and eastern as circular. Even the great scholar of China Joseph Needham, who did so much to rehabilitate Chinese science, made this identification in an important contribution to the subject.[8] In my view it was a characterization of an over-generalized kind that wrongly contrasted cultures and their potentialities in an absolute, categorical, even essentialist, fashion. It is true that in China, apart from long-term calculations of eras, there is a short-term circular calculation of years, by which the name ('year of the monkey') rotates in a regular fashion. There is nothing precisely similar in the western calendar beyond the level of months, which do repeat themselves, and in astrology based upon the Chaldean zodiac that maps out heavenly space, and where these months acquire a similar characteriological significance as in the Chinese years. However, it has to be the case that even for purely oral cultures where time-reckoning is inevitably simpler, everywhere one finds calculations of both linear and circular time. Linear calculation is an intrinsic part of life histories, which move steadily from birth to death. With 'cosmic' time there is a greater tendency to circularity, since that is how day follows night, moon follows moon. Any idea of exclusive calculation having to be made in a linear mode rather than a circular one is mistaken and reflects our perception of an advanced, forward-looking west and a static, backward-looking east.

[7] Lewis 2002: 130–1.   [8] Needham 1965.

Space

Conceptions of space, too, have followed from European definitions. They were also heavily influenced by the uses not so much of literacy as by the graphic representation which developed along with writing. Of course all peoples have some spatial knowledge of the world in which they live, of the world around them and of the heaven above, but graphic representation takes a very significant step forward in being able to map more precisely, more objectively, and more creatively, since one can now study lands that are unknown to the reader.

The continents themselves are hardly exclusively western notions, as they offer themselves intuitively to analysis as distinct entities, except for the arbitrary divide between Europe and Asia. Geographically, Europe and Asia form a continuum, Eurasia; the Greeks made a distinction between one shore of the Mediterranean at the Bosphorus and the other. Though they founded colonies in Asia Minor from the archaic period, nevertheless Asia was very definitely the historical other in most contexts, the home of alien religions and alien peoples. Later 'world' religions and their followers, greedy to dominate space as well as time, have even made an attempt officially to define the new Europe in Christian terms, despite its history of contacts with, and indeed, the presence of, followers of Islam and Judaism in that continent,[9] and despite the insistence that contemporary Europeans (in contrast to others) often give to a secular, lay attitude to the world. Meanwhile the clock of years ticks to a distinctly Christian tempo, so too the present and past of Europe is envisaged as 'the Rise of Christian Europe', to use the title of Trevor-Roper's history.

However, conceptions of space have not been influenced by religion to quite the same extent as time. Nevertheless, the position of holy cities such as Mecca and Jerusalem has controlled not only the organization of places and the direction of worship, but the lives of many people who aimed to make the pilgrimage to these sacred sites. The role of the pilgrimage in Islam, one of the five pillars, is well known, and affects many parts of the world. But from early on Christians too were drawn to pilgrimages to Jerusalem and the freedom to make such journeys was one of the reasons behind the European invasion of the Near East from the thirteenth century known as the Crusades. Jerusalem has also been a strong pole of attachment for returning Jews throughout the Middle Ages but more especially with the growth of Zionism and violent anti-Semitism from the end of the nineteenth century. That argument about space, about Israel as a home which eventually led to the massive return of Jews

[9] Goody 2003b.

to Palestine, strongly supported by some western powers, resulted in the tension, conflict, and wars that have raked the eastern Mediterranean in recent years. At the same time, the stationing of western forces in the peninsula of Arabia is seen to be one reason for the rise of Islamic militancy in this region. In this way, religion 'maps' the world for us in partly arbitrary ways, but this mapping acquires powerful meanings relating to identity in the process. The initial religious motivation may disappear, but the internal geography it generates remains, is 'naturalized' and may be imposed on others as being somehow part of the material order of things. As with time, this is precisely what happened with the writing of history up to this day in Europe, even if the overall measuring of space has been less influenced by religion than time.

But the effects of western colonization are apparent. When Britain became internationally dominant, the co-ordinates of space turned around the Greenwich meridian in London; the West Indies and largely the East Indies were created by European concerns, as well of course as by European orientations, European colonialism, European expansion overseas. To some extent both the extreme west and the extreme east of Eurasia were not in the best position to estimate space. As Fernandez-Armesto points out,[10] in the first half of the present millennium Islam occupied a more central position and was best placed to offer a considered world view of geography, as in Al-Istakhi's world map as seen from Persia in the middle of the tenth century. Islam was placed centrally both for expansion and for communication, lying half-way between China and Christendom. Fernandez-Armesto also comments on the distortions created by the adoption of the Mercator projection for maps of the world. Southern countries like India appear small in relation to northern ones like Sweden, whose size is greatly exaggerated.

Mercator (1512–94) was one of the Flemish mapmakers who profited from the arrival in Florence of a Greek copy of Ptolemy's *Geography*, coming from Constantinople but written in Alexandria in the second century CE. The treatise was translated into Latin and published in Vicenza, becoming a template for modern geography by providing a grid of spatial co-ordinates that could be stretched over a globe, with numbered lines from the equator in the case of latitude, and from the Fortunate Isles in the case of longitude. That work arrived at the time of the first circumnavigation of the globe and the coming of the printing press, both important factors in map-making. The 'distortion of space' to which I referred occurred because orbs have to be flattened for the printed page,

---

[10] Fernandez-Armesto 1995: 110.

and the projection is an attempt to reconcile the sphere and the plane.[11] But the 'distortion' took on a specifically European slant that has dominated modern map-making throughout the world.

Latitude was defined in relation to the equator. But longitude posed different problems, because there was no fixed starting point. Yet one was needed, because of attempts to reckon time for navigation, which became more urgent with the development of frequent long-distance voyages. Research at the Royal Observatory at Greenwich, near London, facilitated by the work of the clockmaker, John Harrison (1693–1776), who built a clock that was accurate on ships at sea, meant that eventually in 1884 the completely arbitrary meridian of Greenwich was chosen as the basis for the calculation of longitude as well as for the calculation of time (Greenwich Mean Time) throughout the world.

Map-making and navigation involved the calculation of heavenly as well as earthly space. Once again all cultures have some vision of the sky above. But the mapping of the heavens was developed by the literate Babylonians and later by the Greeks and Romans. Such knowledge disappeared in Europe during the Dark Ages but continued to be pushed forward in the Arabic-speaking world, as well as in Persia, India, and China. The Arabic world in particular, using complex mathematics and many new observations, produced excellent star charts and fine astronomical instruments, exemplified in the astrolabe of Muhammad Khan ben Hassan. It was on this basis that further European advances were made.

Until recent centuries, Europe did not occupy a central position in the known world, though it did so temporarily with the emergence of classical Antiquity. Only since the Renaissance, with the mercantile activities of first the Mediterranean and then the Atlantic powers, did Europe begin to dominate the world, firstly with its expansion of trade, then through conquest and colonization. Its expansion meant that its notions of space, developed in the course of the 'Age of Exploration', and its notions of time, developed in the context of Christianity, were imposed upon the rest of the world. But the particular problem with which this book deals lies in a broader perspective. It deals with the way that a purely European periodization from Antiquity has been seen as breaking away from Asia and its revolutionary Bronze Age and establishing a unique line of development that leads through feudalism, to the Renaissance, the Reformation, to Absolutism and thence to Capitalism, Industrialization, and Modernization.

[11] Crane 2003.

Periodization

The 'theft of history' is not only one of time and space, but of the monopolization of historical periods. Most societies seem to make some attempt to categorize their past in terms of different, large-scale, periods of time, related to the creation not so much of the world but of humanity. The Eskimaux are said to think the world has always been as it is,[12] but in the vast majority of societies present-day humans are not visualized as being the primeval inhabitants of the planet. Their occupation of it had a beginning which among native Australians was characterized as the 'Dream Time'; among the LoDagaa of northern Ghana, the first men and women inhabited the 'old country' (as *tengkuridem*). With the coming of 'visible language', of writing, we seem to get a more elaborate periodization, the belief in an earlier Golden Age or Paradise when the world was a better place in which to live and which humans may have had to abandon because of their (sinful) behaviour, the opposite of the idea of progress and modernization. Again some envisaged a periodization based upon changes in the nature of the main tools humans used, whether of stone, copper, bronze, or iron, a progressive periodization of the Ages of Man that was taken up by European archaeologists in the nineteenth century as a scientific model.

In recent times Europe has appropriated time in a more determined manner and applied it to the rest of the world. Of course, world history has to have a single chronological frame if it is to be unified. But it has come about that the international calculus is basically Christian, as too are the major holidays celebrated by world bodies such as the United Nations, Christmas and Easter, and that is also the case for the oral cultures of the Third World who were not committed to the calculus of one of the major religions. Some monopolization is necessary in constructing a universal science of, say, astronomy. Globalization entails a measure of universality. One cannot work with purely local concepts. But although the study of astronomy had its origins elsewhere, changes in the information society and particularly in information technology in the shape of the printed book (which, like paper, came from Asia) meant that the developed structure of what has been called modern science is western. In this case, as in many others, globalization meant westernization. Universalization is much more of a problem in the social sciences, in the context of periodization. The concepts of history and the social sciences, however hard scholars may struggle for a Weberian 'objectivity', are more closely bound to the world that gave them birth. For example, the terms 'Antiquity' and

---

[12] Boas 1904: 2.

'feudalism' have clearly been defined with a purely European context in view, mindful of the particular historical development of that continent. Problems arise in thinking about the application of these concepts to other times and to other places, when their very real limitations come to the fore.

So one major problem with the accumulation of knowledge has been that the very categories employed are largely European, many of them first defined in the great spate of intellectual activity that followed after the Greeks' return to literacy. It was then that the fields of philosophy and of scientific disciplines like zoology were laid out and taken up in later Europe. So the history of philosophy, as incorporated in European learning systems, is essentially the history of western philosophy since the Greeks. In recent years some marginal attention has been given by westerners to similar themes in Chinese, Indian, or Arabic thought (that is, written thought).[13] However, non-literate societies get less attention, even though we find some substantive 'philosophical' issues in formal recitations like that of the Bagre of the LoDagaa of northern Ghana.[14] Philosophy is therefore almost by definition a European subject. As with theology and literature, comparative aspects have been brought in rather recently as a sop to global interests. In reality comparative history is still largely a dream.

As we have seen, it has been claimed by J. Needham that in the west time is linear while in the east it is circular.[15] There is a limited truth in this remark for simple, pre-literate societies, who have little knowledge of any 'progression' of cultures. Among the LoDagaa, neolithic axes were sometimes turned up in the fields, especially after rain storms, dating from a period before iron hoes were available. They were looked upon locally as 'God's axes' or sent by the rain god. Not that the people had no idea of cultural change. They knew the Djanni had preceded them in the area and would point to the ruins of their houses. But they had no view of long-term change from a society using stone tools to one employing iron hoes. In their cultural myth of the Bagre,[16] iron emerged with the 'first men', as did most other elements of their culture. Life did not move on in the same way, although colonialism and the coming of the Europeans had certainly led them to consider cultural change and the word 'progress', often associated with education, is in current use; the old is firmly rejected in favour of the new. The linear idea of cultural motion dominates.

[13] For example E. Gilson, in *La Philosophie au Moyen Age* (1997), includes a small section on Arab and Jewish philosophy because they impinge directly on Europe (that is, Andalucia). The rest of the world either had no philosophy or no Middle Ages.
[14] Goody 1972b, Goody and Gandah 1980, 2003.   [15] Needham 1965.
[16] See Goody 1972b, Goody and Gandah 1980, 2003.

But linearity of a kind was already present. Human life proceeds in a linear fashion and although the months and years are seen to move in a cyclical way, that is largely because there is no written schema by which to reckon the passing of time. Just as even in western concepts, the circularity of the seasons is certainly built in. But cultural change takes place in a more obvious way, with each generation of motor car being slightly different and 'better' than the previous one. Among the LoDagaa, the hoe handle remains the same shape from one generation to the next, but change has occurred, and in a realm usually thought of as particularly static, 'traditional'.

Linearity is a constituent of the 'advanced' idea of 'progress'. Some have seen this notion as peculiar to the west and so to some extent it is, being attributable to the speed of change which has taken place mainly in Europe since the Renaissance as well as to the application of what J. Needham and others refer to as 'modern science'. I would suggest that some such notion is characteristic of all written cultures with their introduction of a fixed calendar, the drawing of a line. But this was by no means a one-way progress. Most written religions contained the idea of a Golden Age, a Paradise or natural garden, from which humanity had subsequently had to retreat. Such a notion involved a looking backward as well as in some cases a looking forward to a new beginning. Indeed even in oral cultures a parallel idea of heaven could be found.[17] In the past, there was a clear-cut division, only with the coming of a dominant secularity after the Enlightenment do we find a world ruled by this idea of progression, not so much towards a particular goal as from an earlier state of the universe towards something different, even undreamt of, as with the aeroplane, a function of scientific endeavour and human ingenuity.

One of the basic assumptions of much western historiography is that the arrow of time overlaps with an equivalent increase in value and desirability in the organization of human societies, that is, progress. History is a sequence of stages, each driving from the previous one and leading to the next, until in Marxism finally climaxing in communism. It doesn't take this kind of millenaristic optimism, however, for a eurocentric reading of the direction of history – for most historians, the moment of writing is in the vicinity of, if not identical with, the final target of mankind's development. So, what we define as progress is reflective of values which are very specific to our own culture, and which are of relatively recent date. We speak of advances in the sciences, economic growth, civilization, and the recognition of human rights (democracy, for instance). However, there are other standards by which change can be measured – and, to a

[17] Goody 1972.

certain extent, these are present as counter-discourses even in our own culture. If we take an environmental yardstick, for instance, our society is a catastrophe waiting to happen. If we are talking about spiritual progress (the main variety of progress in some societies, even if questionable in ours), we could be said to be going through a regressive phase. There is little evidence of progression in values on a world plane, despite contrary assumptions which dominate the west.

Here I am especially concerned with broad historical concepts of the development of human history and the way the west has tried to impose its own trajectory on the course of global events, as well as the misunderstanding to which that has given rise. The whole of world history has been conceived as a sequence of stages which are predicated upon events that have supposedly taken place only in western Europe. Around 700 BCE the poet Hesiod envisaged the past ages of man as beginning with an age of gold and succeeding through ages of silver and bronze to an age of heroes, leading to the current age of iron. It is a sequence not too different from that later developed by archaeologists in the eighteenth century, running from stone to bronze to iron depending upon the materials from which tools were made.[18] But since the Renaissance, historians and scholars more generally have taken another approach. Beginning with Archaic society, the periodization of changes in world history into Antiquity, Feudalism, then Capitalism, was seen to be virtually unique to Europe. The rest of Eurasia ('Asia') pursued a different course; with their despotic polities, they constituted 'Asiatic exceptionalism'. Or in more contemporary terms, they failed to achieve modernization. 'What went wrong?', as Bernard Lewis asked of Islam, assuming that only the west got it right. But was that the case and for how long?

What then happened to divide the notion of a common socio-cultural development between Europe and Asia, and lead to ideas of 'Asiatic exceptionalism', of 'Asiatic despotism', and of a different path for eastern and western civilizations? What happened later to distinguish Antiquity from the Bronze Age cultures of the eastern Mediterranean? How did the history of the world come to be defined by purely western sequences?

---

[18] Daniel 1943.

2   The invention of Antiquity

Antiquity, 'classical Antiquity', represents for some the beginning of a new (basically European) world. The period fits neatly into place in a progressive chain of history. For this purpose, Antiquity had to be radically distinguished from its predecessors in the Bronze Age, which characterized a number of mainly Asian societies. Secondly, Greece and Rome are seen as the foundations of contemporary politics, especially as far as democracy is concerned. Thirdly, some features of Antiquity, especially economic such as trade and the market, that mark later 'capitalism', get down-played, keeping a great distinction between the different phases leading to the present. My argument in this section has a triple focus. Firstly, I will claim that studying Antique economy (or society) in isolation is mistaken, as it was part of a much larger network of economic exchange and polity centring on the Mediterranean. Secondly, neither was it as typologically pure and distinct as many European historians would have it; historical accounts had to cut it to the size consigned to it in a variety of teleologically driven, eurocentric frameworks. Thirdly, I will engage with the debate between 'primitivists' and 'modernists' which takes up this question economically, trying to point out the limitations in both these perspectives.

Antiquity is held by some to mark the beginning of the political system of the 'polis', of 'democracy' itself, 'freedom' and the rule of law. Economically, it was distinct, based upon slavery, upon redistribution but not upon the market and commerce. Regarding the means of communication, Grecian with its Indo-European language made the breakthrough to the alphabet which we use to the present day. There was also the question of art, including architecture. Finally, I discuss the problem of whether there were any general differences between the European centres of Antiquity and those in the eastern Mediterranean, including Asia and Africa that surrounded them.

The theft of history by western Europe began with the notions of Archaic society and Antiquity, proceeding from there in a more or less straight line through feudalism and the Renaissance to capitalism. That beginning is understandable because for later Europe the Greek and Roman experience represented the very dawn of 'history', with the adoption of alphabetic writing (before writing all was *pre*-history, the sphere of archaeologists rather than historians).[1] Of course, some written records did exist in Europe before Antiquity in the Minoan-Mycenaean civilizations of Crete and the mainland. But the script has been deciphered only in the last sixty years and the records proved to consist largely of administrative lists, not of 'history' or of literature in the usual sense. Those fields appeared in any strength in Europe only after the eighth century BCE with the adoption and adaptation by Greece of the Phoenician script, the ancestor of many other alphabets, and one which already possessed its BCD (without the vowels).[2] One of the first subjects of Greek writing was the war against Persia which led to the distinction made in evaluative terms between Europe and Asia, with profound consequences for our intellectual and political history ever since.[3] To the Greeks the Persians were 'barbarian', characterized by tyranny rather than democracy. This was of course a purely ethnocentric judgement, fuelled by the Greco-Persian war. For example the supposed decline of the Persian empire from the reign of Xerxes (485–465 BCE) arises from the vision centred upon Greece and Athens; it is not borne out by Elamite documents from Persepolis, Akkadian from Babylonia nor Aramaic documents from Egypt, quite apart from archaeological evidence.[4] In fact the Persians were as 'civilized' as the Greeks, especially among their elite. And they were the main way in which knowledge coming from literate Ancient Near Eastern societies was transmitted to the Greeks.[5]

Linguistically, Europe had become the home of the 'Aryans', the speakers of Indo-European languages coming from Asia. Western Asia on the other hand was the home of peoples speaking Semitic languages, a branch of the Afro-Asiatic family that included those spoken by the Jews, the Phoenicians, the Arabs, the Copts, the Berbers, and many others in North Africa and Asia. It was this division between Aryan and other, embodied later on in Nazi doctrines, that in the folk-history of Europe tended to encourage the subsequent neglect of the contributions of the east to the growth of civilization.

We know what Antiquity means in a European context, although arguments have arisen among classical scholars about its beginning and its end.[6] But why has the concept not been used in the study of other

---

[1] Goody and Watt 1963, Finley 1970: 6.
[2] I use the standard dates. Some scholars would put the transmission much earlier.
[3] Said 1995: 56–7.   [4] Briant 2005: 14.
[5] Villing, 'Persia and Greece', in Curtis and Tallis 2005: 9.
[6] For a valuable recent comment about the end of Antiquity, see Fowden 2002.

civilizations, in the Near East, in India or in China? Are there sound reasons for this exclusion of the rest of the world and for the beginning of 'European exceptionalism'? Prehistorians have stressed the largely similar progression of earlier societies in Europe and elsewhere, differently timed but basically following a set of parallel stages. That progression continued throughout Eurasia up to the Bronze Age. Then a divergence is said to have taken place. The Archaic societies of Greece were essentially Bronze Age, though they extended into the Iron Age and even into the historic period. After the Bronze Age, Europe is said to have experienced Antiquity while Asia had to do without. A major problem for historiography is that while many western historians including major scholars like Gibbon have examined the decline and fall of the classical world of Greece and Rome and the emergence of feudalism, few if any have considered in any depth the theoretical implications of the emergence of Antiquity or of Ancient Society as a distinct period. The anthropologist, Southall, for example, writes of the Asiatic mode that 'the first radical transformation was the Ancient mode of production which developed in the Mediterranean, without replacing the Asiatic mode in most of Asia and the New World'.[7] But why not? No reasons are given, except that the Ancient mode was 'an almost miraculous jump in the question of the rights of man (but not of woman)? It was a transition that took place in the eastern Mediterranean partly by 'migration into the setting of societal collapse', a situation which must have happened frequently enough.

Many see the later history of Europe as emerging from some vague synthesis between Roman and native tribal society, a German social formation in Marxist terms, and there has long been disagreement among Romanists and Germanists as to their respective contributions. But even for the earlier period, Antiquity is often seen as the fusion between Bronze Age states and 'tribes' of 'Aryan' origin participating in the Doric invasions, so that it benefited from both regimes, the centralized 'civilized' urban cultures and the more rural, pastoral, 'tribes'.

From the standpoint of the economy and of social organization more generally, the concept of a tribe is not very enlightening. While the term 'tribal' may be a way of indicating certain features of social organization, especially mobility and the absence of a bureaucratic state, it does little to differentiate the nature of the economy. One finds 'tribes' practising hunting and gathering, others simple hoe agriculture, others pastoralism. In any case what is clear about the emergence of what we perceive as the classical civilization of Antiquity is that it was not constructed directly

---

[7] Southall 1998: 17, 20.

on the basis of 'tribal' economies of any of these types. Rather it was built on societies like the Mycenaean and the Etruscan that were heavily influenced by the many advances in rural as well as in urban life that marked the coming of the Bronze Age, not simply in Europe but primarily in the Near East, the so-called Fertile Crescent, together with parts of India and China. During the Bronze Age, about 3000 BCE, Eurasia saw the development of a number of new 'civilizations', in the technical sense of urban cultures based upon an advanced agriculture employing the plough, the wheel, and sometimes irrigation. They developed urban living and specialist artisanal activity including forms of writing, thus beginning a revolution in modes of communication as well as in modes of production. These highly stratified societies produced hierarchically differentiated cultural forms and a great variety of artisanal activities, in the Red River Valley in China, in the Harappan culture of northern India, in Mesopotamia and in Egypt, later in other parts of the Fertile Crescent of the Near East as well as in Eastern Europe. There was parallel development throughout this vast region and there was some communication. Indeed the Urban Revolution affected developments not only in those major civilizations but also in the 'tribes' that lived on their periphery[8] and which are taken to have in part 'fathered' Greek society.

Childe emphasizes the role played by trade in the classical world, as a result of which cultures, ideas, and personnel were widely diffused. Slaves of course were traded and were not just labourers; 'they included highly educated doctors, scientists as well as artisans and prostitutes . . . Oriental and Mediterranean civilizations, having fused, were joined by commerce and diplomacy to other civilizations in the east and to the old barbarisms of the north and south.'[9] Such exchange took place within as well as between societies.

The 'tribes' on the periphery, those 'barbarians' in the technical sense who did not belong to major civilizations,[10] were affected by these major developments in the urban societies with which they exchanged products, helping to transport goods, and which they saw in transit as possible

---

[8] Childe 1964: 159, 'Even resistance to imperialism generates a "Bronze Age economy" dependent on trade at least for armaments . . .'.

[9] Childe 1964: 248–50.

[10] The notion of barbarian as a contrast to civilized was central to the views of Greeks (and others too), not only about tribal peoples, leading them to devalue other actors. Not all Greek writers divided the world into Greeks and barbarians, however. There were some who considered all humans as similar but the 'other' did take on 'a largely negative characterisation . . . in the wake of the Persian wars' (von Staden 1992: 580). Equally there are writers who recognize the debt to other ancient civilizations, just as there are contemporary scholars who have done the same (the matter is sensitively discussed by von Staden [1992]). I am commenting upon a persistent view.

targets for their greater mobility; raiding the towns and their traffic was a way of life for some. This was the situation described by Ibn Khaldun in his fourteenth-century account of the conflict in North Africa between nomadic Bedouin and settled Arabs (or the equivalents among the Berbers) in which the tribes had greater 'solidarity' (*asabiyaa*) as compared to the peoples that were more technologically advanced,[11] a theme that was taken up by Emile Durkheim in *La Division du Travail* under the heading of 'solidarity'.[12] Most of the great civilizations had similar relationships with neighbouring 'tribes' and suffered from similar incursions, the Chinese from the Manchus, the Indians from the Timurids of Central Asia, the Near East from the surrounding desert peoples, the Doric in Europe. There was nothing unique in this respect about the attacks of the Germans and others upon the classical world, except in so far as they were a major factor in the destruction of the Roman Empire and in the temporary eclipse in western Europe of its extraordinary achievements. However the tribes were not simply 'predators'. They were important too, as we shall see, for their own sakes as well as for solidarity and notions of democracy and freedom, features almost universally associated with the Greeks.

What we refer to as Antiquity obviously had its roots in earlier Greece and in earlier Rome; that narrative is the one that most classical historians pursue.[13] And there is general agreement that Antiquity was built upon an earlier collapse of civilization. In 1200 BCE 'Greece looked much like any near-eastern society.'[14] Just as in western Europe there was later a dramatic break with the fall of the Roman empire, so too there appears to have been a similar collapse of Minoan-Mycenaean civilization in Greece about 1100 BCE. Perhaps that collapse was due to invasion but in any case it resulted in the disappearance of the palace culture. The Greek world was subsequently marked by 'contracted horizons: no big buildings, no multiple graves, no impersonal communication, limited contact with a wider world'.[15]

Although there were resemblances to earlier cultures in the area, especially in language, there is also the question, intrinsic to European history, of what differentiated Ancient Society from the contemporaneous or even older societies that followed the Bronze Age, both in the Near East and elsewhere. Changes, we have seen, certainly took place in the former. Palace cultures disappeared (in the west). The Iron Age emerged, here as elsewhere, bringing a much wider use of metals. But the problem is not an absence of important shifts over time. It comes in making

---

[11] Ibn Khaldûn 1967 [1377].   [12] Durkheim 1893.   [13] Osborne 1996.
[14] Osborne 1996: 3.   [15] Osborne 1996: 32.

categorical distinctions between Archaic and Greek society (that is, Antiquity), differentiated from all others, when these differences might be more profitably conceived in less radical developmental or evolutionary terms, especially if they are primarily of local significance. Archaic society was broadly a Bronze Age society, like the rest of its contemporaries; the Greeks belonged to the Iron Age. But the periods followed one another in the same geographical and commercial sphere, with one merging with another. For instance, Arthur Evans, the archaeologist who uncovered the palace at Cnossos in Crete, claimed the Minoans were 'free and independent', the first European civilization,[16] in other words setting a precedent for the Greeks. Freedom and independence are comparative terms and the Minoans were more dependent on others than he reckoned; they were in fact linked to the Near East commercially and it was from there that supplies of tin and copper came (including from Cyprus) as well as other commodities; tin and copper were needed to make bronze. Cultural links were also present; there is evidence of relations with Egypt, as is proved by the painting in a tomb in the Valley of Kings dated around 1500 BCE, which indicates the existence of relationships between Europe, Africa, and Asia.

Modes of communication: the alphabet

One of the results of thinking in terms of the tribal invasion of Greece by Aryan speakers has been the neglect of Semitic contributions and too much stress being placed upon the Greek contributions to what were undoubtedly developments of great importance. For example, in the modes of communication the Greeks added vowel signs to the Semitic schema and therefore, in the eyes of some scholars, 'invented' the alphabet. The new alphabet became a most important instrument for communication and expression. But in fact a great deal could already be accomplished with the consonantal alphabet, sufficient for the Jews to produce the Old Testament which serves as the basis for Judaism, Christianity, and Islam alike. That was already an enormous historical, literary as well as a religious achievement. So too were the literatures of Arabic and of Indian languages which developed from the Aramaic version of the Semitic script, again without vowels.[17] But these achievements were constantly played down in relation to the Greek, whose position was always assessed from the standpoint of the later European dominance of the world, that is, teleologically. That is the problem of Hellenocentricism.[18]

[16] Evans 1921–35.   [17] Goody 1987.
[18] See von Staden 1992 for a comprehensive and sensitive discussion of this point.

A type of alphabet, one that did not represent vowels but only conso-
nants, had long been available in Asia, from about 1500 BCE, where it had
permitted a big extension of literacy among Semitic-speaking peoples,
Phoenicians, Hebrews, speakers of Aramaic, later of Arabic too. Indeed
the Old Testament, and then the New, used a script of this kind, the
contribution of which has often been neglected by classical scholars concentrating upon the Indo-European languages.[19] Moreover, with other
types of script mankind has performed miracles in terms of accumulating
and diffusing knowledge, for example using the logographic scripts of the
Far East. The Mesopotamians and Egyptians, too, produced substantial
bodies of literature, employing similar scripts, but partly for linguistic reasons they are seen by Europeans as 'oriental' rather than classical. Indeed
many of the supposedly unique achievements of alphabetic literacy were
possible with other forms of writing. The promotion of the alphabet (by
Lenin for example) as 'the revolution of the East' was the counterpart of
his promotion of the nation state in opposition to multinational empires,
since the former supposedly produced the best conditions for the development of capitalism and therefore socialism. It was a very eurocentric
position. Obviously, Chinese script which communicated above the level
of a national language and could be used to teach Confucius in every language was a feature of the multinational empire rather than of national
units, which is why, for cultural-political reasons, the Beijing branch of
the Chinese Communist Party under Mao Tse-tung rejected the alphabet
in favour of retaining the characters.[20]

One of the features of the transition from Archaic Greece to Antiquity was the loss of literacy and of Linear B. The notion of a period
of illiteracy between the late Bronze Age and the Iron Age in Greece
has been contested by Bernal,[21] who sees the West Semitic alphabet as
having been diffused in the Aegean before 1400 BCE and as therefore over-
lapping with Linear B. He suggests that documents must have survived
from that period but none have yet been discovered; papyrus is subject
to serious decay in European climates. However, he recognizes that there
was 'considerable cultural regression' between the twelfth and the eighth
centuries, after the collapse of the Mycenean palace cultures.

Gradually a revival took place. But when literacy returned in the ninth
century, it was not a revival of the Mycenean script but an adapted alphabetic literacy from Phoenicia that assisted in the transmission and in
my view the composition of the Homeric epics. During the intervening
period of 'illiteracy' contacts had been maintained with Ionia and above
all with Phoenicia, and in particular with Cyprus, a half-way house where

---

[19] Goody 1987: 60ff.   [20] Lenin 1962.   [21] Bernal 1991: 4.

iron-working was of great importance in the new Age of Iron which saw the Mediterranean dispersal of the Greeks and Phoenicians with their particular alphabets.

Communications are not only of great social importance but often provide us with a model for a kind of development, from the shift between (purely) oral and written, from the emergence of logographic, syllabic, and alphabetic scripts, from the advent of paper, printing, and the electronic media; in this, one new form succeeded another but did not replace it, as largely did the changes in means of production. There was a different sort of change. Scholars have emphasized the passage of prehistoric or oral societies to literate or historic ones as being of great significance. So it was. One mode of communication builds on another; the new does not make the earlier form obsolete but modifies it in a variety of ways.[22] The same process took place with the coming of printing, which has been seen as an important 'revolution'.[23] So it was, like writing. But speech and handwriting continued to be of fundamental significance for mankind. Perhaps 'mentalities' changed, but at least the technologies of the intellect did, and there were many continuities, in economic as in political history.

The transition to Antiquity

Let us turn to the general problem that Finley, a leading exponent of Greek achievement, poses regarding the emergence of Antiquity. As we have already noted he perceived a unique sequence taking place in Europe; the world of Classical Greece emerges from the (common) Bronze Age to Archaic and then to Classical Greece. The Archaic did away with the palace complexes of earlier times widespread in the Ancient Near East, and there emerged quite different political systems notably in Athens and in Sparta, which introduced democracy and became more individualist into the bargain.[24] The idea that Mesopotamia consisted of highly centralized temple-palace regimes has now been rejected as being a function of the written recordings.[25] Archaeologists 'have tended, perhaps, to overestimate the degree of centralization and power' of states.[26] There was more heterogeneity than this model implies and there were centrifugal as well as centripetal tendencies that manifested themselves in various ways. For example, 'within the cities themselves, the state may have controlled the production of prestige goods, but did not and could

---

[22] Goody 1987.   [23] Eisenstein 1979.   [24] Finley 1970: 140.
[25] For a recent rethinking of the temple-palace civilization of Mesopotamian society, see Stein 1994: 13.
[26] Stein 1994: 13.

not monopolize the specialized manufacture of everyday goods such as ceramics'.[27]

Archaic society 'invented freely'. 'The political structure, made up of magistrates, councils and, eventually, popular assemblies, was a free invention.'[28] They borrowed much from the Near East but whatever they took

> they promptly absorbed and converted into something original . . . They borrowed the Phoenician alphabet, but there were no Phoenician Homers. The idea of the free-standing statue may have come to them from Egypt . . . but it was the Greeks, not the Egyptians, who then developed the idea . . . In the process they not only invented the nude as an art form but, in a very important sense, they 'invented art' itself . . . The human self-reliance and self-confidence that permitted and fostered such questions, in politics as in art and philosophy, lay at the root of the *miracle grec*.[29]

They invented a personal element in poetry too, as well as social and political criticism,[30] producing a new 'individualism' and seeing 'the emergence of rudimentary moral and political concepts'. In Ionia they 'posed problems and proposed general, rational, "impersonal" answers', setting aside myth in favour of the *logos* or reason,[31] encouraging 'rational debate'.[32] These are extraordinarily strong claims but not unusual. However, many among them cry out for qualification. The political 'inventions' we have found elsewhere. While Phoenicia had no Homer, the Semites did have their Bible. As for 'human self-reliance' and 'self-confidence', how does one begin to make a comparative assessment'?

The notion of 'the invention of art' by the Greeks (even if qualified by 'in a certain sense') seems as proprietary as that of the economic historian, Landes, who writes of 'the invention of invention' by the later Europeans. Equally, the claims to the introduction of the personal element in poetry, to social criticism, to a new individualism, to moral and political concepts, to rationality, seem greatly overstated, embodying ethnocentric claims of the superiority of the European tradition over all others. Greek sculpture should perhaps be considered a special case. It does distinguish Antiquity, for there is nothing quite like it in other cultures. However, these other traditions have their own great achievements such as the paintings on Egyptian tombs where gods are not portrayed in a realistic, anthropomorphic manner as in Greece but in a more phantasmagoric, 'imaginative' way. Then there are the magnificent products of Assyrian sculpture. Ancient Greece was preceded by Cycladic, Mycenaean, and Archaemenic cultures, not to speak of the Hittite and Ancient Near East, and clearly owes something to all these substantial artistic traditions.

---

[27] Stein 1994: 15.   [28] Finley 1970:103–4.   [29] Finley 1970: 145–6.
[30] Finley 1970: 138–9.   [31] Finley 1970: 141.   [32] Finley 1970: 142.

What is remarkable about the European inheritance from Greece as far as art is concerned is not so much that it pointed the way forward, but that the whole artistic tradition was decisively rejected not only by early Christianity, but until quite recently by all three of the major Near Eastern religions. Despite Burkhardt's view of the spiritual marriage between Greece and Germany, for well over one thousand years Antiquity, at least its art forms, were virtually dismissed as achievements of the European tradition. There was no question of a progressive movement. Humanism and the Renaissance had to reinvent the past; in significant ways Islam and, until the nineteenth century, Judaism were virtually aniconic, as were early Christianity and later Protestantism. Representation had to be brought back again, certainly in the secular sphere.

Let us try and look at the problem of the contribution of Greece in more particularistic terms. The classical world that emerged certainly gained some advantage with regard to other civilizations, not only in military and technological terms but also in matters of communication, in what I have called the technology of the intellect, referring to the development of a simplified alphabetic script. In a paper entitled 'The consequences of literacy',[33] Watt and I suggested that the invention of the alphabet had opened the way to a new realm of intellectual activity that had been impeded by earlier forms of writing (which was of course one of the great inventions of the Bronze Age). That is a view that I have come to modify in various ways but not altogether to abandon. The Greek adoption of the alphabet was linked chronologically to the extraordinary burst of writing that took place covering so many different spheres that characterized the classical world and formed the basis of much of our understanding of that time. If there is any substance in Finley's claim about individualism, about new poetic styles, about 'rational debate', about greater self-consciousness, about the criticism of myth, this may well be linked to the greater reflexivity which extensive literacy can encourage. Thought is deepened, more probing, more disciplined perhaps, when your words are thrown back at you on the page. The thoughts of others too can be given a different form of scrutiny when they are presented in 'visible language'. It was not only the new alphabet but the fact that writing was being introduced into a culture that had abandoned literacy but was now anxious to catch up. It caught up not only in adopting a new alphabet and in adopting different materials (no longer clay tablets), but in expanding writing into many artistic and intellectual fields, in making a wider use of literacy.

There were some other ways too in which the classical civilizations of Antiquity achieved a certain comparative advantage in particular spheres,

[33] Goody and Watt 1963.

especially in aspects of building technology which produced the massive monuments that still adorn the landscape of Europe and Asia Minor today. Magnificent cities were built, in Greece, in wider Europe and in Asia and later in Rome. That process continued even after the classical period. In the Hellenistic state 'major Greek cities sprang up . . . making it henceforward the most densely urbanised region of the Ancient World'[34]. 'The proliferation of Greek cities in the East was accompanied by an upswing of international trade and communal property.'

Technology and urban life are areas of human activity in which one can trace specific advances over the long term in a way that is difficult to do with other aspects of human life. In other spheres theories to do with the civilization process seem much more difficult to sustain.[35] 'Other cultures' were equally 'civilized' in a very general sense. However, even as far as technology was concerned, the Greeks were not the only builders of cities, even though their ruins were so impressive for later inhabitants of the region. And they benefited like the rest of the Near East from the making of cheap metal in the form of iron, which facilitated construction in many ways. The widespread smelting of iron, from about 1200 BCE, made metal tools much cheaper and at the same time reduced the dependence of small producers on imports by the state or by 'great households'. Iron ore was available almost everywhere, assisting one aspect of the democratic process, not only in Greece.

The supposed uniqueness of European Antiquity was clearly viewed by Finley as intrinsic to the subsequent development of capitalism, just as many have claimed for feudalism. Both had to be unique because Europe's later development was unique. In Finley's eyes 'the European experience since the late Middle Ages in technology, in the economy, and in the value systems that accompanied them, was unique in human history until the recent export commenced'.[36] That teleological approach is shared and justified by other ancient historians. For example, a recent expert writes, frankly and recognizing some teleological problems:

Because ancient Greece and ancient Rome have in the past enjoyed a special status in European thought, in a very few moves one finds oneself back with the political writings of Aristotle, and the practice of democracy in Athens. Time and time again, in pursuing the history of our own society in order to understand its present forms, we find ourselves pursuing myths about ancient Greece and through them the history of ancient Greece.[37]

However that special status in European thought to which he refers does not necessarily indicate uniqueness nor yet ultimate origins. It merely

---

[34] Anderson 1974a: 47.   [35] Elias 1994a.   [36] Finley 1973:147.
[37] Osborne 1996: 1–2.

shows the mythical attributions of post-Renaissance scholars. That does not stop the author from making large claims about the contribution of Greece and the west to world history, particularly to its artistic history.

It is not entirely a European myth that in the classical Greek world we find the origins of very many features which are fundamental to our own western heritage. Whole modes of thought and expression have their fount and origin in Greece between 500 and 300 BC, self-conscious abstract political thought and moral philosophy; rhetoric as a study in its own right; tragedy, comedy, parody, and history; western naturalistic art and the female nude; democracy as theory and practice.[38]

The last sentence makes a very strong claim, even if it is limited to the west but the author seems to say that the world itself owes certain modes of thought to Ancient Greece, which was 'the fount'; that seems an even stronger, and less acceptable, claim.

However, many of these features were present in embryonic form among the Greeks of the pre-classical period. But they were found in other societies too. To talk of moral philosophy as peculiar to Greece, for example, is to neglect the writings of Chinese philosophers, like Mencius. More importantly perhaps, it is to overlook the embryonic moral and philosophical elements in oral works like the Bagre recitations of the LoDagaa.[39] It is true that the *study* of rhetoric as of history may be a feature of written societies and follow from the use of writing, as does 'self-conscious abstract political thought' and other items he lists. But it is an error to suppose that an understanding of the powers of formal speech-making[40] and of politics,[41] for example, needed inventing by the Greeks. They may have treated these features 'more self-consciously' because literacy encourages reflexivity, but that does not indicate an earlier void.

For the classical historian, Osborne, a problem arises because of his insistence on the appropriateness of a 'teleological' approach, on looking at the ancient world for evidence of 'the conditions of our emergence as a civilised society'.[42] Indeed he goes on to suggest that 'In a sense, indeed, classical Greece created the modern world.'[43] Just as one could say that the modern world 'created Greece'. The two are intertwined. What was good about European culture had its roots in Greece; it was part of our identity. Burkhardt actually wrote of a 'mystical marriage' between Greece and his own country, Germany, so that the ancients had to have everything good that marked the moderns. Such claims must arouse a measure of scepticism in a critical reader.

[38] Osborne 1996: 2.   [39] Goody 1972b.   [40] Bloch 1975.
[41] Bayly 2004.   [42] Osborne 1996: 3.   [43] Osborne 1996: 17.

The economy

Much of the uniqueness of Antiquity that was supposed to have set it on
an independent course was connected with advances in literacy, which
made the Greeks very explicit about their own achievements and their
aims. An advantage was attributed to the Greeks in the realm of politics
as well as in art. But there was one area in which the Greeks were seen
by some not as looking forward at all, and that was in the economy.

The influential ancient historian Moses Finley, was very firm on the
fundamental difference between the 'ancient economy' and that of Bronze
Age societies.[44] His view owes a great deal to the work of Karl Polyani but
also goes back to the nineteenth-century controversy that centred on two
scholars, Karl Bücher and Edward Meyer,[45] but more widely involved
both Marx and Weber. Bücher saw the European economy developing
in three stages, the domestic, centring on the *oikos*, the urban, characterized by professional specialization and commerce, and the territorial
or national economy, phases which in turn corresponded to Antiquity,
the Middle Ages, and the modern. Meyer on the other hand laid great
stress on the mercantile activity under the Ancient Economy, that is, on
its 'modern' aspects. The latter approach was consistent with the early
notion of Weber (later that was modified and became closer to Marx)
that Roman society was already marked by capitalism, at least by 'political capitalism'.[46] For some authors a general problem behind this trend
was that, in the words of Garlan, modernizing theories 'often led to an
apology for the system of capitalist exploitation' by insisting on the existence of markets in Antiquity.[47] Finley himself firmly set aside links either
with the earlier Near East or with capitalism.

It is not that the Greeks 'invented' the economy as it is claimed they did
with democracy and the alphabet. Indeed they did not, in Finley's view,
have a market economy at all, but nevertheless developed a different form
from those of the Bronze Age which led later to the unique character of
Europe. But in this view the market itself appeared only with capitalism
and the bourgeoisie. However, whilst his Marxist inclinations forbid Finley to allow capitalist features to seep into the Antique economy, they
oblige him to give an account which distinguishes it from its neighbours
and treats it as a preparatory stage for the subsequent phases of European
history.

In view of its development of capitalism, Finley sees 'European civilization as having a unique history, which it is legitimate to study as a

---

[44] Finley 1973.   [45] Will 1954.   [46] Love 1991: 233.
[47] Cartledge 1983: 5. My translation.

distinct subject'.[48] In this schema 'history and prehistory should remain distinct subjects of enquiry'. That means excluding from consideration 'the important, seminal civilizations of the ancient Near East', commonly thought of as prehistoric, whereas Greece was historic, although the division has little ultimate rationality in terms either of modes of communication or of modes of production; much greater use was made of (alphabetic) literacy for communication and expression in classical societies and possibly greater use of slaves in production, but in neither sphere was this society unique. According to Finley, it is no argument for inclusion in the network of Near Eastern societies to stress the borrowings and the economic or cultural connections between the Greco-Roman world and the Near Eastern; jumping many cultures he claims that the appearance of Wedgwood blue porcelain does not require the inclusion of China as an integral part of an analysis of the Industrial Revolution.

On the contrary, emphasizing these connections is scarcely misleading. I would suggest the emulation of the techniques of making porcelain in Delft and the Black Country, as in the case of Indian cotton, should be considered central to the study of the Industrial Revolution, for it was those very processes, transferred from the east, that formed the basis of the transformations that took place. Regarding the separation of history and pre-history I can see no adequate grounds for such a radical dichotomy at that time on the basis of the nature of the evidence concerning the past, especially if it means a neglect of the important question of the transition from Bronze Age cultures. However, Finley also tries to distinguish the Ancient Economy on more concrete grounds when he writes:

The Near Eastern economies were dominated by large palace – or temple – complexes, who owned the greater part of the arable, and virtually monopolized anything that can be called "industrial production" as well as foreign trade (which includes inter-city trade, not merely trade with foreign parts), and organized the economic, military, political, and religious life of the society through a single complicated, bureaucratic, record-keeping operation for which the word "rationing", taken very broadly, is as good a one-word description as I can think of. None of this is relevant to the Graeco-Roman world until the conquests of Alexander the Great and later the Romans incorporated large Near Eastern territories.

As a result, he adds, 'there is not a single topic I could discuss without resorting to disconnected sections'.[49] The Near East has therefore to be excluded. The Greco-Roman world was essentially one of 'private ownership' whereas the Near East approximates to the notion of Asiatic despotism, that is, if we 'concentrate on the dominant types,

---

[48] Finley 1973: 27.   [49] Finley 1973: 28.

on the characteristic modes of behaviour'. The Mediterranean was an area of rain-fed agriculture (seen as a critical advantage for Europe by other Eurocentric writers such as Mann[50]), specializing in the cultivation of olive trees, whereas the river valleys of Egypt and Mesopotamia needed a complex social organization to make the irrigation systems work. But as Finley recognizes the Greeks under Alexander (d. 323 BCE) and later on the Romans controlled precisely those irrigated areas and to the north of the Mediterranean developed great expertise in water control, though not mainly for farming. In any case water was only one element in this dichotomy. The notion of Asiatic despotism and collective ownership follows nineteenth-century ideas of the east, criticism of which appears in chapter 4 as well as under politics below. So too with the idea of dominance, thought of as related to water control. While it is true that the river valleys with their fertile soils gave exceptional yields and came to be of central importance, Mesopotamia included many rain-fed areas, just as the production of olives was especially important in North Africa, around Carthage for example. The temple complexes Finley mentions were not everywhere present in the Ancient Near East and indeed they also appeared in classical society. He himself notes 'the great temple-complex at Delos'[51] with its detailed financial records. None of the economies in the area conformed to a pure type, and there were many similarities between the economic practices of the different societies – enough to discredit any account which concentrates on Greek uniqueness alone.

Nevertheless in Finley's eyes, and his work is followed by many in the present day, the emergence of Antiquity has to be seen in terms of a specific historical process that took place in Greece and nowhere else. The collapse of the civilization of the Bronze Age (not altogether a unique occurrence) was followed by the Dark Age of the Homeric poems (which some have seen as Mycenaean), the emergence of Archaic Greece with its new political institutions and finally the coming of the classical world.

It is, however, not only the nature of the economy but whether such an institution existed at all that was queried. In a recent review of the general discussion, Cartledge follows Finley (and Hasbroek too) in seeing the polis as 'unique in history' (what is not?) and arguing that '"the economy" was not in fact, and therefore was not conceptualised as, a differentiated, quasi-autonomous sphere of social activity in archaic and classical Greece', that it 'belongs to a class of pre-capitalist economic formations in which the distribution and exchange of commodities takes

---

[50] Mann 1986: 185.   [51] Finley 1973: 186.

quite different forms from those current in the modern world, and are, therefore, pre-economic, most relevantly because of the absence of a system of interconnected price-fixing markets'.[52] This is a wider, more abstract difference that does not distinguish Antiquity from that of Bronze Age societies. Here the inspiration is again Karl Polanyi.[53] In his work on *Trade and Markets in the Early Empires* he saw three general patterns of integration, namely reciprocity, redistribution, and market exchange. These different patterns were associated more or less uniquely with specific institutional frameworks. As we have seen, earlier nineteenth-century notions of the Greek economy in Archaic times were dominated by the idea of control by the *oikos*;[54] market transactions were thought by some authors to have appeared only later. With the advent of Polanyi's powerful voice, which came to dominate classical (but not Near Eastern) studies, shifts in the economy were laid out on a more general theoretical frame, early society being marked by reciprocity and redistribution rather than by trade. Polanyi did admit to some mixture but the trend of his argument moved in favour of categorically different types of 'economy', one pattern excluding the other. Market transfers could emerge only in capitalist societies. But unless one defines the market in a very narrow way, they certainly existed much more widely; even with its largely pre-Bronze Age economies, Africa has long had substantive markets for every village, substantive weekly affairs which operated on broadly market principles, which is what Polanyi meant. That is not simply a personal view but one held by most historians and by most anthropologists in the field. Partly this discussion depends upon a difference being made between substantive markets (a market place), and an abstract principle of market exchange. My own argument is that one does not have one without the other. Polanyi insists on what he calls the embeddedness of the Greek and other pre-capitalist economies, that is, on its undifferentiated character in relation to the social system. But as many commentators have noted, he does this only by ignoring the market elements in these economies. Oppenheim, who had much sympathy for Polanyi's approach, already criticized this omission for Mesopotamia. Many critics have done the same for Greece itself, although others, like Hopkins, recognizing some weaknesses, have defended the idea of categorical differences. After examining the Mesopotamian case and comparing it with recent Mesoamerica, Gledhill and Larsen suggest that, in relation both to Polanyi and Marx, we need to take a more dynamic, less static, view of the economy: 'it may be more rewarding theoretically to focus on the processes that lead to cycles of re-centralization after the "feudalizing" episodes to which all

[52] Cartledge 1983: 5–6.   [53] Polanyi 1957.   [54] Will 1954.

ancient empires are subject than to focus on essentially static questions that are concerned simply with the institutionalization of the economic process under phases of greater political continuity. A long-term perspective clearly suggests that ancient empires are more dynamic and complex in their evolutionary trajectories than is often supposed.'[55] Traders were important both to the government and to themselves in early urban societies, such as Mesopotamia and Central America. Akkadian kings intervened on behalf of merchants venturing abroad, while among the Aztecs refusal to trade served as a pretext for an attack.[56]

The problem is that these economic categories tend to impose exclusivity in relation to each other. Taking a Polanyi view that the ancient economy was dominated by redistribution (and in this sense was non-modern) leads to an over-riding tendency to downplay anything that resembles a market transaction. That is what happens in Finley's study of the Ancient Economy in which his effort in this direction, like Polanyi's, was motivated by a dislike of the market. It was part and parcel of their socialist ideologies. The alternative view of Polanyi, then, which once held considerable sway, no longer has much credence. While Cartledge comes down strongly on Polanyi's side, he recognizes that trade was important, if not in pottery, at least in metals (as it had to be in the age of bronze, less so with the more universal iron), but claims that we need to acknowledge Hasbroek's distinction between an import interest and a commercial interest. Are these distinctions in fact exclusive? As for the generality of earlier societies, we have no evidence, quite the contrary, that Neolithic societies excluded market trade and commerce. Indeed in recent societies of that type the exchange of goods and services, not necessarily for 'money', has been of major significance.[57] While it is possible to envisage substantial markets (market places) that do not operate in the same way as contemporary ones, it is difficult to see them as altogether insulated from the pressures of the factors of supply and demand. Indeed, when working in this type of 'neolithic' situation, I experienced a wholesale change in the value of shell money (cowries) in the early 1980s, when this form of currency became more and more difficult to obtain; supply and demand certainly played a part. Despite attempts of both administrations (in Ghana and in Upper Volta) to substitute their own form of currency, cowries continued to be important for cross-border transactions as well as for some ritual activities. But as they became scarcer and scarcer their value as 'modern' currency went up and up. In my view, the attempt completely to separate off market places and market principles

[55] Gledhill and Larsen 1982: 214.   [56] Adams 1966: 164.
[57] See for example Coquéry-Vidrovich 1978 on the 'African mode of production'.

(supply and demand) from other transactional modes is doomed to failure.

The nature of the early economy and the role of commerce also dominates a recent important collection of essays on trade in Antiquity that turns on Finley's work.[58] One of the authors in this collection, Snodgrass, shows the use of heavy freight for importing iron ore and marble[59] in Archaic Greece, but he adopts a narrow definition of 'trade' as 'the purchase and movement of goods without knowledge or identification of further purchaser'.[60] So most shipments of this period could not be classified as trade because one knew the eventual client. He suggests that a similar situation may have existed even for the Phoenicians who were renowned as the great traders of the Mediterranean.[61] But even if this was the case, his definition is far from the only or even the common-sense notion of trade and seems to have been inspired by a desire to make Greece different and more 'primitive' in a Polanyi-type way.

The alternative to this assumption is not the idea that such commercial transactions were identical with those in the modern world. As Hopkins, following Snodgrass, rightly insists, goods can be exchanged in different ways.[62] But a commercial aspect is normally present, as one sees from Greek trading arrangements and from the recognition that in the final stage in the process of creating an archaic statue the 'client pays artist's and assistant's maintenance for a period of work' as well as for the costs of the marble and its transport.[63] Payment is made in various ways. Again we do not insist that these transactions are identical with modern ones (though in this case they are close to those of Michelangelo at the Carrara quarries during the Renaissance), but they are at least comparable and should be treated as belonging to the same general economic grid. Although some may see Greek commerce as displaying a fundamental distinction between an import interest and a 'commercial' one, others might well perceive the categories as non-exclusive. Although Hopkins considers Finley's model of the ancient economy as being 'by far the best available', he then goes on to propose 'an elaboration' in the shape of seven clauses 'to accommodate modest economic growth and decline'. These suggestions seem radically to modify any Polanyi-type view of the ancient economy such as that espoused by Finley; although he declares the Finley model to be 'sufficiently flexible to incorporate this modest dynamic',[64] it might appear to others that this acknowledgement was

---

[58] Garnsey, Hopkins, and Whittaker 1983.   [59] Snodgrass 1983: 16ff.
[60] Snodgrass 1983: 26.
[61] He claims (dubiously) that they could so easily shift to agriculture.
[62] Hopkins 1983: x.   [63] Snodgrass 1983: 20.   [64] Hopkins 1983: xxi.

rather due to the physical presence at the discussion of this 'charismatic and influential' scholar and that in fact Hopkins pointed clearly to the problems with the 'primitivist' position, without at the same time adopting a 'modernist' one.

Finley's view, then, was not universally accepted by classical scholars. Tandy saw new trade activity and population growth in the eighth century BCE as being critical to the development of Greece, especially in the establishment of colonies overseas, with the traders being mostly *aristoi* ('best men'). That activity in turn led to the development of the *polis*, to 'the collapse of redistributive formations'[65] and to the growth of what he calls 'the limited market system, which proved to be the machine that generated the eventual consequences of the economic and social shift: the beginning of private property, land alienations, debt, and the polis'.[66] For him this represents the beginning of the capitalist world, a conclusion that puts him firmly in the 'modernist' rather than the 'primitivist' camp; later on the mercantile economy got firmly established. In this discussion, however, Tandy simply pushes the 'primitivism' of the *oikos* further back to pre-Archaic times where the absence of markets still remains questionable, with the implication that this type of economy, one capable of ultimately leading to capitalism, remains a European prerogative.

Despite the dispute among ancient historians between the 'modernists' and the 'primitivists', despite the use of Polanyi's categories of exchange transactions and of the claims of substantivists, their idea of 'primitive' economies (and society generally) was ill-informed. These ideas make a categorical distinction either between the ancient economy and the preceding ones (as in the work of Tandy) or alternatively between the ancient world and subsequent economies, in particular 'capitalist' ones, as in the work of Finley. There are two problems here. Firstly, earlier societies differ very much among themselves, as between the urban communities of the Bronze Age and the hunting and gathering societies of the K'ung bushmen. To see these all as 'primitive' in an undifferentiated way is a very simple-minded approach. An example of the gathering together of all pre-literate cultures under the one rubric is in Tandy's attempt at comparison of these 'simple' societies with Dark Age Greece. He sees the terms 'small-scale' and 'pre-industrial' as euphemisms for 'primitive', employed in order to avoid upsetting those scholars who find comparisons between archaic Greece and the K'ung San of the Kalahari offensive. Regardless of terminology, the fact remains that he draws close analogies between eighth-century Greek society and non-Western 'primitive' communities; until the organization of the polis, for him, the early

[65] Tandy 1997: 4.   [66] Tandy 1997: 230.

Greeks were 'primitive' in this sense and not what we call 'western'.[67] The comparison is not so much offensive as inadequate; there may well be non-western societies that can be compared with Archaic Greece but the latter is certainly much closer to 'modern' society than the Bushmen of the Kalahari – who had never experienced the urban revolution of the Bronze Age. Lumping together such heterogeneous societies as Bushmen, 'primitives', and Archaic Greece may be consistent with ideologically informed projects as those of Finley and others, but receives little support from the kind of data available to anthropologists.

Secondly, while the emphasis on different types of exchange varies in particular contexts, it is a fundamental error not to recognize the possibility that reciprocity (as in contemporary families) can exist side by side with market transactions. The study of the latter in Africa, for example,[68] does not imply that the political economy is 'capitalist' in any nineteenth-century sense, only that substantive markets are very common both for short-distance and for long-distance trade. The market developed from well before Greece until the advent of industrial capitalism. Weber saw the growth of *latifundia* with its surplus production as giving birth to 'agrarian capitalism'.[69] In this he followed Mommsen, but is criticized by Marx who objects to the very idea of capitalism in relation to ancient society.[70] Marx uses the term for a specific mode of production, to which the notion of the factory system was intrinsic. Clearly that system only emerged as an important feature in later times; however, fundamental 'capitalist' features already occur much earlier.

It should be added that both Finley (in a groundbreaking article on marriage in Homeric Greece) and Tandy make use of anthropological comparisons, but they tend to do so, particularly Tandy, as we have seen, in an a-historical, a-sociological way, comparing Antiquity to an undifferentiated 'primitive' society. That approach is encouraged by the modernist–primitivist controversy, as well as by the work of Marx who paid little attention to pre-capitalist formations, except in *Formen* (1964), by that of Weber, who saw traditional societies as the residual case, the left-over from the analysis of more complex systems (1968), and by Polanyi who treated them as the inverse of market societies. As we see from the title of Polanyi's essay on 'our obsolete market mentality,'[71] these positions are often highly ideological, introducing a particular attitude regarding modern society and the ubiquity of its market activities. But such activities are not in themselves to be associated only with the modern world. We do not intend to take up the position of the 'modernizing'

[67] Tandy 1997: 8.   [68] Bohannan and Dalton 1962.   [69] Love 1991: 18ff.
[70] Marx, *Capital*, 1976, vol. I, 271.   [71] Polanyi 1947.

historians of the classical world. The contemporary western economy is certainly very different. But that does not mean that there are no elements in common, such as trade and markets, even if these have very differing dimensions. Not to recognize the presence of market activities in the ancient world is to blindfold oneself.[72]

As we have seen there can be little doubt that the position of many scholars on this subject derives from an ideological view of markets and an opposition to their taking over increasing areas of human life, as they have constantly done, undoubtedly with some detrimental effects. But the attempt to characterize societies either in Antiquity[73] or the Ancient Near East[74] as non-market is as utopian and unrealistic as those who perceived a 'primitive communism' and absence of 'private property' in Neolithic or in hunting and gathering societies. These societies were more collective than later ones in certain respects; but they were also more individualised in others.[75]

The question of markets is obviously related to the position of merchants and of ports (*emporia*) which has been discussed at length by many authors. Mossé, for example, concludes that the former were men of 'modest origins' with few connections to the life of the city. The 'world of the *emporium*' was marginal to Athens. 'Commerce belonged to the private domain.'[76] However merchants interacted with the rest of the community, for example, if they needed to borrow money from other citizens in order to conduct their commercial activity, and for this purpose the institution of the maritime loan was available, 'the basic mechanism' of which 'survived through Hellenistic, Roman, medieval, and modern times until well into the nineteenth century',[77] testifying to the continuity of trade, trading practices and 'emporia' over two thousand years. Indeed the institutions existed yet earlier and in other civilizations, wherever there was elaborate trade and towns, casting yet more doubt upon the approach of Polanyi, Finley, and others. Not that differences in trading systems were absent, but there were also similarities that are very significant for the understanding of cultural history. So Polanyi's claim that 'merchants never existed in Mesopotamia simply does not stand up to closer scrutiny' according to Gledhill and Larsen.[78] Equally the claim that Ancient Greece did not have an economy[79] should perhaps be treated in the same way in view of the work of Tandy[80] on the power of the market

---

[72] They are constantly stressed by the Marxist prehistorian, Gordon Childe (eg. 1964: 190, where he sees 'an international body of merchants' responsible for the diffusion of the alphabet).
[73] Finley 1973.   [74] Polanyi 1957.   [75] Goody 1996a.   [76] Mossé 1983: 56.
[77] Millett 1983: 37.   [78] Gledhill and Larsen 1952: 203.   [79] Finley 1973.
[80] Tandy 1997.

in early Greece, of Millett[81] on lending and borrowing in ancient Athens
and of Cohen[82] on Athenian banking.

Polanyi did however raise quite explicitly the important question
to which we have referred of the differences between Greece and
Mesopotamia, between Antiquity and the Bronze Age societies of the
Near East.[83] At one level the problem is straightforward. Greece belongs
not to the Bronze but to the Iron Age, with abundant supplies of that
cheaper metal, making tools and arms much more widely available. But
Polanyi is referring to his categories of exchange – reciprocity, etc. Despite
noting what he called the broadly distributional basis of those earlier societies, he also saw other transactional modes as of great economic significance. Commercial activities emerged but in Mesopotamia they were
interpreted as administered trade, carried out by means of equivalences
(fixed prices), special-purpose money, and ports of trade – but no markets, an opinion shared by Finley, who, as we have seen, talks about the
monopoly exercised by great palatial, or temple, complexes. As Gledhill and Larsen, the latter an important scholar of the Mesopotamian
economy, point out, this statement is quite inadequate;[84] even where no
market places existed, markets certainly did. Although Polanyi claimed
there was no word for that institution, at least three are found. Moreover exchange was not confined to 'administered trade'; merchants often
acted on their own account and the better-off used their gains to purchase houses. The two authors write of the private archives of Kanesh in
Anatolia consisting of 'letters, contracts, accounts, bills of lading, legal
texts, verdicts issued by various authorities, notes and memoranda'.[85]
They provide evidence of partnership contracts (*commenda*) of both the
familial and the non-familial kinds, of trading risks (which the contracts
were intended to spread), and of the profit and the loss. To argue in this
way is not, as they insist, quoting Marx, to 'smudge over all historical
differences and see bourgeois relations in all forms of society',[86] but to
recognize continuity as well as discontinuity.

One of these continuities, I have suggested, lies in the sphere of trade,
whose importance and diversity had been emphasized for Bronze Age
societies by the prehistorian Gordon Childe. When urban civilization
developed in Mesopotamia, the fertile flood plain gave abundant return
to farmers but did not provide many basic materials, including wood,
stone, and metals. All these materials had to be imported, largely along
the major rivers. For transport had been revolutionized, 'metallurgy, the

[81] Millett 1991.   [82] E. E. Cohen 1992.   [83] Polanyi 1957: 59.
[84] Gledhill and Larsen 1982: 203.   [85] Gledhill and Larsen 1982: 209.
[86] Marx 1973: 105; Gledhill and Larsen 1982: 24.

wheel, the pack-ass and sailing ships provided the foundation of a new economy'.[87] Trade therefore became increasingly important, leading to the establishment of merchant colonies as at Kanesh in the second millennium. It became 'a more potent agency in the diffusion of culture than it is today. Free craftsman might travel with the caravans seeking a market for their skill, while slaves would form part of the merchandise. These, together with the whole caravan or ship's company, must be accommodated in the home city. Foreigners in a strange land would demand the comforts of their own religion . . . If cults were thus transmitted [an example is given of an Indian cult being celebrated in Akkad], useful arts and crafts could be diffused just as easily. Trade promoted the pooling of human experience.'[88]

The problem with Polanyi's position, and that of many of his followers, is that it adopts a categorical, holistic rather than a historical approach to economic activities, seeing them *either* as redistributive *or* as market, whereas in practice no such exclusive opposition exists. Different practices are present at the same time in different social contexts, for example, reciprocity in the family, the market outside, redistribution by the state. Of course there are varying emphases on these modes of exchange that relate partly to differences in the modes of production; at least at the level of the means of production one can point to substantial differences over time, as for example, between hoe and plough cultivation. But that change does not introduce nor eliminate markets. We need a much more nuanced treatment of continuity and discontinuity, of 'modernism' and 'primitivism'. What we need in fact is to consider the problem of exchange transactions in terms of a grid, explicit or implicit, so that we can assess the range of possibilities (in columns) against specific societies or modes of production (in rows). That approach would be subtler than the usual historical one of dealing in categories, often exclusive. In this way we could test the hypothesis of Greek uniqueness in a more satisfactory way.

Politics

A parallel definition to that of the economy, similarly narrow, is often used for politics, with the result that certain general features are totally appropriated for Ancient Greece. In this context politics is seen as 'the policy or policies pursued by states, rather than the processes that lie behind their adoption',[89] a restricted view that clearly excludes non-state societies as well as an enormous range of activity that many would recognize

---

[87] Childe 1964: 97.   [88] Childe 1964: 105–6.   [89] Cartledge 1983: 14.

as political. 'Primitive democracy', often a feature of small-scale societies, is given no room for consideration.

As a consequence the study of politics gives rise to a set of problems parallel to those of the economy. For example, Finley rejects the possibility of Marx's use of class in Antiquity (since there is no market) and sees both classes and markets as emerging only much later (with 'capitalism'). What he finds on the other hand are status-groups of the Weberian kind (characterized by 'styles of life', rather than the economic classes seen by Marx). Yet he is not altogether consistent, for at one point he writes of the emergence of a 'middle class of relatively prosperous, but non-aristocratic, farmers with a sprinkling of merchants, shippers and craftsmen'[90] around 650 BCE when they made their appearance as the subjects of lyric poetry. This group constituted 'the most important military innovation in all Greek history' being organized in a phalanx of heavily armed infantrymen, called hoplites, who provided their own arms and armour. The 'phalanx for the first time gave the communities of more substantial means an important military function'. He also attributes the origin ('for the first time') of other enduring features of modern political life to Ancient Greece, especially democracy and freedom. Indeed some authors attribute politics itself to that source and a recent classical scholar has boldly entitled his book *The Greek Discovery of Politics*.[91] And in a recent article Žižek argues that what he and others call 'politics proper' appeared for the first time in Ancient Greece when 'the members of the demos (those with a firmly determined place in the hierarchical social edifice) presented themselves as the representatives, the stand-ins, for the whole of society, for true universality.'[92] Politics here appears to refer to democracy alone but it is also used to apply to any activity at a governmental level as well as the manipulation of authority at less inclusive levels ('parish-pump politics') and of systems that have no constituted authority ('acephalous').

In this sphere as in others, the Greek contributions to subsequent socioeconomic developments were highly important for Europe and hence for the world. But to confine political activities (or their discovery) to Greece in such general terms or to exclude economic action means using those concepts in highly specific ways. One possible restriction of the sphere of the political is to claim that it does not exist as such unless it is separated institutionally and not embodied in society, as Polanyi does for the economy. However, the fact that there is a process of social evolution the result of which is the growth of complexity leading to the partial 'disembodiment' of activities and their embodiment in substantive institutions

[90] Finley 1970: 101.   [91] Meier 1990.   [92] Žižek 2001.

does not mean that one cannot profitably use the category of economics, politics, religion, or kinship before that takes place. Indeed anthropologists have always proceeded on the basis that one can, and that is the case with the very notion of a social system in the work of Talcott Parsons and many other sociologists. The approach of some ancient historians to this question creates an unnecessary conceptual gap between scholars dealing in different historical periods and types of society.

There are three aspects of the politics of the classical tradition that are seen as different from other, contemporary societies and as being transmitted to western Europe: democracy, freedom, and the rule of law. Democracy is assumed to be a characteristic of the Greeks and opposed to the 'despotism' or 'tyranny' of their Asiatic neighbours. That supposition is invoked by our contemporary politicians as representing a longstanding characteristic of the west in contrast to 'barbarian regimes' in other parts of the world. The modern aspect of that question I examine more fully in a later section (chapter 9) – here I will concentrate on the ancient world. In his discussion of democracy, Finley recognizes the possibility that 'there were prior examples of democracy, so-called tribal democracies, for instance, or the democracies in early Mesopotamia that some Assyriologists believe they can trace'.[93] But whatever the facts, he observed, their impact on history, on later societies, was small. 'The Greeks, and only the Greeks, discovered democracy in that sense, precisely as Christopher Columbus, not some Viking seaman, discovered America.' 'It was Greek writing provoked by the Athenian experience that the eighteenth and nineteenth centuries read . . .' That was obviously the case, but it represents a totally European and literary appropriation of history, of the 'discovery' of democracy. If we suppose, with Ibn Khaldun for example, that tribal democracies existed elsewhere, while they may not have provided a model for nineteenth-century Europeans, they certainly did so for other peoples. The Greeks, of course, invented the word 'democracy', possibly were the first to give the term a written shape for others to read, but they did not invent the practice of democracy. Representation in one form or other has been a feature of the politics and struggles of many peoples.

One of the 'tribal' peoples with whom I worked, the LoDagaa, constituted a non-centralized, acephalous group of the kind so clearly described by Fortes and Evans-Pritchard in *African Political Systems*,[94] societies in which there was minimal delegation (or imposition) of authority and no institution of chiefship of the kind that marked their neighbours in northern Ghana, the Gonja. Such groups relished the absence of political

---

[93] Finley 1985: 14.   [94] Fortes and Evans-Pritchard 1940.

domination, their freedom, even though they had no specific word with which to describe it. They regarded themselves as being quite free in the same sense as Robin Hood and his band were free.

The presence of such polities was particularly marked in regions such as Africa that practised simple hoe agriculture with shifting cultivation. But 'republican' groups of this kind are reported even in the context of more complex (Bronze Age) agricultural systems, often in hill areas less easy for any central government to control. For example, Oppenheim[95] reports them for Mesopotamia, and Thapar[96] for India. In China a similar kind of polity, closer to the Robin Hood type of Primitive Rebels or of Bandits,[97] existed on the 'water margins'. In North Africa I have referred to the work of the great historian, Ibn Khaldun, on the desert tribes. In Europe we find groups of this kind in some hill areas which escaped the clutches of states, as with the Scottish and Albanian clans. But even more on the margins is the organization of pirate ships which was often based on 'democratic' principles, as if having escaped the authority of states the communities chose to operate a more cooperative system, of a kind similar to that envisaged in some North American colonies. So, words apart, there is no sense in which the Greeks can be said to have 'discovered individual freedom' or democracy. Moreover, the contrast with the Ancient Near East smacks too strongly of the disputed idea of Asiatic or other despotisms which has so long characterized European thinking about oriental cultures.

Even strong central governments are rarely left to rule without taking into account 'the people'. Sometimes this produced violent interruptions. Protest, resistance, 'freedom' movements in various parts of the world, arose independently of any stimulus from Ancient Greece. It cannot be supposed that the popular uprisings that marked the state of affairs in post-war Iraq in 2004, at least among the Sunnis, had anything to do with that inheritance. The same was true of earlier movements in India or China. Neither their impetus nor their origin lay in Greece or Europe,

---

[95] Oppenheim 1964.

[96] Thapar 1966. In a more recent book (2000), Thapar presents an overview of early India and briefly discusses 'tribal' society in a developmental framework as she had previously done in an essay entitled 'From lineage to state', where there is the evolution from one to the other. While this is a perfectly valid framework, it sets aside the problem that not only do lineages persist within states, but 'tribal' societies continue to exist side by side with states. She therefore overlooks the question of the 'articulation' of different political systems, a situation that offers alternative models to the inhabitants (as is the situation in northern Ghana). I do not mean to imply that one can transfer the representative procedures of 'tribal' societies to more complex systems but wish to point out that not only do such alternatives co-exist but that they may stimulate what I regard as a widespread human desire for representation.

[97] Hobsbawm 1959, 1972.

though their modern manifestations may sometimes do. They are related to the permanent problem of the delegation or imposition of power in centralized polities and consequently to 'the frailty of authority' that often marks them.

The effect of the classical world on later European or global history is not straightforward. The west may look upon Athenian democracy as a model but that was not the only type of regime that existed in Greece. 'Tyranny' was also present. Neither tyranny nor democracy had the same values placed upon them as at present. Indeed Finley sees tyranny as often being introduced by popular demand, breaking the aristocratic monopoly of the *demos*. 'The paradox is that, standing above the law and above the constitution, the tyrants in the end strengthened the *polis* and its institutions and helped raise the *demos*, the people as a whole, to a level of political self-consciousness which then led, in some states, to government by the *demos*, democracy.'[98] Tyranny therefore is said to prepare the way for democracy (much as slavery does for freedom), certainly an optimistic view of the world. In any case there was an oscillation between the two, not a direct development, since many in Antiquity thought democracy a bad thing. In Europe too democracy did not definitely take on an unambiguously positive value until the nineteenth century[99] and the development of centralized governments whose rapidly increasing bureaucracies and military required continual financial contributions, by taxation, from the masses. Even then some political thinkers still advocated a stronger rule of the 'best', the 'few', the 'elite'.

How different in fact was Greece from its neighbours? Difference certainly existed but it is always a question of assessing its extent. Most classicists make extravagant claims for its unique contribution. Davis writes of our inheritance of democracy, of the 'Athenian revolution', of how the Greeks 'rightly thought that compared with any others they were notably civilized'.[100] But other societies are disregarded. Castoriadis too sees Greece as 'creating democracy'. He even writes that 'the interest in the other starts with the Greeks. This interest is but another side of the critical examination and interrogation of their own institutions.'[101] One cannot doubt that the Greeks did think a great deal about their institutions; this was an aspect of their extensive use of literacy providing increased reflexivity.[102] But to regard them as initiating an interest in the other is to lose track of the nature of human society itself. Interest in the other has been a constant of man's behaviour, though it could

---

[98] Finley 1970: 107.   [99] Finley 1985: 19.   [100] Davies 1978: 23, 64.
[101] Castoriadas 1991: 268.   [102] Goody and Watt 1963.

and did take many different forms. To regard this feature as an aspect of the 'modernity' of Athens is once again to misunderstand the nature of human society as well as the concept of the modern.

The notion of their invention of democracy is equally suspect. The idea that much simpler societies already displayed democratic features was often expressed in European thought. There was of course the Hobbesian view of early societies as engaged in a war of all against all which could be constrained only by introducing an authoritarian leader in the shape of a chief, an early form of state organization. But there was also the view of philosophers like Kropotkin and sociologists like Durkheim who saw early societies as characterized by 'mutual aid' or by the mechanical solidarity of segmental systems. Both these authors influenced the thinking of the anthropologist Radcliffe Brown (known to his colleagues in Trinity College, Cambridge, as 'anarchy Brown') who developed the notion of segmentary politics in stateless lineage societies that dominated the discussion of African political systems to which I have referred. Segmentary systems practised a mixture of direct and representative democracy as well as reciprocity of a positive and negative kind, together with 'distributive justice'.[103]

One major way in which the choice of the Athenian people was determined was by means of election (here, by written token). However, this procedure was not confined to Greece. In Davis's discussion of the beginnings of democracy, Carthage is mentioned in his survey only in connection with wars, never for its political system. Phoenicia gets treated in an even more summary fashion. But the Phoenician colony of Carthage voted annually for their magistrates, or *sufes*, who appear to have been the supreme authority in the time of Hannibal. Some have seen the term as synonymous with *basileus* or *rex*, others consider the institution to be derived from Rome, but Semitic experts point to the two suffetes conjointly exercising authority in Tyre in the fifth century.[104] 'Some have proposed linking the regular institution of the annual collegial suffetate in Carthage with a "democratic revolution" supposed to have occurred in the Punic city at the outcome of the first Punic War', a hypothesis inspired by Polybius, the Greek historian (*c.* 205–123 BCE), who was taken to Rome in captivity and accompanied Scipio at the destruction of Carthage in 146 BCE. He wrote: 'In Carthage the voice of the people had become predominant in deliberations, whereas in Rome the senate was at the full height of its powers. For the Carthaginians, it was the opinion of the greatest number that prevailed; for the Romans, that of the elite

[103] See for an even simpler society Barnard 2004.   [104] Lancel 1997: 118.

of its citizens.'[105] In other words, a type of representative democracy was at times practised in the People's Assembly not only in Carthage but in Asia, in the mother city of Phoenician Tyre.

In fact it is correct to compare the political arrangements in Greece with those of the West Semites of Phoenicia, partly as the result of similar geographical conditions. Both were 'broken, geographically dismembered territories without a central organizing axis';[106] in Phoenicia the mountains of Lebanon with their forests came down to the sea, in Greece the coast was hilly with narrow valleys. In both cases, the inhabitants looked towards the sea rather than the land. These conditions were consistent with 'the free world of the numerous small . . . city states' which was often contrasted with the 'Oriental military bureaucratic despotisms of Egypt and Mesopotamia'. But the contrast is not altogether correct, as Astour remarks, for Mesopotamia started out from small city-states 'and strong survivals of municipal autonomy of larger cities existed even under the truly despotic neo-Assyrian empire. But even Assyria started out as an almost republican city-state.'[107] In some cases magistrates were appointed for an annual period by selection among the better-off residents.[108] Childe refers to these early Mesopotamian city states as 'primitive democracies'. As a consequence, there is no sharp distinction between Oriental despotism and the democracy of the *polis*, whether of Greece or of Phoenicia. Regarding Mesopotamia, where 'city-states' abounded, Adams writes: 'Yet forty years later his successor in the kingship of Uruk was still constrained to share with an assembly his decision-making powers concerned with warfare'.[109] It is this affinity between the two that Astour sees as the basis for the early Semitic colonies in Greece and later the Greek conquest of the Phoenician coast.

I would suggest that the desire for some form of representation, to have one's voice heard, is intrinsic to the human situation, though there are often authoritarian voices among the elite raised against the practice, and these voices may prevail over long periods. Indeed Finley[110] suggests that even in modern times many representative democracies became elite institutions as a result of the professionalization of politics, which annual elections on the Carthaginian model would do something to combat;[111] there would be more turn-over, more recall, more citizen participation.

---

[105] Polybius VI, 51; Lancel 1997: 118. Unfortunately the bulk of Polybius's history has been lost.
[106] Astour 1967: 358.   [107] Astour 1967: 359, n. i.   [108] Oppenheim 1964.
[109] Adams 1966: 140.   [110] Finley 1970.
[111] An understanding of Carthage, unlike the classical societies of Europe at that time, is limited by the lack of documentary evidence. But that may be the result of the destruction or disposal of the libraries (Lancel 1997: 358–9). Aristotle, too, 'praises the democratic principles of Carthage' (Fantar 1995: 52), with an elected senate that had

The second of the three aspects of politics supposedly inherited from Greece is 'freedom', a feature again associated with their explicit and self-promoting ideology though they certainly practised slavery extensively, as did the Romans. That form of labour continued in later Europe, despite the frequently claimed commitment to freedom; indeed in the Carolingian period slaves were an important part of the continent's exports. Various forms of servile labour continued virtually until the Industrial Revolution, which some have also characterized as wage slavery since individuals had no direct access to the means of production and were therefore bound to work for some employer. Freedom is therefore a more complicated feature than might be thought. And, as Isaiah Berlin pointed out, there is a distinction to be drawn between the negative and positive concepts of liberty, between freedom from interference and coercion, which is seen as a good thing, and freedom to achieve self-realization, which easily slides into a justification for the coercion of others.[112]

Despite these evident lapses, the notion of freedom as a European attribute, inherited from the Greeks, returns time and again. In discussing the failure of later Muslim societies to 'modernize', Lewis goes through many alternative answers to the question of 'what went wrong', running from the presence of fundamentalism to the absence of democracy. He himself comes down in favour of 'the lack of freedom – freedom of the mind from constraint and indoctrination, to question and enquire and speak; freedom of the economy from corrupt and pervasive misman-agement, freedom of women from male oppression, freedom of citizens from tyranny'.[113] Although it is often considered to be virtually a west-ern monopoly, freedom used in these wide contexts has little meaning. Freedom of the mind seems to imply secularization, which is certainly one factor in developing new solutions, new knowledge. If you reject or qualify religious answers, you inevitably open up others. But for many that solution presents its own problems and people may simply prefer to limit the scope of religion without taking the road to full-time secu-larization. However, in considering Lewis's question, the Near East also fell behind in the 'knowledge revolution' which affected those mental operations of which he speaks for more concrete reasons. Partly, as I have suggested, it was because of the absence of the printing press as a

many responsibilities, including for declaration of war, a popular assembly which elected magistrates (*sufes* or *shophat*) for a year's office. Fantar speaks of Carthage as 'profoundly democratic, giving preference to collegial structures' (p. 57). Personal power was abhor-rent, tyranny condemned; there was respect for the rule of law and individual rights were recognized, for which liberty is an appropriate word.

[112] Berlin 1958; Finley 1985: 6.   [113] Lewis 2002: 177.

key to the circulation of information, as well as the Industrial Revolution and the growth of trading networks (Atlantic and Pacific) which preceded and followed it. With the opening up of the great Atlantic sea-ports, those networks of exchange between western Europe and the rest of the world largely bypassed the Near East. These are more concrete, specific factors than the highly generalized freedoms of which he speaks.

Moreover, freedom is a relative, not an absolute concept. Freedom for the Shiites in Iran is not freedom for the Sunnis, Kurds, or other minorities; it is determined solely by the majority of a more or less arbitrary electorate, yet 'democracy' in whatever form is one aspect of freedom for the many. Electoral procedures can work where people are voting for policies; where the reference group is primordial in character, ethnic or religious, they can hardly be called representative. Freedom for one group is subordination for another. There can be no freedom for the aboriginal inhabitants of Australia or the United States. For them freedom would be seen as the defeat of the majority, consisting of incoming conquerors, hardly something the loud protagonists of universal freedom would accept.

Freedom, Finley insists, is the obverse of slavery. Slavery, he argues, was linked to freedom, obviously a kind of paradox.

The Greeks, it is well known, discovered both the idea of individual freedom and the institutional framework in which it could be realized. The pre-Greek world – the world of the Sumerians, Babylonians, Egyptians and Assyrians; I cannot refrain from adding the Mycenaeans – was, in a very profound sense, a world without free men, in the sense in which the West has come to understand that concept . . . One aspect of Greek history, in short, is the advance, hand in hand, of freedom *and* slavery.[114]

Some historians have also tried to relate the achievements and singularity of the classical world to its use of slavery, to the slave mode of production in Marxist terms. Certainly the total control of the labour force would have been invaluable for the construction of the immense building works that marked that world. But other forms of labour organization have achieved similar ends. In any case the extent of slave labour, always stimulated by military conquest, is unclear. Many activities in the classical world were carried on by other forms of labour, some of which constituted modalities of servile labour not so different from slavery itself. In any case we do not have any clear idea about the comparative levels of the use of slave labour in the various Bronze Age civilizations. It is sometimes argued that while slavery existed in them all, only in the classical

---

[114] Finley 1960: 164.

world was it 'dominant'. Dominance is a difficult concept to utilize, as Love points out.[115] Certainly slavery was widespread, largely as a result of the state's aggressive military policy as well as its commercial success. But in any case, other forms of labour were also significant, especially in the urban and craft sectors. The problem of slavery in the Ancient Near East is discussed by Adams.[116] He concludes concerning Finley: 'Seen in this light, the controversy between Soviet economic historians characterizing early state society as "slave" society and Western specialists insisting on the relatively small numbers of slaves in some respects becomes more a matter of nomenclature than of substance.' The characterization of 'slave societies' depends upon slavery being a 'dominant' institution of classical times whereas in Mesopotamia it was marginal.[117] The extent of slavery is clearly important but in the classical Mediterranean slavery was not unique as an institution, the prevalence of which can be exaggerated. The concept of 'freedom' certainly did not depend on numbers.

While Finley argues for the centrality of slavery to social life in Greece (it was 'a basic element in Greek civilisation'[118]), he also recognizes the wide range of other types of labour contributing to the work force. In the country smallholders took on temporary paid work, especially at harvest; there was 'a symbiosis between free and slave labour'.[119] In towns there was a more evident pool of casual labour. However, 'the more advanced the Greek city states', the more likely they were to have had 'true slavery'. But, while it was central to Greece, slavery was certainly not the only or even main, source of labour, either in agriculture or elsewhere.[120] Nor is it clear that a measure of freedom did not mark societies elsewhere; non-slave labour certainly existed in Mesopotamia.

However, the alternative contention lies at the crux of Finley's view of Antiquity, which he sees as differing from the great Bronze Age societies of the Ancient Near East partly because of the absence of irrigated agriculture but also because they 'discovered individual freedom' as well as practising slavery. Childe also sees Greek philosophy of the Iron Age preoccupied by the question of the individual and society (as was Indian philosophy), which in more concrete terms he considers as being the personal speculation of individuals emancipated from complete dependence on the group by the advent of iron tools and coined money.[121] However, more cautiously he argues that these concerns appeared even in the Old

---

[115] Love 1991.   [116] Adams 1966: 103–4.   [117] Adams 1966: 96–7.
[118] Finley 1960: 69.   [119] Finley 1960: 155.
[120] 'Slave society' Bernal sees as introduced at the time of the invasions of the Sea Peoples on the Levantine coast, leading to a replacement of monarchical but commercial Bronze Age cities by ones dominated by a temple (1991: 8).
[121] Childe 1964: 224.

Stone Age, so that notions of freedom and the individual were not unique to Greece. That seems entirely correct.

Finley is rightly 'concerned with the language used to describe these statuses' and it is in this context that he and others ('it is well known') can talk of the 'discovery' of freedom. He justifies his point by the claim that no Near nor yet Far Eastern language (including Hebrew) provides a translation for the word freedom, *eleutheria* in Greek, *libertas* in Latin. Since an institution approximating to slavery existed in the other societies he mentions, whether or not it can be considered 'basic' or 'dominant', it seems inconceivable that there was no recognition of the difference between slavery and its absence, even if there was not a single noun to designate it. While slavery had been present among the groups with whom I worked in northern Ghana, there was no specific word used to describe being free; nevertheless people had no difficulty whatsoever in making the distinction between a 'slave' (or 'pawn') and other people. Indeed, if you were not a slave (*gbangbaa*), it was assumed you would be free and there was no need for a specific marker.

The third contribution that Antiquity is supposed to have made to politics was in providing the rule of law, a feature predominantly associated with the Roman tradition. Certainly the Romans developed an elaborate code of written law, as did other literate societies. But it is quite mistaken to suppose that even oral cultures were not governed by law in a wider sense, as Malinowski[122] and countless anthropologists have argued, above all perhaps Gluckman in his detailed study of law among the Barotse (Lozi) of Zambia.[123] Indeed the notion of the 'rule of law' has been interpreted by members of literate cultures in altogether too narrow a fashion. Textbooks have been written on Nuer Law, on Tswana Law and on many other systems; such oral law has often been incorporated in the written codes of the new nations of which they form part. It is true that recent events in Sub-Saharan Africa might give the impression that the security of the law was lacking in that continent. But so too might recent events in Iraq, the Balkans, or in eastern and at times even in western Europe. The use of military force wherever it occurs is the opposite of the rule of law, even though the latter may emerge as one of the results of such actions.

If we move to a more specific level, the widespread idea that individual property rights are an invention of Roman law – or of the west – completely overlooks the sophisticated analysis by anthropologists of the jural order in oral cultures. What agricultural society could operate without having excluding (but not necessarily exclusive or permanent) rights

---

[122] Malinowski 1947.   [123] Gluckman 1955; 1965.

to the plot being cultivated? The LoDagaa of northern Ghana, an oral culture where there was no overall shortage of farm land, marked the boundaries of plots very clearly with stones, often having black crosses painted on them warning of the trouble (largely mystical) that would come from encroachment. Boundary disputes, if not frequent, certainly took place here, as in all neighbouring societies. And they were often resolved by recognized jural procedures, by moots, intermediaries, or threats of violence. More complex written cultures had of course their own methods, including registration and deeds, and were found in all the post-Bronze Age societies. Written 'contracts' were used in China as 'documents of declaration', including the transfer of land – and had been since the Tang period. One example from nineteenth-century Taiwan begins: 'The executor of this contract for the irrevocable sale of dry field land . . .'.[124] The vendor goes on to say that he has consulted close kin to determine whether they wanted to buy and, since the answer was negative, proceeds with the sale 'because my mother needs money'. The transaction is put into writing 'because we fear that oral agreement is unreliable', thus realizing that in principle it was also possible to transfer rights in land orally, without recourse to written procedures, but less certain.

The idea that such rights were absent until the advent of Roman law in Europe was held by many historians. For example, Weber first assumed, following his teacher Mommsen, that the original condition of man was 'essentially communal';[125] so too does Marx. However, it is one thing for nineteenth-century historians to make this assumption; it is quite another for twentieth-century practitioners to do the same. Earlier scholars had a paucity of documentation and fanciful notions about the past. Later writers have access to a wealth of studies of recent societies with vaguely similar political economies which demonstrate the validity of Maine's notion of a hierarchy of rights in land, some located in the individual, others in particular groups. His grid dispenses with earlier dichotomies of individual and communal, categories that fail adequately to characterize the tenurial system of societies either in the past or in the present. Pre-literate societies too have hierarchies of rights, including both what can crudely be called individual and collective.[126] It is true that there are obvious methodological dangers in comparing the jural arrangements of Antiquity with the result of even a sophisticated study of a near-contemporary pre-literate judicial system like that carried out by Gluckman in Zambia,

---

[124] Cohen 2004: 41.   [125] Love 1991: 15.
[126] On this general problem of collective and individual, and the way this crude dichotomy has bugged historical and sociological analysis, see Goody. 1996a: 17.

where the evidential base is strong. But such a procedure is clearly to be preferred to the generalized assumption about a communal phase, which pertains to the realm of myth rather than of history. The neglect of alternative 'sources' is partly a matter of ignorance, of the isolation of the respective disciplines, that makes for a deficient history.

Religion and 'Black Athens'

Part of the solution to the general problem of Greek culture is suggested by scholars who have started not from the uniqueness of classical society but have tried to establish connections and continuities with the Aegean and with the Middle East, particularly Egypt and the southern Levant in the work of Bernal, but Mesopotamia and the northern Levant in the case of others. Inflating the role of Greece, downplaying their mercantile activity and their market economy, means neglecting the wider context of Greek achievements, their contacts with Phoenicia and Egypt together with their importance as traders in the seas around their shores, in the eastern Mediterranean and in the Black Sea. These are the main contentions of the critique made by Bernal in *Black Athena*.

The accepted interpretation of the cultural history of Ancient Greece is referred to by Bernal[127] as the Aryan model, one that depends upon the notion of an invasion of Indo-European speakers (or of Indo-Hittite in his more inclusive category), which is held to have had far-reaching consequences for the branching away of European history from that of its neighbours, and a rejection of the influence of Semitic influences (and of Afro-Asiatic, the larger family to which those languages belong) from the eastern shores of the Mediterranean. That model leads to the desire to play down the connections not only with Phoenicia but with Egypt, which he considers made a major contribution to Greek civilization, as indicated in the title to his major work.[128] The Aryan model, in Bernal's eyes, made 'the history of Greece and its relations to Egypt and the Levant conform to the world-view of the nineteenth century and, specifically, to its systematic racism'.[129] He rejects that approach in favour of what he calls 'a revised Ancient model' which accepts ancient stories of Egyptian and Phoenician colonization of Greece, accepts in other words that Greece was influenced by contacts from across the eastern Mediterranean, affecting its language, its script, and its culture more generally, as Herodotus had originally suggested (hence 'the Ancient model').

One of the problems with Bernal's account is his argument that the shift of emphasis from the Ancient to the Aryan model only comes in the

---

[127] Bernal 1987, 1991.   [128] Bernal 1987: 72.   [129] Bernal 1987: 442.

nineteenth century with the development of racism and of anti-Semitism. Certainly these sentiments grew stronger at that time, with the world domination of Europe following the Industrial Revolution. But Bernal sees the appearance of these attitudes as a new development linked to the emergence of Indo-European philology in the 1840s, which produced an 'extraordinary reluctance' to see any connections between Greek and the non-Indo-European languages.

However, in my view the tendency to reject the eastern connection goes back to more general problems of 'roots' and of ethnocentrism, aggravated by the expansion of Islam from the seventh century[130] and the defeats involved in the Crusades and the Christian loss of Byzantium. At that time the opposition between Europe and Asia took the form of one between Christian Europe and Islamic Asia which inherited the earlier stereotypes of 'democratic' and 'despotic' respectively. Islam was conceived as a threat to Europe, not only militarily, which it became early on in the Mediterranean, but also morally and ethically; Muhammad is consigned by Dante to the eighth circle of the Inferno. At the broadest level, ethnocentrism divides all of us from the others and so helps to define our identity. But it is a bad guide to history, especially to world history.

A further reason why Bernal seems to me mistaken in his late date for the development of ethnocentric attitudes is because he recognizes that the 'wellspring' of the Renaissance and of the humanists was 'classical literature'. At that time Greek and Roman thought was privileged above all others and provided humanism 'with much of its basic structure and method'. The possible links with the Near East, with Semitic and Afro-Asiatic cultures, including Carthage, were set on one side, as was the influence of Islam, which at the time of the Renaissance had already been present in Europe, in one way or another, for many centuries. Antiquity proved to be a refreshing contrast to medieval Christianity, and Antiquity was Greece and Rome, whose writings one could read.

Bernal, on the other hand, thinks there are sufficient parallels in, for instance, religion and philosophy to assert that Greek religion is basically Egyptian and was the result of colonization. Some of the evidence derives from linguistic comparisons; however, my limited experience of the philology of African languages suggests that these comparisons are often too tenuous and hazardous to form the basis of profound cultural conclusions. In any case religions, to take one example, underwent constant invention and decline, obsolescence and creation, which makes it less profitable to look for borrowings in, for example, the case of the

[130] Goody 2003b.

bull-cults on which Bernal places much importance. Any cattle-raising group is potentially likely to have a type of such a cult; again, all such cults fail to deliver from time to time and may then be replaced by new ones. I would therefore give more place to what anthropologists have called independent invention in this sphere than I think his hypothesis appears to allow. That does not happen everywhere; the influence of Egyptian hieroglyphics on Minoan writing is generally accepted, as is the influence of the Egyptian column on Greek architecture. But with religious cults invention is often independent.

Of course the influences work in both directions. Egypt was affected by its constant communication with the Levant and with its recruitment of soldiers and sailors from that area. During the Hyksos period, the rulers were foreigners who established themselves at Avaris (Tell al-Dab'a) in the Delta and pursued a vigorous trading policy with Asia, with ready access to the turquoise mines at Serabit el-Khadim and the trade through donkey caravans. Egypt lacked a sea-going fleet at this time and may have welcomed Minoan protection.[131] Much pottery was imported; fragments of Minoan wall painting were found in Avaris that have relations with the Thera wall paintings at Akrotini.[132] During that period 'contacts between Knossos and the Delta were more profound . . . than they had previously been'.[133]

The theme of the possible Egyptian contribution to Eurasian religion was taken up by Freud in his monograph on *Moses and Monotheism* (1939). There he notoriously claimed that Moses was an Egyptian who derived his monotheism from the 'heretic' Pharaoh, Akenaton. Of the likelihood of such an influence I cannot judge. I would add however that the possibility of a switch to monotheism, and back again, as some Protestants would claim happened in Christianity, is an ever-present possibility in many human societies as the result of a Creation myth that emphasizes the uniqueness of the process. One reason is that Creation is viewed as a unique act (often of a Creator God) while lesser deities tend to proliferate as intermediaries.

Freud's contention was that 'the rule of Pharaoh's empire was the external reason for the appearance of the monotheistic idea'.[134] Political centralization led to religious centralization. But many missionaries and anthropologists have reported, if not monotheism, at least the existence of a Supreme Deity in simpler cultures, a deity who is a Creator God and who created lesser deities. In Africa he becomes the *deus otiosus*, who

[131] Bietak 2000:40.   [132] Davies and Schofield 1995; Sherratt 2000.
[133] P. Warren, 'Minoan Crete and Pharaonic Egypt', in Davies and Schofield 1995: 8.
[134] Freud 1964 [1939]: 108.

is rarely worshipped, yet the fact that he created the universe raises the possibility that he may return to a more active existence. In this context, the appearance of monotheism is not difficult to understand.

Despite some reservations I have no doubt at all about the correctness of Bernal's main contention that

(a) in this neglect 'racial' factors have played a significant part. But I regard these factors as being of a much more long-standing origin than he suggests and as being linked to notions of cultural as well as racial superiority;

(b) connections between Ancient Greece and the Near East have been greatly neglected; the marginalization of Phoenicia and Carthage are obvious examples of this process. The religion of Carthage was influenced both by Greece and by Egypt.

Bernal is not alone in trying to establish a higher degree of commonality between Mediterranean societies than is usually recognized. The insistence on a connection between the Semitic-speaking peoples of the Asiatic coast and the Greeks has been at the core of the work of a number of Jewish Semitic scholars, notably Cyrus Gordon.[135] He undertook a pioneering study of the grammar of Ugaritic, analysing that newly discovered Semitic language from the tablets found in the north Syrian town which provided evidence of the earliest alphabetic script. Gordon attempted to link the Phoenician settlement of Ugarit with Crete, and in 1955 published a monograph entitled *Homer and the Bible* concluding that 'Greek and Hebrew civilizations were parallel structures built on the same east Mediterranean foundations.'[136] The notion was heretical for many at the time. Since the Second World War, however, the earlier rejection of Phoenician influence on Greece has been modified. The idea of Phoenician settlements not simply on the islands but at Thebes on the mainland, has become more acceptable;[137] so that the influence on Iron Age Greece is now seen possibly to have begun as early as the tenth century.

Phoenicians were voyaging throughout the Mediterranean. They were a coastal community that had to look abroad for trading opportunities, especially in metal, and developed alphabetic writing as a simple way of recording transactions. One sees very well how the Phoenicians became traders, both in wood and in metals. The mountains of Lebanon virtually come down to the sea from Sidon northwards. Even Tyre has a limited coastal strip. So the cedars of Lebanon were exchanged with Egypt for the building of boats (Egypt had no timber), and with Israel for the construction of temples, in return for grain. And they travelled throughout

---

[135] See also the work of his colleague Astour 1967, as well as Ward 1971.
[136] Bernal 1987: 416.   [137] Bernal 1991: 6.

the Mediterranean to Carthage, Cadiz, and even to Cornwall, to search for metals, in the last two places particularly for tin to use in the making of bronze. One result of their travels was the very considerable colony of Carthage, established in present-day Tunisia. They were even said to have led an Egyptian expedition that circumnavigated Africa in about 600 BCE. In any case, they were the great sea-farers and rich merchants, not only of the Aegean but of the whole of the Mediterranean. While some nineteenth-century scholars such as Beloch vigorously denied the presence of Phoenicians in the Aegean before the eighth century BCE, archaeological evidence indicates 'thriving commercial relations between the Aegean world and the eastern Mediterranean coast during the second millennium' and in the Minoan and Mycenaean periods.[138] Indeed, the author Jidejian claims that the Cadmus story 'reflects an early western Semitic penetration into mainland Greece'.[139] According to Herodotus, Cadmus, the son of the King of Tyre, who was sent to search for his sister, Europa, ended by founding the Greek city of Thebes. It was the Phoenician Cadmus who brought the alphabet to Boetia in Greece and there are stories of Phoenician settlements in Rhodes and elsewhere; the tradition of Cadmus founding the dynasty of Oedipus persisted in the ancient world. So they certainly had many contacts with and influences upon not only the ancient Near East, but what we call the classical world, of which they were essentially a part.

In the work of most classicists the concentration on Greece and Rome has not only played down the contribution of Phoenicia to the emergence of the alphabet (750 years before Greece in the consonantal sense) as well as the literate achievements in Semitic languages, but has also relegated Carthage, initially a Phoenician trading community and later a considerable empire in the western Mediterranean, to the margins of history. Not simply to the margins of history but to that of 'barbarian' status, partly because of the insistence of the Romans on their practice of child sacrifice, the evidence for which is open to a number of doubts. In any case it is not clear why that is any more barbaric than certain events in the Old Testament, such as the sacrifice of Isaac, nor yet the exposure of illegitimate infants in Rome, or certain Spartan practices which, however, get largely interpreted as giving rise to discipline. What is clear is that a highly accomplished civilization, a rival as well as a predecessor of Rome, has been excluded from the category of Antiquity in much the same way as the societies of the Near East, even though it was the contemporary

[138] Jidejian 1996: 66.
[139] For a cautious evaluation of the connections between Egypt and the Aegean between 2200 and 1900 BCE, see Ward 1971, especially 119ff.

and counterpart first of Greece and then of Rome from the fifth century when the scattered *emporia* were united.

One problem in our knowledge of the contribution of Carthage and Phoenicia to Mediterranean culture is that we have so few of their own written records. The Phoenicians clearly kept records of various kinds since they had an alphabet. Moreover Josephus later wrote that 'among the nations in touch with the Greeks, it was the Phoenicians who made the largest use of writing both for recording affairs of life and for the commemoration of public events'. He further comments that 'for many years past the people of Tyre have kept public records, compiled and very carefully preserved by the state, of the memorable events in their internal history and in their relations with foreign nations'.[140] None of these documents have survived but they may have been written on perishable papyrus imported from Egypt rather than on more enduring tablets. Phoenician inscriptions, mainly short, have been found in all the coastal towns but otherwise little or nothing remains, unless we extend our horizon to Judaism.

That is why, although they were a major part of the ancient world, the Phoenicians did not leave the literary or artistic heritage bequeathed by the Greeks and Romans. As far as the literary heritage goes, the libraries of Carthage were destroyed or disappeared as the result of the town's destruction by the Romans in 146 BCE. There is evidence of their agricultural knowledge not only in the advanced farming they practised but also in the translation into Latin of a text book on the subject.

The dismissal of the role of the Semites in the eastern Mediterranean therefore contradicts the widespread evidence of the sea-faring Phoenicians in that region. The Phoenicians inhabited a number of well-known 'city-states' (as they are described) along the Levant coast mainly in present-day Lebanon, stretching from Acre in Israel/Palestine to Ugarit in Syria.

Conclusion: Antiquity and the Europe–Asia Dichotomy

The Greeks were defined as different not only by themselves but by later Europeans. What do classicists like Finley see as the driving force behind the presumed differentiation from the rest of the Near East, with which it was actively exchanging goods and ideas? The supposed political differences hardly seem sufficient in themselves. Whatever the special characteristics of the world of Antiquity, what is lacking in scholars' accounts is how and why Europe and the Mediterranean diverged from the generality

[140] Bernal 1991: 6.

of post-Bronze Age societies in such a way as to be considered a distinct (and possibly progressive) societal type and mode of production. Their achievements in terms of knowledge systems, of sculpture, of drama, of poetry were immense but regarding the existence of a special societal type, we have expressed our doubts. The dominance of slavery has been selected by many commentators as the crucial difference of classical societies. Its prevalence, I have shown, had both advantages and disadvantages as far as the growth of the culture and of the economy were concerned. In any case it did not perhaps constitute such an enormous distinction between the western and eastern modes of livelihood as the dichotomy between Ancient and Asiatic modes would suggest. The use of slave labour may have been extensive but there seems to have been little difference in the technical means of production. In Antiquity the widespread use of iron, a much cheaper metal than copper or tin, universally available, had important consequences, but that was the case with all the societies in the region.[141] Whatever other developments took place, notably in water engineering and in crop development, were broadly continuous with what preceded them. At these levels the contrast was less marked than most classical historians allow.

The very notion that what occurred in the east represented 'Asiatic exceptionalism' and that the western sequence of events was 'normal' embodies an unwarranted European assumption, based on the vantage point of the nineteenth century, which asserts that it pointed to the only road to 'capitalism'. And that idea arises from a conflation of capitalism, in the broad sense in which the historian Braudel often employed the term, with the development of industrial production, a much more specific economic event, often seen as involving 'productive investment' (though that is a general factor even in agricultural societies). While western Europe itself became 'exceptional' in the nineteenth century, it is not apparent that earlier on it was out of line with other major civilizations, except in terms of its advantages in the era of the 'Great Voyages' perhaps related to technical developments in 'guns and sails' and following its adoption of printing long practised in China, to an alphabetic script using movable type. That development permitted the more rapid circulation (and accumulation) of information, an advantage which the Chinese and Arabic civilizations had earlier enjoyed because of their use of paper, and in the first case of printing.

The effect of differentiating the Ancient from the Asiatic development of post-Bronze Age civilization creates an explanatory problem relating to that supposed divergence. At the same time it pushes back the question

---

[141] Childe 1964, chapter 9.

of the origin of capitalism to the supposed roots of European culture. Because already in Antiquity, according to many classicists, Europe was pursuing the right path in that direction, whereas Asia had gone astray. Until recently that was the view of the majority of 'humanists' who saw European culture as springing from the achievements of Roman and Greek society in a quite unique way. These achievements have some-times been put down to 'Greek genius', as did Burkhardt in a manner that is difficult to discuss from a straightforward historical or sociolog-ical point of view. Sometimes they have been seen as connected with the invention of the alphabet in a way that neglects the Asiatic (Semitic) roots of systematic phonetic transcription as well as the very considerable achievements of other systems of writing.[142] Sometimes Greek science (or logic) is given a unique status with regard to later developments, an idea that would seem to have been refuted by Needham's encyclopaedic work on *Science and Civilization in China*.[143,144] Each of these factors appeals to some extent to the means of communication and made some contribution to later developments at the time of the Renaissance but it is difficult to accept a categorical distinction in the levels of achievement between east and west, Europe and Asia, before that period. Indeed most would accept that until then cultural and economic attainments were not greatly different and that mercantile 'capitalism', urban cultures, and lit-erate activity were present elsewhere at least to the same degree.

[142] Goody 1977.
[143] Needham, *Science and Civilization in China*, 1954. This is not always Needham's con-clusion as he is inclined to see 'modern science' as emerging only in the west for reasons that go back to the Greeks. I comment in a later chapter upon this suggestion.
[144] This subject has been sensitively approached by G. E. R. Lloyd (1979) from a somewhat different point of view.

3   Feudalism: a transition to capitalism or the collapse of Europe and the domination of Asia?

The word feudalism is used in a variety of ways. Often it refers in ordinary speech to any hierarchy that is not elected, not achieved, such as the original House of Lords. In more technical language, we may follow Strayer's distinctions: 'One group of scholars uses the word to describe the technical arrangements by which vassals become dependents of lords, and landed property (with attached economic benefits) became organized as dependent tenures of fiefs. The other group of scholars uses feudalism as a general word which sums up the dominant forms of social and political organization during certain centuries of the Middle Ages'.[1] In his introduction to Marc Bloch's study, *Feudal Society*, Postan makes a similar distinction between those Anglophone speakers who assess military fiefs and Soviet scholars who discourse on class domination and the exploitation of peasants by landlords. Like Bloch, Postan prefers the latter approach.[2] Here we use the term to refer to a period that followed classical Antiquity in Europe.

The shift to feudalism from Antiquity

In western eyes feudalism has often been seen as a transition to capitalism and as a 'progressive' phase in the development of the west, a phase which other societies could not have attained in the same way. Its absence, like that of Antiquity, excluded others from the path to modernity. However, this period demonstrated little that was definitely intrinsic to the later expansion of mercantile and emergence of industrial capitalism except in so far as a regressive phase is sometimes followed by more vigorous innovative action, as has been argued for the Dark Age in Greece – the advantage of backwardness. Revival came partly through contact with the east and was not a purely endogenous growth. It was not the Merovingians and Carolingians who were heirs to the Roman Empire but rather Constantinople. 'Seen as part of world history, the West was reduced

[1] Strayer 1956: 15.   [2] M. Postan, foreword in Bloch 1961.

68

to a forgotten corner of the world whose centre was now in the eastern Mediterranean basin, namely, the Byzantium Empire, and later also the Arab countries.'[3] Indeed the centre probably lay even further east.

Despite this exclusive view of feudalism, some form of great estate, with obligations attached, existed almost everywhere in post-Bronze Age cultures. Moreover urban cultures continued to develop in the east with some hiccups but nothing like those in the west, which in this respect was marked by 'occidental exceptionalism'. Its collapse did not spread to the eastern Mediterranean, where in many respects towns and their urban culture, as at Constantinople or Alexandria, continued earlier developments, especially economically, for they persisted as craft centres, as homes for educational establishments and as entrepots for trade, especially with the east.

Decline in the west, continuity in the east

While the timing of the shift from Antiquity to Feudalism may be questionable, the events themselves were not. At least in the west a dramatic collapse took place. So the critical feature of the west was not the progressive development of culture from the Roman period, as many have chosen to assume, but the disastrous decline of urban cultures with the collapse of that empire. The political economy of western Europe was always more fragile than in the east, less profoundly based on the urban revolution of the Bronze Age. Consequently it was much more liable to collapse when the empire weakened. Clearly the aspect of collapse, then later a renewal, was very important in European feudalism and Southall sees this as central in all feudalisms which he consequently considers widespread.[4]

That collapse in western Europe was partly the result of the external fact of barbarian invasions as well as of the rise of Christianity and Christian power, but many authors have also seen it as due to internal factors such as the weaknesses (contradictions) of the slave mode of production, and possibly due to a longer-term economic decline since 200 CE or else to a decrease in population. The process of production has also been held to account in so far as there was a big expansion of large estates (*latifundia*), which became increasingly self-sufficient, a development that has been spoken of as an early feudalization. Some have seen the problem as one of exporting industry rather than the products,[5] as a result of which there was no expansion. Committed to the export of bullion in exchange for goods, the Roman economy became bankrupt.

---

[3] Slicher van Bath 1963: 31.   [4] Southall 1998.   [5] Childe 1964: 283.

Much has been written about the decline of social life with the end of the Roman Empire.[6] The north suffered most severely, especially Britain 'where cities, together with Christianity, seem practically to have disappeared';[7] the same happened in the Balkans, though other areas did much better, especially southern Spain. Even in northern Italy three-quarters of the hundred municipium survived until 1000 CE. Nevertheless the collapse of the west has been seen as paradigmatic for world history, the fall of Antiquity and its urban centres leading to the prevalence of feudalism, the later stages of which saw the emergence of capitalism. A recognition of the different history of the west and that of the east and south of the Mediterranean puts the general course of events in a very different light.

What it is important to ask is how far the collapse of Rome affected the empire in the east as well as in the west. European historians have looked at these events very much from the standpoint of western Europe, excluding eastern Europe as well as the east more generally. Even during Roman times there were significant differences between the east and the west of the Empire. The east was more closely connected to Asian trade, with huge Roman cities like Palmyra and Apamea being constructed in the Levant and in western Asia generally. The difference is clearly out-lined in Anderson's *Passages from Antiquity*. The west was less diversely populated, less urbanized and its political economy was not itself based on the complex civilizations of the Near East which had existed in Egypt and the Levant. It was marked by rain-fed rather than irrigated agriculture, with fewer towns and less trade. The west was in decline: the rural areas had taken over from the cities where activity had become greatly diminished.[8] The rich estates (*latifundia*) had expanded, incorporating peasants and artisans into their closed economies. The Romans changed the economic base by introducing more complex farming, often organized around the villa, and in some parts around the *latifundia* as well, which were based on extensive slave labour. There was therefore some elaboration in the western countryside. Further mechanization took place and water wheels spread in late Antiquity.[9] But the east was less affected by invasions, urban life was more active and the peasantry resisted the

---

[6] The concept 'decline' is used with reference to specific criteria (e.g., rate of literacy) and has to be taken in context of our earlier discussion (chapter 1) of 'progression' as distinct from 'progress'. The latter involves a value judgement about superiority in all fields. The concept of 'progression' dismisses the notion of complete relativity in all spheres and recognizes that a movement has occurred in a number of fields, for example, in modes of production and modes of communication.

[7] The following section was first given as the Tillion lecture in Aix in March 2004.

[8] Petit 1997: 336.   [9] McCormick 2001: 10.

settler system implied in *latifundia*. In towns such as Carthage, Athens, Constantinople, Antioch, and Alexandria, higher education continued.

In the eastern Mediterranean, according to Childe, city life, with all its implications, went on:

> most crafts were still plied with all the technical skill and equipment evolved in Classical and Hellenistic times. Farms were still worked scientifically to produce for the market. Barter did not entirely oust the money economy, nor did self-sufficiency paralyse trade completely. Writing was not forgotten. Indeed, at Alexandria and Byzantium scientific and literary texts were studiously copied and preserved. Greek medicine was practised in public hospitals with the blessings of the Church.[10]

The west suffered more but cathedral cities arose, travel continued, as did the manufacture of glass; the use of water wheels expanded.

The argument has been made that Roman prosperity depended upon the interdependence between one region and another. Ward-Perkins disputes Finley's emphasis on local economies but recognizes that all parts of the empire were not as tightly linked. When Rome collapsed as a polity, so did the overall economy which depended upon it, but with different results in the west and in the east. Especially the 'fifth century is a period of growing prosperity in the east and of marked economic decline in the west'.[11] The Mediterranean world in 600 CE bore strong similarities to the pre-Roman period of around 300 BCE – a developed commercial economy in the east extending to Carthage, Sicily, and southern Italy, 'barbarism' in the west. That difference was partly because the east, and to some extent the south, were more closely integrated into the exchange economy of Asia. By the seventh century, Italy and even Byzantium 'look very different from the contemporary (and by this time Arab) Near East, where there is much more evidence of continued economic complexity and prosperity'.[12]

How different were towns and markets in the east? It has been asserted that Islamic cities and markets fell into a distinct category from those in the west or even those further east.[13] There may well have been some general characteristics that differentiated them but these variants were swamped by similar problems, similar features, a similar organization of people massed together. Outsiders have a constant tendency to exaggerate the differences (which are often 'cultural', of the surface) and neglect the similarities (which are often 'structural', more deep-seated). Take the urban situation. In the Far East this has been described as a peddler economy;[14] in the Near East, it is a bazaar economy, and always opposed

---

[10] Childe 1964: 290.   [11] Ward-Perkins 2000: 382.   [12] Ward-Perkins 2000: 360.
[13] Goitein 1999.   [14] van Leur 1955.

to western economy.[15] In fact these low-level methods of selling small portable commodities have their structural parallels in the markets, shops, and travelling salesmen of the west. They are in any case only one aspect of the total economies of these different societies, where the forms of trading, banking, and investment are much more alike. So too with the town, whether it is walled or not, whether there are streets occupied by a single craft, whether the rich and poor live cheek by jowl, these are important but not determining features for the growth of the economy; the town carries on its business in a variety of circumstances.

The west lost touch with these developments; from the fourth century the gradual disappearance of knowledge of Greek cut them off from Constantinople until the Renaissance. The collapse of the Roman empire had been accompanied by the growth of Christianity which had a profound effect on artistic and intellectual life. As in the other monotheistic religions, the church was initially against many of the arts, especially theatre, sculpture, secular painting. The predominant sway of dogmatic belief could mean a restriction in the range of intellectual enquiry. We have seen that in the west the emperor Justinian did not encourage the teaching of philosophy, which was open to attack from Christianity because it raised questions such as whether the world was created or uncreated, or about the relation between the human and the divine, problems on which that religion had already pronounced authoritatively. In many cases there was even some diminution of knowledge. Of few spheres was this clearer than medicine, since the dissection of the human body ('made in God's image') was now forbidden.

During the early centuries of the Christian Era, learned doctors came to Rome, including Galen. He was heir to the great tradition of the Hellenistic medical school at Alexandria, where Herophilus practised anatomical dissections. But dissection of the human body was by then illegal, and Galen was forced to depend upon the examination of animals. After the fall of Rome, learning was no longer held in such high esteem, experiment was discouraged, and originality became a dangerous asset. The historian of science, Charles Singer, writes of the anti-scientific character of Christianity in relation to medicine, which underwent a period of 'progressive disintegration'.[16] 'During the early Middle Ages medicine passed into the widely diverse hands of the Christian Church and Arab Scholars . . . Disease was regarded as a punishment for sin, and such chastening demanded only prayer and repentance.'[17] In one respect he claims that Christianity may have helped: with the use of nuns more humane

---

[15] Geertz 1979, Weiss and Westerman 1998.   [16] Singer 1950: 215.
[17] Guthrie and Hartley 1977: 890.

nursing developed, which provided great benefits for the sick. However, hospitals were certainly not a Christian invention and nursing took place in the great hospitals in Baghdad and elsewhere. The only real contribution the west made towards the preservation of medical knowledge, if not its increase, was the translation into Latin of Greek medical texts, which were retained in some monasteries.[18] A somewhat more dynamic picture is presented by eastern Christianity. Persian Christians from the Nestorian church assisted the transmission of classical medical knowledge by translating texts into Arabic. From Persia too came the physician Rhazis (al-Razi, second half of the ninth century) as well as Avicenna (980–1037) whose principal work, *The Canons of Medicine*, was being used at the medical school in Montpelier as late as 1650. But the Arabs added little in anatomy or physiology of their own; they had similar restrictions to the Christians about cutting up the human body. In the west, dissection began again only with the founding of medical schools in the twelfth century. At that time a renaissance and indeed extension of knowledge of this kind saw the building of the magnificent anatomy theatres of the north Italian cities, Milan, Florence, and Bologna, in the first two of which Leonardo da Vinci performed some thirty investigations. The history of investigative medicine thus presents a résumé of the decline and fall of much knowledge in the medieval west.

But in the east and south there was a different situation, at least commercially. The eastern Mediterranean as a whole was less dependent for its prosperity on trade with the ex-Roman north and west. In Syria during the first centuries CE the desert entrepot of Palmyra imported a wide range of goods from further east, from China as well as from India, which are recorded in a famous Tariff dated 187. The Tariff specifies many items of trade, including slaves, purple dye, aromatic oils, olive oil, salted goods, cattle, as well as prostitutes. The Syrians have been called the middlemen of Antiquity. Their vessels went everywhere and Syro-Phoenician bankers were present in all the markets. Palmyran merchant communities resided at Doura-Europus on the river Euphrates in the east and at Rome in the west. Excavations have produced silk yarn and jade from China, as well as muslin, spices, ebony, myrrh, ivory, pearls, and precious stones. Glass came from Syria, green glaze pottery from Mesopotamia, some wares from the Mediterranean through Antioch, and many other items of the luxury trade.[19]

In Carthage and the Maghreb in North Africa, the power of Vandal rule is no longer seen as one of such economic decline, for overseas trade continued as before, there and under the subsequent Byzantine conquest

---

[18] See Reynolds and Wilson 1974: 122ff. [19] Browning 1979: 16–18.

right up until the Arab invasion. African exports of red-slip ware, fo.
example, persisted to the seventh century. With the Byzantine invasio▪
in 533, the situation did not greatly change. More investment seems t▪
have been made in cities like Carthage, and commerce was diverted from
Europe to Constantinople and the east when the Arabs arrived in th▪
middle of the seventh century. The province was still rich in oil an▪
wheat, and valuable goods were being imported from the east, though
these later declined.[20]

City life and particularly commercial activities suffered more unde▪
Christianity in the north than under Islam in the south. In the east, ▌
have argued, the commercial centres were particularly linked with long-
distance trade, whereas in the west this far-flung exchange largely collapsed with Rome. Instead we see the emergence of 'cities of prayer', o▪
towns in which the dominant element had become ecclesiastical, partly
because of the collapse of commerce that had flourished with the Roman
state, partly because of the rise of the church. That rise meant the shift o▌
funding from the municipality to the ecclesia. As has been remarked, 'I▪
is characteristic of the age that the balance of munificence shifts from the
old civil projects of baths and theatres to religious building.'[21] In Islam
too there was the problem of funding the religious establishment, but
the needs were less demanding. There were magnificent mosques and
later madrasahs, which were often supported by the markets attached to▪
them, but an establishment without bishops and, in general, without full
time clergy and having no monastic culture, meant lower demands on
the economy.

We learn from the work of Goitein, the historian who spent his life
working on the medieval Jewish manuscripts found in a Cairo cemetery
in the late nineteenth century, as well as from other sources, that this city
remained as much a centre of trade with the further east as it had done in
the Roman period.[22] Jewish and Muslim traders were constantly visiting
the Malabar coast of western India, just as eastern Indians were coming
to Egypt.[23] The same was true of Constantinople. Needham refers to a
Chinese scholar coming to Baghdad, and Europeans continued, sporadically, to travel the land route to China. That did not mean the decline
of the trade with the west counted for nothing. While the Near East was
inevitably affected by the European downturn, the main focus of its trade,
however, lay elsewhere. Western Europe lay at the end of the line. If its
demand for eastern luxuries, spices, textiles, perfumes, ceramics, fell off,
there were other markets. Trade with North Africa continued, as we see

[20] Cameron 2000.   [21] McCormick 2001. See also Speiser 1985.
[22] Miller 1969.   [23] Ghosh 1992.

from the case of the merchant trading between India and Tunis that first
attracted the attention of the historian Goitein to this commerce. The
Near East had its own active markets which needed to be supplied. So
commerce continued in an easterly direction even when the westerly route
had become of marginal importance. India remained a goal for traders of
the Near East as the whole history of the settlement of Jewish, Christian,
and Muslim communities on the Malabar coast testifies, leaving a major
mark on the Geniza documents. There are many references to the trade
in pepper with south-west India in the well-known traders' handbook,
The Periplus Maris Erythraei, composed around 50 CE by a Greek pilot,
as well as in other Roman sources. Trade with India remained of great
importance from Roman times onwards. The entrepot of Muziris, situ-
ated near the present-day Cochin, being the supposed landing place for
the missionary St Thomas and the Syrian (Nestorian) Christians,[24] was
an important centre for Alexandrian shippers, as we see from a papyrus
recording a written contract about 150 CE for the transport of goods from
a Red Sea port to the customs–bonded warehouse in Alexandria. While
it had been assumed there was a decline in this trade between the second
and fourth centuries, that does not seem to be altogether the case. Indian
merchant ships were still transporting pepper to Egypt for the Roman
market in the sixth century. Indeed there continued to be a major trading
centre in western India for Christians, Jewish, and Muslim communities
up to Geniza times and later.

Meanwhile Turkey and Syria provided alternative markets for goods
from China, Iran, and the Caucasus. Their exchange was oriented mainly
in a non-European direction. It was this eastern commerce into which
Venice, followed by the towns of western Italy, Parma, Genoa, Amalfi,
gained a foothold, picking up trade as the European economy gathered
momentum in the new millennium with the Crusades and the entry of
western Europe into the Mediterranean.

For Venice was not the only Mediterranean power to re-open commerce between Europe, Asia, and Africa. One of the Italian towns that
was founded on the revival of trade in the eastern Mediterranean was not
from there or from Tuscany, the homes of the merchant families in Florence (Medicis) and of Prato (Datini), but from Campania, specifically
Amalfi (and Ravello), near to Salerno to the south and Naples to the east,
under Angevin rule. The towns became very active in merchant activity
(*mercatantia*) from an early period. Already, in 836, the Lombard princes
had given the Amalfians an 'unusual freedom to travel'.[25] They were
quick to take advantage of that liberty and traded grain, oil, and lumber

---

[24] Gurukkal and Whittaker 2001.   [25] Caskey 2004: 9.

with Byzantium, Syria, and Egypt for silks and spices, some of which they then sold in Aghlabid North Africa and Sicily for gold, a rare commodity in the west of that time. Amalfian merchants traded with Constantinople, Cairo, and Antioch and even Cordova as early as the tenth century, with a sizeable community in Jerusalem in the eleventh. Indeed Byzantine and Fatimid currencies were widely in use in local transactions in that period, giving some idea of the impact of long-distance trade in the region. The Italian towns renewed part of an easterly oriented trading network with Byzantium and the East, stimulated by Lombard rule. This revival owed little to Antiquity or feudalism but represented a more general take-up of mercantile culture.

The activities of Amalfi brought the town prosperity. This was, however, not a purely Christian or western achievement, as the south's diverse population included Jewish and Muslim communities as well as Christian, all participating in the commercial activity: this was a multicultural society, a fact that is reflected in the arts that were promoted by *mercatantia* around Amalfi, for example the bronze doors of the cathedrals were made in Constantinople about 1061. This commercial activity is described by Caskey as 'nascent capitalism',[26] which in fact clashed not only with Christian values but with other values promulgated by the Abrahamistic religions concerning usury. Merchant activity was contested by religion, here as elsewhere, but it clearly won out in the end; the contribution of merchants to those regimes was part of this very process.

Much of this art in Amalfi was commissioned by merchants, especially the house of the Rufolos of Ravello who were celebrated by Boccacio in one of his early *novella* about commercial existence. But the story also illustrates the dangers as well as the achievements of merchant life. For the family was charged with corruption and the father executed in 1283 by the Angevin, Charles of Salerno, later king Charles II of Sicily, where they had ruled from 1265 at the behest of the Pope.[27]

Southern Spain, like parts of Italy, remained integrated in the Mediterranean trading network, due to its Islamic connections. Obviously the Muslims, who may well have assisted in the collapse of European commerce in the Mediterranean,[28] maintained contact after 711 CE with their conquests in Spain. Traffic between Andalucia and the African mainland continued and developed;[29] the same was true of Sicily and 'Ifriqua' (Tunisia). Looking at the Mediterranean from the vantage point of

---

[26] Caskey 2004: 8.   [27] Hodges and Whitehouse 1983.
[28] As has been discussed by the Belgian Henri Pirenne 1939, as well as by Hodges and Whitehouse 1983.
[29] See Constable 1994.

contemporary western Europe can seriously distort the picture as far as culture and history are concerned. We need to re-orient, as Frank has demanded,[30] since the east did not suffer to the same degree as the west. The continuation of economic, scientific, and urban culture in the east and south in the post-Roman period was critical much later in enabling western Europe to catch up after the collapse of Rome and the period of early 'feudalism', associated with the loss of trade and urban life and with the consequent stress on agriculture and the countryside.

The role of the army also differed in the east and west. It was an important institution for maintaining law and order internally and for defence and conquest abroad, as well as providing a market for goods (such as sigillata ware) and services. In contrast to the west, 'the East managed to survive with its military institutions relatively intact'.[31] The army 'remained an institution under imperial authority, not an independent force capable of dictating to its nominal masters'.[32] The west on the other hand was dominated both by military force and by tribal bands. Inevitably local lords assumed military duties in relation to their territories and the inhabitants, conditions that provided a baseline for feudal decentralization and military duties. Once again this form of social organization appears as a western reaction to decline rather than as a progressive stage in the march of civilization.

Wickham's discussion of the shift from the ancient world to feudalism, for example, makes no reference to democracy, quite the opposite. The ancient is characterized by the strong central government of Rome with its large armies sustained by increasingly heavy taxation, larger than the rent people were paying. The objections to taxation encouraged farmers to place themselves under landowners, who took responsibility for tax as part of the rent. The landowners themselves were prepared to shift allegiance to Germanic regimes for tax reasons, the military was being organized on a local rather than a national basis so that, in the longer run, the hated taxation disappeared and rents and local services prevailed. But not immediately; the landowners were the first to make this move after 568.[33]

The shift to feudalism

There was no generalized transition from Antiquity to feudalism except in the west and in the minds of its scholars. In any case, even in the west feudalism did not appear immediately after the fall of Antiquity. In his

---

[30] Frank 1998.   [31] Whitby 2000: 300.   [32] Whitby 2000: 305.
[33] Wickham 1984: 20.

account of the transition from Antiquity to feudalism, Anderson recognized the 'catastrophic' rather than the 'cumulative' events at the end of
the ancient world. But the regression in Europe is seen as clearing the way
'for the dynamic subsequent advance of the new mode of production born
of their [Antiquity's] demolition'.[34] This new mode arose out of 'the concatenation of Antiquity and feudalism'. He argued that it was the element
of Antiquity that was absent in the nearest equivalent to feudalism outside Europe, namely Japan, similar as it was in many other respects.[35] At
the same time, he writes negatively about Roman agriculture and extends
his comments to the whole economy, remarking on the gap between the
intellectual and political achievements of the Greco-Roman world and
'the cramped economic earth beneath it'.[36] Indeed its 'superstructural
heritage' survived, in compromised form, through the Church which had
helped to destroy the polity. The 'superstructural civilization of Antiquity
remained superior to that of feudalism for a millennium – right down to
the epoch that was consciously to call itself the Renaissance, to mark the
intervening regression'.[37] He sees the endurance of the Church as bridging this gap, for it became the custodian of literacy. Nevertheless it was
literacy of a highly restricted kind, one that deliberately excluded much
classical learning.

So for Anderson it was not the 'superstructure' but the 'infrastructure', the economy, that was seen as progressive in the medieval period.
He writes of the contrast in the classical world between its static economy (as compared with the dynamic basis of feudalism) and the 'cultural
and superstructural vitality' of that world. At times Childe too tended to
play down the Roman contribution arguing that it 'had not released any
new productive forces'.[38] This view maintains that the widespread use
of slaves in Roman agriculture inhibited advances in technology, since
manpower was cheaper than machines. For Childe, slavery impeded 'the
expansion of industry'.[39] Despite its emergence from a collapse in western Europe, 'feudalism' is said to be progressive partly because of the
idea, most strongly expressed by traditional Marxist historians, that 'the
slave mode of production led to technical stagnation; there was no impetus to labour-saving improvements within it'.[40] These authors however
chose to ignore the fact that the period saw many 'improvements', as
a consequence of which certain statements about slave societies require
modification.[41] Also, the slave mode of production does not automatically lead to economic stagnation; despite, or possibly because of the use

[34] Anderson 1974b: 418.   [35] Anderson 1974b: 420.   [36] Anderson 1974a: 136.
[37] Anderson 1974a: 137.   [38] Childe 1964: 280.   [39] Childe 1964: 209, 268.
[40] Anderson 1974a: 132–3.   [41] White 1970.

of slaves, the agriculture of Roman villas produced a surplus not only to provide a high standard of luxury living for the upper class but also enough wine, for example, to be exported to other countries, together with pottery, textiles, and furniture.

Improvements were not necessarily 'labour-saving' because, as Boserup has argued,[42] advances in technology may involve more work rather than less. If improvements mean that one can produce the same amount of goods with one slave rather than two, there must be an incentive for their adoption. In Sicily and in Carthaginian domains large estates worked by slaves or serfs were run on 'scientific capitalist lines'.[43] Indeed, all over Europe the Romans established 'capitalist forms'.[44] That is not a contradictory notion. In their analysis of the slave production of sugar in the Caribbean, Mintz and Wolf describe the innovative use of machinery as 'capitalism before capitalism'.[45] Getting rid of slave production was seen as one of the positive effects of the fall of the Roman Empire in the west, although slavery certainly did not disappear entirely. 'The notion of Antiquity is used only of Greece and Rome, as is the associated "slave mode of production"',[46] but in Europe some authors have seen slavery at least as continuing over a much longer period until 'feudalism' was eventually established.[47] Even later on Europe was heavily involved in the capture and sale of slaves to the Muslim world, which became one of its major exports.[48] Still for many authors, the slave mode of production disappeared with Antiquity, and from this perspective, feudalism, like Antiquity before it, is seen as a progressive step along the path to capitalism. However, that is not the only view of the medieval economy. 'Considered economically', writes the historian of European agriculture Slicher van Bath,[49] 'the manorial system was not very satisfactory. People produced little more than was needed for their own consumption, capital was not accumulated and there was almost no division of labour.' Initially at least, there was a decline in production, just as there was undoubtedly a decline in learning and in the 'superstructure' generally. The recovery was slow.

There are more positive views of Roman agriculture than Anderson's, ones that necessarily modify the idea of a progressive leap to feudalism. Hopkins,[50] who offers qualified support to Finley's view of the Ancient economy, argues that total agricultural production rose with more land being brought under cultivation. In the heavier lands of the north, a much stronger plough was employed, drawn by a team of oxen and equipped

---

[42] Boserup 1970.   [43] Childe 1964: 244.   [44] Childe 1964: 276.
[45] Mintz and Wolf 1950.   [46] Anderson 1974a: 47.   [47] Bonnassie 1991.
[48] McCormick 2001.   [49] Slicher van Bath 1963: 37.   [50] Hopkins 1983: 70–1.

with an iron mould-board and coulter to turn over the soil instead of jus
scratching the surface as did the Mediterranean plough. Population too
increased, and the number of inhabitants in towns where most craftsmer
and petty traders lived. That increase entailed a growth in the demand
for food as well as in the division of labour and in per capita productivity
Much of the latter had been achieved by the first century CE as the resul
of the diffusion of standards of productivity which had been established
earlier in various parts of the eastern Mediterranean. It occurred because
of advances 'in the wider use of iron tools, in some improvements ir
agricultural instruments (e.g. screw presses), and in the mere existence o
agricultural handbooks, which were symptoms of attempts to rationalize
the use of labour, particularly slave labour'.[51]

Outside agriculture there was also an increase in productivity since
now muscle power 'was supplemented by levers, pulleys and ratchets, by
fire, by water (for mills in late Antiquity and for mineral washing), by
wind (for ship-sails not mills), and by technical competence'. There were
'technical advances' in building (with the use of concrete for instance),
in rotary mills and in methods of improving the air flow in iron smelting,
as well as in transport, in larger units of production, bigger ships. In all
these activities the use of iron, a cheaper metal, as ore was available almost
everywhere, helped greatly in developing some forms of mechanization.

It was not simply 'cultural superiority' in the limited sense of 'high
culture' and the 'superstructure' that the Romans displayed, since they
changed the face of much of Europe with their urban buildings, viaducts,
hypocausts, theatres, and baths. They also created legal codes, literary
works, educational establishments, and performances of various kinds.
None of this would have been possible without a flourishing economy. It
was one that employed slave labour very widely both in the rural sphere
and for building these vast urban conglomerations – Rome itself, smaller
provincial centres in Britain as well as magnificent towns like Palmyra
and Apamea in Syria. All this is much more than the froth on a static
infrastructure. And it surely makes the feudal period seem not so much
dynamic (as some have claimed) as puny and marginal.

However, the early Middle Ages did show some improvement in agriculture. There were changes in the use of the plough,[52] but these were
mainly extensions of earlier practice. In addition there were a number of
inventions 'which were a great advance on the Roman era. Some of them
were taken over from other parts of the world, but there were already
signs of that technical sense which was later to be so characteristic of
west European civilisation.'[53] No-one doubts the technical achievements

---

[51] Hopkins 1983: xvi.   [52] Slicher van Bath 1963: 69.   [53] Slicher van Bath 1963: 70.

of later Europe. But it is difficult to see how inventions adopted from abroad can be signs of a west European technical sense; that view represents typical eurocentricism expressed in technological terms. 'We had it later, therefore we had it earlier', 'it' being a hypothetical technical 'sense', an aspect of our inherited mental makeup. In fact, the advance of such imported technologies were surely a mark of the inventiveness of others, especially the Chinese.[54] The major inventions adopted at this time, according to Lynn White (1962), were the spur, the horseshoe, and the water-mill. The spur, primarily of military value, came to Europe by way of the Arab countries, like many improvements in horses and their management. The horseshoe arrived at the same time as the new harness (head-collar) in the ninth century, possibly from the Byzantine Empire, which improved horse traction just as the spur improved mobility. The water-mill, used for Chinese blast furnaces as early as 31 CE, appeared in Europe in late Roman times, drawing water from the aqueducts for the purpose of milling; it spread very slowly to Arabia in the fourth century, then into western Europe, reaching Britain in the eighth century. In Europe these machines were first used for grinding corn and only later for extracting oil, beating bark for tanneries, rolling metal, sawing timber, pulverizing dyes, and after the thirteenth century for paper. In English the word 'mill' became a general term for any mechanized plant, as in Blake's famous line, 'dark Satanic mills', where they are the icons of the Industrial Revolution.

Despite these gains, civilization as a whole was in decline, as Anderson acknowledges. How long did it take for public theatres and baths to return to western Europe? How long before the educational system could hold up its head? How long before a sophisticated cuisine returned? How long before secular art and literature made a significant appearance? When all that eventually happened, we speak of a Renaissance, the rebirth of classical culture. But it was a long wait, punctuated by periodic revivals, as in the so-called 'renascences' of the Carolingian period and of the twelfth century.

The Carolingian revival and the birth of feudalism

The collapse of the Roman Empire did not lead automatically to the birth of 'feudalism', although some have seen feudalism foreshadowed in the self-enclosed estates of later Rome.[55] The characteristic feudalism of the Middle Ages in western Europe, held by many to be unique, was preceded by a Dark Age so that some see it as beginning only with the Carolingian

---

[54] Hobson 2004: 50ff.   [55] Coulbourn 1956; Goody 1971.

state of the eighth and ninth centuries, which Anderson characterizes as 'a real administrative and cultural revival' throughout the west. But the main achievement of this era lay in 'the gradual emergence of the fundamental institutions of feudalism below the apparatus of imperial government'.[56]

The great estates of the Carolingian feudal rural economy, it is claimed, were a distinctive phenomenon 'that expressed and exacted economic dynamism', with peasant farming making a contribution in return for rents and labour.[57] It is on those great estates that 'the beginning of the European economy' has been traced.[58] Some of those estates were very large but rarely completely self-enclosed. So that, from the eighth to the tenth centuries there was already a general trend 'to monetize the dues of rural households'[59] and to participate in market operations. At the same time, some estates invested heavily in water-mills, although these were already more widespread in later Antiquity than had been thought.[60] After countless excavations, a variety of urban crafts has also been revealed on the estates. Some of them even had their own dependent traders, as a result of which commerce began to expand slowly, especially in the north, as did the population.

Not only the 'causes' of feudalism, but even its timing and its distribution is subject to much debate, which relates to the Carolingian period. The former obviously depends significantly on the latter, on whether 'it is a purely European phenomenon and when it appeared (or disappeared)'. In an important review of the final volume (XIV) of the *Cambridge Ancient History*, Fowden queries the advisability of the periodization that sees 'Antiquity' in the west as ending in 600 CE, or worse with Constantine in 310 as did the earlier edition.[61] The latter date neglects the fact that in the east the New Rome 'had an emperor as well as a bishop, and was to continue in that happy state for another eight and a half centuries'.[62] Indeed the emperor Justinian (482–565) 'genuinely had a vision of a reunited Roman Empire'. So his successors looked to the east, especially after the Muslim invasions which cut communications with the west. Fowden insists that the spread of Islam has to be seen in the context of Judaism and Christianity as 'a fresh, clearer vision of the divine' that established a continuum from Afghanistan to Morocco, bringing together the southern, the eastern and the western parts of the Mediterranean. To adopt a date of 600 CE is to exclude any consideration of Islam which is then seen

---

[56] Anderson 1974a: 139.   [57] McCormick 2001: 7.   [58] McCormick 2001.
[59] McCormick 2001: 9.   [60] McCormick 2001: 10.   [61] Fowden 2002.
[62] Fowden 2002: 684.

as belonging to a quite different Asiatic world. That would be to overlook the continuities at all levels, so he concludes that a better marker for the shift would be 1000 CE.

A tradition in French scholarship has followed a similar direction, concentrating upon later political changes which have been viewed either as radical (that is, as a revolution) or as gradual (as a mutation). This tradition places 'feudalism' considerably later than even the Carolingian period, around 1000 CE. It has been described by some French historians as 'a brutal rupture, a "social tempest"'.[63] However, another group criticizes the whole notion of radical change, calling instead for a more sensitive, gradualist model. They reject the case for a particularly violent period between the relatively stable governments before 1000 and after 1200, especially one that led to dramatic economic change, and claim there are no grounds for assuming that seigneurial violence was an instrument by which the ruling class established a new kind of servitude.[64] Nevertheless for both groups, feudalism is still perceived as an essential prelude to a European modernity. 'The feudalisation of the eleventh century is seen as a necessary precondition for the birth of the modern state.'[65]

A precursor, because modernity is not regarded as a characteristic of the earlier period. In the emergent 'feudal mode of production' it has been said that 'neither labour nor the products of labour were commodities'; the mode of production was dominated by land and by a natural economy.[66] Another author has written that 'The fall of the Roman Empire and the transition from Antiquity to the Middle Ages can be seen, from an economic point of view, as a relapse from a money to a natural economy.'[67] However, he argues, the 'natural economy' eventually developed an urban aspect.

What constitutes a 'natural economy' is far from obvious but it is clear that this account is oriented purely to western Europe, dependent on the collapse and return of towns (elsewhere, as we have seen, there was greater continuity). In this view the east, whose history was deemed to be so different, would have had no Middle Ages (what would they have been middle between?) and no 'feudalism'; for towns continued to flourish as did manufacture and trade, although with some different emphases than in the west. That was true of the east of the Mediterranean too. Cities and even city-states continued to exist, in Syria for example through to the time of the Crusades.[68] Even in Italy 'the urban civilization of Late

---

[63] Barthélemy 1996: 197.   [64] White 1996: 218.   [65] Barthélemy 1996: 196.
[66] Anderson 1974a: 147.   [67] Slicher van Bath 1963: 30.   [68] Maalouf 1984.

Antiquity never wholly foundered, and municipal political organisation –
blended with ecclesiastical power . . . flourished from the 10th century
onwards'.[69]

One of the problems about defining change in social life in the very general terms of modes of production is that the latter are not only categorical
in their definition but tend to get interpreted in a restricted way, based
on a radical distinction between infrastructure and superstructure. But
the 'infrastructure' is much affected by what goes on at another level,
and developments in knowledge systems are often of profound importance for the economy. In that sense they play a significant part in the
infrastructure. In any case even agricultural production depends not only
upon technology in a limited sense but also on transport (for example,
on the construction of Roman roads), on techniques of plant breeding
and dissemination, as well as on organization and personnel.

Despite these justified queries about the nature of feudal developments,
the broad course of human history has nevertheless been traced by western scholars in terms of what happened in their part of Europe. Antiquity
and feudalism are part of a unique causal chain leading to western capitalism. Everything beyond, in Marx's phrase, was 'Asiatic exceptionalism'. Looking at the situation from a broader world perspective, it
is surely the west that was 'exceptional' at this period. It had suffered
what all are agreed was a 'catastrophic collapse' that was only slowly
overcome in many spheres. Like other authors such as Lynn White, the
historian Anderson stresses the technical advances that were made in
the medieval period, which he contrasts (questionably) with the 'static'
economy not only in Asia but in Roman times. For example, he comments on the fact that while the Romans had taken over the water-mill
from Palestine and thence from Asia, they did not make any general
use of it (although there is new evidence of wider employment). Water
was an element that was only gradually harnessed over time in both
east and west. The Romans certainly made significant moves along that
path, with aqueducts, hypocausts, and complex systems of water supply as at Apamea in Syria or the Pont du Gard in Provence. It seems
a restricted view of the political economy to concentrate only on agricultural technology in a limited sense, in which in any case Rome was
by no means static if one considers the introduction and extension of
crops, the use of water-mills, and the overall success of their productive
system.

As for the progressive nature of European society during the feudal
period, the productivity of western agriculture undoubtedly improved

[69] Anderson 1974a: 155.

 over time but from a low point of departure. However, it was never
remotely as productive as the irrigated agriculture of the Near East, nor
of North Africa and Southern Spain, much less the Far East,[70] where
[b]y the thirteenth century China had thus become what was probably
the most sophisticated agriculture in the world, India being the only conceivable rival'.[71] Some have even spoken of 'a Green revolution' in the
Middle Kingdom by the sixth century CE, others later.[72] In Europe, agriculture did improve between the eighth and twelfth centuries. But by how
much? There is a radical difference of opinion between those like Anderson and Hilton, who regard it as a highly 'progressive' development, and
others who are less impressed with its achievements.

Cavalry warfare

In respect of the means of destruction rather than the means of production or of communication, the development of feudalism in Europe
has also been linked to the advent of cavalry warfare.[73] Horsed combat
arrived much earlier than most historians recognize as feudal, for they are
more concerned with a different set of political and economic changes.
That form of combat, and its associated knights, was the result of international events. Europe underwent many challenges from its eastern steppe
frontier between 370 and 1000 BCE experiencing intense waves of Asian
migration as the result of disturbances as far away as China.[74] The penetration of the Avars into the continent meant that a number of Germanic
peoples were displaced into Italy, Spain, Gaul, and England, while Slavs
occupied much of the Balkans. One of the responses of the rulers was
military, the emergence of shock cavalry making use of the eastern stirrup which enables the rider to fight in the saddle with lance or sword.
Western historians often see this cavalry as the creation of Charles Mar-
tel at the battle of Poitiers in 733, leading to a victory that they were
convinced, by epic and by legend, had saved Europe from the heathen
Muslims. In fact, for the Muslims that expedition was little more than
a minor raid.[75] They themselves were much more concerned with their
contemporary rebuff at Constantinople. In any case the essentials of the
new military technology that supposedly saved Europe also came from the
east.

The stirrup was certainly known in China in the third century CE, where
it was made of bronze and cast-iron. Mounted shock cavalry had been

---

[70] For the Islamic contribution to agriculture, see Watson 1983 and Glick 1996.
[71] Elvin 1973: 129.   [72] Hobson 2004: 56.   [73] White 1962; Goody 1971.
[74] Hobson 2004: 105.   [75] Goody 2003b: 23–4.

used by the Persians and Byzantines as well as by Islamic armies, while 'horsed soldiers firing arrows' appeared in the Near East many centurie before. All forms of specialist horsed warfare require a considerable out lay on equipment[76] and it is suggested that the expensive obligation to provide shock cavalry lay at the basis of the feudal system. Horsed war riors needed to recoup their expenses either from booty or from the loca peasantry whom they could claim to defend. This expectation also existed among the horsemen of the ruling estate of the Gonja in West Africa but their domination was more limited since the recompense had to be in wa booty rather than in peasant dues; indeed I argued against the identifi cation with European 'feudalism' since production with the hand-held hoe, as distinct from the plough drawn by the ox or horse, produced little or no 'surplus' either for themselves or for their rulers. But there were nevertheless some comparisons to be made, in techniques, in support and in attitudes.

In sum, we do not have to accept the medieval period in Europe as a 'progressive' stage in evaluating the development of society, although much European thinking would wish us to do so.[77] That number includes those subscribing to the five-stage theory of development of human soci- ety, the 'communal' or 'tribal', the Asiatic, the ancient, feudal, and bour- geois (capitalism),[78] stages that are seen as necessarily proceeding from one to another. The 'ancient stage' is 'a history of cities founded on . . . agriculture', in which a slave economy predominates, though it also had a few traders. But feudalism was a subsequent outcome of that situation though it hardly represents an advance of Europe over Asia.

During the medieval period there were certainly improvements in the quality of life but to regard feudalism as progressive in comparison with the irrigated production, the continuing cities, and the developing cul- tures of the Near and Far East seems wide of the mark. Western advantage did not really manifest itself until after the Renaissance based upon the manufacturing and commercial achievements of Italian towns, primarily in textiles, for it was they who pointed the road in Europe to industrial capitalism and finance as well as signalling an advance in learning and in aesthetic pursuits. This advance rested on changes not only in the mode of production but also in the mode of communication, with the tardy arrival of the printing press and of paper, both eventually from China but now employed using an alphabetic script.

---

[76] Goody 1971: 47.

[77] In using the term 'progressive', I refer in this context essentially to technological progress, which as I have suggested is capable of some measurement.

[78] Hobsbawm 1964: 38.

The upswing of trade and of manufacture

The work of historians of medicine has uncovered the first stage in the appropriation of the Arabic science by the Carolingian physicians of Europe, an acquisition that reflected the re-establishment of long-distance commerce in the Mediterranean and that affected more than the economy alone. This was part of a wider rebirth that has been called the Carolingian Renaissance and which involved not only an increase in learning and the construction of schools but also the development of trade and manufactures: 'a glance at silk imports makes the case in a way that affords sporadic but telling quantification'.[79] Trade really began to pick up in Europe with the reciprocal ventures with the Levant which started at the end of the eighth century but only reached a significant level by the tenth and eleventh 'through the quickening of trade between Venice and southern Italy on the one side and the Near Eastern countries on the other'.[80] Mediterranean trade with the west then opened up (it had continued between eastern and north African ports), a renewal some have seen as the very 'origins' of capitalism. So it was, to a large extent – for the medieval west. For the expansion of trade meant re-establishing contacts with the great entrepots of the eastern Mediterranean, with Constantinople and Alexandria as well as with many smaller centres, none of which had suffered the same kind of collapse as the towns in the west and where a mercantile economy had long been established. Those contacts paved the way for the slow recuperation of Europe, bringing the benefit of luxuries as well as of more everyday products, of technological improvements, of classical scholarship, of literary and scholarly influences.

Dependent traders worked for the large religious houses and great estates in the Carolingian period, and independent ones in the urban economy. So commerce led to the revival of many towns in Italy which provided an altogether different focus to the centre of the so-called 'natural economy' in Carolingian Europe where feudalism is said to have developed. The towns had significantly collapsed in western Europe, not in the east, and now, stimulated by eastern trade, they revived. Trade in Europe then started to pick up at the end of the eighth century, not only along the northern route in the Baltic, through Russia and to Iran, but even in the Mediterranean where spices (and medicines), incense, and silks began to be exchanged for wool, fur, tin, Frankish swords, but especially slaves. The latter became one of Europe's most important exports, continuing down to the Turkish period. In this way, 'Europe's small worlds came to be linked to the greater worlds of the Muslim economies'[81] – 'the

---

[79] McCormick 2001:23.   [80] Slicher van Bath 1963: 34.   [81] McCormick 2001: 797.

rise – and economic consolidation – of Islam changed the nature of an emerging European economy'.[82]

In medieval England, overseas trade depended very much upon the production of wool and cloth and its export to Europe, where the greatest profits were not in manufacture but in the associated activities, long-distance trade and usury. The textile industry became of central importance to the growth of the European economy and, most notably in the Renaissance, to the revival and expansion of its cultural activities that were based upon its success. First to be established was the local woollen industry. Silk followed, initially imported and later manufactured locally, and lastly cotton, again imported, then woven in Europe, and constituting the very basis of the Industrial Revolution in England. In an earlier form of industrial production silk had spread from China to the Islamic world and taken root in weaving at Bursa in Turkey. There too, as in the west, Indian cotton was much appreciated and its bulk import gave rise to complaints, similar to those against silk, about the outflow of bullion required for its purchase.[83] For the eastern trade was not simply a matter of 'peddlers'[84] as some have maintained, but of large-scale imports and exports, a major commercial undertaking. That massive importation eventually led to the local production of cotton both at Bursa and Aleppo, adapting imitations of Indian designs, as was done with the famous Iznik tiles in Turkey that copied the Chinese.[85]

Wool was first exported raw, later as cloth, and eventually played an important part in the trade with the Near East. Woollen textiles were the main growth sector in manufactures in the west, productivity in which 'probably more than trebled with . . . the horizontal treadle loom'.[86] The production of cloth was greatly improved with this new loom, the earliest form of which appeared in Europe in the tenth century. This type had long been known in the east, from the Shang period in China. So too had complex reeling devices for thread that seem to have provided the basis much later for the water-driven silk-reeling machines of Lucca and then Bologna.[87]

The production of silk had undergone considerable development in China, well before mechanical processes had developed in Italy and later, with other textiles, in Britain. Elvin describes a large water-powered hemp-spinning machine which was based on one used in the Northern Sung for reeling silk and spooled by a treadle, drawing a number of filaments from a tub of boiling water in which the cocoons of silkworms

[82] McCormick 2001: 718.   [83] Inalcik 1994: 354–5.   [84] Steensgaard 1973.
[85] Inalcik 1994: 354–5.   [86] Anderson 1974a: 191.
[87] Elvin 1973:196; Poni 2001a and b.

were immersed.[88] In the thirteenth century this machine was adapted for hemp thread and driven by animals or water. Elvin compares it with the late seventeenth-century, early eighteenth-century, flax-and-silk spinning machines illustrated in Diderot's *Encyclopédie*, commenting that the resemblances are so striking that 'suspicions of an ultimate Chinese origin, possibly via the Italian *filatorium* for spinning silk, are almost irresistible'.[89] In other words not only the production of silk but its mechanization began in China and fed into the manufacture of textiles in Europe which was characterized by a process of 'import substitution' for both silk and cotton.

Developments in the textile industry were central to the revival of trade in Europe, both in the export of woollen cloth and in the import of silk, for which it was often exchanged in the Near East. The product of both was assisted by the move towards mechanization and even industrialization. In Europe the use of hydraulic machinery in the textile industry began in Italy in the wool-district of the Abruzzi in the tenth century where water was used to operate the large hammers for beating wool felt,[90] a process that also probably derived from China.[91] The town of Prato, adjacent to Florence (their production was not always distinguished abroad), depended upon the development of Roman canals and mill ponds (*gore*) for the washing and processing of wool as well as for the hydraulically driven machines.

The textile industry in Prato emerged in the twelfth century, based on the plentiful waters of the river Bisenzio. It was especially suitable as a place for finishing wool because of the availability of fuller's clay in the area. Early that century we find records of woollen cloth being dried along the ditches around the walls. In the twelfth century the development of manufacturing, which had taken place elsewhere in Eurasia, led to the shift from domestic to what is described as industrial production. The brisk trade in cloth meant that there were many money-changers in town although full banking activity was found only at the end of the century. By 1248 the wool merchants and pannaioli organized their own corporations, which included some immigrants from Lucca and from the wool-producing parts of Lombardy.[92] In 1281 a merchant of Prato was already trading in silk and ermine at Pera, the Frankish quarter of Constantinople organized by the Genoese, for the trade of wool and silk was central to European and Near Eastern exchanges. By the end of the twelfth century merchants were going to the Fairs of Champagne

---

[88] Elvin 1973: 195.   [89] Elvin 1973: 198.
[90] See Duhamel de Monceau, *Il Lanaioli*, 1776.
[91] Needham 2004: 223, referring to water-powered hammers.   [92] Cardini 2000: 38.

and in the thirteenth to the papal court at Avignon. At the end of that century it was another merchant of Prato working as a tax collector for the French king who inspired Boccaccio to write the opening story of the *Decameron* (1358).[93] Banking and textiles were often closely associated, here as elsewhere, in India for example.

By the thirteenth century, there were sixty-seven mills in Prato used for processing both grain and textiles. The great expansion of the manufacture of wool in that town is credited to Francesco di Marco Datini (1335–1410) whose statue stands in the centre of the square in front of the Town Hall. Datini left vast quantities of letters and account books that were discovered walled up in his house and provide an index of the extent of mercantile literacy. He had no children, so left his wealth to a foundation that took care of the poor. In his travels he went to Avignon when the Papal court (a great market for textiles) was established there and returned to build a factory dealing with every phase of production including dyeing. The development of the textile industry and the related commerce took place at the same time as that of book-keeping in Italy – the one needed the other. So Prato itself was populated by accountants, lawyers, and traders as well as by successful merchants like Datini.

The wool merchants not only manufactured textiles but also dyed and finished wool and cloth bought in from elsewhere, from Lombardy and from England where the best quality wool was produced and where the activities of merchants and bankers working especially within the wool trade are reflected in the name of Lombard Street in the centre of the City of London. These were the earliest international bankers in that town. English wool fed into the continental trade and led to the considerable prosperity of East Anglia, with its fabulous 'wool churches' and the home of the wool-sack on which the Chancellor of Exchequer traditionally sits. The wool was exported to Flanders, principally to Bruges, where it was used by Flemish weavers who enriched the town in buildings and artistic activity, giving rise to the Flemish Renaissance in the fourteenth century. In Tuscany it was the trade in textiles that laid the foundations of the artistic triumphs of the Renaissance. These activities began with the painters (*i primi lumi*) of the late twelfth and thirteenth centuries, precisely the time when the wool trade in Prato got going and when European accountancy developed. The Medicis were themselves textile merchants as well as bankers with a residence in the wool district of Abruzzi near Aquila and had close connections with Prato where they built the church of Santa Maria delle Carceri next to the castle.

---

[93] See also I. Origo 1984 [1957] *The Merchant of Prato: daily life in a medieval Italian city*, Harmondsworth: Penguin.

What was critical in the revival of the medieval economy was exchange, including long-distance exchange, especially in the Mediterranean, which in turn stimulated production. 'The urban economy of the Middle Ages was throughout indissociable from maritime transport and exchange.'[94] The Arabs had dominated the inland sea in the early years of their expansion. But it was partly cleared of Islamic fleets in the eleventh century, at about the time of the First Crusade and the opening up of the Atlantic route from the Mediterranean to the Channel by the Italian fleet. The advent of the Turks changed that situation and their navy became an important factor at least until their defeat at the battle of Lepanto (1571). But exchange remained critical for the renewal not only of the economy, but of knowledge and ideas.

Other feudalisms?

Preoccupied by the notion of feudalism, some European scholars have searched for its presence or indeed its absence around the rest of the world. Coulbourn has looked for it in Asia, especially Japan;[95] others have found it in the heart of Africa.[96] For these scholars, any vaguely decentralized regime was up for consideration (and most regimes display a measure of local autonomy as between the centre and the periphery). More specifically, they have looked for military obligation attached to landholding. Again that was not too difficult to find. So in some cases the notion of feudalism became imposed upon non-European regimes as in Africa.[97] However, the search for universal feudalism is mistaken, for while the political conditions that are commonly regarded as feudal were widespread, European and Asian society was based upon plough agriculture which gave birth to a very different system of land tenure than in Africa.

One problem with the wider, unrestricted view of feudalism is how to explain the apparently unique dynamism of the European theatre. 'No historian has yet claimed that industrial capitalism developed spontaneously anywhere else except in Europe and its American extension.'[98] This view holds that it is because of the earlier feudal social formation that Europe gained its 'economic primacy' which led uniquely to the Industrial Revolution and the subsequent transformation of societies everywhere. The commitment to 'western exceptionalism', to the unique significance of the direct line of progression between Antiquity and capitalism through feudalism slants history in a particular direction. We need

---

[94] Slicher van Bath 1963: 193.   [95] Coulbourn 1956.   [96] Rattray 1923.
[97] Goody 1971.   [98] Anderson 1974a: 402.

to consider that the primacy of the nineteenth century (or earlier) does not necessarily go back in any causal way to the medieval period, to a unique feudalism. Indeed, how can the early uniqueness thesis be reconciled with the notions of Chinese scholars about 'shoots of capitalism' under what Elvin calls a manorial system (and Needham 'bureaucratic feudalism') or of the ideas of Nehru and others about India's route to capitalism having been inhibited by the colonial conquest? How can it be reconciled with the view of those scholars such as Pomeranz and Bray who see parts of China and 'Europe' as level-pegging economically and culturally until the end of the eighteenth century?

Although we have discarded the idea of an African feudalism because of the great disparity in the productive systems, the situation in Asia, where these were societies with complex types of production, was different. The notion of 'sprouts of capitalism' in Asia has been proposed by some and vigorously denied by more orthodox eurocentrists. Marx's correspondent, the young Russian historian Kovalevsky, argued that feudalism of a kind arose in India, a proposition to which both Marx and Anderson objected suggesting that it neglected the different political and legal situation in Europe. There is something to be said for both points of view. European feudalism was of course unique, as are all social formations; nevertheless the property relations in those different regimes do have something in common. This is a situation in which the constitution of a sociological grid would be useful, attempting to show which elements of 'feudalism' were present or absent in different regions. The critical question is whether any unique features in Europe contributed in a significant way to the emergence of industrial capitalism. That is assumed in many 'evolutionary' arguments of those supporting 'western exceptionalism' but are these arguments based on anything more than temporal priority?

Most scholars see feudalism as a stage intrinsic to the development of capitalism and therefore confined to Europe. Anderson for example considers that nowhere outside that continent (except possibly in Japan) was there a feudal stage that could develop into capitalism. Feudalism in Europe did so since, as we have seen in discussing Antiquity, it was considered to be partly based on the 'Germanic system' that was characterized by an aggregate of separate homesteads and therefore implied a greater potentiality for 'individualization' than the antique system in which individuals were representatives of the Commonwealth, as in a corporation. The situation was similar in societies with intensive agriculture, living in tight settlements and participating in collective labour. Many thoughtful scholars have seen this vague attribute, individualism, as an essential feature of entrepreneurial capitalism as opposed to earlier 'collectivism', and as one of the crucial contributions made by feudalism to development of capitalism in Europe. It is a view we will later dispute. In Anderson's case the feudal mode of production is looked upon as emerging from the coming together of the inheritances of the earlier slave and the tribal modes – 'the combination of large-scale agrarian property controlled by an exploiting class, with small-scale production by a tied peasantry'.[99] The former is thought to permit the growth of autonomous towns 'in the interstitial spaces' as well as a separate church and a system of estates,[100] providing for the 'parcelization of sovereignty'.

Thus the feudal outcome could only occur in the west of Europe. Not only Africa and Asia, but even eastern Europe all had different regimes. The situation was less clear-cut in Byzantium which was marked by the earlier contrast between the western and eastern parts of the Roman empire, the subsequent development of which was however seen by Anderson in the following terms: 'Late Byzantine feudal forms were the end-result of a secular *decomposition* of a united imperial policy' whereas western feudalism was 'a dynamic *recomposition* of two dissolved anterior modes of production [tribal and slave], in a new synthesis which was to unleash productive forces on an unprecedented scale'.[101] At best, he argues, the process in Byzantium 'released a certain intellectual effervescence' but commerce in the capital had been 'captured' by Italian merchants rather than by locals. In fact, however, commerce in Constantinople involved both locals and foreigners in its very nature (as in Venice or London), and that was even more true of Bursa and other cities in the Near East.

Overall, Byzantium is considered economically stagnant in agriculture and manufacture (except for the introduction of some new crops and the wider use of the water-mill). However, one major breakthrough took place in Constantinople where 'state plants . . . enjoyed a monopoly role in the European export market until the ascent of the Italian mercantile towns',[102] which later appropriated much of the production of that region. Even the technique of processing silk in Turkey is said to have been 'purloined from the Orient rather than an indigenous discovery'. But what then constitutes a truly 'indigenous' discovery? Many basic inventions regarded as critical for the rise of the west, came from the Orient. The same could be claimed of the production of silk in Europe, a major economic factor in the Italian Renaissance. Silk-worms were said to have been smuggled to Byzantium from the east in the staves of Nestorian monks. Roger II of Sicily in turn kidnapped silk weavers from the

---

[99] Anderson 1974b: 408.   [100] Anderson 1974b: 410.   [101] Anderson 1974a: 282–3.
[102] Anderson 1974a: 275.

Byzantine towns of Thebes and Corinth in 1147. From there silk production spread to Lucca in northern Italy and that town again attempted to maintain a monopoly of the technology. However, its practices were taken by immigrant workers to Bologna where yet more complex techniques of mechanized silk-reeling were developed before they shifted yet further north. From there a critical part of the process of mechanization was pirated by an English silk merchant at the beginning of the Industrial Revolution in that country. When we are considering the characterization of Turkey as a backward Asiatic power, we have to recall the similarities (not identities) of the system of land tenure, whether or not designated feudal, and the active manufacturing and commercial sectors in its towns, especially in Europe and the Mediterranean.

There seems to be widespread agreement that a partial exception to the claim that feudalism was absent in other parts of the world, even for many European historians, was the case of Japan;[103] one suspects that the perception of this particular pattern is a backward projection from Japan's early achievements in industrial capitalism (often seen as contrasting with China's experience, a judgement that has turned out to be distinctively premature). Japan is claimed by Anderson to have developed a similar system to Europe in the fourteenth to fifteenth centuries, although its estates differed in never having had a demesne or home-farm. However, he argues that Japan did not of itself produce capitalism which it is questionably said to have borrowed from Europe. Moreover its 'feudalism' did not provide the 'economic dynamic of the feudal mode of production in Europe which released the elements for primitive accumulation of capital on a continental scale',[104] preparing the way for the ascent of the bourgeoisie. Like Braudel, Anderson sees the full capitalist mode as being launched only by the arrival of the Industrial Revolution which was built upon a 'market-centred landlordism' and a bourgeoisie. Japan may have had feudalism but it never had Absolutism, which, in an original contribution to the debate, Anderson considers an essential precursor to capitalism. Consequently he is critical of those scholars who follow the tendency of some writers and look upon the successive phases of socio-economic development as universal and so see feudalism as a world-wide phenomenon.[105] This view he understands as a reaction against assumptions of European superiority, but nevertheless insists on a narrower definition of the feudal mode of production as the combination of large landownership, with 'judicial and constitutional systems

---

[103] On Japanese feudalism see also Bloch 1961: 446. For him, feudalism is a type of society not confined to Europe – Japan passed through such a phase.
[104] Anderson 1974b: 414–15.   [105] Anderson 1974b: 401.

becoming . . . external elaborations; the parcellized sovereignty, vassal hierarchy and fief system are irrelevant'.

Wherein lay the supposedly unique characteristics of earlier Japan? Like Western Europe, it is claimed, feudal agriculture had generated 'remarkable levels of productivity'.[106] Agricultural productivity, however, was surely no greater than in other areas of monsoon Asia, such as Indonesia, South China, or South India. These regimes were also highly urbanized and displayed 'a pervasive market-oriented landlordism'. They traded vigorously with the west, especially in spices, and they had long been the centre of a complex system of exchange that included textiles from India as well as many 'cultural' imports, Sanskrit, Buddhism, Hinduism, temples and items of largely secular significance. Despite the levels of productivity attributed (uniquely) to Japan, the impetus to capitalism is said to have come 'from the outside', an opinion which ignores the fact that there were also indigenous developments, here as elsewhere in Asia, at least in mercantile capitalism.

Anderson argues that Japan is the exception in Asia, in that it easily 'adopted' capitalism. The argument remains highly eurocentric since it does not grant the east, even Japan, the possibility of developing capitalism unless by borrowing from the west. One reason he gives for its incapacity to develop on its own is the absence of Antiquity. Japanese feudalism, Anderson suggests in his original contribution, was the result of the slow disintegration of 'a Sinified imperial system'.[107] What distinguished Europe was not simply the disintegration of the Roman empire but 'the perdurable inheritance of classical Antiquity',[108] that is, 'the concatenation of Antiquity and feudalism'. In Europe there persisted a 'remanence' of the earlier mode; the classical antecedence prepared the way. The rebirth of Antiquity eventually produced the Renaissance, 'the crux of European history'; for Japan 'nothing remotely comparable to the Renaissance touched its shores'.[109] There was obviously no need for a rebirth if there had been no death (or decline). Since neither 'feudalism' nor 'Antiquity' were to be found elsewhere, they could not have been linked (in concatenation) outside Europe.

This claim founders upon an obvious problem: whilst for feudalism an attempt is made by historians, however unsatisfactory, to define its characteristics, 'Antiquity' is basically a historical period in which Greece and Rome were dominant, largely undefined economically, and was so specifically geographical that it even excluded major trading partners (and rivals), Carthage, the Near East, India, and Central Asia.

---

[106] Anderson 1974b: 418.   [107] Anderson 1974b: 417.   [108] Anderson 1974b: 420.
[109] Anderson 1974b: 416.

Nevertheless, Japan is often seen to provide a parallel to Europe, a view based not only upon the formal similarities between the two, but, more significantly, upon the outcome. 'Today, in the second half of the twentieth century, only one major region outside Europe, or its overseas settlements, has achieved an advanced industrial capitalism: Japan. The socio-economic preconditions of Japanese capitalism, as modern historical research has amply demonstrated, lie deep in the Nipponic feudalism which so struck Marx and Europeans in the later nineteenth century.'[110] Again, this is a highly teleological perspective. While that opinion may have been possible to sustain in 1974, it was soon no longer adequate, and 'modern historical research' has been found wanting. With the growth of the Four Little Tigers, especially Hong Kong, and now China itself, one must decouple the growth of capitalism from the pre-existence of feudalism in Asia (unless one takes the other and probably even less satisfactory tack of universalizing feudalism). Economically Japan is no longer unique. With Braudel, I would argue that a decoupling between capitalism and feudalism was always necessary, just as we should also decouple the relation between capitalism and industrialization, for industrialization has obviously characterized socialist regimes as well as capitalist ones. Both exist in a wider range of societies than is often supposed and have long done so.

In Europe, the procession towards capitalism from feudalism started with what is seen as the very different evolution of cities under what Anderson calls parcellization (deemed 'irrelevant'); they had 'the municipal legacy'. In the countryside it was the inheritance of Roman law that is claimed to have made possible the decisive advance from conditional to absolute private property;[111] the advent of capitalism is related to this 'legal order', through 'a written civil law'. The revival of Roman law in Bologna was accompanied by 'the reappropriation of virtually the whole cultural inheritance of the classical world'.[112] Included in these developments was said to be the institutionalization of diplomatic exchange (which seems a particularly eurocentric claim when looking at China and the Muslim world) and the emergence of a form of state, Absolutism, which did away with the parcellization of feudalism, and prepared the way for capitalism. Absolutism occurred at the time when commodity production and exchange developed, dissolving 'primary feudal relations in the countryside'.[113] But with centralization in Europe, supposedly absent in that form from other parts of the world, one also found the consolidation

---

[110] Anderson 1974b: 415.   [111] Anderson 1974b: 424.   [112] Anderson 1974b: 426.
[113] Anderson 1974b: 429.

of absolute private property, another feature seen as a necessary precondition of capitalism.

There are several problems with this account. Firstly, it is a legalistic interpretation that confines the nature of law to written law. Clearly all human groups have 'law' in a wider sense that includes customary 'law'; so, too, all enter into 'diplomatic' relations with their neighbours and have some form of 'private property'. Secondly, German tribes were more likely to be members of corporate groups than Roman citizens; yet paradoxically such membership is supposedly the basis of the 'free labour' of capitalism. Thirdly, there is the ethnocentric treatment of 'individualism' pursued by so many European scholars. Many 'tribal' peoples have been shown to stress their existence as individuals, as for example in Evans-Pritchard's classical study of the Nuer of the Sudan. In any case, as I have argued elsewhere, the capitalist organization of work, in a factory for example, demands a greater suppression of individualistic tendencies than either hunting or farming.[114] The life of a solitary individual Robinson Crusoe or of a settler on the frontier is not the normal experience for the majority of people, and more closely resembles the life of earlier forms of hunting and gathering societies rather than of later modes. Finally, this discussion of the contribution of feudalism to capitalism appears to neglect the role of the towns (which Marx recognizes as the nucleus of later developments), towns that grew within feudalism and gradually dominated rural-based relationships, but whose history goes back to the Bronze Age, and which were flourishing in post-Antiquity almost everywhere outside of western Europe. Marx does consider the possibility of capitalism developing from Rome or Byzantium but argues that wealth from trade and usury was not as yet 'capital'. In fact investment took place in trade and manufacture, in the production of silk textiles as well as in the manufacture of paper and in agriculture. Trade and usury too were of course essential to later developments, as were the 'free' peasantry and urban craft producers. It is the two latter that develop into the industrialized labour force.

Feudalism is therefore seen as a decentralized polity that allowed for developments 'in the interstices' and that encouraged a modicum of freedom. The east, beginning in the Near East, was thought to be marked by irrigated agriculture and by despotism, which were seen to go together in what was called the 'Asiatic mode of production', the problem with which we see in the following chapter. 'Despotic' systems were believed to be incapable of providing the background necessary for the growth of

[114] Goody 1996a.

capitalism (though 'Absolutism' apparently did). But they were obviously quite compatible with the existence of towns, with large-scale manufacture (of silk textiles in Turkey for example or of cotton in India), even with a measure of mechanized production. They also conducted complex exchanges between Europe on the one hand and Asia on the other. How could other societies participate in this important exchange of goods and techniques if they had such different socio-economic bases? Were not the elements of capitalism distributed very much more widely than many scholars assume, as we will discuss with the work of Braudel?

4 Asiatic despots and societies, in Turkey or elsewhere?

In the later Middle Ages, the nearest major non-European, Asiatic power to Europe was Turkey. Since the fourteenth century her armies had been attacking existing European and Christian space, including Byzantium and the Balkans. Much earlier Europe had been invaded by Islam (the 'Moors') from North Africa, in Spain, advancing into Sicily and into the Mediterranean generally. The Moors and the Turks had become the epitome of the non-European forces ranged against the continent and they were typically seen as despotic in character, as lacking the Christian virtues and marked by cruelty and barbarism: they were Muslim.

In European eyes, Turkey was generally seen even by intellectuals as a despotism, especially after the seventeenth century. In *The Prince*, Machiavelli described the subjects of the Porte as being ruled by one master, and as consisting of his slaves or servants. Some years later the French author, Bodin,[1] contrasted European monarchies with Asian despotisms unrestricted in their dominion, a situation never to be tolerated in Europe.[2] Others saw the critical difference between east and west as due to the absence of a hereditary nobility[3] or as the result of the lack of private property in Turkey,[4] both seen at the time as instruments for protecting man and his earthly goods. The French philosopher Montesquieu believed that under eastern systems assets were always liable to confiscation;[5] that insecurity was the epitome of Oriental despotism, opposed in principle to European feudalism, where a man's property was safe.

Of course the notion of Turkish 'despotism' changed over time. In the early part of the sixteenth century, Ottoman institutions were compared favourably to those in the west by Venetian ambassadors. After 1575 the relation is reversed.[6] 'If the principles on which his power was based were at variance with those of the Venetian republic, the empire was nonetheless a construction of imposing beauty, an admirable order.'[7] What reversed the situation? Matters had changed in Istanbul; there was

---

[1] Bodin 1576. [2] Anderson 1974b: 398. [3] Bacon 1632. [4] Bernier 1658.
[5] Montesquieu 1748. [6] Valensi 1993: 71. [7] Valensi 1993: 98.

more 'tyranny'. The Atlantic powers had brought in an excess of American bullion which had affected the economy. Lepanto had been a great military defeat. But above all, in Valensi's eyes, there had been a reinvention of Aristotle, or invention of the concept of the despot, 'the separation of Asia (or the Orient) from Europe: the concept of oriental despotism'.[8] The spectre of pure power came to haunt Europe.

So Turkey became the type case of Oriental despotism in the early modern period just as earlier in Antiquity Persia had done for Greece. As we have seen in chapter 2, Greek ethnocentric attitudes became integrated into western scholarly historiography and cultural analysis. The dichotomy they established between their own democratic systems and what they perceived as the despotic Persian 'other', merged with the later European opinion of the Turks to produce, in European thinking, a paradigm which was held to be characterized by what Marx designated 'Asiatic exceptionalism'. However, all were heirs to the Bronze Age civilizations which stretched from the Fertile Crescent of the Near East right across Asia to China, and which were also the foundation of European developments beginning with Antiquity. So the implied opposition between European and Asian societies is of little analytic value as far as the earlier history is concerned. During the opening years of the present era, for instance, there were two great empires in Eurasia, Rome in the west and China in the east. In terms of development, there was little to divide them. Both were built on Bronze Age economies and organized themselves using literate knowledge systems and communication, in one case employing a form of the Phoenician alphabet, in the other an elaborate logographic script using 'characters'. In terms of knowledge systems, they were in many cases comparable, as Needham has shown with botany.[9] In the case of both Rome and China, economic and cultural achievements were built on analogous developments which began in the Bronze Age. However, whilst both Rome and China practised plough agriculture – a practice that was widespread in the cultures which emerged from the urban Bronze Age societies which stretched across Eurasia, in China geographic conditions favoured large-scale irrigation in the river valleys. This gave rise to the notion of Asiatic despotism, since central control was deemed to be necessary to the organization of such an enterprise. These developments comprised many craft activities involved in urban construction, manufacture, and exchange, including writing.

The urban revolution of the Bronze Age also produced more pronounced economic stratification since with the aid of animal traction,

---

[8] Valensi 1993: 98.   [9] Needham 2004.

essential to that change, one man could farm a much greater area than
with the hoe. That made differential ownership of greater significance,
since with more land an individual could employ others as well as animal energy to produce a surplus for the urban markets serving the non-
farming population. Land became a value in quite a different way than
under hoe farming. Throughout Eurasia, the economy of the major societies was based not only on similar techniques of production but also on
broadly similar labour practices, more servile with the slavery of the west,
somewhat less so in the east. Later on, to bronze was added iron, a more
'democratic' metal that was used both in peace for the plough and in
war for weapons. Also involved in the social differentiation encouraged
by agricultural practices was the exchange of natural and manufactured
products, luxury items over long distances, but everyday over shorter
ones, made easier by the use of wheeled vehicles as well as water transport. Writing was just one of the specialist activities that grew up under
the 'Urban Revolution' which introduced what many have understood as
'civilization' in what were huge conglomerations compared to earlier settlements. That situation led to 'cultural' as well as to politico-economic
stratification throughout the major societies of Eurasia. The specific ways
in which every society dealt with these emerging social divisions gave rise
to a variety of political systems – and it is not my purpose to obliterate the
difference in governance and organization between the various cultures.
However, this variation took place within the broad framework that Eric
Wolf termed 'the tributary state', more centralized in the east, less so in
the west,[10] but without the violent dichotomies that the notion of a typical
Asiatic despotism presupposes.

   A recent world history of the last millennium by Fernandez-Armesto
does try to adjust the balance produced by earlier European accounts; in
it, 'western supremacy' is seen as 'imperfect, precarious and short-lived'.
Leadership was passed from the Atlantic to the Pacific, where it existed at
the beginning of the millennium, and remained there much longer than
Europeans have often supposed:

During the eighteenth century, despite the long reach of some European empires,
China's was by almost every standard still the fastest-growing empire in the world.
It also looked like the homeland of a more 'modern' society . . . a better educated society, with over a million graduates; a more entrepreneurial society with
bigger businesses and bigger clusters of mercantile and industrial capital than
anywhere else; a more industrial society, with higher levels of production in more
mechanised and specialised concentrations; a more urbanised society, with dense
distribution of population in most areas; even for adult roles – a more egalitarian

[10] Wolf 1982.

society, in which the hereditary gentry shared privileges similar to those of their western counterparts, but had to defer to scholar-bureaucrats drawn from every level of society.[11]

A consideration of even a selection of those features leads not only to a revaluation of China's position in world history up until the eighteenth century, but certainly dismisses any notions of static oriental despotism.

Indeed the whole idea of Asiatic despotism is grossly inadequate. *The Great Learning* of Confucius sheds an interesting light on the nature, at least the ideal nature, of the Chinese polity. Far from offering the typical picture of an Asiatic despotism, the argument runs that 'anyone who loses the support of the people loses the state'.[12] That support directly depends on the virtue of the ruler. The requirement to enlist the support of the people implies a kind of consultative process, certainly not an autocratic rule. The ruler must help his people to lead 'prosperous and happy lives', that is what the mandate of Heaven involves.

It is, then, apparent that a binary opposition between Europe and despotic Asia is hasty and founded on ignorance or prejudice. In the remainder of this chapter we will further explore those issues that are perceived to distinguish the abnormal and tyrannical east from the healthily and democratically developing west, and analyse the validity of this discrimination by looking more closely at the recent paradigm of Asiatic exceptionalism, Turkey.

I want to discuss three aspects of Ottoman society in order to query certain aspects of these eurocentric perceptions of Turkey and to reflect upon European notions of the periodization of history and historiography more generally. These are the adaptation of firearms as a case study which allows us to question the notion of 'Islamic conservatism', the organization of agriculture (and the idea of the 'peasant as slave'), and the level of trade, usually seen as state regulated (whilst I will argue that Turkey displayed a certain degree of mercantile capitalism).

The discussion will allow us to conclude that in these respects, as in matters of government, Turkey was more similar to Europe in the polity, in the economy, and in 'cultural' matters than has often been assumed. The armed forces readily adapted to guns and gunpowder, just as the military soon built up a naval force in the Mediterranean. Peasants held a similar status to those elsewhere and were not all slaves of the emperor. Most importantly the so-called despotic rule did encourage trade, including private enterprise, and encouraged the development of a mercantile economy especially in the trade in silk and paper (and their manufacture),

---

[11] Fernandez-Armesto 1995: 245.   [12] Confucius 1996: 46.

and spices. There was a vigorous development in all these spheres, which was in the end defeated not so much by internal blockages as by the shift of textile manufacture to Europe and to the opening of the sea routes by the Atlantic powers both to the east (for spices and textiles) and to the Americas for bullion and agricultural products, thus marginalizing the earlier achievements of the Near East. Whilst most of this chapter is devoted to an analysis of Turkey, as one of the traditional extreme negatives on the scale of European values, in the concluding section of the chapter the discussion will move to the Far East – another type-cast 'antonym' of the dynamic, democratic west. Here we will look more deeply into the similarities, already announced in broad outline, between the two opposite sides of Eurasia.

The Sultan's army

The view of Turkey as a despotism goes hand in hand with the idea of 'Islamic conservatism', for example regarding the Ottoman's supposed technological inferiority[13] associated with the eurocentric approaches of authors such as K. M. Setton,[14] E. L. Jones,[15] and P. Kennedy.[16] This entails their resistance to adopting technological innovations made by others and the tendency to subordinate all matters of advances in knowledge, as well as economic and social life, to ideologically determined rather than practical considerations, under the guidance of an autocratic dictate from the secular or religious authority, leaving no room for the personal initiative or the 'free will' which supposedly characterized the very different European situation.

Whilst it was probably Europe which first adapted the use and development of firearms, the Ottomans, faced with an enemy using these weapons, soon followed. They did so rapidly, pragmatically and effectively, collecting the materials for guns and gunpowder, manufacturing their own weapons and organizing the very considerable productive effort and associated techniques, even changing the structure of the army.

'The "discovery" of gunpowder, the appearance of firearms and especially their employment in warfare'[17] was a feature of the late Middle Ages. Gunpowder had been made in China in the seventh or eighth century CE and according to Needham 'the "true" gun, hand-gun, or bombard . . . appeared in . . . about +1280'.[18] Within decades these weapons had reached both Islamdom and Christian Europe. It is not known precisely how gunpowder and firearms reached Turkey. Gunpowder-based

---

[13] Ágoston 2005: 6.   [14] Setton 1991.   [15] Jones 1987.   [16] Kennedy 1989.
[17] Ágoston 2005: 1.   [18] Needham 1986b: 10.

devices are reported among the Mongols from the 1230s,[19] and from the middle of that century they were instrumental in introducing them to Iran, Iraq, and Syria; proper firearms were introduced late in the four-teenth century. Europe seems to have recognized very rapidly the value of the new weapons, and developed them in the form of cannons (the Chi-nese employed the first kind of cannon in the thirteenth century accord-ing to Needham[20]). They were being used in sieges in the 1320s and 1330s as well as on ships. By the middle of the century they were being used in Hungary and the Balkans, by the 1380s the Ottomans knew of the weapons. In the Ottoman conquest of Constantinopole in the 1450s, can-nons were employed. In the early fifteenth century they were installed on European ships in the Mediterranean, which enabled them to dominate at sea.

The manufacture of cannons was a complicated task. The Ottomans used bronze, since they had access to supplies of copper: the other Euro-peans used mainly iron, which was less expensive but also heavier and more risky. Both bronze and iron required foundries with a complex division of labour and work organization. This was true throughout the Mediterranean. For the large Arsenal of Venice, Zan writes of an indus-trial plant employing a huge work force that upset the guild system. The Ottomans developed many foundries (*tophane*) throughout the realm, at Avlonya, Edirne, and other towns, including the Ottoman Imperial Foundry (Tophane-i Amire) in Istanbul. As in western Europe, ships with cannon were built at the Istanbul arsenal.

'In the late fifteenth and early sixteenth centuries, the Imperial Cannon Factory, Armory (Cebehaneni Anire), Gunpowder Works (Boruthane-i Amire) and Naval Arsenal (Tersane-i Amire) gave Istanbul what was probably the largest military-industrial complex in early modern Europe, rivaled only by the Venetian Arsenal.'[21] The Istanbul foundry produced up to 1,000 guns a year (usually fewer) and employed a varying number of workers, 62 cannon casters in 1695–96, with an array of other tech-nicians and between 40 and 200 day-labourers.[22] While the Ottomans made some very large cannon, used in sieges, they also produced other weapons. As Ágoston has shown, the common European idea of their being unable to produce smaller ones by mass-production techniques is mistaken. While mass-production was perhaps a new technique in Turkey, so too it was in the west, though there are some precursors, characterizing all the new arsenals and foundries making ships and guns, and Turkey was not slow to adopt both techniques and labour practices, which have been defined as 'capitalist'.

---

[19] Ágoston 2005: 15.   [20] Needham 1986b: 4.   [21] Ágoston 2005: 178.
[22] Ágoston 2005: 181.

So there was no question of Islamic technological conservatism. When Ottoman technological receptivity was coupled with widespread mass-production capabilities and superior Ottoman logistics, the Sultan's armies gained clear firepower superiority over their immediate European opponents by the mid-fifteenth century.'[23] They were able to maintain their firepower and logistic superiority against the Austrian Habsburgs and Venetians until the very end of the seventeenth century.

Neither can they be accused of 'organizational conservatism'. The Ottomans had a standing army in the form of the Janissaries long vefore the European powers. With Murad I (1362–89) the need for an independent army was recognized, 'a force that would stand above the various religious, cultural and ethnic groups'.[24] The Janissaries were recruited by the *devşirme* (collection) system whereby Christian males between fifteen and twenty were periodically rounded up and Ottomanized. After training they were paid by the Treasury and came under the direct command of the Sultan. Among their neighbours, the first standing army seems to have been that of the Austrian Habsburgs who only possessed permanent troups of any importance during the Thirty Years War (1618–48), that is, some 250 years later.

Together with the larger cannon they produced, this development demonstrates that the Ottomans were innovative in military matters. The ease with which the Turks adapted to the requirements of their military situation, both technologically and in terms of organization, suggests a different dynamic in Turkish society than is generally envisaged by scholars committed to the notion of Asiatic exceptionalism and the uniqueness of Europe, at least with regard to the issues of conservatism and the technological inferiority that is supposed to inhibit change. Those historians who recognize the achievements of Turkey in this field tend to insist that the technology was borrowed and was part of the foreign workforce. Attention has been called to the numbers of foreign workers employed in the armament industry and sometimes in the armed forces. In the European view, Ottoman achievements have sometimes been interpreted in terms of 'dependency theory', which sees them as being unable to establish an industry of mass-production on their own, as being a 'third-tier producer'. However, this does not constitute proof of Turkish waywardness or incapacity, as it was common practice for other powers to recruit abroad, especially German metal workers, as in the case of Spain. As for foreign members of the armed forces, think of Othello, the Moor of Venice, commanding the army in Cyprus, or the British Admiral Slade in the Turkish Navy.[25] So 'borrowings' were not a Turkish privilege, and

---

[23] Ágoston 2005: 9.   [24] Ágoston 2005: 22.   [25] Yalman 2001: 271.

Europeans were 'lenders' of workforce as well. Neither is this use of a workforce from other countries to be regarded as either conservative or inferior. To recognize the advantage of a new instrument or method – or workforce – and act upon it shows an adaptability totally at variance with common European notions of Asiatic inflexibility. They were not simply recipients of armaments (who was not?), but 'important participants in the dynamics of organized violence in the Euro-Asian theatre of war'.[26]

That is the correct way to think interactively of technology transfer and development, rather than simply in terms of who was first in developing an innovation, for example in industrial processing. Questions of superiority and inferiority then take on a different perspective.

Peasants as slaves?

One European argument has been that the workforce in Turkey was quite unlike that of the west, where slavery developed into feudal serfdom, because the peasantry always remained in a more servile state. But was that really the case? Were they capable of being bought and sold like chattels? Did they have no kinship rights? The Porte certainly had periods of strong central rule but to see Turkish peasants as 'slaves' of the sultan is to take rhetoric for reality. In fact Ottoman agriculture was based on leasehold farms under what is known as the çift-hane system. That system of peasant family farms is analysed by the Turkish historian, Inalcik, in relation to Chayanov's work on Russia.[27] He makes the claim that it fits the same general frame as Europe. That type of family tenancy was as important as the guilds were for the Turkish towns.[28] Both were actively maintained by the state bureaucracy by means of systematic surveys. In other words, demographically, economically, socially, the systems were comparable. The household farm unit consisted of a married couple, a certain area of land (5–15 hectares), and a pair of oxen. The ideological insistence on the state ownership of land was largely a device to maintain this system and to protect the peasant from division, incursion, or over-exploitation. State protection was also important since this holding constituted the basic fiscal unit.

The state was very protective of its farmers and herders, if only for fiscal reasons, and that protection included asserting the general right to gain a living. Peasants and nomads could be settled on newly conquered lands in return for various obligations. Since the state itself was unable to use all the 'feudal' labour services, it converted some into cash. Taxation was based upon the family farm ('a legally autonomous

---

[26] Ágoston 2005: 12.   [27] Chayanov 1966.   [28] Inalcik 1994: 143.

unit')[29] which had marked the late Roman period and persisted after the decline of the Empire. The state's role was in fact little different from the eminent domain vested in the rulers of European societies, which enabled them to tax, conscript, and judge their subjects. The peasantry was both 'dependent and free', like most tenants everywhere, protected by central government against incursions by landlords or tax collectors.[30]

Ottoman land tenure then is much more complex than is perceived by those who characterize Turkey as a despotic state in an Asiatic mould, a notion which was not at all confined to Marxist writers but represented a more general European view of the eastern 'other'. Since it was essentially a conquest state, it was the fact of conquest that established the overall rights in state land (*miri*), but there is disagreement as to whether those rights are vested in the *umma*, the community of the faithful, or in the sultan as its representative. Indeed, as we have seen, the conquerors left the indigenous peasant communities in place, simply acting as 'rent' gatherers.[31] The state took over 'eminent domain' and since its programme of continuing conquest required an army, it needed the support of taxes on the land.

'Land and the peasant may belong to the sultan', as a Persian saying declares. But the notion of the rights implied by the word 'belong' has to be very carefully understood. Indeed the Turkish civil law code was closely linked to Roman-Byzantine practices.[32] As in Roman Law, rights in land consisted of 'eminent domain' ('ownership'), possession, and usufruct, the two latter of which were fully entrusted to farmers in a variety of ways. Although it was not an easy transaction, under certain circumstances state lands could be sold by peasants; in this event they needed to establish 'absolute ownership' under Islamic Law.[33] As in Europe, eminent domain meant only the ultimate right of legal control, but 'pure ownership' (*mülk mahz*) could be established by a subject and the peasant used this possibility to transfer lands to a religious foundation; in this context Inalcik employs the term freehold, though as everywhere this 'freedom' was subject to wider controls.

The peasant could also use his rights for commercial purposes. In some cases, particularly from *waqf*, that is, endowed, and freehold land, 'the peasants collected a large amount of surplus wheat which they sold for export to distant markets in the urban centres of the empire and in Europe'.[34] In other words they were connected to the market and the production of cash crops – cotton, sesame, flax, and rice. Private ownership rights of this kind were sanctioned by Islamic law, a fact that an Islamic

---

[29] Inalcik 1994: 174.   [30] Inalcik 1994: 145.   [31] Inalcik 1994: 104.
[32] Inalcik 1994: 105.   [33] Inalcik 1994: 117.   [34] Inalcik 1994: 126.

state could never ignore; the 'rule of law' covered property rights as well as many others. The tensions between the secular and religious author-ities meant that the rights of peasants – and those of craftsmen – were defended from too heavy impositions by either. Indeed in the Ottoman empire, as elsewhere, there was always a tension between the state and the church, between the authority of the sultan and that of the *quadi*, constituting a sort of 'parcellized sovereignty' that has been seen as a unique characteristic of European feudalism, as we discussed in a previ-ous chapter.[35] The interests of state and church were by no means always identical, in theory allowing for a similar room for manoeuvre in the town and the country, as has been claimed for Europe.

Despite their materialist approach, many writers with a Marxist back-ground have concentrated on highly abstract rights (rather than practice), using the broad and exclusive categories of state ownership, communal or individual ownership. But as Henry Maine emphasized, in all societies we find a hierarchy of 'estates' in land, with some rights vested in the individual cultivator (or his household), some in wider groups of kith or kin, some in the local landlord, and some at a more inclusive political level. There are many variations in the rights vested at the different levels and it is an error to see all possible rights as located at one level only in any particular society. In the sphere of agriculture, where most indi-viduals made their living, there was considerable differentiation of rights related to the tools and methods of farming, most basically in whether dry or wet (irrigated) cultivation was practised, whether it was carried out with the plough or the hoe, or whether it was shifting or permanent in character; there were other differences that were more shaded. Secondly, there was differentiation with regard to rights in land. The complexity of Ottoman land-rights, and the superficiality of the earlier European view, are well brought out in a recent study of land ownership (the military 'fief') in Islamic (Hanafite) jurisprudence in Egypt from the Mamluks to the Ottomans.[36] The 'hierarchy of rights', whilst differently distributed from Europe, appears at least equally complicated, both in practice and in the course of the changing debate conducted by lawyers, although there is little theorizing around these issues in the political ideology or specula-tions about their misty origin.[37] The debates took place around the nature of these rights and were undertaken by a highly sophisticated legal profes-sion. Their varied conclusions have of course had an influence on public affairs, especially when matters come to court, but part of the debate is an attempt to formulate in writing the existing complexities of social life in relation to property. It should be added that, unlike much European

---

[35] Inalcik 1994: 128.   [36] Mundy 2004.   [37] Mundy 2004: 143.

egal thinking, the advent of Islam and the change of regime did not wipe he slate clean of existing rights although it did do some reorganization, is undoubtedly happened in many other 'conquest' situations.

Apart from peasant territories, grants of land were made to the military and to administrators in return for specific duties. It has been argued convincingly' that since it was revocable, the Arabic term *iqta* should be translated as 'administrative grant' rather than fief.[38] But clearly the concepts are very close and like the Chinese system which has been described as manorial[39] (and as 'bureaucratic feudalism' by Needham) again need to be examined by means of a sociological 'grid' rather than on a present-absent basis starting from purely European experience. When this is done even notionally, the situation can be seen as much closer to Europe than many theories assume. Indeed, existing conditions in the Islamic Near East at the time of the Turkish advance have recently been compared to early Europe. At Saladin's death in 1193, the regime resembled that of 'a monarchy bound by ties of lordship and clientage, dependent on dissolving loyalties, threatened at a moment when the suzerain of subordinate lords is weak'.[40]

Agriculture could never have remained at a purely subsistence level; it had to produce a surplus. Istanbul was a huge town, larger than any in the rest of Europe, and its provisioning was of great concern to the Ottoman rulers, as it had been to its Christian and Roman predecessors. Most of the grain came from the area north of the Crimea where commercial farming developed on a huge scale, at one point providing corn for Venice too. But parts of the country produced cereals for the town while much of the area around the capital itself was devoted to livestock-raising and to the farming of fruit and vegetables. The peasants were never involved simply in subsistence production; trade and the market were always relevant. Istanbul was in a similar position to many of those towns on the northern shore of the Mediterranean under Roman rule, which was supplied under the system known as 'anona' (a form of 'dole'). In many ways, the towns were comparable to those to the west and the east; Turkey was part of the Mediterranean world but all large urban sites had the problem of supply, often from peasants.

Trade

If agriculture were in a basically similar position to the rest of Europe, so too was the status of towns and of trade. Trade was both public and

---

[38] C. Cahen 1992, Mundy 2004: 147.   [39] Elvin 1973: 235.
[40] Fernandez-Armesto 1995: 90.

private, requiring a bourgeoisie which was not entirely under 'despotic' control, indeed that cast doubt on the notion of 'despotism'. The Roman and Byzantine empires had placed commerce, the circulation and sale of merchandise largely under state control;[41] the Ottomans followed suit. However, trade also involved partly independent merchants and a bourgeoisie, as well as government servants. The House of Mendes, run by Moroccan Jews expelled from Christian Spain, had a network of agents in the principal towns of Europe and 'controlled a large portion of international commerce'.[42] 'Every European country aspiring to mercantilist expansion, as a prerequisite for economic development, sought these economic privileges from the Sultan', that is, the trading privileges into the capital that following Venice the Italian cities had earlier enjoyed.[43] 'The West depended, at least at the beginning, on supplies from or through the Ottoman Empire for its newly rising silk and cotton industries.'[44] The battle of Lepanto in 1571 and the advent to the Mediterranean, in 1580–90, of the Atlantic seafaring powers, the British and the Dutch with their guns marked a turning point; the region was opened up to the new Levant companies of those nations. So the first successful charter companies in the west were the Levant companies, dealing with the Near East rather than with India and beyond, and were established well before the founding of the East Indian Company.

During the sixteenth century 'the Ottoman empire played a determining role in world trade'.[45] Istanbul was the meeting point of the north–south route to the Black Sea and Danubian ports, and the east–west route to India and the east. There was not only the western link to Venice and Genoa, but from 1400 a vertical north–south trade route through Damascus-Bursa-Akkerman-Lwow by which oriental goods reached Poland, Muscovy, and the Baltic countries; that path followed an earlier one from the Baltic to the Near East that marked the opening up of European trade in the Carolingian period.[46] Imports from the west were mainly woollen cloth (and bullion as always) which were exchanged for 'oriental goods' including local products, silk, and carpets. It was mainly but not only in luxuries. Some Roman moralists had been very concerned about the loss of bullion to the east in return for those products. They saw the east as the home not so much of despotism as of luxury, an indulgence in which would greatly affect the Roman military virtues. But the trade remained of great importance.

---

[41] Inalcik 1994: 198.   [42] Inalcik 1994: 213.
[43] Braudel 1949. In Europe the history of Turkey had often been treated from a distinctly one-sided point of view. However Braudel's work on Philip II saw that Islamic empire as an intrinsic part of the Mediterranean world.
[44] Inalcik 1994: 3.   [45] Inalcik 1994: 4.   [46] McCormick 2001.

Trading operations covered both Europe and Asia. The Byzantine political and economic dominance of the Black Sea had collapsed by 1204 when Venice became supreme on the Western Aegean and at Istanbul while Genoa conquered the eastern Aegean and established colonies around the inland sea. Turkey later destroyed the Latin colonies in that region and restored the old Byzantine imperial tradition, controlling the sources of supply itself. For Mehmed the Conqueror was inspired by the idea of reviving the eastern Roman Empire and the Porte needed to take control of the Black Sea in order to provision Istanbul with wheat, meat, and salt. The trade of silk, cotton, and hemp of northern Turkey for the agricultural products of the northern Black Sea, meant that Asia Minor 'industrialized' in these respects even before Western and Russian manufactures had a chance to compete in the late eighteenth century.[47] There was also a very active presence of Turkey and Egypt (nominally at least under Turkish sovereignty for long periods) in the Indian Ocean. At one point the Turks tried to assist the Indonesian Muslim kingdom of Aceh as a trading partner with men and arms in order to resist the European navies then active in the region. Although it had started as a land-based power, on reaching the Mediterranean Turkey had shown great adaptability in creating a navy that for long dominated the sea. Then the opening of the American continent, bringing cheap silver, cotton, and sugar (the latter previously available only through trade with Islam), changed the whole balance of opportunity.

The silk industry

Trade encouraged one particular sphere of manufacture, virtually an industry, in which Turkey became the dominant player and which greatly affected the rise of the west, of Italy in the first place. That was silk.

Raw silk first reached Byzantium from China by way of Persian intermediaries, either by the land route or through the Indian Ocean. The Emperor Justinian tried to break this Persian monopoly, especially after the Mongols had intercepted the direct route, by seeking alternatives – in the south from Ethiopian merchants of Aksum, in the north from among people in the Crimea and the Caucasian kingdom of Lazica as well as from the Turks of the steppes. Silk became the 'commodity of prime interest'. Some time before 561, Justinian's agents smuggled silkworms into Constantinople, leading to the establishment of a complete silk industry that was intended to liberate the country from dependency on the east and

---

[47] Inalcik 1994: 275.

in fact became 'one of medieval Byzantium's most important economic operations'.

Silk cloth had also made its way from China to Europe as early as the sixth century BCE. With the opening of the Silk Road in the second century BCE, the material arrived in larger quantities. After 114 BCE 'a dozen caravans a year loaded with siks crossed the deserts of central Asia from China'.[48] Syria, Palestine, and Egypt imported both raw silk and fabrics and a silk-weaving industry eventually began to flourish. By the fourth century CE its manufacture had spread to Persia and then to Byzantium, an industry that was inherited and developed by the Turks. Silk was introduced into the Islamic part of Spain during the rule of the emir Abd al-Rahman II (755–788) of Cordoba at a time when he adopted the title of Ummayad Khalif. He took on the monopoly of minting money and, following the Abbasid and Byzantine examples, organized the royal manufacture of luxury textiles. Mulberry trees, silkworms, and Syrian weavers were introduced and silk workshops were set up near the alcazar in Cordoba as well as in Seville and Almeria. Like the techniques, many of the motifs came from the Near East, some of Persian (Sassanid) origin.[49]

Indeed silk 'formed the structural basis for the development of the Ottoman and Iranian economies'.[50] In this process Bursa became 'a world market' by the fourteenth century, with many western merchants using the ports of Ephesus and Antalya. However, the Genoese in Pera-Constantinople traded directly with Bursa, which was under Ottoman rule at the time. Genoese merchants even travelled inland to buy directly in the towns of Tabriz and Azov. Silk demonstrates the close links between the manufacturers and merchants of Europe and the Near East, especially Turkey. At first silk cloth arrives from the east as a luxury product, then Europe imports raw silk and makes its own cloth, finally it takes over the whole production process, including the cultivation of silkworms and mulberry trees. That process shows the way the regions are interlocked, and the process by which ideas and techniques are transferred between one area and another. We need to look at Eurasia not so much in terms of dichotomies and barriers between Asian and European systems, whether on the political level (despots) or any other, but rather in terms of the gradual flow of goods and information across the landmass. Far from initiating the early phases of mechanization, large-scale production, and marketing of textiles that began in the east, including Turkey, silk was only later developed in Europe; in any case its production was a matter of import substitution. 'Along with the highly developed native woollen

---

[48] Childe 1964: 249.   [49] Reynal 1995.   [50] Inalcik 1994: 219.

industries, silk became the principal source of international exchange and wealth for Western countries from the thirteenth to the eighteenth centuries.'[51] Fashion, it has been argued,[52] was the wheel of the expanding economy and the use of silk cloth among the elites, increasingly following the Crusades, gave rise to a flourishing luxury industry.

Apart from Spain, silk was gradually produced in Europe. In Italy Salerno was using raw silk in the ninth century and in the Po Valley by the tenth, acquiring the techniques from Greece and the Near East, that is well before Roger II of Sicily was bringing in silk workers from Greece. However, the real breakthrough came in the towns of northern Italy, an expansion that may have been encouraged by difficulties with the supply of silk cloth from the Near East as the result of the Mongol invasions and other disturbances. Silk weaving took place in the town of Lucca as early as in the thirteenth century, many weavers having fled from Sicily after the French conquest in 1266.[53] They began by using raw silk imported through Genoa from the Caspian area, from Persia, Syria, and 'Romania', a trade that was certainly stimulated by the burgeoning commerce with the east.[54] Silk cloth was of course aimed at the luxury market, at the courts of princes, rich abbeys, and great cathedrals, and eventually successful merchants. An attempt was made to limit the consumption of this material by sumptuary legislation to the court and to certain elite categories, but eventually these restrictions collapsed. Trade inevitably expanded. The merchants sold their cloth at the fairs of Champagne and from the end of the twelfth century in Paris, Bruges, and London.[55] Supply and demand increased. Their manufacturing success was copied in Bologna and Venice, although Florence continued to specialize mainly in woollen cloth, especially made with English wool, becoming probably the most important industrial city in Europe in the fourteenth century.[56]

There is therefore an interesting progression in the manufacture of textiles in the east and west. Mechanization was initially a slow process but one in which the efficiency of looms was gradually improved, not everywhere at once but often stimulated by changes elsewhere as the result of communication. That process developed further in China with the use of water power to drive machines for twisting thread, a process that later got taken up in Europe. So too did the production of raw silk

---

[51] Inalcik 1994: 218.   [52] Reflecting the thesis of the German economist Sombart.

[53] Some sources place silk weaving in Lucca already in the eleventh century.

[54] Arizzoli-Clémental 1996.

[55] E. de Roover did some of her research for *La Sete Lucchesi* (1993) in St Paul's Cathedral, London.

[56] Tognetti 2002: 12.

itself. By then Turkey, erstwhile a major player in the manufacture and trade of silk, had handed over its primacy to Europe – which it resembled in terms of the organization of its commercial enterprise to such an extent that any stark contrasts between the two are misplaced.

The spice trade

It was not only in the manufacture of silk and its exchange (mainly for bullion) that Turkey and the other Islamic countries around the Mediterranean displayed mercantile activity of the kind that is associated with mercantile capitalism, and which involved a certain degree of private enterprise and initiative, a response to market demands, and the combination of manufacture and trade. Apart from silk, trade was also affected by the other shift occurring in the spice trade that had also spurred Portuguese, Dutch, and English colonization in the east. Earlier Turkey, like the Near East more generally, had again been an important player. Writing of that country, Kellenbenz claims that 'the capitalist spirit found in the commerce in pepper one of its most important fields of activities'.[57] This commerce was largely in the hands of individual merchants who frequented the great khans and caravanserai scattered throughout the territory; it was a trade that involved capitalist enterprise in the same way as European traders.

Spices had already reached Europe from the east in the classical period and it was a highly significant factor in exchange in the Near East, in India and in China over a long period. Local pepper formed an important part of the diet in Black Africa but in the Mediterranean region it had to be imported from the east, a commerce in which local merchants were heavily involved from early times. As with the silk trade, the Turks took over the well-established Byzantine commercial traditions after they conquered Constantinople. Earlier, Islam had spread to South-East Asia, to Malaysia and Indonesia and its traders remained active even after the Portuguese opened up the sea route to Western Europe, with their first cargo of spices arriving in Lisbon in 1501. However, ships from India and Aceh in Sumatra, mainly belonging to Muslims, continued to supply the Red Sea despite Portuguese opposition. Then Muslim ships took their cargos through to the Persian Gulf where in 1546 the Ottomans had established a base at Basra. So there was never any complete diversion of the spice trade; the Ottomans continued to have direct links with the Islamic kingdom of Aceh, which they tried to support politically

---

[57] H. Kellenbenz, 'Le commerce du poivre des Fugger et le marché international du poivre', *Annales: Economies, Sociétés, Civilisations*, XI (1), 1956: 27, quoted in Inalcik 1994: 344.

nd militarily; Venice continued to be the recipient of some eastern pices.

With the coming of the English and Dutch to the Indian Ocean and vith the loss by the Portuguese in 1622 of the port of Hormuz that con-rolled the Gulf, there was an enormous expansion of the trade with the Atlantic powers. In addition, the result was that there was a fundamental geo-political shift to the Atlantic with the development of trade with the Americas, the substitution by colonial production – sugar, tobacco, cof-ee, and cottons, all brought in from the Americas.[58] It was Venice and he Ottomans that suffered from this diversion from the eastern Mediter-anean when the Atlantic economy took off.

Sugar was an epitome of this shift in production and trade. It was one of he most important 'spices', the production of which had been brought from South Asia to Persia and then by Arabs to the eastern shores of he Mediterranean. The Turks were heavily involved, so too were Chris-ian kingdoms under the Crusaders. The organization of work retained significant aspects throughout. 'Estates growing sugar cane, remarkably similar to the later plantations of the Americas, emerged in the Crusader kingdoms of twelfth- and thirteenth-century Palestine. By the fourteenth century, Cyprus had become a major producer.'[59] These estates were created by the Hospitalers and by Catalan and Venetian families who employed Syrian and Arab slaves as well as local peasants. The labour force was mixed. Sugar spread westwards to Crete, North Africa and to Sicily where it flourished even after the Norman invasion of the twelfth century. Since the Moorish conquest many centuries earlier the crop had also been cultivated in the Iberian peninsula, based on the use of Christian and Muslim slaves, and the sugar was marketed throughout Europe, fre-quently by Italian (Genoese) merchants. In the fifteenth century slaves were imported from Black Africa, which the Portuguese were actively exploring at the time. From the Algarve, sugar production and its related organization moved to Madeira and other Atlantic Islands, and later to colonial America.

Production in the Mediterranean had been improved by the use of a millstone for crushing the cane. The industry gradually became more mechanized. Somewhere in that region or on the Atlantic Islands, a new system developed consisting of two rollers cogged together; the cane no longer had to be cut up and more juice was extracted. It was in the Canary Islands that a complex sugar industry developed which has been described as 'capitalist' (again under Genoese management),[60] and cer-tainly substantial capital was required for the *engenhos*, the machines that

[58] Inalcik 1994: 353.   [59] Schwartz 1985: 3.   [60] Schwartz 1985.

were used to crush the cane. Traders became producers, investing capi
tal and employing machinery, in ways that became increasingly complex
The whole enterprise was highly market-oriented from the beginning, bu
now the produce was exported to northern Europe. In the West Africa
island of Sâo Tomé conditions were particularly favourable for the large
scale acquisition of African slaves and therefore to the growth of the kine
of enterprise that eventually formed the model for the industry in Brazil
The latter began as early as 1516, even before an organized governmen
was established there in 1533, a third of a century after Cabral's dis
covery of that vast region. In South America these enterprises employee
considerable numbers of European craftsmen as well as Indian and late
black slaves. Consequently the structure of society, based from the begin
ning on commercial agriculture, was mixed both ethnically and profes
sionally, providing a model for mechanized capitalist enterprise in othe
areas.

In the course of time Turkey became unable to compete with the west ii
its production of a range of cheap goods, cotton, woollens, steel, mining
its earlier hold on the preparation of sugar was broken by the migratioi
of cane to the Canaries and to Brazil, so that the refineries in Cyprus anc
Egypt were forced to close, the technology now being taken up in th
Atlantic and producing what Mintz and Wolf called 'capitalism before
capitalism'.

A static society?

These manufacturing and trading activities suggest that Turkey car
hardly be regarded as the 'static economy' which is supposed to char
acterize despotic states. The same holds for the society as a whole. This
alleged inflexibility has been attributed not only to its assumed despotic
character but also to Islam; the oft-cited example is the rejection of the
printing press that had been used in China for many centuries. On the
contrary, I have argued, the society was open to many influences and
many changes. The restriction regarding the printing press (and perhaps
other innovations, such as the clock) has nothing to do with a reluctance
to change. Rather, it has primarily to do with religious beliefs and as such
quite specific. Due to the wrongful generalization on the basis of what are
specific solutions to specific problems, the question often arises as to why
the Islamic world appears to have been willing to hold on to these beliefs
longer than either Christianity or Judaism, which appears to be the case.
The establishment of an independent secular power was slower. It has
sometimes been said that in contrast to other religions, particularly Islam,
Christianity allowed for secularism, a thesis that has been maintained by

Bernard Lewis: 'Secularism in the modern political meaning – the idea that religious and political authority, church and state are different and can or should be separated – is, in a profound sense, Christian.'[61] That assessment seems to me unsustainable. It is true that Christ told his followers 'to render under Caesar' what was his, emphasizing the distinction between church and state. But that distinction became less clear-cut with the establishment later in Europe of the Holy Roman Empire, with rulers claiming to be defenders of the faith. Religion dominated most areas of life in medieval Europe. There were counter-currents of scepticism, even agnosticism, that ran through this, as through other religions. But in general secular thinking was post-Renaissance, even post-Enlightenment, when it achieved a more permanent status. That constituted an important development. Even later, the old ways persisted in some respects in places like the South of the USA, despite its modern economy, not to speak of orthodox Jewish communities in various parts of the world. Islam differs only in degree and timing. Moreover, it too experienced periods of humanism when secular learning flourished. There seems little general difference in these religions until the Renaissance.

What a brief examination of the Turkish situation, focusing on government, the peasantry, and trade, emphasizes, is that it is an error to concentrate the analysis on one particular aspect of the regime, especially when the argument depends upon seeking out differences. The search for difference is of course important when trying to account for 'modernization'. Europe did develop a very advanced knowledge system after the advent of printing and an equally strong economy after the Industrial Revolution, having achieved a certain advantage in guns and sails somewhat before that time (though the extent of this advantage has been queried).[62] But to link this achievement to political systems (European democracy versus 'Asiatic despotisms'), to differences in land tenure ('absence of feudalism') or to the legal system (supposedly no tradition of Roman Law in the case of Turkey) is to project the present back into the past in an unacceptable manner and to engage in a front-to-back reading of history.

In any case, as far as the production of knowledge was concerned, the Islamic world held a distinct advantage until the coming of the printing press. The manufacturing and exchange economy was equally developed, with the Near East being the centre for silk textiles and other luxury products. These developments were not greatly inhibited by supposedly 'despotic' regimes or features such as the claimed absence of law, of independent towns, or of freedom! Towns were inherited from the ancient

---

[61] Lewis 2002: 107.　　[62] Hobson 2004: 189.

world and developed guilds, markets, and charitable foundations (*waqf*)
as in the west. Islamic law had its base in Roman jurisprudence and in th
post-Judaic codes of the Near East. Legal discussions reached a simila
kind of complexity to those in Europe.[63] The activities of both peasant
and merchants received legal protection from the courts in which wome
could appear as plaintiffs. The notion of Asiatic despotism is revealed a
a way that Europe denied those states legitimacy, first in Ancient Greec
and subsequently in the scholarship of post-Renaissance times. It is
concept that needs to be abandoned.

The Ottoman empire, which lay at the centre of these developments
was no static Oriental despotism from the economic point of view. 'By an
standards, [it] remained highly dynamic until well into the seventeenth
century.'[64] The same author remarks that 'the Ottoman state from th
fifteenth to the seventeenth centuries could outstrip in efficiency and
match for adaptability its western competitors, many of whose tradition
it shared'.[65] The shared traditions were important; Turkey was not sim
ply some Oriental other, either in the economy or the polity. 'In the six
teenth century, Turkish political thought kept pace with developments i
western Christendom. The great Ebu us-Sud produced a justification o
absolutism that revealed a thorough command of Roman law.'[66] Turke
is described as 'a state of extraordinary resilience'; only 'the treacherou
hindsight' of historians 'has foreshadowed its early decline'. Adaptabilit
was equally to the fore. The Turks, dependent at first on horsed cavalry
became a very significant naval power on reaching the Mediterranean
their engineers developed 'a quick grasp of gunnery'. The author goes o
to praise 'the far-sightedness of Istanbul in relation to the adaptation o
maps'; it was interested in the world-wide discoveries of Columbus and
others, which in the end so strongly affected their situation.[67]

Cultural similarities in east and west

While Turkey was the nearest non-European (Asiatic) state, the main target of post-Enlightenment criticism was China. In the eyes of many Europeans, that huge country was destined to remain 'traditional', 'static',
'despotic', even backward. In earlier publications I have attempted to
show on the contrary that in many ways the culture of China ran a roughly
parallel course to the European one.[68] I began with the family and marriage, arguing that firstly the demographic figures gave little evidence of

---

[63] Mundy 2004.   [64] Fernandez-Armesto 1995: 220.
[65] Fernandez-Armesto 1995: 222.   [66] Fernandez-Armesto 1995: 223.
[67] Fernandez-Armesto 1995: 219.   [68] Goody 1982, 1993, 1996a.

a non-European pattern as far as household size (MHS) was concerned and that this fact was connected with a measure of 'individualization' of the conjugal pair.[69] That occurred in dowry systems where parental property was transmitted to daughters as well as to sons at their marriage or later by inheritance, giving rise to the features of 'the woman's property complex' (endogamy in marriage, particular strategies of management and of heirship such as adoption and woman-centred unions, etc.). Such a system seemed to characterize all the major post-Bronze Age societies of Eurasia. Their advanced agricultures entailed marked economic stratification ('classes') under which such transfers obviously varied and parents attempted to maintain or improve the position of their daughters as well as their sons after marriage. The entire sibling group received parental property, though not equally. To make the point about the convergence between Europe and Asia, we can contrast that situation with the one prevailing in sub-Saharan Africa under hoe cultivation where economic and social differences of this kind were minimal and did not affect who one married (or the size of marriage payments) except perhaps in the case of some traders.[70]

There were similar parallels in other 'cultural' matters which suggest convergence rather than divergence. Similarities between east and west suggest that the divergence which historians have made with the notion of both Antiquity and the subsequent *isnad*, or genealogy, to western capitalism, leaving as marginal a 'despotic', even backward, Asia, is quite inadequate to account for the levels of complexity. I have argued that in Europe elaborate culinary practices, known as 'haute cuisine', could be distinguished from more simple stratified forms of cooking and those again from the broadly undifferentiated cooking that was found even in politically stratified societies in Africa, where among other things the agricultural economy could not sustain such differences.[71] Simple stratified cooking accompanied all the major post-Bronze Age societies of Eurasia but in some of these we find the further development of an *haute cuisine* in which connoisseurship played a prominent part in court circles and among elite groups, including merchants and the haute bourgeoisie. *Hautes cuisines* of this kind were to be found in China,[72] in India, in the Near East,[73] as well as in classical and modern Europe.[74] While this may appear to be a superficial matter, the question of cuisine bears upon stratification (class) and the very food we imbibe.

It was the same with the culture of flowers, the way that different societies cultivated and used them for aesthetic, ritual, and related purposes

---

[69] Goody 1976. [70] Goody and Tambiah 1973. [71] Goody 1982. [72] Chang 1977.
[73] Rodinson 1949. [74] Goody 1982.

such as gift-giving and worship.[75] Once again, what may seem marginal goes to the heart of cultures, not only of the rite of the gift but of agriculture and stratification. The pre-colonial countries of sub-Saharan Africa not only produced no domesticated floral varieties of this kind but made virtually no use of wild flowers in ritual or in other social contexts. That was very different from China, India, Europe, and the Near East. In their economies, African cultures had more use for the fruit rather than the flower, for the edible rather than the decorative. In Eurasia, the cultivation of flowers was often a specialist occupation. Floral varieties were developed for the gardens of courts and other elites and they were also grown for the market; the market provided blooms for worship (but not in the Near East), for communication (gifts, presentations) as well as for decoration. In parts of China, fruit trees in blossom were cut down and placed in vases in merchant houses at New Year as an offering, in a gesture of 'conspicuous waste'; one did not wait for the fruit. And there developed an expertise in the culture of flowers for 'aesthetic' purposes just as there did with cuisine, an expertise that marked all the major post-Bronze Age societies. And it was not only political but mercantile elites that took part in these activities, so it is not surprising to find them linked to the development of commerce and even industry. Indeed, contrary to many European ideas, the delight in fine food and flowers was even more developed in the east than in the west.

Cultural similarities extended to a whole range of other artistic activities. The kabuki theatre appeared in Japan at roughly the same time (in the early seventeenth century) as secular drama developed in Renaissance Europe and appealed to similar mercantile and bourgeois audiences. Novels began to be composed in China in the sixteenth century even before those in eighteenth-century Europe, and yet earlier in Japan, if we count the *Tale of Genji* (eleventh century). Some parallel developments in these matters were due to the world-wide system of exchange that existed between merchant groups. Such groups owed their existence to the exchange of goods, an exchange that necessarily involved the communication of ideas and know-how as well as commodities. That is how the manufacture of paper and silk were transferred over the centuries from east to west. Other features such as glass-making[76] and the use of perspective in painting passed in the other direction. Some graphic motifs such as the acanthus and the lotus travelled in one direction and dragons in another.[77] But in addition to such forms of intercultural communication, there was another process at work, internal elaboration (or social evolution). Starting with the Bronze Age, urban societies produced

[75] Goody 1993.   [76] MacFarlane and Martin 2002.   [77] Rawson 1984.

increasingly complex artisanal and intellectual activities, one building on another over time, as in many changes in technology.[78] Thus there was an internal dynamic in such societies, only partly prompted by the 'market', which resulted in parallel socio-cultural developments in different parts of the world. The notion of totally divergent patterns emerging out of the Bronze Age in Eurasia seems highly questionable at least if we adopt an 'anthropo-archaeological' approach to the modern world.

What I am suggesting here is an alternative to a 'cultural' account of differences between one society and the next. Such an account tends to be static and places human groups in an almost biological framework, though clearly involving cultural units (which have been called memes) rather than physical ones. This alternative has to be more dynamic, taking into the reckoning the external exchange of information and the internal development and communication of more complex behavioural forms over the long term. Cultural or social development of this kind is quite a different process from biological evolution, though in some cases it operates along 'selectionist' lines. However, a possible but not inevitable outcome of the analysis of cultures in terms of 'deep structure', tracing homologies (similar building blocks) between the various components, is a genetic one that has led to branches of 'cognitive anthropology' searching for built-in structures of the mind. Such 'structures' undoubtedly exist, but only along with more dynamic processes referred to above that arise from 'social evolution', that is, from 'external' communication and 'internal' development. It is these that are important in considering the long-term development of Eurasian societies and the arguments in favour of understanding those cultures in a frame, partly interactionist, which would exclude the radical separation of any major component as 'despotic'. In this context, any comparative advantage that one society may gain is strictly temporary.

A more dynamic account of cultural history looks for convergence as well as divergence from a common base rather than a categorical distinction between 'despotic' and 'democratic' powers. Such a position is suggested by Eric Wolf's classification of states in both east and west as 'tributary', the eastern sometimes being more 'centralized' than the western but both belonging to one general category. By 'tributary' I understand a state which requires monetary support from its inhabitants and which therefore opens the way back to the 'rule of the people' who provide that funding. And a similar parallelism is perhaps indicated by Needham's description of the west as having 'military feudalism' and the east

[78] Singer 1979–84.

as having 'bureaucratic feudalism'. Both writers eschew the notion c
'Asiatic despotism'.[79]

In my opinion Wolf's notion solves the problem that I find in man
other accounts, Marxist and others, of 'Asiatic exceptionalism' and 'ori
entalism', in other words, the question of developments from the paral
lelism of the Bronze Age societies to the supposed diversity of Antiquit
and after. But it requires a very radical conceptual shift, abandoning th
notion of a distinct European sequence of modes of production, of com
munication, and of destruction. Instead we have to see the growth of th
'tributary state' throughout Eurasia, the development of parallel urba
civilizations, the increase in the exchange of goods and ideas over tim
and therefore the appearance throughout Eurasia of mercantile capital
ism, of markets, of financial activity, and of manufacture. There is n
room for Asiatic despots, Asiatic exceptionalism, or Asiatic modes of
dramatically different kind.

[79] Wolf 1982, Needham 2004.

Part Two

Three scholarly perspectives

5   Science and civilization in Renaissance Europe

In the next three chapters I want to discuss three major writers on history. They are not necessarily the most recent, although Needham's conclusion appeared in 2004, but they are the most widely quoted and the most influential historical scholars who have played an important part in the contemporary understanding of world history. First of all there is Joseph Needham, originally a broad-ranging biologist who spent the latter part of his life studying the history of science in China and wrote and edited a magisterial series entitled *Science and Civilization in China* (1954–), in which he showed that Chinese science had been equal, if not superior, to that of the west until the sixteenth century. For the subsequent period he tried to explain what has been called 'the Needham problem', why the west took over. In the following chapter I discuss the influential work of the German historical sociologist Norbert Elias, who looked at *The Civilizing Process* which he sees as achieving its zenith in Europe following the Renaissance. Thirdly, I examine the writings of the great French historian Fernand Braudel, who in his *Civilization and Capitalism, 15ᵗʰ– 18ᵗʰ Century*, discusses various forms of capitalism in different parts of the world, but concludes that 'true capitalism' was a purely European development.

These authors are addressing, in their different ways, a very real problem, namely the comparative advantage obtained by Europe following the Industrial Revolution of the late eighteenth century and in some respects following the Renaissance of the sixteenth. That advantage has to be explained. But I argue that their explanations are flawed since they either take that advantage back to a distant past, or also privilege later Europe in a questionable way, so that they distort world history rather than illuminate it.[1] More recent writers have done little better, making similar assumptions about European uniqueness, the bourgeoisie, capitalism, and even civilization. These approaches may in some cases appear to have been modified by a different appreciation of world history or even

---

[1] Of course, only in certain ways; I am in complete agreement with most of their writings.

by a measure of cultural relativism, but in fact they display the sam
eurocentrism as much of history and the social sciences.

In the following three chapters, I look at some general features tha
have attracted historians. Firstly, Europe was held to have invented cer
tain characteristic institutions which had heralded capitalism; there wer
the universities of the twelfth century and the trading towns, both sup
posedly differing radically from their eastern counterparts. Then there
was the notion that in the course of its history, in any case going back
to Antiquity, Europe has a unique claim to certain virtues and practice:
such as democracy, freedom, individualism, family. In chapter 10, I dis
cuss the claim made by many highly respected historians that Europe
has a similar status regarding the emotion of love (or at least romantic
love). These claims again seem to be highly ethnocentric and teleological
stemming from attempts to account for the later domination of the worlc
by projecting advantage backward in quite unsustainable ways.

Following feudalism, a period held to be singular to the west, and highly
significant for its modernization, was the 'Renaissance'. Its achievement:
are often seen by European scholars in the humanities as centring upor
the arts. But art was very much linked to politics and to the economy. A
recent commentator has described the situation in the following terms:

> Early fifteenth-century Renaissance art emerged as a result of the enhancec
> power of a predominantly urban and commercial elite keen to display their wealth
> through the commissioning of lavish art objects, and the eagerness of a church
> to manufacture and distribute a coherent theological position to the faithful . .
> [Art objects] looked backwards to a classical past rather than biblical precedent
> to provide new political ideologies with intellectual credibility and authority.'[2]

Certainly there was a great revival in those branches of the arts, especially
theatre and sculpture (not to mention secular painting and music) that
had initially been suppressed or commandeered by the church.

At a slightly later period, a Renascence (or the early Renaissance)
reached Flanders. Jan Van Eyck (c. 1395–1441), working for Philip the
Good (1419–67), Duke of Burgundy, was said to have developed if he
did not invent the art of oil painting and produced the 'Adoration of
the Lamb' (1432) in Ghent; Rogier van der Weyden of Tournai followed
him (1399/1400–1464) and visited Rome, where he was welcomed by
Humanists, taught there and became painter for the Medici as well as for
the king. Hans Memling (c. 1430/5–1494) worked significantly for representatives of the Florentine Medicis and for the new Hanseatic League

---

[2] Brotton 2002: 138–9.

it Lübeck.[3] At that time Bruges was the largest trading city in Europe,[4] known for its mercantile activity, bringing spices and other goods from the Orient but especially English wool, which formed the basis of the economy, providing the raw materials for the famous Flemish weavers. This activity brought them into close contact with Lübeck on the Baltic, headquarters of the extensive League, as well as with the fairs of Champagne and with Florence, Spain, and countries to the south. The flourishing economy and the burgeoning renascence went hand in hand, since it was the rich merchants, and the clergy and government they maintained, who supported the wealth of decorative and artistic work that adorned the town.

In his account of the Italian Renaissance, Brotton asks whether the term has in fact 'been invented to establish a convincing myth of European cultural superiority'.[5] Certainly that is the way the Renaissance was often perceived. In the last volume of his *History of France* (1855), the historian Michelet wrote that it meant 'the discovery of the world and the discovery of man . . . Man refound himself', an event that in his view was not so much European as French. In a similar way Burkhardt in Switzerland and Pater in Oxford developed almost nationalistic ideas of the 'spirit' of the Renaissance celebrating 'limited democracy, scepticism towards the church, the power of art and literature and the triumph of European civilization over all others'.[6] In other words, it was 'humanism', with the human, like the Renaissance or the rebirth itself, being appropriated by the west, that 'underpinned nineteenth-century European imperialism', justifying European dominance over the rest of the globe.

The east was not thought capable of activity of this kind. However there was a shift in the predominant views of China in the west. Critical comment had existed previously (as for example in Vico, Hume, Rousseau, and Dr Johnson), but Jesuit missionaries to that country reported favourably on many of its institutions, ideologies, and attitudes. The positive element largely disappeared after the Industrial Revolution when the more general view was that the country was backward, despotic, and unchanging. In the eighteenth century Europe had been much influenced by Chinese art and decoration but the German historian Winckelmann saw only the Greek artistic tradition as displaying the true 'ideal of beauty', with Chinese art being much inferior and stagnant. The linguist Humboldt thought the language inferior, the poet Shelley

---

[3] Van Eyck's early work (early fifteenth century) had been influenced by Burgundian illuminated painting.
[4] In the fourteenth century, Letts 1926: 23. Probably 40,000–50,000 inhabitants, but 100,000–150,000 in the eyes of the chroniclers.
[5] Brotton 2002: 20.   [6] Brotton 2002: 25.

that their institutions were 'stagnant and miserable', Herder was scornfu
of their national character, De Quincey saw them as antediluvian, Hege
believed China represented the lowest level of world-historical develop
ment (for whom it was a 'theocratic despotism'). Comte, Tocqueville
and Mill saw it as inferior, barbarian, or stationary.[7] Sinophobia even
took on racial overtones in the work of Gobineau and other Europeans
while the philosopher Lucien Lévy-Bruhl saw 'the Chinese mentality' a
'ossified'.[8]

Accepting a certain scepticism around the Renaissance these chap
ters will explore how scholars have adopted the eurocentric notion of it
uniqueness and its contribution to the development of capitalism, an
the way in which it provided the economic, social, and epistemologi
cal basis for later European intellectual and ideological developments, in
other words for modernity. There was no Chinese equivalent of the word
'modernity' or for 'capitalism' which even in English were nineteenth
century inventions. However, in the case of the Chinese their absence
was deemed to show a fundamental problem, and to signal Chinese inca
pacity to attain to the European successes of the last few centuries.

There was, for most European authors, no progress towards the mod
ern world without the Renaissance – hence the modern world is a purel
European phenomenon, as are all the advances that derived from it: cap
italism, secularism, a dynamic art system, modern science. As we have
seen, the more extreme version of this view moves the origin of European
pre-eminence at least to feudalism, or even to well before the adven
of Antiquity and Christianity, but even in more prudent formulation
the fact remains that Europe is seen to have outdistanced its potentia
competitors since the transformations initiated by the Renaissance at the
latest. In this context 'modernity' was seen as separable from capitalism
I shall take as my point of departure for analysing the accuracy of these
claims the magisterial work of Joseph Needham on Chinese science which
he has done so much to reintegrate into world history. Nevertheless when
he discusses the advances of western science in recent centuries, he falls
back upon accepted notions of the uniqueness of the Renaissance and the
rise of the bourgeoisie, of modernization, of capitalism and of 'modern
science'.

However, while all renascences were unique, all literate societies had
them at some point. The tracing of a common line from the Urban Rev
olution to 'modernity' means that all societies in that tradition had a
bourgeoisie, as we will see, and at least a mercantile capitalism. The Ital
ian Renaissance did lead chronologically to modernity in the west and to

---

[7] Brook and Blue 1999: 91–2.   [8] Brook and Blue 1999: 82.

modern science', but it is the uniqueness of the general features in the background of Europe to which these are attributed that is the problem. 'Modernity' is conceived as a purely western phase, but even the criteria for its emergence, though stated in categorical terms, are far from clear.

This use of the western concept of 'modern' is analysed in an interesting way by Brook in relation to its adoption by Chinese scholars, and his words are very relevant to the problem of 'modern science'.

Since the rupture from the past was the key discursive moment in telling the history of the modern, the pre-modern had to be conceived of as being of a different essence than the modern world, incompatible with the modern but still providing a bed from which the modern could grow to overcome it. As it separated modern from pre-modern, modern history discredited the pre-modern as a source of contemporary value or meaning.[9]

The achievements of the Renaissance, to which Needham refers, were not of course confined to art. For at that time changes in education took place, following the needs of mercantile and administrative activity; so that both the content and the reach of the systems were greatly extended as it became more concerned with secular activities. Universities had developed earlier, picking up from earlier institutes of higher education such as madrasas, and their curricula; although still dominated by religion, they included a range of other subjects. From the fifteenth century in Britain grammar schools and their equivalents proliferated at a municipal level (church schools had reappeared much earlier, in the tenth century); similar developments took place elsewhere. Then, in the middle of that century, Europe developed printing, the mechanization and industrialization of writing that had been present in the Far East since 868[10] but now used with a limited alphabetic script instead of thousands of characters. That process, which made possible the rapid and accurate production of many copies of works, was critical in the growth of schools and universities, as well as in the development and transmission of information in other ways.[11]

Brotton's account emphasizes the importance of the contribution of the east (principally of Turkey) to the Renaissance in Europe, both commercially and in terms of knowledge.[12] The singling out of Europe is curious

---

[9] Brook and Blue 1999: 115   [10] Bloom 2001: 36.

[11] The Chinese were often criticized by Europeans for not having an alphabet. It is unclear what difference this would have made to the natural sciences.

[12] I find a problem with regard to Brotton's assertion that 'there were no clear geographical or political barriers between east and west in the fifteenth century'. Only in the nineteenth century, he claims, do we find the 'belief in the absolute cultural and political separation of the Islamic east and the Christian west that has obscured the easy exchange of trade, art, and ideas between these two cultures'.[12] That dating seems much too late, as in

if we remember that the Renaissance was not determined purely inter
nally. But we also need to take into account 'renascences' that took plac
in Europe at other times, and in other cultures as well. In itself rebirt
is not a unique phenomenon, as we have earlier argued in the context o
humanism. Indeed in any written culture the possibility of going back t
earlier phases of history and of having a rebirth (as of Antiquity) is alway
present; the written word enables us to do precisely this. Our own immer
sion in the culture of western Europe since the Renaissance, together wit
our reading of accounts of European art historians, inevitably we mean
that we give pre-eminence to that tradition. Despite such inevitable pre
dispositions arising from culture, the European Renaissance was not a
unique as is often supposed. Parallels existed. In all societies descend
ing from the cultures of the Urban Revolution there was a growth o
artistic and 'cultural' forms along with rising standards of living in othe
mercantile and bourgeois communities and in the societies in which the
were embedded. The growth occurred in Renaissance-type development
at different times, but regularly in the general course of urban societie
becoming more complex. The period called the Renaissance is know
by many historians as the early modern, a formula which looks for
ward to a birth rather than backward to a death and a rebirth. Wha
made the process more spectacular in Europe was the extent to whicl
knowledge and the arts (and indeed family life itself) had been limitec
by the adhesion to a specific world religion, namely Christianity. The
Reformation of that religion, which was again a looking-back to earlie
written texts, represented the rejection of certain established beliefs anc
opened up the possibility of the same happening to secular knowledge
In any case it pointed to a more restricted sphere for the sacred, anc
family life too was no longer dominated by the rules of the Catholic
Church.

Needham's view not only of the Renaissance but of the development o
capitalism is not only eurocentric but follows Weber, another Protestant
in its attribution of significant 'progress' to the economic ethic of that religious sect. 'The success of the Reformation involved a decisive break with
tradition, and Europeans were not slow to reach the conclusion that there
could in fact be real change in history, and that the Lord would truly make
all things new. Protestantism, with its direct access to God, meant literacy'[13] producing for the first time 'a really literate labour force', sweeping

Bernal's case linking the separation with imperialism. There was exchange much earlier
but there was also a black side which saw opposition on the religious front, as we see from
the expulsion of the Moors, the pogroms against the Jews, and the attacks on Christian
communities.

[13] Needham 2004: 63.

away class barriers; after the Renaissance 'an "industrial revolution" was bound to follow', as was 'modern science'. In fact, while Protestant countries did see a rise in literacy rates, that increase was rather small and soon followed by Catholic regions. In any case it was in the latter, especially in Italy, that the commercial revolution in Europe, the early development of the mechanical production of silk and paper and the advances in banking, credit, and accountancy, all had taken place – most of them influenced in one way or another, by eastern imports. Needham is again reading back teleologically, from later developments, or perhaps from his own ideological position. Moreover, the early Europeans transferring part of western science to China were not Protestant but were in fact Jesuit missionaries like Ricci.

What was peculiar about the west was that for many centuries systems of communication and learning had been restricted, not only by the dictates of the church (as happened in Islam and Judaism, which too had their humanistic periods) but also by the absence of paper (which was essential to the Muslim world and which originated in China). A Renaissance took place in the west when it opened out to the east, partly because the earlier collapse of the west had had such dulling consequences that had rightly given rise to the phrase 'the Dark Ages' for the initial period. To overcome these restrictions, a Renaissance was certainly necessary. When it came, the west experienced a burst of knowledge, of artistic activity, in part secular, stimulated by the wealth flowing from the increase in trade with the Levant. This aspect of the Renaissance was peculiar to the west, since the east had never suffered so extensive a collapse, a collapse that was accompanied by a dramatic ideological change in the shape of the coming of Christianity.

Nevertheless the east did experience periods of greater or lesser activity in the sphere of knowledge and the arts, which were partly connected with the level of trade, as in the west. Zafrani refers to 'humanistic' periods in the Islamic and Judaic traditions, when secular rather than religious learning flourished. There was frequently a tension in Islam between Hellenistic learning ('ancient science') and religious texts, which were held by the orthodox to be the fount of all understanding. So while some rulers and rich merchants collected what knowledge they could in their libraries, others might dispose of such collections on theological grounds. In Europe the movement was more unilineal, in Islam more fluctuating – the rejection and revival of secular knowledge, particularly that derived from the Greeks, shifted over time and place. In Islam we find similar fluctuations with regard to the use of figurative art which despite religious interdictions flourished in Persia as well as in Egypt and in India at the Mughal Court. Courts often escaped the restrictions associated with religious beliefs. At the same time there was a general quickening of trade and manufacture which led to a vectorial change throughout Eurasia. Everywhere the bourgeoisie, essential to conducting these activities, strengthened their participation in society and strengthened too their contribution to knowledge, education, and the arts.

That is why, as I have mentioned in the previous chapter, we find developments in *haute cuisine* and the culture of flowers happening in urban contexts right across the major societies of Eurasia. We find similar parallels in the theatre of the west in the sixteenth century and of Japan somewhat later, as well as in painting and the emergence of the realistic novel in both China and the west. While recent writers on the European Renaissance such as Burke and Brotton have shown the importance of Near Eastern culture in that development, their analysis does not go far enough. We need to take into account the renewal of cultural developments throughout the major 'civilizations' over time. But this process was more marked in western Europe because of the earlier trough after the collapse of Rome and the advent of Christianity, and because of the impact of the sudden change in the modes of communication resulting from the adoption of printing and paper using an alphabetic script. China of course had long had a competitive advantage in respect both of printing and of paper, but Europe now made a great impact because of the advantage of backwardness in the breakthrough to modernization.

In Europe, these developments provided a great burst of activity including the development of 'modern science'. The Italian Renaissance is generally associated with developments in the arts, though these were not the only significant achievement of this period. The so-called 'scientific Revolution' or birth of 'modern science' was another. It forms the background to one of the great works of the history of mankind, Joseph Needham's *Science and Civilisation in China*, rightly compared to Gibbon's *Decline and Fall of the Roman Empire*. As Elvin remarks in an introduction to the 'last' volume (VII, part 2), 'One's conception of the world has been transformed',[14] transformed by 'the revelation of a Chinese cultural universe whose triumphs in mathematics, the sciences, and technology were often superior, and only rarely inferior, to those of western Europe until about 1600'. Nevertheless, while its contribution was often essential to the west as well as the east, only in a limited way has it been assimilated 'into the bloodstream of the history of science in general'.

Needham spent some fifty years documenting the growth of Chinese science in a study of epic proportions. However, it is not his work on

[14] Needham 2004: xxiv.

science in China on which I wish to comment, but his attempt to explain why, despite the earlier advance, it was the west not the east that made what he sees as the breakthrough to 'modern science'. The paradox has been called the Needham problem. Following the lead of a number of western social historians, his explanation assumes a close connection between the development of science and the rise of the bourgeoisie, the growth of capitalism.

At the beginning of this vast project Needham writes 'Our original question was: why had modern science originated only in Western Europe soon after the Renaissance?'[15] But he adds 'one train can hide another. We soon came to realize that there was an even more intriguing question behind that, namely, why had China been more successful than Europe . . . for fourteen previous centuries?' The first question was one to which Needham returned in his 'final' remarks whose composition was spread over several decades. These were based on the presumption of a leap forward in Europe after 1600 to 'modern science', that is, a science involving a combination of the experimental method and applied mathematics. The problem he posed was how did it come about that with this early advance both in science and in the economy in China, it was the more backward Europe that achieved the leap forward not only to 'modern science' but also to capitalism. In offering an answer he concentrates on the spheres of the polity, the economy, and the internal characteristics of knowledge systems.

For Needham, Chinese science was in advance of western science right up until the Renaissance. Most telling is the graph he produces in the volume on Botany which shows that Europe and China were about equal in their recognition of botanical species at about 400 BCE, in the time of Aristotle's pupil, Theophrastus. After that, however, European knowledge fell away while in China a steady advance took place until the sixteenth century when Europe made a sudden spurt and overtook it.[16] This he suggests was due to the birth of 'modern science' which is defined as 'the mathematicization of hypotheses about Nature, and the testing of them vigorously by persistent experimentation'.[17] The Greeks did little experimentation and the Chinese used it primarily for practical rather than theoretical purposes. 'Modern science' is seen, very generally, as arising 'pari passu with the Renaissance, the Reformation and the rise of capitalism'.[18]

However, Needham regards some elements of western advantage that assisted the advent of modern science as being present even earlier than

---

[15] Needham 2004: 68.   [16] Needham 1954: xxx.   [17] Needham 2004: 211.
[18] Needham 2004: 210.

the Renaissance. For the west had the benefit of Euclid whereas the east did not develop the idea of 'geometrical proof'[19] (nor indeed of trigonometry). These he sees as deriving from and connected with 'the public nature of Greek city life' since the public circulation of ideas require their more explicit and detailed justification (as well as the absence of the Babylonian division of the circle into 360 degrees). Following Weber and others he sees the town in Europe as being unique and as contributing to the development of science by promoting the bourgeoisie and its values. Moreover, the east did not have the benefit of the tradition of the Greek city-state; 'Athens gave rise, when the Renaissance came, to Venice and Genoa, to Pisa and Florence, and these in their turn to Rotterdam and Amsterdam . . . and finally London . . . In these cities . . . merchant could shelter from interference by the feudal nobility . . . until the day they should come forth . . .'.[20] So here he too sees a kind of urban life and its bourgeoisie (and capitalism) as unique to the west, inherited in a direct line from Antiquity. He also looks at the difference between 'military feudalism' in the west and 'bureaucratic feudalism' in the east, which he thinks influenced the process and restricted growth in the east.[21] In a sense, this attempt to interpret European history as offering that continent certain long-term advantages stood in contradiction to his emphasis on the achievements of Chinese science.

It is obvious that there have been important developments in Europe in all spheres, in the economy, the class system, and 'natural philosophy'. However, Needham's argument assumes that 'the rise of the bourgeoisie' happened in no other civilization in the world, not in India, Southeast Asia, nor China. In the west, military-aristocratic feudalism (which differed from the 'bureaucratic feudalism' of China) 'was replaced' by the bourgeoisie who were more willing to experiment, for 'exact knowledge meant greater profits'. It is in that contrast between the two feudal structures that he finds much of the answer to his question. But just as in Europe part of the aristocracy engaged in commercial and financial affairs, so the Chinese mandarinate could and often did participate in trade while 'in retirement' and even at times 'in office'. They could thus wear two hats, not just government official/local grandee and landlord gentry, but also official gentry and commercial investor. They used their past in government and its connections to provide them with institutional support not available in the legal code.[22]

---

[19] Needham 2004: 210.   [20] Needham 2004: 211.
[21] The phrase 'bureaucratic feudalism' was used by the Japanese Marxist historian Moritani Katsumi (Brook and Blue 1999: 138).
[22] I am indebted for these remarks to Dr J. McDermott.

But there were other and earlier bourgeoisies; other merchants and manufacturers were interested in profit and in 'exact knowledge' even if they were not always as successful in the search. Moreover it is not altogether accurate to claim that in Europe the aristocracy were actually replaced by the bourgeoisie. The latter gradually achieved greater power and influence, but they had existed in Europe long before the Renaissance, in Chaucer's company travelling to Canterbury, in Lucca, Venice, and Palermo, but also in Near Eastern towns such as Istanbul, Cairo, and Aleppo as well as much further east. Indeed they existed ever since the Urban Revolution of the Bronze Age, becoming increasingly important with the growth of the exchange economy. And that economy could not exist only in one country or continent, but was Eurasian-wide. The notion of uniqueness depends very much on the definition of 'modern' in qualifying capitalism and science. In the following sections on the polity and the economy I want to consider at greater length some of the factors Needham sees as causing the differences between China and the West in his attempt to account for the later (temporary?) imbalances in scientific achievement following the Italian Renaissance.

The polity and the bourgeoisie

The bureaucratic system of the mandarinate is praised by Needham for its early introduction of an administration based upon 'achievement' (examinations from the second century CE) rather than the largely ascriptive recruitment practised by other types of 'feudalism'. Needham considers that the early Chinese state and the bureaucracy, though basically 'non-interventionist', did a great deal to forward early science, with the construction of astronomical observatories (as elsewhere, of course), keeping millennial records and organizing encyclopaedias and scientific expeditions.

By contrast, science in the west was generally 'a private enterprise' and therefore hung back. Indeed in his words the 'social and economic system of medieval China was much more rational than medieval Europe'.[23] It encouraged science in the early period but subsequently acted as a brake when, according to Needham, the private enterprise of the bourgeoisie provided a better base for advance: 'Yet State Science and medicine in China were not capable of making, when the time came, that qualitative leap' leading to modern science in the west.[24] That failure he thinks was in part due to the nature of the bureaucracy which did not encourage competition. But what promoted science in the early days was surely capable

---

[23] Needham 2004: 9.   [24] Needham 2004: 18.

of promoting it later on, unless that possibility is excluded automatically by the very way one specifies a 'qualitative leap' to the 'modern' from the 'early', which partly derives from a nominalist problem. The assumption underlying Needham's analysis effectively means denying that earlier China had a bourgeoisie which, like guilds, he sees as inhibited by the mandarinate. The absence of the bourgeoisie (and of a monetary system), is thought to explain the failure to develop both modern (or indeed any) capitalism in China and 'modern science'.

While it could be argued that China in the past was not modern because of a lack of a bourgeoisie, the presence of the mandarinate and therefore the absence of capitalism, in the past century the country has embraced not only socialism (which Needham sees as compatible with its earlier bureaucracy) but also 'capitalism'. While it might be possible to see capitalism as a purely western import, it is more reasonable to see western procedures as compatible with eastern forerunners. Certainly the alternative represents altogether too crude a level of analysis and is neglectful of the whole history of the east. The notion of a qualitative leap in European science must leave open the possibility of China rapidly catching up with the west in the way that is more difficult for Africa. The socio-economy of China was of quite a different order and much closer to that of Europe than the views of Marx, Weber, or even Needham would allow.[25] The possibility of a breakthrough in China was much more likely than these authors, looking backwards from present advantage, took account of.

The major cultures of Eurasia did of course differ in their achievements in knowledge at any one moment, but they were part of an interconnected system of exchanging units where the more 'backward' mainly caught up with the more 'advanced' within a measurable length of time. Needham's perception is certainly not altogether wrong but it is phrased in a vaguely Marxist, eurocentric way. He acknowledges that at an earlier point he was much attracted to Wittfogel's notion of 'Oriental Despotism'. But that hypothesis tried to link economy (irrigation) and polity (despotism) in too tight a fashion; water control differed in its demands and organization, but in any case 'bureaucratic' control was seen as a better description than 'despotic'. That is certainly an improvement. The claimed absence of the bourgeoisie in China draws from euromarxism which, taking a nineteenth-century stance, sees capitalism as a specifically European phenomenon. That was a notion to which Needham subscribed in calling

---

[25] The Chinese lineage of 1500–1950 had no equivalent in Europe, but the work of Faure (1989) suggests that it did not inhibit commercial developments in the way Weber suggested. That was certainly true in China overseas.

attention to the uniqueness of the Greek tradition as well as in standard comments on the medieval communes.

The 'bureaucratic state' that marked China is said to have wanted to preserve social stability rather than further economic gain; it was to its advantage 'to maintain the basic agrarian social structure than to engage in, or even permit, any forms of commercial or industrial development whatsoever'.[26] That statement follows the assumption of a categorical developmental scheme that sees agricultural societies as being succeeded by commercial ones. But such a scheme is highly simplified. Even neolithic societies already depend on trade and commerce for some purposes, as we have argued in relation to markets; all have some artisanal element that involves the exchange of goods and services. That component of society was radically increased by the Urban Revolution of the Bronze Age, which affected China as much as any other of the great civilizations. Of course, the agricultural activity of these societies was of fundamental importance for the bulk of the population, but innovative spheres were to be found in the towns which were often highly commercialized. These states comprised both agricultural and urban sectors and were ideologically complex.

While leading elements in the 'dominant' rural-based sector might despise trade, the bourgeoisie developed their own values. These did not 'dominate' the whole society until much later, but they nevertheless had long provided an alternative focus, promoting the uses of literacy and the arts outside the court, the clergy, and the administrative process. The Third Estate existed, even when it was not formally represented in government. And as Needham himself notes for China, rich merchants might play a role at court, apart from having a central part in urban life, especially in the coastal cities.[27] Moreover, a country that produced vast quantities of goods under commercial and industrial conditions well in advance of Europe, partly for export, partly for the huge internal market, could hardly be said to reject commerce, even though some elements of the society were ambivalent about trade. However, that ambivalence is no reason to argue that there was no 'genuine' bourgeoisie.[28] As Braudel remarked of towns, 'a town is always a town'; so too its inhabitants always include an incipient bourgeoisie. The mandarinate may have inhibited its development and that of the guilds (as happened in other civilizations) but it could not and did not suppress them altogether. From the standpoint of social history Needham failed to allow sufficiently for the admixture of commerce and agriculture, and for the increasing part the former played in political and social life generally. The denial of the existence

[26] Needham 2004: 61.   [27] Needham 2004: 50.   [28] Needham 2004: 8, n. 22.

of a genuine estate of this kind seems to be a function of teleologi
cal history of a palaeo-Marxist kind. If there was no bourgeoisie (and
no monetary system), that absence is thought to explain the failure to
develop both modern (or indeed any) capitalism and 'modern science' in
China.

This argument about the later inhibitions on China's development of
capitalism is more nuanced than Weber's view that 'officialism', that is
the scholar-officials of the bureaucracy, were the greatest impediment
Needham sees this bureaucracy as initially providing a stimulus to development, Weber as it being universally detrimental. Merchants, Weber
claims, were always suppressed, anyhow after the Sung dynasty. In this
argument Weber was followed by the distinguished French historian of
China, Etienne Balazs, who wrote of the 'despotic power of scholar officials' (who were however recruited widely by examination) and whose
existence inhibited the rise of the bourgeoisie and hence the nature of
Chinese towns.[29]

As a case-study of how ideology can impact upon research findings,
Balazs's intellectual trajectory is interesting. He worked closely with the
historian, Braudel, at the École des Hautes Études in Paris and clearly
influenced his thinking on China, as we will see in chapter 7. A recent
commentator suggests that Balazs was affected by his own personal history and by the political vicissitudes he had experienced.[30] Early on he
took an uncompromising position regarding China's 'failure' to build
on the achievements of the Sung economy. Zurndorfer writes of his
'search in the endless volumes of statistics, countless troves of personal
records, or bulky government reports in the hope of finding some evidence
to support his idea that merchants continuously suffered under officialdom, or that peasants were always the victims of an overbearing, relentless
state'.[31] Balazs was led to move from 'these stereotyped accounts of imperial China' to explore 'the complexities of the relationship between state
and society' as the result of the publication in 1957 of a volume of 'Essays
on the Debate on Sprouts of Capitalism in China' issued by the People's
Republic. He then became especially interested in developments in mining during the Ming-Qing era when the state vied with private enterprise.
Investigating the organization of production, labour conflicts and profits
from iron, silver, and copper mines, he concluded that the state did not
hinder private enterprise when it was not in its interest to do so. As distinct

[29] See Zurndorfer 2004: 195.   [30] Zurndorfer 2004: 193.
[31] Zurndorfer 2004: 234–5. The word personal should not be taken too literally. As Dr
MacDermott points out to me, what we have is some merchant guild books, account
books but nothing really personal. He also suggests that it is a mistake to see traders in
China as a class of 'merchants', as literati also took part.

from his earlier 'literary' studies that were inevitably skewed towards the concerns of the literati and the bureaucrats, he now used information on workers and local merchants.[32] So he came to recognize that there was 'a sort of bourgeoisie' outside the state bureaucracy and that China did develop 'a sort of capitalism'. However, he qualifies this point by arguing that the legal position of the merchants meant they had to resort to bribery and were never able to achieve 'autonomous' consciousness.[33] Instead they encouraged their sons to become officials and invest their profits in land. While he was influenced by 'the sprouts of capitalism' debate and the material it led him to study, he rejected the attribution by Chinese Marxists of the concept of feudalism to the long stretch of the country's history (in a manner parallel to Elvin's objection to Needham's usage) but at the same time tried to account teleologically for the later 'failure' of China to develop modern capitalism by concentrating on the legal aspect of the position of the merchants. These, however, appear to have behaved in a manner not so different from merchants in other parts where engaging in trade was seen as less prestigious than holding land, a position that was everywhere modified over time.[34] Needham, too, repeats the old complaint that merchants and their profession were 'not the way of life classically most admired in China',[35] so that merchants used their wealth to become 'educated gentry'. So too they did in Europe.

It is not just Needham, Weber, and Balazs who entertain conflicting views on the development of capitalism and science in China. The whole Marxist tradition has been divided on China's position in world history. Essentially Marx himself saw China and Asia as a whole excluded from the main progression of human societies from the ancient, to the feudal to 'bourgeois' modes of production. China he described as the 'rotting semi-civilization of the oldest State in the world'.[36] Two quite different approaches developed among Marxist writers. After the October Revolution, some were more concerned with efforts to promote the anti-imperialist and peasant struggles in China, especially local communists who did not want to think of China as permanently excluded from modern developments.[37] To them, a more dynamic history seemed called for. One group saw earlier China as feudal (*fengjian*), which would leave space for a progressive movement forward following the Marxist five-stage

---

[32] Zurndorfer 2004: 214.
[33] Dr McDermott points out that merchants could not have welcomed this autonomy which may well have led them to bankruptcy.
[34] Smith (1991: 9) argues that the large part played by the state in the early Sung period contained the seeds of 'capitalism'.
[35] Needham 2004: 59.   [36] Blue 1999: 94.   [37] Brook 1999: 130ff.

theory; China was therefore not excluded from the usual history. Some even saw the country as having been dominated by commercial capital in recent centuries. Others believed it to be still marked by an Asiatic mode in one of its variant forms, as in Wittfogel.[38] Eventually in 1931 the Soviet leadership decided against the static notion of an Asiatic mode, a notion that was brought back to European historiography with a flourish in the 1960s.[39]

The development of commerce in a 'feudal' society was seen by some Chinese Marxists as the growth of 'the sprouts of capitalism' that occurred in the east as in the west.[40] This position, as against that of euromarxists, seems eminently reasonable. It meant the rejection of the Asiatic mode, and the acceptance of a universal 'feudalism', a concept that is watered down until it refers to any highly stratified agricultural society, of the general type that is bound to arise out of the stratification of agricultural production following the Bronze Age and the introduction of the animal-drawn plough. Like the west, China was seen to experience the emergence of what Gates (1989) calls 'a petty-capitalist mode of production' at the expense of the 'tributary mode', even though the government tried to resist its encroachment. However, money won through, for example the 'New Whip' reforms of the tax system in 1581 meant the payment of taxes in money rather than in kind.

How did this situation affect intellectual history, especially the history of science? Recall that in the west the notion of a leap is linked not only to the 'meteoric rise of modern science' but to the advent of 'capitalism' and of the Renaissance. However, the leap was not totally confined to the west. For China, Needham speaks of the 'fusion' of eastern and western astronomies by the mid-seventeenth century.[41] Indeed a figure in his volume on *Clerks and Craftsmen*[42] shows the points in time at which the west caught up in scientific achievement ('the transcurrent point') as well as the points of fusion.

Regarding astronomy, mathematics, and physics, the west caught up in 1600 and fused some thirty years later. That hardly suggests one needs to look for some deep-seated causal features in the so-called failure to develop modern science, but rather for some more contingent ones. By contingent I refer to features of the so-called 'internalist' model of science but not necessarily confined to such developments alone; there can be no general opposition between 'internalized' and 'social' explanations.[43]

---

[38] Wittfogel 1931: 57.   [39] Godelier 2004, Hobsbawm 1968.
[40] Brook and Blue 1999: 153.   [41] Needham 2004: 28.   [42] Needham 1970.
[43] Needham 2004: 22.

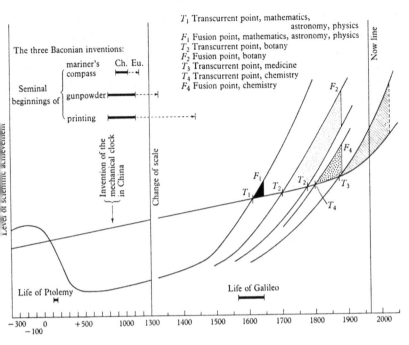

Figure 5.1 Graph showing transcurrent and fusion points for Chinese and western science. From Needham (1970), *Clerks and craftsmen*, Fig. 99.

The economy and law

One of the political factors Needham saw as inhibiting internal trade was the absence of 'law and order'. The roads, he argues, were at the mercy of bandits, the towns had large numbers of semi-employed individuals, the police force was too small. But how did this situation differ from eighteenth-century Britain with its highwaymen, urban poor, local constables-and the feuding of its 'Highland clans'? Yet Britain managed to trade internally and to develop a factory system. As we have seen in earlier chapters, 'law and order' was certainly not the prerogative of the west in the way some analysts presume. All societies placed sanctions on violence, all managed to trade, all encountered problems in so doing.

Needham also notes that business commitments in China were honoured in ethical principles, 'not enforced by law'.[44] But 'gentlemen's agreements', which are sanctioned reciprocity, are still common in

[44] Needham 2004: 60.

business circles and the recourse to courts of law, which is apparentl
what Needham refers to, is not the only means of conducting busines.
especially in long-distance exchange between different jurisdictions. Bu
that was equally true in the heyday of Victorian England when capitalisn
was triumphant; in some circles there too one found 'a built-in anti
commercialism' so that its absence hardly explains why Europe 'took of
and China did not. Once again the author is thinking teleologically an
looking for profound and long-standing 'social' differences, which do no
seem altogether relevant.

Another problem that Needham sees with Chinese trade is its failur
to develop a credit system,[45] which meant that trade could not expand
nor merchants, nor capitalism, nor therefore 'modern' science. He write
of 'the underdevelopment of the monetary economy in China', which h
contrasts with a 'modern monetary system'.[46] So that an individual coul
not 'extend his business operations beyond his personal presence'.[47] Th
suggestion seems quite unrealistic. Even in purely oral cultures one find.
a measure of credit.[48] In written cultures such as China this process i
much extended; indeed that extension of credit was one of the early use
of literacy, in Mesopotamia, in China, and elsewhere. His proposition
which is denied by Elvin on behalf of economic historians more generally
is certainly at odds with the huge exports of bullion from Europe an
America; no serious economic historian, he remarks, would now see th
Sung as being 'seriously under monetized'. Needham does admit ther
was a later revolution in money and credit but it was not followed, h
claims, by any institutional change. He also mentions merchants witl
accountants as assistants, indicating a considerable level of guild an
mercantile activity, but remains critical of those scholars, mainly Chinese
who see 'Han industrialists' as 'capitalist *entrepreneurs manqués*',[49] wh
claim 'budding capitalism' under the Ming, and in the Sung perceive a
'renaissance' and a 'commercial revolution'. All were 'abortive' because
there was 'a fundamental institutional incompatibility between the centra
bureaucratic administration of an agrarian society and the development
of a money economy'.[50] But they were abortive only from a teleologica
point of view, which is part of a palaeo-Marxist (albeit Christian) mindset that sees China as lacking a bourgeoisie and as incapable of proceeding
along the path to capitalism.[51]

This perception of the Chinese economy unable to make the grade
in independent mercantile activity is curious until one understands its

---

[45] Needham 2004: 55.   [46] Needham 2004: 55.   [47] Needham 2004: 58.
[48] Goody 1986: 82ff.   [49] Needham 2004: 57.   [50] Needham 2004: 57–8.
[51] Needham 2004: 52.

ideological background. It is obliquely criticized by Elvin in his introductory remarks when he writes: 'Leaving aside the issue of hierarchical eminent State domain, which was important up to and during the first millennium but rarely later', we see much variation within China. He criticizes Needham's notion of 'bureaucratic feudalism'[52] because the changes over 2,000 years were too great to allow any single label 'to work equally for all periods'.[53] The usage is part of Needham's propensity to 'biologize' Chinese history by stressing 'continuity', 'wholism', almost as inherited ('instinctive' is a word he uses) characteristics of the 'Chinese mind' which he compares, often favourably, to the heritage of the 'Religions of the Book', since the country was not dominated by a single religious ideology. 'There was plenty of private mining from the Sung through to Chhing times, and private instruments of credit were extensively used during the Sung as they were under the Chhing, which also saw the rise of private financial institutions like the "money shops". Under the Chhing the long-distance transfer of funds was handled above all by the Shansi banks, which were technically private though in a sort of symbiotic relationship with the government'.[54] Elvin's account presents a very different picture of credit and commercial operations than the one expounded by Needham, a picture that is much more in line with the rest of east Asia[55] and closer to Europe, once again cutting at the roots of assumptions of earlier European advantage. The key to the apparent contradiction between what Needham had to say about earlier Chinese science and his views on the economy is contained in Elvin's remark that it 'seems likely that he was personally uncomfortable with the prospect of explaining a logic of Chinese historical development that might prove too different from the immobile and eurocentric formulae of the Soviet and Chinese Marxism of his time'. There was therefore to be no bourgeoisie before European capitalism.

The notion that confined these developments to Europe was firmly espoused by Needham.[56] He follows Wallerstein[57] and of course Marx and many other nineteenth-century writers in seeing the rise of capitalism as unique to Europe; so too was the bourgeoisie which arose out of the collapse of earlier European society (seigneurs, the Church, etc.). And 'with the bourgeoisie arose modern capitalism hand in glove with modern science'. But these questions all involve nominalist problems, such as the supposed boundaries between town-dwellers and the bourgeoisie.

---

[52] For earlier usages of 'bureaucratic feudalism' in a Chinese context, see Brook and Blue 1999: 138. The general result of the Social History Controversy (1928–37) was that imperial power in China was 'feudal', though some preferred 'despotic'.
[53] Needham 2004: xxx.   [54] Needham 2004: xxix.   [55] Goody 1996a: 82ff.
[56] Needham 2004: 209.   [57] Wallerstein 1992.

Wallerstein sees these 'structures' as being characteristic of 'the capitalist/modern' historical system, private property, commodification, and the sovereign 'modern' state. Rights of ownership are in no sense singular to the modern western world. We have contracts for land sale as early as we have writing, although subject to 'eminent domain' which he recognizes as widespread. In early societies there were certainly more property rights which were shared with kin and sometimes neighbours, but nevertheless individual property rights existed and were fiercely defended, even in the absence of a state and written law. In the simplest agricultural societies, some commodification existed, though land was often *extra commercium*.[58] The commodification of land was also rare in such societies but nevertheless perfectly comprehensible. Institutionally, the 'modern' west was far from unique, which is why Asia has made such spectacular advances in 'capitalism' in recent times.

Wallerstein discards what he refers to as the civilizational (as distinct from the conjectural) accounts of the causes of capitalism – those associated with the names of Marx, Weber, and others, opting for a more contingent explanation. He sees as the essence of capitalism 'the continuous search for profit' which occurred only in western Europe, effectively in the sixteenth century. It occurred when the crisis of feudalism pushed the landed class into capitalist enterprises. The continuous pursuit of profit is difficult to measure. Profit was certainly a feature of earlier mercantile activity; the endless pursuit he speaks of seems to be associated with technological invention, especially the development of industrialization and mechanization. Certainly the tempo increased, but the bourgeoisie were already engaged in the search for profit, and it seems to be their existence and gradual take-over of the economy which Wallerstein's discussion of the changing role of land-owners perhaps underplays. While he analyses clearly the changes that occurred in western Europe, and subsequently elsewhere, that history does not need to be written in such categorical terms.

In my own usage, the bourgeoisie were international. Of course, they had more power in some places than in others. But the extensive exchange of goods and ideas that took place along the Silk Route, by sea as well as by land, could not have happened without them and without financial instruments. Merchants were required as well as artisans and in some cases manufacturers; so too were lawyers, bankers, accountants, not to speak of schools and hospitals. And it was along these trade routes that various religions, which too played their part in the economy by organizing fairs and pilgrimages, spread to the east, not mainly by aristocrats,

---

[58] Goody 1962: 335.

conquerors, nor by bureaucrats but by merchants, as witness the presence of Jews, Christians, and Muslims on the west coast of India, as well as in China itself. They were involved in mercantile activity which is normally reciprocal, and led to the creation of merchant communities in India (the Banias for example, and the Jains) as well as in China (Cheng Ho and his fellow Muslims in Beijing, for example). These merchant communities developed their own sub-cultures which displayed some notable similarities, encouraging the growth of literary forms such as the realistic novel, of performance arts such as the theatre, of secular painting and sculpture, again breaking out of purely religious confines, developing the cultivation of food and of flowers which, as with some other arts, they gradually took over from the aristocracy. In this and in other activities they were crucial in the spread of knowledge between east and west.

As for the rural economy, Needham writes of Chinese technology being so successful that it inhibited increases in production because it led to the numerical growth of the labour force, meaning there was little incentive to further mechanization, as would have happened with a scarcity of labour. As we have seen in chapter 3, that argument is similar to the one that has been applied to slave labour. Further steps were needed. What was required to bring Chinese agriculture 'into the modern world' were advances in technology 'not thinkable without the appearance of modern science'.[59] Yet modern science was not possible without capitalism, in agriculture and in the towns. So we come the full circle. However not only was Chinese farming already highly successful in feeding the many, but it was also very diversified; in the south rice cultivation required very different intensive techniques than the extensive farming along European lines in the north. Was there then really a case for demanding advances in 'technology' apart from the breeding of new varieties, which represents a continuation of old ways? With its minimal use of non-human labour, Chinese farming might be considered ecologically in advance of extensive mixed holdings of the European kind.

Water-power was applied not only in farming but very widely to the textile industry in the thirteenth and fourteenth centuries, 'challenging comparison with what happened in Europe in the eighteenth'.[60] It was 'those same spinning, doubling and twisting machines that must have inspired the Italian silk industry of very little later'. Why did factory production 'not quickly ensue?' Needham asks. He attributes this 'failure' to a variety of general factors, including as we have seen to 'the inhibition of a monetary economy' and the bureaucratic state. That hardly seems

---

[59] Needham 2004: 62.   [60] Needham 2004: 60.

an adequate explanation; the former does not seem so 'backward' and the latter earlier encouraged developments in this very field. We need to look more closely at Needham's notion of 'modern science' which holds the key to some of these contradictions.

'Modern science' and the internal characteristics of knowledge systems

In selecting the west as the only region in which 'modern science' spontaneously developed, Needham is led to adopt an implicitly eurocentric standpoint. The west 'spontaneously' developed modern science, whereas the recent Chinese Nobel prize winners supposedly achieved these goals only through a kind of imitation. We consider two of the main characteristics he singles out as the cornerstones of 'modern science', mathematics and experiment; but is so-called 'modern science' best looked upon as a purely western development when the numerical basis for its calculations came from Asian place systems and where the idea of experimentation must have applied very much more widely for any technical success to have been achieved?

Beside the economic and political context Needham also mentions influences internal to knowledge systems and their mutual interaction. Gradual changes in one area are seen to have given rise in a different area of thought to conditions favourable to the complete overhaul of current practices and models. Needham discusses Christianity, which encouraged an attitude towards nature said to be unlike that of any other religion, education which was rapidly expanding and aided the wide spread of knowledge, and the advent of the printing press and the appearance of how-to-do-it manuals, again making information and thought much more widely available.

Religion is the one of the factors used in explanation of what he sees to be the apparent paradox of the qualitative leap in western science when compared with its Chinese counterpart. Needham follows Roszak and other writers in suggesting that the capacity of the west to adopt a 'scientistic' point of view was connected with the 'aggressive intolerance' of Hebrew monotheism, together with its offshoots, Christianity and Islam, in favour of the 'desacralization of nature' embodied in the 'fuss about ideology'. These attitudes to nature are seen by others, according to Needham, as the result of Christianity's struggle with 'paganism'[61] and were reinforced by earlier Greek atomism, which was a 'mechanical materialism'. That reification of nature is claimed to have initiated the more

---

[61] Needham 2004: 93, quoting Pallis and Lynn White.

object-based approach characteristic of 'modern science' rather than the holistic, practical engagement of non-European cultures. But once again the west was not alone. India not only had 'advanced atomic speculations' but also a tradition of materialistic, atheist thought (the *Lokāyāta*).[62] Confucius too displayed a considerable measure of scepticism regarding the supernatural.

All written religions initially faced the same problem of confronting local 'animistic' ones that Christianity had with paganism, a confrontation that was never altogether complete. The argument is obscure, but it is simply not the case that the objection to idols as explanations of natural events, which supposedly cleared the intellectual air, was an attitude confined to the Near Eastern religions; it was also characteristic of early Buddhism, as indeed of Platonism and many other systems of thought. Indeed I have suggested it is a universal tendency in language-using animals.[63] Once again Needham focuses on the west in order to explain 'modern science'. But there are other possibilities to be explored.

The whole existence of a binary conceptual division between 'modern' and earlier science is thrown into doubt by Elvin's introduction. He writes: 'as of about 1600, China possessed in varying degrees *all* of the styles of thought identified by [the historian of science] Crombie as the eventual key components of science . . . with the apparent exception of the probabilistic, which hardly yet existed at this time even in Europe'.[64] 'The revolution in Europe after 1600, *in so far as there was one* [my italics], lay mainly in the *acceleration* with which these styles both developed and interconnected, rather than in any fundamental qualitative innovation – probability excepted.' That is a radically different position from Needham's and obviously throws doubt not only on the idea of a 'qualitative leap' (anyhow at the level of scientific thought) in the west, but also of the explanations, in terms of the bourgeoisie, religion, the Renaissance, and capitalism. The singularity of modern science or technology has also been queried by a number of recent authors.[65] It is argued that in this feature Europe had earlier been backward so that significant change could not be accounted for in terms of some west European affinity for a tradition of scientific knowledge. Certainly such racist or cultural explanations must be rejected.

Elvin tries to qualify the divisions between science and technology on the one hand, and between modern and earlier science on the other, modifying the terminology employed by many historians of science. He criticizes the 'slightly Brahminical disdain' among those scholars of the

---

[62] Goody 1998: 211.   [63] Goody 1997.   [64] Needham 2004: xxviii.
[65] Wallerstein 1999: 20.

higher sciences towards attempts to make sense of rough and ready but complex phenomena such as moving water. He is also dubious of the validity of the division between science and technology adopted by many historians of science, a division that appears intrinsic to Needham's concept of 'modern science' on which so much of the argument regarding the 'Needham problem' depends.

The 'Needham problem'

Needham nevertheless insisted on trying to answer the question of why the spark of scientific knowledge caught fire in Europe, which is what has been called 'the Needham problem'. It has been suggested that, following the practice in some Islamic circles, teachers such as Roger Bacon in Europe began systematically to probe the qualities of the natural world (against the background we have noted in the previous section), although as Elvin points out, a similar movement was also found among Chinese alchemists. It has also been suggested, as we have seen, that with the advent of printing, the production of handbooks on how-to-do-it again encouraged such enquiries, but printing had also been established in China long before.

What differences can we see in the European situation? The continent had fallen far behind in the accumulation of knowledge, as we see from Needham's remarkable summary diagram in his last contribution to *Science and Civilisation in China*[66] (see Table 5.1).

When Europe was largely cut off from its eastern neighbours in the early Middle Ages, it turned in on itself and on its dominantly religious culture. With the expansion of trade and contacts with the rest of the world, especially with Islamic Europe and the Islamic Near East, a realization of its backwardness in matters of trade, knowledge, and invention would have made itself felt. Trade picked up, knowledge flowed in from abroad, as did information and inventions from the east including from India and China, usually by way of merchant contacts passing along the great band of Muslim societies that stretched across Asia. The recovery of knowledge was extraordinarily rapid, depending upon the particular field. The speed had surely to do with 'the advantage of backwardness'. Within a relatively short space of time the inferiority regarding the east was overcome.

Another of the features deemed to be responsible for the sudden European recovery of knowledge after the Renaissance was the expansion of education, in universities and in schools, partly promoted by the advent of printing bringing about the ability to disseminate rapidly and in large

---

[66] Needham 2004: xx, see figure 2.

Table 5.1 *Transmission of mechanical and other techniques from China to the west*

		Approximate lag in centuries
(a)	Square-pallet chain-pump	15
(b)	Edge-runner mill	13
	Edge-runner mill with application of water-power	9
(c)	Metallurgical blowing-engines, water-power	11
(d)	Rotary fan and rotary winnowing machine	14
(e)	Piston-bellows	*c.* 14
(f)	Draw-loom	4
(g)	Silk-handing machinery (a form of flyer for laying thread evenly on reels appears in the + 11th century; and water-power is applied to spinning mills in the + 14th century)	3–13
(h)	Wheelbarrow	9–10
(i)	Sailing-carriage	11
(j)	Wagon-mill	12
(k)	Efficient harness for draught-animals: breast-strap (position)	8
	Collar	6
(l)	Crossbow (as in individual arm)	13
(m)	Kite	*c.*12
(n)	Helicopter top (spun by cord)	14
	Zeotrope (moved by ascending hot-air current)	*c.*12
(o)	Deep drilling	11
(p)	Cast iron	10–12
(q)	'Cardan' suspension	8–9
(r)	Segmental arch bridge	7
(s)	Iron-chain suspension-bridge	10–13
(t)	Canal lock-gates	7–17
(u)	Nautical construction principles	>10
(v)	Stern-post rudder	*c.* 4
(w)	Gunpowder	5–6
	Gunpowder used as a war technique	4
(x)	Magnetic compass (lodestone spoon)	11
	Magnetic compass with needle	4
	Magnetic compass used for navigation	2
(y)	Paper	10
	Printing (block)	6
	Printing (moveable type)	4
	Printing (metal moveable type)	1
(z)	Porcelain	11–13

Source: Needham 2004: 214.

quantities both text and diagrams.[67] However, this was not a uniquely European feature either, as we see in chapter 8. Elvin writes of the error that some historians have made in considering the presence of the 'university' in twelfth-century Europe as being the magic variable regarding the origins of 'modern science'. For he finds 'analogies to universities in China',[68] the best known of which was the 'Great School' run by the government during the Sung dynasty. It had mathematics, medicine, and examinations. In addition, the 'academies', much more widespread, offered instruction, debate, and training.

Elvin also considers a proposal that two factors may be involved, firstly the conception of nature as a repository of decipherable secrets, possibly derived as we have seen from a strand of the Islamic tradition which most notably stimulated Roger Bacon in the thirteenth century. The second relates to the vulgarization of knowledge leading to 'a barrage of how-to-do-it manuals' which was obviously linked to the advent of printing. Nevertheless Elvin rejects this suggestion because he sees Chinese alchemy as broadly equivalent to the first (the tradition of enquiry) and the long series of Chinese how-to-do-it books on farming and crafts (though not so easily available to the moderately literate) as a partial equivalent to the second (vulgarization). For example, Kubla Khan authorized the compilation of *The basic elements of agriculture and sericulture* which in its 1315 edition was printed in 10,000 copies.[69] So we need to look more deeply at the context.

What this situation emphasizes is that the gap between Europe and China was less profound than much theory assumes. It would seem that it only needed a spark to set the train of intellectual events in motion, a spark that could have been provided by Galileo (as Elvin infers). The great advance could have been partly the result of the sleeper awakening; the very backwardness of western science – it permits freedom of development – largely held back in my view by the dominance of the Christian church and its world-view, was liberated, in part at least, by the countercurrents of the Renaissance, by the reversion to the models of Rome and Greece that were not dominated in the same way by a world religion. The secularization of large areas of knowledge, aided by the advent of printing to Europe, by the questioning of the Reformation, and by the growth of schools, of universities and of humanism, could be held to have contributed to these changes, as could the growth of trade, of overseas adventure, and of the series of events that encouraged enquiry and promoted capitalism.

However, whilst these events have provoked a radical change in the European intellectual climate, this can not be regarded as anything but an

[67] Ong 1974.   [68] Elvin 2004: xxvii.   [69] Needham 2004: 50.

awakening for Europe – be it one that gave it a temporary advance over its Far Eastern counterpart. Certainly, science did not make its first appearance in history in Renaissance Europe, for the simple reason that it had long existed elsewhere. The distinctions with which Needham operates, between early and modern science, science and technology (disputed, we have noted, by Elvin, among others), come out of a habit of regarding developments in post-Renaissance Europe as the zenith of accomplishment and seek to justify a preference which otherwise might seem arbitrary. The Needham problem, posed as such, does not exist. The questions that ought to be asked refer to whether European primacy in terms of modern science is to be regarded as an undisputable fact. Needham has taught us that European science did not appear in a scientific desert, rather that there existed in other parts of the world solid systems of knowledge which were, in his estimation, overtaken by Europe – but only after its prolonged passivity. Whether European leadership is unassailable remains an open question.

The fact that it did make good use of science after the Renaissance is undisputable, but needs explanations of a less categorical kind than the ones we reviewed in this chapter. In Elvin's view the Needham problem is even now far from solved. He concludes his review by suggesting that we look at more specific variables than Needham had selected. Elvin insists upon the 'disaggregation' of variables in a manner rather different from Needham's approach to social factors. For example, for universities he suggests that what is needed to sustain the argument about European advantage is a more specific analysis of the institutions. What specifically was it about the European institutions, he asks, that led to rapid scientific advance? He claims the same approach is needed for the notion of probability which he sees as one of the scientific ideas that China had not formally developed by 1600. Nevertheless while there was no statement of general principles on the subject, there was a very significant practical knowledge of probabilities embodied in the use of board games, some of which travelled from the west like backgammon, others from the east like dominoes. That practical knowledge may not have been framed as a general theory because it constituted a professional secret of gamblers. One does not broadcast secrets on which one's livelihood depends. But gamblers possessed the elements that could have produced 'a basic calculus of probabilities'. Since the figures were never published, 'so the codification, generalisation and progress usually associated with public availability never occurred'.[70] This situation provides an excellent example of the way that literate expression seems to make explicit and hence

---

[70] Elvin 2004: xxxiv.

more 'theoretical' the principles of science, the development of which depends ultimately upon developments in the mode of communication.

Once again the notion of a grid would seem more appropriate than categorical distinctions that tend to identify each tradition with one pole. What we then find is the concentration of various characteristics in one tradition at one time, varying over the years, with the more 'disinterested' activity linked to 'science', the more immediately useful to 'technology', but neither being totally distinct from the other. Neither can be unilaterally associated with one continent rather than another.

There are other problems within binary categories that do not allow of plurality and contradiction. In a speculative passage Needham sees the possibility of a solution in China to some of the ethical dilemmas that 'modern science' poses, because China has for 2,000 years had 'a powerful ethical system never supported by supernatural sanctions'.[71] He is referring here to Confucianism. But China's belief systems also embodied Buddhism, ancestor worship, and local deities.[72] What it lacked (and that was important for knowledge, as we have seen) was a single overarching religious ideology, as in Christianity, Islam, or Judaism. That plurality certainly opened the way for wider enquiries into 'nature'. But there were in fact plenty of 'supernatural' agencies' and 'supernatural sanctions'. Needham singles out Confucianism but that is an example of a tendency to point to one element (the most literate) in the totality of a society's belief systems and to link this with other aspects of the culture one is trying to explain, as a number of historians and sociologists do in different ways. But it is a distinct error to overlook the diversity and contradictions in belief systems at any point in time and one that makes for unsatisfactory history.

A related problem which I mentioned before with the use of categorical distinction is the tendency (it is no more than that) of regarding such distinctions as more permanent than can be justified. As a biologist, Needham avoids the recourse to 'racism' as it is normally understood but his history is often affected by references to the heredity disposition of cultural trends. Thus he talks of the 'most noble ethical *instinct*' of the Jews.[73] At another point he writes of the Chinese 'genius'.[74] These usages may be metaphorical but they appear to display an almost biological belief in cultural continuity, a notion that requires careful handling and much modification. My comment here seems at one with Elvin's

---

[71] Needham 2004: 84.

[72] At one time Needham attributed to Daoism a central role in the history of Chinese science but the idea is no longer current.

[73] Needham 2004: 85, my italics.   [74] Needham 2004: 69.

point that Needham sees Chinese culture and society as unchanging over time, a totally ahistorical view; he does the same over space, treating the empire as homogenous as a nation state. He always leans towards continuity. Once again a grid can be a better guide to the fluctuations, changes, and reversions to earlier models that occur in the historical process.[75]

The problems with Needham's social history can be seen especially clearly in his prognostications for China's future. Instead of copying the west, the development of a 'socialist form of society would seem to be more congruent with China's past than any capitalist one could be'.[76] How he would have interpreted the present arrangements in China is not certain but many would no longer see them as 'socialist'.[77] In any case, the examples of Hong Kong, Singapore, and Taiwan do not seem to bear witness to any incongruity of the kind he is thinking of. Needham's categories are too exclusive, both for the present and for the past.

Quite apart from the overemphasis on cultural or historical continuity, there are other difficulties about Needham's attempt to explain what he sees as the 'unique' development of modern science in the west, along with the Renaissance, the bourgeoisie, and capitalism. Let me insist that these in no way diminish the enormous advance he made in the understanding of Chinese achievements. But we come up here against the same problem that we will find even with Braudel's account of 'capitalism' and with Weber's discussion of the nature of the medieval town, not to speak of his view of the contribution of aesthetic Protestantism. All these explanations suffer from an unjustified concentration on post-Renaissance Europe, which saw extraordinary developments in science and technology as well as in other fields. But when these are set aside as 'modern' in contrast to all other forms, the 'Needham problem' is posed in a categorical, essentialist way that fails to allow for the subsequent developments in the economies, the polities, and the scientific achievements of the east. Those developments require a different type of long-term historical–cultural account. If you start with contemporary Europe or European science as the point of reference, everything else is bound to seem deviant, as lacking something. That is a general problem for contemporary European historians looking backwards or elsewhere. Difference takes on a somewhat negative evaluation, since recent European science becomes the norm and everything else is found wanting, a failure that needs accounting for.

---

[75] See Needham's denial of 're-emergence', Needham 2004: 51.
[76] Needham 2004: 65.
[77] The effects of the Chinese socio-economic revolution on Chinese history are discussed by Brook and Blue 1999: 155ff.

6   The theft of 'civilization': Elias and Absolutist Europe

Much of the history of the world has been written in terms of civilization and civilizations, of the larger units of post-Bronze Age society, often perceived as cultures clashing together in the manner discussed by Samuel Huntington.[1] From an ethnocentric position, the struggle is seen as one in which the west always wins out. Some prescient scholars do recognize that victory, if it should be so regarded in an interactive world, may be temporary while a few may even look upon the respective achievements of earlier centuries as being more equal than is often assumed. The more extravagant ethnocentric claims involve not only presenting contemporary or recent advantage as virtually permanent, but interpreting that advantage in terms of the evolving aspects of European society alone, at least since the sixteenth century and often long before. An influential example of such an approach is the study of the sociologist Norbert Elias entitled *The Civilizing Process*,[2] in which the author's intentions to elucidate this process are qualified by the limitations of his approach to human cultures.

Civilization is a word used in a variety of ways. It is widely employed in contrast to barbarism, both concepts that take their particular form in the Greek world and its view of its neighbours in the north, in the south, and in the east. The latter term began life as a highly ethnocentric notion for the despised other but it also had a more solid rationale since the inhabitants of cities (*civis*, a citizen) used the term 'barbarian' for those outside its walls, with more rural practices. Eventually the pair of words got taken up by western anthropologists and archaeologists without any element of moral evaluation to refer to the 'culture of cities', civilization, to complex societies based on plough agriculture, artisanal production, and the use of writing that emerged in the Bronze Age around 3000 BCE,[3] and barbarism to those practising a simpler, hoe agriculture.

However, in common speech the ethnocentric, evaluative usage continued. In colonial situations, one constantly heard the word 'barbarian' in

---

[1] Huntington 1996.   [2] Elias 1994a.   [3] Childe 1942.

the mouths of Europeans to refer to the members and 'customs' of other cultures with whom they came in contact. Today one hears it applied with equal frequency, always pejoratively, to immigrants from other lands or to active resisters who do not play by the normal rules. The counterpart, 'civilized', has returned in a basically European context in Elias's widely acclaimed book.

My aim in this chapter is to use the kind of material available on Heian Japan, China, and other eastern cultures to query Elias's confinement of civilization to a purely European context, which I regard as 'the theft of civilization' by Europe. Secondly, I want to juxtapose Elias's project in *The Civilizing Process*[4] with his experiences in Ghana where he taught towards the end of his life and so elucidate his more general attitude to what anthropologists refer to as 'other cultures' (especially the 'uncivilized', 'barbarian') with a view to showing the self-congratulatory nature of this approach.[5] Thirdly, some methodological considerations seem appropriate, to explain the distance between the data that was available to Elias and his interpretive conclusions. Some will consider Elias's thesis as *passé* but it still has an important following in France, as in the work of the distinguished historian, Roger Chartier, in the Netherlands, in Germany, and among sociologists in Britain, where a coterie of interesting followers publish the journal *Figurations*. New editions of his works continue to appear and raise the question of the comparative study of civilization in an acute form.

Elias's enterprise takes as a starting point Kant's declaration that 'we are civilized to the point where we are overburdened with all sorts of social propriety and decency'.[6] The 'we' is Europe. His actual study begins with a discussion of the 'sociogenesis of the concepts of "civilization" and "culture"', that is, of how the very broad folk notion of civilization in Germany developed into a quasi-analytic term. In this view we are civilized, the others are savages – or pagans (country-dwellers) or even a lumpen proletariat in our midst. He sees the concept of civilization (in its general function and its common quality) as expressing 'the self-consciousness of the West', summing up everything in which the west believes itself to be superior to other societies and as indicating its special

---

[4] Elias 1994a [1939].
[5] A version of this chapter was originally written as an ethnographic comment upon my encounter with Norbert Elias in Ghana in the context of the recollections of that country he published in a series of interviews. I was led to expand on the question of sociological and anthropological approaches which his sojourn there raised and to consider that experience in terms of his broad thesis about the 'civilizing process'. Later I was asked to expand these latter remarks in relation to his theoretical stance and those of other major social theorists of the twentieth century.
[6] Kant 1784; Elias 1994a [1939]: 7.

character in relation to modernization. (Modernization is my term; he refers to 'the progress of the West'[7]). This notion of progress is one he criticizes in the work of other sociologists[8] but here he justifies his own usage by claiming to be employing the words of the people themselves. That adoption of the actor's terminology obviously contributes to the eurocentric aspect of his work, since the speakers are Europeans. So that the usage comes to sound very like the way humanism came in some circles to refer to our own particular achievements at the time of the Renaissance or before.

Elias's attempts to 'historize' the concepts of civilization and culture are of interest since, in contrast to scientific concepts, he understands their usage as inextricably bound up with a particular social context. But that consideration greatly complicates their analytical use as it leads him to take a stance based purely on the western social context. Civilization is everything the west thinks it has achieved as well as the associated attitudes. But then other complex societies have similar views about their achievements in relation to others. In this respect, his usage is very different from the one adopted by historians of early societies, where civilization is associated with the word 'civil' in quite another way (rather like 'gentility') and refers to the culture of cities, the result of the Urban Revolution of the Bronze Age. We have to understand Elias's endeavours in a totally different, evaluative, frame of reference.

Elias's claim refers to the emergence of both social and psychological patterns of behaviour. In the first case he speaks of 'sociogenesis', in the second of 'psychogenesis'. His claim is that after the Middle Ages behaviour was increasingly censured socially, leading to the sociogenesis of the feelings of shame and delicacy, and, more generally, to civilized behaviour. This in time becomes internalized, the mechanisms of civilization are moved from external coercion to internal censorship, shame becomes guilt (an idea that relates to Freud). The whole process from 'Naturvolk' to civilization has been completed only once in history – in modern Europe. According to Elias, these developments have their origin in the shift from feudal society to absolutism. Social organization becoming ever more hierarchical and complex, it imposed tighter restraints upon behaviour which in time became internalized.

Before proceeding with an analysis of his claims, Elias takes pains to bring out his theoretical and methodological interests. He is particularly concerned with the way in which the predominant type of sociology current in his day – he refers mainly to Talcott Parsons – had become a sociology of 'states' (static) and had set aside a consideration of problems of long-term social change, 'of the sociogenesis and development of social

---

[7] Elias 1994a [1939]: 4.   [8] Elias 1994a [1939]: 193.

formations of all kinds'.[9] An important achievement of Elias was that he kept alive the tradition of historical sociology, rejected by many 'post-modernists' and others, the tradition that was exemplified in the works of Marx and above all those of Max Weber.[10]

I do not wish to suggest that comparison is the only strategy history, anthropology, or the social sciences can adopt. Clearly there is a place for those who wish to concentrate upon the Nuer, upon the wider frame of Nilotic studies, or upon medieval Bosnia, even upon modes of behaviour in Renaissance Europe. There may also be a place for a mode of enquiry that embraces neither intensive study nor systematic comparison, but involves general speculation on the human story. I myself would prefer to see this listed under a separate designation, for example the 'philosophic anthropology' as practised by Habermas is a possibility here. But if one wants to say something about the differences between certain types of society (however defined), or even to imply the existence of such general differences, there is really no alternative to systematic comparisons. In a recent book Pomeranz acknowledges that much of classical social theory has been eurocentric but argues that

the alternative favoured by some current 'post-modernist' scholars abandoning cross-cultural comparison altogether and focussing almost exclusively on exposing the contingency, particularity, and perhaps unknowability of historical moments – makes it impossible even to approach many of the most important questions in history (and in contemporary life). It seems much preferable instead to confront biased comparison by trying to produce better ones

by seeing both sides of the comparison as deviations rather than as seeing one as the norm.[11] That goal should remain an important aim for all the social sciences, and it is one with which the work of Weber and Elias urges us to engage.

Despite the problems with aspects of his approach, Elias has had some influence on the development of sociological analysis but always in the European context. One example is Mennell's interesting study on the development of food in France and England, which is historical in content but has been given a sociological frame. An aspect of that frame is the

---

[9] Elias 1994a [1939]: 190.
[10] For Elias had worked with his brother, Alfred Weber, and had joined the circle of Marianne Weber at Heidelberg, becoming an assistant to the sociologist, Karl Mannheim, with whom he later met up again in London. And that approach Elias applied to the fascinating topic of 'manners'. He is also very much preoccupied, as we have seen, with development over time. That was the case, but Parsons saw advantages in the synchronic analysis of social action. Indeed the diachronic analysis, in the work of authors like Comte, Spencer, Marx and Hobhouse, is dismissed by Elias himself partly on evidential grounds and partly because of an ideology that assumed development was always for the better, a movement in the direction of progress.
[11] Pomeranz 2000: 8.

'figurational sociology' of Norbert Elias, intrinsic to his approach but in fact rather obscure.

> The word 'figuration' is used to denote the patterns in which people are bound together in groups, states, societies – patterns of interdependence which encompass every form of co-operation and conflict and which are very rarely static or unchanging. Within a developing social figuration, modes of individual behaviour, cultural tastes, intellectual ideas, social stratification, political power and economic organisation are all entangled with one another in complex ways which themselves change over time in ways that need to be investigated. The aim is to provide a 'sociogenic' explanation of how figurations change from one type to another . . .[12]

Like Mennell, Elias produces some interesting historical sociology about Europe. That necessarily involves the analysis of events over time, and it is change and continuity with which he is trying to deal in introducing the notion of 'figurations'. But what does it in fact do that is not already done by numerous sociological or anthropological concepts? Very little. Moreover, there is always the problem with Elias's work that the figurations, like civilizations, have little comparative basis. Mennell refers to Elias's suggestion[13] 'that it is one of the peculiarities of western society that the reduction of contrasts in culture and conduct has been meshed with the co-mingling of traits deriving initially from very different social levels'.[14] I doubt very much that this feature is uniquely western; certainly no shadow of proof is presented.[15] Nor are we offered any understanding, either in his original work or in his comments on Ghana, of the range of human society, behaviour, or figurations as a whole. And while one can certainly do valuable scholarly work without such an understanding, its absence gravely inhibits the analysis of a feature as general as the 'civilising process'.

Rightly in my opinion, Elias argues that we should set aside the ideology of the social sciences and attempt to improve the factual basis. But the

---

[12] Mennell 1985: 15–16.   [13] Elias 1994a [1939]: ii, 252–6.   [14] Mennell 1985: 331.

[15] A more elaborate critique of Elias has been offered by Hans-Peter Dürr, to which a sensitive reply has been given by Mennell and Goudsblom (1977). In my view the attempt to show Elias as concerned, intellectually and empirically, with the east and with the other is basically a failure. He started from a Weberian point of view, as I tried to show, both in the opening remarks in his book and in his African experiences, and he never managed to overcome a eurocentric vision. In their later comments, both these authors have modified Elias's notions, Mennell by stressing the complementary process of de-civilization, Goudsblom by taking 'civilization' back not simply to the sixteenth century and 'state formation', or even to the Bronze Age and its cities, but to man's invention of fire, which some have seen as the beginning of culture itself. The first modification takes care of the Nazi experience, the second of the exclusion of Ghana and the 'Naturvolk'. Both modifications point up the relevance of my critique and run, I believe, in a different direction from the main thrust of Elias's argument.

problem with his study is that the factual base is restricted – nor is it clear in his earlier monograph to what extent a notion of 'progress' is intrinsic to his concept of civilization, of centralization and the internalization of constraints in the development of manners. There has been much discussion of the nature of Elias's concepts of 'progress' and of 'process' and their relation to earlier notions of evolution and development, but in his major book he is certainly dealing with vectorial transformation over time, both of society and of the personality.

He also draws attention to the paucity of work on 'the structure and controls of human affects' except for 'the more developed societies of today'. He appreciates the need for evidence from other societies, but considers he has tackled the question, both with regard to differentiation at the socio-political level ('state controls') and to the relationship with long-term changes in affect control, the latter being manifest in experience 'in the form of an advance in the threshold of shame and revulsion'. The notion of such an 'advance' is critical. Although he wishes to replace metaphysically dominated sociological theories of development by a more empirically based model, he rejects the notion of evolution 'in the nineteenth-century sense' or of unspecific 'social change' in the twentieth-century one.[16] He rather looks at social development in one of its manifestations, namely the process of state formation over several centuries together with the complementary process of advancing civilization; anything else seems to be the product of *naturvolk*. He claims he is 'laying the foundation of an undogmatic, empirically based sociological theory of social process in general and of social development in particular'.[17] One would have expected a generalized *naturvolk* to be the first casualty of such an enquiry. However, he goes on, social change (seen as 'structural') must be regarded as moving towards 'greater or less complexity' over many generations.[18] It is not easy to discuss the applicability of this theory to other contexts because of its great generality. At the same time he confines the notion of state formation and civilization to the modern period in Europe. From a theoretical point of view such a purely European focus is unsustainable, especially as the process of state formation was discussed by other German writers (such as the anthropologist Robert Lowie) in a much wider context.

The civilizing process

Elias starts the preface of his major book with the words: 'Central to this study are the modes of behaviour considered typical of Western civilised

---

[16] Elias 1994a [1939]: 184.   [17] Elias 1994a [1939]: 184.   [18] Elias 1994a [1939]: 184.

man.' His thesis is that in the 'medieval-feudal' period, Europe was not civilized. The 'civilizing' of the west came later. How did behaviour and 'affective life' change after the Middle Ages? How can we understand 'the psychical process of civilization'? Specifically, he claims, there was a shift in 'the feelings of shame and delicacy'; the standard of what society demands and prohibits changed. The threshold of socially instilled displeasure moved, and so the question of 'sociogenic' fears emerges as one of the central problems of the civilizing process, which is marked by the internalization of social sanctions. Some peoples, he suggests, appear more childlike, less grown-up than ourselves; they have not reached the same stage in the civilizing process. While Elias does not claim that 'our civilised mode of behaviour is the most advanced of all humanly possible modes of behaviour', nevertheless the very concept of civilized 'expresses the self-consciousness of the West'.[19] By this term western society, he remarks, seeks to describe its superiority.

He draws attention to 'the notion that people should seek to harmonise with and show consideration for each other, that the individual may not always give way to his emotions'; that notion emerges both in France, especially in court literature, and in England.[20] These ideas are seen as absent from feudal society and arose out of the court life of the absolutist monarchies of post-medieval Europe; 'related social situations, life in the *monde*, led everywhere in Europe to related precepts and modes of behaviour'. In other words the civilizing process is seen as linked to the 'modernization' of Europe.

Part of this process was the development of manners with the rise of the state from the Renaissance to recent times, with bodily functions becoming ever more concealed, both in word and in deed, with mediators gradually being introduced between food and mouth, with movements, gestures, and postures more deliberately formal. The evidence comes from manuals on behaviour (which Elias thinks should be taken more seriously than what we now call 'books of etiquette'), or from the French 'manuels de savoir-faire', as well as from other written and visual sources. Both the instructions and the behaviour were class-based, aimed at upper elements of society, or rather at teaching the middle what the upper should be doing. Such manuals, like many books on cooking and other forms of stratified behaviour, are directed at the bourgeoisie rather than at the aristocracy itself, at those who want to be rather than those who are. At the same time they distinguish the 'upper' in general from the 'lower', especially as these groups, or components of them, were in the process of changing their position in society.

[19] Elias 1994a [1939]: 3.   [20] Elias 1994a [1939]: 27.

One of the problems with Elias's exposition is that, whilst some elements in this behaviour, such as the use of the fork, were clearly new to Europe, striking aspects of these patterns of behaviour are reminiscent of earlier classical models. Such models obviously played an important part in the course of the Renaissance in Europe, which was in many ways a rebirth rather than a birth (sociogenesis).[21] As with so many facets of European culture, societies were going through a process of re-civilization, not only of recreating but of retrieving what had often been lost following the collapse of Rome. High–low differences did not of course disappear in the Middle Ages, even before the period that saw the development of 'courtoisie' and chivalric honour. Nevertheless, for a considerable period in the medieval west little stress was given to bourgeois culture, to the culture of towns ('civilization'), that had existed in the classical world. Even among the nobility, some graces had vanished.

Elias attempts an account of European social life following the Middle Ages. Though he is concerned with the socio-political changes after feudalism, he does not make the great socio-economic transformation of 'capitalism' or industrialization central to his study, as did Marx and Weber. The work of the former he rejects because of the author's identification with the industrial working-class and his belief in the progress of mankind; while the latter's historical method in setting up ideal types ran against Elias's concern with process rather than with abstraction, distinction, separation. In contrast to later 'civilization', Elias's interest took him back to the Middle Ages in Europe; what happened before and elsewhere was of little concern. He does not deal with civilization in Antiquity nor in the east.

This thesis is treated as a question of unilineal development that took off in Europe at the time of the Renaissance. As a consequence of ignoring the process of civilization in earlier and other cultures, it comes to be seen as an aspect of modernity, as part of a comprehensive process that should include the socio-economic changes marking the advent of capitalism (in the Weberian or Marxist account) as well as the developments of knowledge systems; to these Elias gives scant attention. Another problem with his account is that the kind of restraint and etiquette that is manifested in the manuals Elias examined is a feature of all major systems of stratification. By major systems I mean those associated with post-Bronze Age civilizations, which extended from eastern Asia to western Europe. Indeed beyond those areas to parts of Africa and Oceania, because Muslim

---

[21] Elias writes of the sociogenesis of the concept of civilization, of institutions (absolutism), even of sociogenetic laws. He appears to be referring to their origin in the social.

missionaries spread new forms of 'restrained' behaviour, including certain practices of cleanliness, to many other cultures, as also happened in China when educational institutions spread Confucian manners, rites, and ideologies throughout that immense land. Perhaps even outside that range, for in the more 'culturally egalitarian' but stratified states of Africa, special behaviours of this kind are attached not so much to groups ('classes') as to individual office-holders, to chiefs for example, another instance of the kind of restraint Elias observes, unconnected to hierarchies like those that defined Eurasian stratified societies. This suggestion points to the weakness of his particular developmental view, not of course of all developmental views but of those that take as their model relatively short-term developments in Europe and see the emergence of class-differentiated behaviour (in a particular cultural situation) as a unique event rather than as a recurrent process.

That European focus and the aversion to abstraction also differentiate him from the French sociologist, Durkheim.[22] Marx and Weber certainly incorporated material on Asia into their work; indeed they saw that as essential to account for the development of capitalism in Europe. They knew rather little of 'other (simpler) cultures' in a more general way. Durkheim however did, and he worked on a much broader canvas in considering human development. Although Elias frequently discusses the division of labour, he fails to mention the broad comparative work of the influential French sociologist, concentrating only on events in the early modern period from a narrower perspective. Had he done so, given his strong psychological interests, he might have paid more attention to the internalized aspects of the division of labour that Durkheim took into account under the rubric of organic and mechanical solidarity, the former referring to the nature of relationships in simple, undifferentiated, societies, the latter to the way groups and individuals link together in complex ones. He discussed these forms of the division of labour under the heading of moral density, a concept that was taken up by anthropologists such as Evans-Pritchard. For Elias too an interest in social origins was always paralleled by one in psychogenesis[23] since he rightly sees the internal and the external, the social and the individual, as being very much two sides of the same coin.

Despite his lack of long-term historical depth from the standpoint of cultural analysis, we need to consider seriously Elias's constant stress on sociogenesis, an interest in the emergence of institutions which in the twentieth century anthropologists dealing with pre-literate cultures had rejected as being of little or no value. However it was a problem that

---

[22] Elias 1994a [1939]: 3.   [23] For instance, on p. 26.

historical research had opened up for Elias. The psychological aspects are inevitably more problematic to investigate because of the nature of the evidence but the emergence of institutions, providing there is some reasonable historical, comparative, or even theoretical basis, constitutes a perfectly valid field of enquiry.

This brings us too the central example, namely, the sociogenesis of absolutism[24] which in turn he perceives, like Anderson in his work *Lineages of the Absolutist State*,[25] as occupying 'a key position in the overall process of civilization' which is clearly similar to the notion of despotism we discussed in Chapter 4. The process of the formation of absolutism is related to the way 'increased constraint and dependence came about' and refers to the Kantian discussion about civilized man being 'overburdened' by 'social propriety' that we have seen is central to his whole enterprise. Sociogenesis, social development, is always accompanied by an internalized 'psychogenesis', the social constraints of absolutism by the control of the super-ego. His resort to Freudian concepts is indicative of the fact that he takes a similar view of social progress to that author's in *Civilization and its Discontents*.[26]

The common pool of ideas from which Elias and Freud draw is indicated in Freud's *The Future of an Illusion*,[27] described by the English translator and editor, James Strachey, as turning on 'the irremediable antagonism between the demands of instinct and the restrictions of civilization'.[28] 'Civilization is something which was imposed on a resisting majority by a minority which understood how to obtain possession of the means to power and wealth',[29] that is, paradigmatically under conditions of absolutism, not by means of a democratic system as the later ideology required. The 'masses are lazy and unintelligent' according to Freud[30] and have to be controlled by coercion, at least until education enables them to internalize controls when they will cease to hate civilization and recognize its benefits, including the sacrifice of instinct.

The notion of civilization is very similar to that used by Elias and its benefits include the recognition of beauty, cleanliness, and order; baths were important in this process and the use of soap becomes 'a yardstick of civilisation'.[31] Indeed the passage seems to propose the very programme for the elaboration of Elias's thesis about the growth of civilization in Europe. Moreover the emphasis moves from the material to the mental.

---

[24] Elias 1994a [1939]: 269.   [25] Anderson 1974b.
[26] Elias 1994a [1939]: 249. Although no specific reference is made to Freud in the original version, this absence is rectified in a subsequent footnote where the debt is thoroughly acknowledged.
[27] Freud 1961 [1927].   [28] Strachey 1961: 60   [29] Strachey 1961: 6.
[30] Freud 1961 [1927]: 9.   [31] Elias 1974 [1939]: 93.

According to Freud the sense of guilt is 'the most important problem in the development of civilisation'; 'the price we pay for our advance in civilisation is a loss of happiness through heightening the sense of guilt'.[32] And in the well-known letter he wrote to Einstein, *Why War*,[33] he states:

> The *psychical* modifications that go along with the process of civilisation ['an organic process'] . . . consist in a progressive displacement of instinctual aims and a restriction of instinctual impulses.[34]

The general line of argument, the view of civilization, the notion of restraint and repression, the control of instinctual (animal) nature, the role of authority (absolutism in the shape of the father) in the process, these themes are very similar in the two writers and help explain Elias's attitude to what he called *Naturvolk* when he visited Ghana and encountered the native population. The rise of the state is directly connected with the control of feelings and behaviour. In considering this proposition, we should note that the claim was not unique. That notion of state control associated with the internal behaviour of the citizens has its parallels elsewhere, in Japan for example: indeed one suspects that such a claim is part of the post-facto justification for a state's very existence. In his commentary on the great eleventh-century Japanese novel, *The Tale of Genji*, the critic Bazan writes: 'To express themselves in feelings is the nature of the people; to rest in ritual and righteousness was the beneficent influence of the former kings.'[35] In other words the conditions that are thought to have aided the emergence of civilization during absolutism are not dissimilar from those characterizing the so-called Asiatic despotisms. So there is nothing particularly European about this notion of the role of the state. And it is in any case obviously a theoretical error to see state sanctions as the only method of controlling behaviour, of making 'laws', except from a purely terminological point of view. In simpler societies reciprocity exists very widely as a social sanction, without any necessity for the actions of the state.

Those actions are seen as influencing manners, just as manners are linked to internal changes. Elias concentrates upon aspects of everyday behaviour, the increasing use of tableware (especially the fork), of handkerchiefs, and so forth. Rising consumption over this period, associated with mercantile expansion, did see a series of substantial changes in western cultures, including the elaboration in matters of dress and table manners. But we need to ask ourselves if it is satisfactory simply to select a particular set of cultural factors and then to disregard others which seem

---

[32] Freud 1927: 134.   [33] Freud 1964 [1933].   [34] Freud 1964: 214.
[35] McMullen 1999.

to go in a contrary sense? As well as changes in personal manners, one needs to take account of the increase in warfare and violence, including those aspects that led to Elias himself having to flee his native Germany, as well as less constrained behaviour in the area of sex, of violations of property rights and other forms of criminal action which we experience in contemporary life.

Concerning violence, he claims that 'we see clearly how the compulsions arising directly from the threat of weapons and physical force gradually diminish, and how those forms of dependency which lead to the regulation of the affects in the form of self-control, gradually increase'.[36] The proposition is highly questionable, at least at the level of society, taking into account the use and threat of weapons in the twentieth century; we experience this daily on our TV screens and on our streets. Yet he claims that social facts fit in with the general notion of increasing self-control. As we have seen, that thesis is vaguely based on the contrast with '*Naturvolk*' with their supposedly freer feelings, on the notion of a shift from (external) shame to (internal) guilt, on Freudian and similar visions of instinctive drives and impulses gradually being brought under control by society. For Elias sociogenesis (as in absolutism) seems to be connected with shame, psychogenesis (as in the super-ego) with guilt.

There are further problems with Elias's thesis: firstly that all social life, everywhere, involves giving some consideration to other individuals, some taking into account, some measure of restraint on the emotions and on behaviour, even for reciprocity's sake. While he may be right about his account of the historical development of table manners in Europe, that has little to do with the overall notion of the development of consideration for others, which he presupposes.[37] That consideration we certainly find elsewhere. And indeed, as we have seen above, in some respects a lack of consideration in other spheres appears to grow *pari passu* with developments in table manners; today's violence in family and street is not a mirage and it is difficult to reconcile Elias's Whiggish approach (despite his claim to have rejected the idea) with the fact that at the time he was writing Nazis were murdering Jews throughout Europe, clicking their heels with handkerchiefs stuffed in their pockets and blowing their noses in a refined way. A book on civilized behaviour demands an adequate consideration of such contradictions.

---

[36] Elias 1994a [1939]: 153.
[37] For comments on this substantive aspect of his work, see E. Le Roy Ladurie, *Figaro*, 20 January 1997 and *Saint-Simon* (Paris 1997), Gordon 1994, and the defence by Chartier, 2003.

Secondly, the major problem with Elias's analysis of civilization is that it is entirely eurocentric and does not even begin to consider that a similar process occurred in other cultural areas. Let us leave aside the earlier societies of the Bronze Age, for which the term 'civilization' is often used, and consider the recent cultures of the east. The comparative historian, Fernandez-Armesto, writes of the subtleties of the court culture of Heian Japan as presented in Murasaki's *The Tale of Genji* which I mentioned before. 'In Christendom at the time, aristocratic thuggery had to be restrained or at least channelled by the Church. Noble hoodlums would be at best slowly and fitfully civilised, over a long period, by a cult of chivalry which always remains as much a training in arms as an education in values of gentility. From this perspective, the existence on the other side of the world of a culture in which delicacy of feeling and the arts of peace were spontaneously celebrated by a secular elite seems astounding.'[38] Using a concept similar to Elias, he speaks of Japan as manifesting 'a collective project of self-restraint', seen as a key term.[39] Nor is that the only similarity. For he adds, 'judged alongside some other eleventh-century court cultures, the values of Heian are not as bizarre as they seemed by the standards of Christendom'. For example, al-Mu'tamid, ruler of Seville, shared with Japan 'an epicene appreciation, a love of gardening, a talent for poetry, and a homo-erotic appetite'. The differences were less than Europeans often assumed.

Elias would certainly admit that the civilizing process was also happening in China (although this country is mentioned only four times in the course of this long book on civilization, including twice in the later notes) but his problematic and mode of explanation leaves little or no room for the inclusion of other 'civilizations', let alone 'other cultures', for it is highly eurocentric. That situation occurs partly because of his attitude to the 'general regularities' in customary behaviour which systematic comparison discovers, for he sees the value of these regularities as lying '*solely* in their function in elucidating historical change'.[40] But both structure and change are essential aspects of the study of society. One can understand why he was so opposed to the American sociologist, Talcott Parsons, and the tradition of highly generalized comparison he represented and which included such a strong emphasis on 'synchronic' analysis. But Elias himself altogether avoids any wider comparison with other societies, except a standardized *Naturvolk*.

My observation of contemporary society suggests that what is often seen as the civilizing process in terms of manners or civility is not one

---

[38] Fernandez-Armesto 1995: 20.   [39] Fernandez-Armesto 1995: 22.
[40] Elias 1939: 534, my italics.

of straightforward amelioration, but is much more ambiguous. We pride ourselves on changes in our treatment of children (as in the work of Ariès), of animals, of women, of prisoners of war, etc. There is some basis for these assertions but are the attitudes really internalized in the way Elias, taking a generalized Freudian line, suggests? Why then are our children in danger from abuse, mainly within the family but from outside paedophiles as well? Why do we have so many 'broken families'? Why Guantanamo Bay, Abu-Ghraib, and the abandonment of the Geneva Convention?

At a technological level there has undoubtedly been an advance in civilization in the sense of urban-based cultures. They have become more complex. There has been a parallel shift from luxury cultures to those of mass consumption, which has had the effect of partly generalizing the manners of the upper groups to others. In certain respects, their manners were always more restrained than those of lower groups. But that restraint does not necessarily represent an internalization of earlier forms of external behaviour. Although that is a common view held in the west, in folk ideas as well as in Freudian social theory, there is little evidence that our behaviour is more restrained internally than anyone else's. In all societies behaviour is sanctioned both internally and externally; the parallel notion that some cultures are guilt cultures with internal sanctions (us) and others shame cultures with external ones (them) seems quite egocentric and unsustainable. It is a eurocentric notion widely held of the other, that they are less restrained than us, as in the case of the wild Caliban in Shakespeare's *Tempest*. This idea, which rests on little evidence worthy of the name, has in turn been integrated as a premise in numerous theories concerned with other aspects of social life and its career began long before Elias. For instance, the famous demographic historian, the Revd Malthus, writing at the turn of the nineteenth century, saw the late marriage of the 'European marriage pattern' as being evidence of self-restraint and an ability to control the population, an opinion about restraint that for China has been decisively rejected by Lee and Wang.[41]

'What lends the civilising process in the west its special and unique character', Elias writes, 'is that here the division of functions has attained a level, the monopolies of force and taxation a solidity, and interdependence and competition an extent, both in terms of physical space and of numbers of people, unequalled in world history.'[42] Could that really be said of the sixteenth century? In any case he does not examine the history of any other part of the world and if he did so, given his initial question about post-Renaissance manners, he might still have ended up like Weber in seeing

---

[41] Lee and Wang 1999.   [42] Elias 1994a [1939]: 457.

Europe as 'unique'. Which of course it is bound to be. But the implication is that it is unique in respect of the factors leading to the civilizing process (or to capitalism). In a recent book Pomeranz has effectively queried these assumptions[43] in a manner that seems quite correct.[44]

Western society, Elias asserts, developed a 'network of interdependence' encompassing not only the oceans but the arable regions of the earth (in the expansion of Europe), creating a necessity for an 'attunement of human conduct over wider areas'. 'Corresponding to it, too, is the strength of self-control and the permanence of compulsion, affect-inhibition and drive-control, which life at the centres of this network imposes'.[45] Having elaborated this relationship between terrestrial expansion (European colonialism) and psychological interdependence, producing permanent self-control (more complex super-egos), he sees this in turn as related to punctuality, to the development of chronometric techniques, and to the consciousness of time as well as to the development of money and 'other instruments of social integration'. Those developments include 'the necessity to subordinate momentary affects to more distant goals',[46] starting with the upper and middle classes. All this concerns 'western development' and 'western societies', with 'their high division of labour'.[47] High, note, rather than more complex. There is certainly more planning, and hence delayed gratification, in such societies, associated with the reckoning of time. But that often involves external controls as much, or more than, internal ones which he sees as preponderant in this type of society. And we must not lose sight of the fact that apart from such 'attunement', state formation led to violence within and without the boundaries, to colonialism and oppression as well as to 'pax Britannica'.

In the introduction that he added to the 1968 edition, Elias takes pains to bring out his theoretical and methodological interests.[48] We need to look at Elias's work in the wider context of social theory and analysis where the obvious comparison is with Max Weber. Weber had an important effect in encouraging a comparative approach on sociology. However his discussion was sometimes of limited value, as the notion of a single category of traditional authority was far too restrictive and did not correspond to what one found in practice. Traditional was simply a residual category for Weber and so too it became for Elias. In the second, while he was extremely knowledgeable about the major Eurasian civilizations, unlike Durkheim Weber knew virtually nothing of non-literate societies, and little enough of 'peasant' ones. Such a wider interest was very

[43] Pomeranz 2000.   [44] Goody 1996, 2004.   [45] Elias 1994a [1939]: 457.
[46] Elias 1994a [1939]: 438.   [47] Elias 1994a [1939]: 459.   [48] Elias 1994a [1939]: 190.

limited in the German sociological tradition from which Elias emerged. More stimulating was Weber's major problematic and the way he tried to test his suggested answer cross-culturally. But while he reviews the situation in the major Eurasian societies, he does so from the standpoint of nineteenth-century Europe without giving sufficient weight to the achievements of others nor yet to their points of view. Elias offers no such comprehensive review. He begins with Europe and ends with Europe. In other words his original thesis adopts a similar approach to those discussed by Blaut in his *Eight Eurocentric Historians*.[49] Elias would have qualified for a ninth place (though there are many other candidates) because of his statements about Europe's advantages in the civilizing process (and particularly regarding the internalization of restraint) without any review of non-European materials.[50]

As I have said earlier, his major work concentrates entirely upon Europe and the development of the civilizing process in the period following the Renaissance. This he sees as manifested in increasing self-restraint, in the internalization of controls over affect, which he contrasts explicitly with what took place in the Middle Ages (such as uncontrolled bouts of drinking) and continues to happen in simpler societies among the *Naturvolk* as in Ghana, with their sacrifices, rituals, scanty clothing but greater directness. With Weber, as with Elias, the focus came firmly back to historical comparison, though talk of the *Naturvolk* and of the assumption of some ideal type of traditional society brought one perilously close to the wider speculations of nineteenth-century anthropologists against whose procedures and results the fieldworking anthropologists of the interwar period with their 'static' observations had struggled so strongly and to much purpose.

Elias does not see every development as proceeding in a straight line. After the First World War, there was a 'relaxation in morals'[51] but this was 'a very short recession' which he claims did not affect the general trend. Nevertheless Elias asserts that 'the direction of the main movement . . . is the same for all kinds of behavior'.[52] Instincts are slowly and progressively suppressed. While this point of view is commonplace in the west, it is not easy to find any empirical support. For instance, more revealing bathing costumes (and clothing for women's sport) presuppose 'a very high standard of drive control'. Why does that observation apply to us and not to the scantier clothing of simpler societies? Indeed when one examines the

---

[49] Blaut 2000.
[50] As with many writers, there has been change over time. I am talking about the original work.
[51] Elias 1994a [1939]: 153.   [52] Elias 1994a [1939]: 154.

problem of increasing constraints from a different angle, the notion of a general progression disappears, although there may have been changes towards stricter and laxer controls over time.

Later on towards the end of his life, Elias turned to consider the most dramatic of recent political events, the rise of Nazism (or more broadly Fascism), which some consider should have had its place in any account of the overall changes in human society. He now sees the Nazi period as manifesting a process of 'decivilization', of 'regression', but that seems to avoid the main issue. Both the Fascist ideologies and activities in Germany and Italy, like the World Wars, are surely an intrinsic part of the development of contemporary society that has led to our present situation, and not some kind of 'regression', a social equivalent of Freudian psychological processes.

That concept of regression seems to relate to the problem of phylogeny and ontogeny. There is little doubt that in most contexts Elias equated the childhood of the race with the childhood of the human being, the phylogenetic with the ontogenetic (although children did not go through all the phases of the civilizing process); the *Naturvolk* or primitive needed to have his emotions and behaviour controlled, as was the case with children who required disciplining in the same way (with fear playing its part in both cases). That notion is now generally regarded as misleading. As has often been pointed out, *Naturvolk* have themselves already been through a long process of socialization, of denaturing, and to see them as lacking in self-control is unacceptable. In acephalous societies without elaborate systems of authority there are possibly more 'internalized' constraints, certainly reciprocal ones – which may of course take the form of 'negative reciprocity' in the violence of vengeance and the feud. That Elias would later have understood had he learnt from the studies on Ghana undertaken by Fortes with his psychological and indeed psychoanalytic background, which Elias neglected.

The change in the structure of affects is related by Elias to the change in the structure of the social formation, in particular the shift from the 'free competition' of feudal society to the monopolization of power by the absolutist monarchy, creating the courtly society. In a differentiated culture, that increased central control is seen as offering greater 'freedoms' to its members, entailing a shift from external constraints to internal ones, though the logical basis of this transformation seems open to question. And the shifting basis of being 'free' adds to those doubts.

However, the process of what he calls state formation, the sociogenesis of the state, is analysed exclusively from the standpoint of western Europe, which is of course where he sees the civilizing process as taking place. No indigenous African society was considered by him as having a state at all, though he lived within the shadow of the Kingdom of Asante. His approach contrasts with that of Weber, who was concerned with the sociogenesis of capitalism (and the internalized religiously based constraints of Protestants) and discussed at great length the reasons why Asian societies did not, could not, give rise to capitalism. Nevertheless the questions are linked together.

No need to consider *Naturvolk* in this civilizing process but it is unacceptable that there is no reference to other urban societies, especially as this might have led him to query the notion of a special 'social personality structure' in the west. The question he raises is whether the long-term changes in social systems, 'towards a higher level of social differentiation and integration',[53] are accompanied by parallel changes in personality structures. The problem of long-term changes in affect and control structures of people constitutes an interesting question and is not one that has been much discussed, historically or comparatively, certainly in terms of affect and emotion. However, there has been considerable interest in social control, including internalized sanctions, the question of shame and guilt, and the relation of segmentary (non-centralized) political systems to moral and jural solidarities which was raised by Durkheim (and only much later in the German tradition with its overwhelming concern with the state). The comparison and history of 'affect' presents greater problems of evidence and documentation, at least in the absence of written sources; indeed that situation throws some doubts on a dependence on the text alone for examining 'mentalities', and most anthropologists, discomforted by Levy-Bruhl's 'primitive mentality', would tend to follow G. E. R. Lloyd in his extensive criticisms of such an approach. That is not to deny the possibility of long-term changes, possibly directional ones, at the level of affect, even if anthropologists more frequently take a relativistic or sometimes universalistic line ('the unity of mankind') about such topics, demanding a scepticism about such questions as 'the invention of love' in twelfth-century France or eighteenth-century England, the evidence for which depends entirely on the written record.

As we have seen Elias's failure seriously to examine other cultures leads him into several kinds of problems. Firstly, his sequence of development privileges western Europe and its development from feudal to courtly (of the sixteenth and seventeenth centuries) to bourgeois society. Secondly, his vision totally underestimates the social constraints in the simpler societies, certainly with regard to sex, violence, and other forms of

---

[53] Elias 1994a [1939]: 182.

interpersonal behaviour. The fact that 'primitives' may go about scant-
ily clad does not mean they do not have strong internalized feelings
of shame and embarrassment. Thirdly, the alternative hypothesis is to
over-interpret, as I think he sometimes does, the material culture as an
index of a psychological state; material culture involves development and
'progress' which is much more questionable with psychological states.

What remains problematic in his analysis is not the interlocking of
human beings in a wider perspective (society, culture, figuration), nor
the relationship of the individual to the *social* (as distinct from society),
questions that were more clearly discussed by Durkheim and further analysed by Parsons in *The Structure of Social Action*,[54] a study that Elias does
not take fully into account. The problem that is most worrying lies in the
nature of the nexus between social structure and personality structure.
How mental stages correspond to social ones is a question that lies at the
heart of his problematic. No one would deny that there are some such
relationships. But it is very easy to interpret those as too tightly linked,
too closely associated. Elias posits the western world as going through
a series of linked stages of this kind. He writes of the emergence of a
conception of the relation between what is 'inside man' and 'the external
world' that is found in the writings of all groups 'whose power of reflection and whose self-awareness have reached the stage at which people are
in a position not only to think but to be conscious of themselves, and to
reflect on themselves as thinking beings'.[55] But what is this stage which
is formulated in such a vague way? It seems to assume the existence of
a more primitive mentality that excludes the possibility of self-awareness
and fails to look for particular social factors leading to this supposed
breakthrough, such as the power of the written word to promote reflexivity of this kind (as well as the role of individuals, social groups, and
institutions that developed such an approach, including 'philosophers',
other intellectuals, and schools). Can we properly speak of a 'stage in the
development of the figurations formed by people, and the people form-
ing these figurations'?[56] That again seems to be putting the problem at
a too general, non-sociological, non-historical level. This he also does
when he sees the shift from a geocentric view of the world as resulting
from 'an increased capacity in men for self-detachment in thought';[57] that
particular development of the civilizing process led to 'greater self-control
by men'. Many historians of science would put the relationship round
the other way and offer explanations that did not require the notion of
an autonomous civilizing process bringing about greater 'affect control',

---

[54] Parsons 1937.   [55] Elias 1994a [1939]: 207.   [56] Elias 1994a [1939]: 20.
[57] Elias 1994a [1939]: 208.

greater self-detachment. Indeed going to the roots of Elias's hypothesis, it is difficult to accept the construction of a prima mobile of this abstract kind which is not simply descriptive but causal – 'a civilisation shift . . . that was taking place within man himself',[58] flattering as that may be to our own egos.

Even granted there were directional changes in behaviour linked to centralization in Europe, why disregard what happened in other societies such as China when one is dealing with 'civilizations', as we have seen he does? There too the development of manners, the use of intermediaries (chopsticks) between food and mouth, the complicated rituals of greeting and of bodily cleanliness, of court constraint as contrasted with peasant directness – as for example in the tea ceremony, all these present parallels to Europe at the time of the Renaissance that should have attracted his attention and led to geographical (cross-cultural) analyses rather than to one confined to Europe – especially given the more general psychological thesis he was attempting to substantiate. Stick to Europe if you will, but not if you are making more general claims. And that was precisely what Elias was doing, viewing in a Weberian fashion what was happening here in Europe as the unique path to modernity.

What I want to establish is firstly that western Europe was not inventing civilized manners for the first time, let alone manners *tout court*. No society is without its table manners, its formalized ways of eating, and none without some attempts to distance bodily functions from the generality of social intercourse. Equally, in most stratified societies the behaviour of upper groups is more formalized than that of lower ones. I say most because in Africa, even in state systems, these differences of behaviour are relatively small, partly because of the nature of the economy, partly because of the related systems of marriage and succession to high office. In what have been referred to as 'primitive states', there is little hierarchical differentiation of behaviour, in manners as in culture more generally. But in Europe and Asia major states are stratified not only politically but in terms of culture too; all have experienced the Urban Revolution and its concomitants.

In a discussion of manners, however, we cannot ignore the fact that the west suffered a 'significant regression'[59] from the point of view of body baths and bodily cleanliness from the fifteenth to the seventeenth centuries. Baths, 'an invention from Rome' (a doubtful contention), were found throughout medieval Europe, private as well as public, with both sexes bathing naked together. Baths were even subject to seigneurial

---

[58] Elias 1994a [1939]: 209.   [59] Braudel 1981: 329.

dues.[60] However, after the sixteenth century when Elias sees the civilizing process taking off, they became rarer, partly due to the fear of disease, partly to the influence of preachers, both Catholic and Calvinist, who 'fulminated against the moral dangers and 'ignominy of the baths'.[61] There was not a single bathing establishment in London in 1800. Some indication of the advanced state of affairs in the east is that in the Persian city of Isfahan, under the great Emperor, Shah Abbas (1588–1629), the city had 273 baths at a time when these were indeed scarce in the west. Soap production was low, though this is said to have been lower still in China, a country that was without the benefit of underwear (that appeared, Braudel claims, in Europe in the second half of the eighteenth century). But the Chinese nevertheless had toilet paper a thousand years before Europe, a fact he does not mention; paper is only discussed in connection with printing and money, the presence of which is said to have redeemed China's 'backwardness', which was a result of living near primitive countries 'in their infancy'.[62] When baths were finally reintroduced to Europe they were known as 'Chinese baths'[63] and Turkish baths. But of course earlier Christians in Europe had often destroyed the Roman baths, for similar reasons that Braudel ascribes to the sixteenth century; they encouraged immorality and were associated with pagan rituals, including Jewish and Islamic practices. Their revival in the medieval period may have been connected with the Crusades and with Muslim influence.

It was not only baths but cleanliness more generally that was the problem. In Rabelais, Gargantua was visited by his father who asked if he had been kept clean while he was away. Yes, the son replied, none cleaner because he had invented a special ass wiper.[64] He had used various pieces of cloth, including his mother's gloves – 'nicely scented with cunt flavour'.

Then I wiped myself with sage, with fennel, with dill and anise, with sweet marjoram, with roses, pumpkins, with squash leaves, and cabbage, and beets, with vine leaves, and mallow, and *Verbascum thapsus* (that's mullein, and it's as red as my asshole), and lettuce and spinach leaves – and a lot of good it all did me! – and mercury weed, and purslane, and nettle leaves, and larkspur and comfrey. But then I got Lombardy dysentery, which I cured by wiping myself with my codpiece.

Then I wiped myself with the bedclothes, the blankets, the bed curtains, with a cushion, a tablecloth (and then another, a green one), a dishcloth, a napkin, a handkerchief, and with a dressing gown. And I relished it all like mangy dogs when you rub them down.

---

[60] Cabanès 1954.   [61] Braudel 1981: 330.   [62] Braudel 1981: 452.
[63] Braudel 1981: 330.   [64] Braudel 1981, chapter 13.

'To be sure,' said Grandgousier, 'but which ass wipe did you find the best?'

'I'm getting there,' said Gargantua. 'In just a minute you'll hear the *tu autem*, the real heart of it. I wiped myself with hay, with straw, with all sorts of fluffy junk, with tag wool, with real wool, with paper. But:

Wipe your dirty ass with paper
And you'll need to clean your ass with a scraper.'

By the sixteenth century, when he was writing, paper had come into Europe from the Arab world and had made an enormous difference in so many ways, not only for communication. Earlier in the fourteenth century in *Piers Plowman* Langland describes how people cleansed themselves with leaves.

And seten [sat] so til evensong, and songen umwhile [from time to time],
Til Glotoun hadde yglubbed [guzzled] a galon and a gille.
His guttes bigonne to gothelen [rumble] as two gredy sowes;
He pissed a potel [pot full] in a Paternoster-while [the time it takes to say the Paternoster],
And blewe his rounde ruwet [horn] at his ruggebones [backbone's] ende,
That alle that herde that horn helde hir nose after,
And wisshed it hadde ben wexed [scoured] with a wispe of firses [furze].[65]

Experience in Ghana

Some of Elias's problems with other cultures can be seen from his comments on his experiences in Ghana in his *Reflections on a Life*. There, in response to his interviewers, he explains how in 1962 it was suggested that he take up the chair of sociology in Ghana for two to three years. He accepted, though he was then over sixty, noting 'I had an immense curiosity for the unknown.'[66] As a result he developed a 'deep liking for African culture' in a way that for anthropologists strongly resembled the attraction of nineteenth-century writers to the *Naturvolk*, a category that even included the Ancients. 'I wanted to see all that with my own eyes – the entrails spilling out, the blood spurting': . . . 'I knew in Ghana that I would see magic arts, that I would be able to see animal sacrifices, in vivo, and I did in fact witness many things – experiences which have lost their colour in more developed societies. Naturally, this had to do with my

[65] Langland, B version, Passus 5, lines 339–45.   [66] Elias 1994b: 68.

theory of the civilising processes, the emotions were stronger and more direct.' The more natural (instinctive), the less civilized (restrictive).

How did he learn about 'primitive culture', his interlocutor asks him in this book of interviews? 'I did a lot of fieldwork with my students. I began to collect African art, and some of my students took me to visit their homes. There I learned how formalised and ritualised Ghanaian life is: the student stood behind his father's chair and behaved towards him almost like a servant. The old type of family certainly is still very much in force in Ghana.'

He recalls driving to a village 'deep in the jungle' with his chauffeur (there is a picture of the author with his cook and driver). He reached the village and 'realised for the first time what it means not to have any electric current'. In other words his comments on the 'other' concerned their technology rather than their attitudes. The inhabitants betrayed equal curiosity and surrounded him, saying 'a white man has come', asking about his wife (he was a bachelor). He rather than they was the odd man out, arriving in a chauffeur-driven car, without a wife. Elias fails to draw the evident conclusion from this encounter – that for each culture, the 'other' represents the deviation from the norms of civilized behaviour, civilized in the sense of obeying social regulations that are often internalized to the extent of appearing self-understood. He himself, with his peculiarities, was the aberration in the Ghanaian village, the one who disregarded the norms of co-habitation.

On another occasion he went to the area that was to be flooded by the new Volta River dam and was amazed that people worried about what would happen to their local gods when the waters rose. This active concern with gods, and there are many of them, he sees as related to people's greater insecurity. He applies this thought to personality structure: 'one has to conclude that the super-ego is constructed differently from ours, for all these gods and spirits are representations of the super-ego'.[67] Whereas we presumably know only one God and have less segmented super-egos. In this way Ghana helped him see (or confirmed his belief) that Freud needed to be developed further in a comparative direction and in accordance with his own notion of the civilizing process. 'I thought that super-ego and ego formation in simpler societies would be different from ours, and this expectation was fully confirmed in Ghana', as we have seen.[68] Looked at in another frame of reference, there is shame (external) rather than guilt (internal). In the former, 'It is not enough to rely on an inner voice to restrain oneself.' To achieve restraint 'they [his African

[67] Elias 1994b: 71.   [68] Elias 1994b: 70.

friends] have to imagine there are beings outside them which force them to do this or that. You see it everywhere if you go to such a country.' In other words, a kind of external restraint is there (contrary to his other assumptions about the unrestrained nature of sacrifice) but the controls and sanctions are different.

However, this difference is not because they are more 'childish', as his interlocutor suggests; that view of Africans Elias now understands is a colonialist one. Our way of life is only possible 'because our physical safety is incomparably greater than theirs'.[69] While there are some upper-class Ghanaians who are 'on the same intellectual level we are . . . no less educated and self restrained', the mass of the people erect their little altars and call upon 'fetishes'. Such religious activity (Elias is an out-and-out humanist) appears to be identified with unrestrained and uneducated behaviour; it is an aspect of social security, or its absence.

The perception of such behaviour lies behind his enjoyment of their artistic manifestations. Their art

expresses emotions far more strongly and directly than the traditional art of the nineteenth century or Renaissance. And that fits in very well with my theory of civilising processes; for in the Renaissance there was *an enormous advance of civilisation*, expressed not least in the attempt to make paintings and sculptures as realistic as possible. In the twentieth century there was a reaction against that. One can also relate it to Freud: what happened in psychoanalysis – that on a new level a higher degree of affect expression could be permitted is also seen in non-naturalistic art, which has a far greater resemblance to dream. African sculptures have the same quality. There are frightening masks and friendly masks, but they all give stronger expression, if you like, to the unconscious.[70]

The Renaissance is seen as part of the European process of civilization, which became a model for the rest of the world. Artistically it involves realism which seems to imply restraint, the restraint involved in the realization of objective reality. For Elias, the theories of Freud represent a reversion to the acknowledgement of the primitive and his lack of restraint, though it is not obvious how Elias's developmental theory encompasses such long-term reversals. He himself relies heavily on a popular version of Freud. At the same time he sees Freud as needing to be supplemented. The notion of the super-ego would be different in other (that is, simpler) societies, a notion that he found was fully confirmed in Ghana, as we have seen. However, the evidence he uses is simply the multiplicity of shrines to which people refer their actions, a superficial observation to

---

[69] Elias 1994b: 71.   [70] Elias 1994b: 72–3 (my italics).

anyone with any acquaintance of the societies concerned.[71] Once again these are hazardous conclusions about the native life drawn from considering material objects. He remained distant from African religion, as is brought out in the use of the old-fashioned word 'fetish' for a shrine and in his anxious curiosity to see a blood sacrifice. Had he not heard of, let alone seen, a kosher or Muslim killing of an animal, or experienced a 'Christian' slaughterhouse in Chicago or elsewhere?

Problems with Elias's overall theory of social process emerge clearly in these comments on Ghana. At one point people slaying chickens at their shrines are seen as indicating a greater freedom of emotional expression. That is in line with the folk-notion of *Naturvolk*. At the same time he mentions the student showing excessive restraint before his father. The two comments indicating freedom and restraint run in contrary directions. Contradictory statements both seem to fit the theory, suggesting that the psychological and sociological interpretations are each suspect. It would be very difficult to say if the LoDagaa of northern Ghana, with whom I spent several years, were more or less restrained than the contemporary British; any assessment would have to depend on the context of the particular activity, not on an overall categorization. At funerals they showed grief but generally in ritualized ways that seemed to restrain or channel it. All rituals were restrained including sacrifices. But life was nevertheless undergoing many changes, with the addition of schools, of migrant labour and missions. In fact, I did not see African religion as

---

[71] I met Elias briefly when he was Professor of Sociology at Legon. It must have been in 1964. My impression was of a scholar deeply embedded in the European experience and totally committed to Weberian categories, at least when we talked about local political systems. He appeared to have read very little about this 'unknown' place, which was receiving a great deal of scholarly attention at the time, and he gained his knowledge from what he called his 'field trips', driving out to a village with chauffeur and students. It was little informed by scholarly work on 'other cultures'. As an anthropologist who had by then spent several years in Ghanaian villages, I was unhappy at this notion of 'fieldwork' and at what I saw as the non-comparative, eurocentred kind of sociology he practised. I had myself worked with the comparative sociologists George Homans (also a historian) and Lloyd Warner (also an anthropologist), both of whom tried to take into account the full range of human behaviour. For similar reasons I found the idea that one could gain any profound insight from a casual collection of African 'art' from itinerant traders to be highly questionable. One could not altogether approve the collecting and exporting of African objects about whose use one knew or understood little. That was too reminiscent of those predatory members of the scholarly tribe who, though later justifying themselves on grounds of conservation, were more concerned with acquisition and display than with an appreciation of the cultural context or with the meaning of such objects to the actors themselves. Most expatriates started an art collection – it was not difficult as every evening Hausa entrepreneurs with their wares visited the colonial-style bungalows on the campus; such transactions represented the complete decontextualization and commoditization of African art, but they provided something tangible to take back home.

unrestrained as the Pentecostals who were then preaching in the Wa market some fifty miles away (led by the American 'Holy Jo', as he was known to all and sundry). In local practice, killing a chicken was carried out to discover the truth about a troubling situation, possibly as an offering to a deity, but it never displayed the orgiastic qualities, nor even the 'freedom', that Elias attributes to the act. Many of the differences that come from his superficial observations about 'civilization' disappear in a more intensive and thorough examination. There is no real reason to assume that his attribution of psychological states and his sociological analysis were equally suspect in his European work. But why the great gap between the observations on Europe and those on Ghana?

His problem about understanding Ghana touches upon the roots of the theory about the progression towards restraint intrinsic to the civilizing process. That is by no means confined to the author himself but is often part of the folk beliefs of Europe. He sees African art as achieving a more direct expression of feeling. The practice of blood sacrifice and the worship of a plurality of 'fetishes' are uninhibited actions that civilization has taught us to restrain in favour of prayer and monotheism. All these aspects of Ghanaian society are judged as closer to uninhibited feelings, marked by the absence of restraint. However, in the highly ritualized (and restrained) behaviour of the Ghanaian university student standing rigidly behind his father's chair, he seems to acknowledge that all social life demands some restraint, some control of behaviour that would otherwise lead to a war of all against all. Ritual plays its part. So too does language which intervenes between affect and its expression.

By juxtaposing Elias's experience in Africa and his theory of the 'civilising process' I have tried to show that contrary to his claim that they were mutually self-supporting, experience and theory were in fact contradictory. They should have been recognized as such had the author given more profound attention to enquiries into the local scene, to attempts to understand contemporary behaviour, rather than imposing a pseudo-historical, pseudo-psychological, pseudo-philosophical concept of *Naturvolk* on what he saw. In this he followed the folk-notions of Europeans in their idea of the civilizing process, setting aside the more firmly based studies of pre-historians and of comparative sociologists.

7   The theft of 'capitalism': Braudel and global comparison

Antiquity, feudalism, and even civilization have been claimed as unique to Europe, thus excluding the rest of the world from the path to modernity and to capitalism itself, since all those phases are seen as logically leading into one another in successive stages. There is little disagreement about Europe's dominant position in the nineteenth century after the Industrial Revolution had given them a comparative economic advantage. But the argument turns around the earlier period. What was it that predisposed Europe to achieve this advantage? Did that continent invent 'capitalism' as many have supposed? Or is this claim by historians yet another example of the theft of ideas?

In this chapter I want to look at attempts by distinguished scholars at global comparison regarding 'capitalism', which end up by affirming Europe's privileged position not simply with regard to the Industrial Revolution, about which there may be some agreement, but with regard to other, wider, and earlier features of the west that are thought to have stimulated that change. I will concentrate upon Braudel's contribution and comment indirectly on the way in which all these writers have deviated from 'objectivity', despite their best intentions. They have privileged the west to an overwhelming degree, thus depriving the east of its rightful place in world history.

The French historian Braudel made a determined effort to view 'capitalism' in a world-wide context. So too did the German sociologist Weber before him. The latter concentrated upon comparing the economic ethic of various 'world religions', concluding that only ascetic Protestantism provided the proper ideological base for the development of 'capitalism' (though as we have seen he changed his mind about Ancient Rome). I do not want to argue that Weber was wrong in his programmatic pronouncement, only that he did not fully realize what was involved. And if he did so 'theoretically', he did not do so 'analytically'. He makes great efforts to be 'objective' when considering the nature of the 'economic ethic' in different religions (Ancient Israel, India, and China, as well as Europe) in relation to the rise of capitalism but he then comes down firmly in favour of the Protestant variety. That focus has been equally firmly rejected by many other historians, but principally by the great French historian of the Mediterranean himself. Braudel saw market 'capitalism' as being much more widely distributed, while some scholars even identified it for ancient societies. Nevertheless, he argues that 'finance capitalism' was distinctly European and discusses in depth the reasons why this was so.

Weber is more direct in his treatment of capitalism, linking it unilaterally with the west. He makes great claims for objectivity in comparative analysis,[1] yet comes to the conclusion that he saw the development of the scientific spirit as more significant in the west and as linked to its notions of rationality. Take the process of disenchantment of the human mind which marked the growth of meaningful scientific knowledge by the process of intellectualization. This process has, he writes, 'continued to exist in Occidental culture for millennia' and constitutes 'progress'.[2] That notion of progress, of 'continuous enrichment of life', is the key to civilized man, and was essentially western.

Weber writes at one point that 'an "objective" analysis of cultural events', which proceeds according to the thesis that the ideal of science as the reduction of empirical reality to 'laws', is meaningless for such events. It is meaningless for a variety of reasons. One relates to his definition of culture which is 'a finite segment of the meaningless infinity of the world process, a segment on which *human beings* confer meaning and significance'.[3] This definition is very different from the classical definition of the English anthropologist E. B. Tylor,[4] which embraces all human action and beliefs. Yet it is one that was important to the schema of Talcott Parsons,[5] now largely abandoned, and to the American scholars who followed him. I myself cling firmly to the wider definition of Tylor in which culture covers all known human activities, material and spiritual, and would query the utility of this idea of Weber's, on which his discussion of objectivity depends, because it is in practice impossible to

---

[1] Weber's essay on comparison, which has been translated as '"Objectivity" in Social Science and Social Policy', constituted the introductory remarks of a new editorial board for the journal *Archiv für Sozialwissenschaft und Socialpolitik*. He explained that the difference he perceived between the natural and the 'cultural' sciences lay in the fact that 'the significance of cultural events presupposes a *value-orientation* towards these events. The concept of culture is a *value-concept*. Empirical reality becomes "culture" to us because and insofar as we relate it to value ideas' (Weber 1949: 76). His argument is based on the need to make an 'unbridgeable distinction' between 'empirical knowledge' and 'value judgements' (Weber 1949: 58). Both are important topics for reflection although 'those highest "values" underlying the practical interest are and always will be decisively significant in determining the focus of attention of analytical activity in the sphere of the cultural sciences'. But what is valid for us 'must also be valid for the Chinese' (Weber 1949: 58).
[2] Weber 1949: 139.   [3] Weber 1949: 80–1.   [4] Tylor 1881.   [5] Parsons 1937.

establish a field of enquiry that centres upon the values of the observer (which he rightly says are important in the selection of topic), much less those of actors (in the way most sociologists take the notion of value orientation). In any case few scholars would in practice wish to limit their analyses in this way, though there are some anthropologists who try to follow Parsons's view that the entire field turns on beliefs and values, the domain of 'cultural science'. While values cannot be treated like science, he does aim for a measure of objectivity in his comparative analysis, especially in his broad aim of considering the origins of capitalism. What Weber failed to appreciate was the difficulties in the way of achieving objectivity, in separating 'fact' and 'values' in view of the extent of their interpenetration, determining a good deal more than 'the focus of attention'. The difficulty is to be seen in his own work, especially in relation to the European origins of capitalism.

When Braudel turns his attention to capitalism, he accepts an important number of western propositions about east–west differences relating to its growth, including that concerning the unique nature of the European city, deriving from the north Italian commune of the tenth century. But he is very much against Weber's attribution of a primary role to Protestantism in creating the 'spirit of capitalism'. Fernandez-Armesto also criticizes the religious aspects of the 'Weberian thesis' in discussing the Atlantic empires, whose emergence has been 'used as evidence that Protestantism was superior to Catholicism as an imperialist faith and as proof that Protestants inherited the talents for capitalism that in the middle ages had been particularly evinced by Jews'. He comments, 'Every part of this thesis seems, to me, to be misguided.'[6] The Atlantic empires of the southerners were more extensive, lasted longer, and were more profitable than those of the Protestant countries. 'The preponderance of northern powers in nineteenth-century world struggles did not begin . . . nearly as early as is commonly supposed.' And even then religion had little to do with that preponderance. What mattered was geographical position.

I do not want to comment further on Weber's original attempts at global comparison. He was of course primarily concerned with the economic and cultural dominance of the west in recent times and his acute analyses of India and China always have the prevalence of western capitalism as their background. In fact he does not limit himself to the development of industrial capitalism in nineteenth-century Europe but understandably looks back to the pre-conditions, specifically to the Reformation (hence the Protestant ethic), to the Renaissance and to the 'Age of Exploration'

[6] Fernandez-Armesto 1995: 238.

and even further back to the 'unique' nature of the European city, at times even to Rome. That route has been taken by most commentators on the situation. Marx and Wallerstein[7] both go back to the Age of Exploration, pushing Europe's advantage backwards in time from the nineteenth century.

The idea of global comparison is a historian's notion associated with recent European history. What is being compared? The phrase basically refers to the kind of questions that interested Marx and Weber in the nineteenth and beginning of the twentieth centuries and pertains ultimately to the origins of (European) capitalism. Written from the standpoint of Europeans after the First and, in Weber's case, the Second Industrial Revolutions, that enterprise sought an answer to the question of why Europe 'modernized' while other major civilizations in Asia did not, or in the words of a recent pursuer of the same kind of question, *Why some nations are so rich and some are so poor*, the subtitle of the recent book by the economic historian, David Landes. An important question, but the search got off on the wrong foot.[8]

In the first place, these comparisons were far from global. Weber wrote interestingly of China and India. The rest of the world was marked by traditional societies, exercising 'traditional authority', hardly a helpful sociological or historical concept because they were treated as residual, what was left over. India and China were brought into the picture as background to Europe's 'capitalism'. Secondly, Marx in his important discussion touches upon the analysis of other societies from an economic point of view, examining a variety of modes of production and their associated social formations. He had carefully studied Lewis Morgan's *Ancient society*, which was an ambitious attempt to undertake global comparison of the range of human societies. Morgan's was one of many efforts to construct a more systematic, a better evidenced, history of man's development than had emerged from earlier philosophical efforts such as those of Vico or Montesquieu. But while this work represented an improvement on the speculative works of the philosophers, it still adopted a teleological attitude with regard to Europe.

Braudel's approach to capitalism, modernization, and industrialization, which is indeed global, is presented in the three volumes of his major work on *Civilization and capitalism 15th to 18th century*. The first is entitled 'The structure of everyday life';[9] the second 'The wheels of commerce',[10] the third 'The perspective of the world'.[11] The first volume deals with what he calls 'material life' which he sees as 'lying underneath

---

[7] Wallerstein 1974.   [8] Goody 2004: chapter 1.   [9] Braudel 1981 [1979].
[10] Braudel 1982 [1979].   [11] Braudel 1984 [1979].

the market economy' and comprises what we eat, what we wear, how we live. The second level (that of the economy) is the world of the market, the world of commerce. The third level, which is a 'shadowy zone' 'hovering above the market economy', is the world of finance, 'the favoured domain of capitalism', and without which it is 'unthinkable'.[12]

Braudel was a historian of the very first rank. His *Structures of everyday life*[13] is described by his colleague Zeldin as 'brilliant' and by another, Plumb, as 'a masterpiece'. I want to review one aspect of his work both admiringly and critically, from the standpoint of new developments in world history which attempt to modify certain eurocentric biases. These any western scholar inevitably has. Braudel certainly displays less than, say, Weber or Marx and considers a wide range of comparative material on everyday life. Moreover he is much subtler about the question of European advantage.

Nevertheless his sources are inevitably largely European and partake of some of those prejudices about that advantage. Certain of these are minor, others major. Consider some of the minor first, as these set the tone of his presentation and in fact refer to wider issues of advantage. Seen as 'the great innovation, the revolution in Europe', according to Braudel, was not paper but 'alcohol', distilled liquor, though a name like alembic clearly indicates an Islamic provenance (ultimately Greek).[14] Nevertheless, referring to the rest of the world, he asks 'Did the still give Europe the advantage over these people?'[15] However, Europe was in fact slow to adopt distilled alcohol. Leaving that slowness aside, why is it the Europeans who were considered to have the advantage, even at earlier periods? The question seems to have been answered in advance and any alternative perspective is missing. For example, other drinks are treated in the same way. At about the time of the 'discovery' of alcohol, Europe, supposedly at the centre of the innovations of the world, is said by Braudel to have discovered new drinks, both stimulants and tonics; that is, coffee, tea, and chocolate. But all three came from abroad; coffee was Arab (originally Ethiopian); tea, Chinese; chocolate, Mexican.[16] Clearly the sense in which Europe 'discovered' these beverages, innovated, is very limited indeed; what it did was concerned with marketing and consumption. Nevertheless Braudel is led to claim their discovery for Europe, presumably because of its later 'discovery' of 'capitalism', which promoted both. However, later on New Guinea equally could be said to have discovered, innovated, these beverages when they arrived on its shores. The idea that Europe was ('always'?) at the centre of innovations is greatly exaggerated,

[12] Braudel 1981: 24.   [13] Braudel 1981.   [14] Braudel 1981: 241.
[15] Braudel 1981: 247.   [16] Braudel 1981: 249.

especially in the context of food in which they were certainly behind China or India; indeed Braudel himself recognizes that 'there was no real luxury or sophistication of eating habits in Europe before the fifteenth or sixteenth centuries. In this respect Europe lagged behind the other Old World civilisations.'[17] That comment seems to be correct. Wherein, therefore, lies the European advantage in this sphere?

He seems particularly eurocentric about matters to do with the house, including food. In relation to the consumption of meat, Europe had 'a privileged position' relative to other societies.[18] So too of course did hunters and gatherers. Equally, we could take a different standpoint and assert that China and India were privileged, in a more ecologically friendly way, with regard to the consumption of fruit and vegetables. Preferences for a vegetarian diet are given no value, whether based on taste, religion, or morality. As with beverages the spread of commodities like sugar and spices round the world is dealt with basically from a European point of view, even though all these items were discovered by others. Braudel quotes with approval the writer Labat, who remarks of the Arabs that they did not know the use of tables; it might equally be claimed that Europe did not have the divan or the carpet until they arrived from the east. The 'advantage' is always seen as European (which it may have been later in terms of distribution and marketing). His section on 'the slow adoption of good manners'[19] in Europe seems to show a similar kind of bias as Elias's in favour of European behaviour, for it is widely thought by others that at an earlier period the Far East had a more elaborate and exacting etiquette. He quotes one European observer as saying the Christians do not sit on the ground like animals,[20] implying that others did and were. The table and chair 'implied a whole way of life'[21] and were not present in early China until after the sixth century. The chair 'was probably European in origin', for the sitting-up position is said not to be found in non-European countries and represented 'a new art of living'. Whether or not that was the case (and the statement seems very dubious), to give this change in the sixth century such an importance (a change in 'life-styles') is hardly compatible with the view that Chinese society was unchanging and 'stood still',[22] a conclusion that he derives from the consideration of one feature, clothing, the use of which is certainly not a general factor in human behaviour.[23]

His argument is that changing fashion indicates a dynamic society, following the opinion of Say in 1829[24] who wrote disparagingly about the

---

[17] Braudel 1981: 187.   [18] Braudel 1981: 199.   [19] Braudel 1981: 206.
[20] Braudel 1981: 285.   [21] Braudel 1981: 288.   [22] Braudel 1981: 312.
[23] Bray 2000.   [24] Say 1829.

'unchanging fashions of the Turks and other Eastern peoples', that 'their fashions tend to preserve their stupid despotism'.[25] It is an argument that could apply equally to our own villagers, who wore the same clothes day in and day out and rarely changed them, and perhaps to all those men who wear evening dress on special occasions. However, even when changes occurred in Europe, such 'fashionable whims' only affected a small number of persons and then did not become 'all-powerful' until after 1700, when people broke away from 'the still waters of ancient situations like those we described in India, China and Islam'.[26] Change was on the side of the privileged few but nevertheless he does not consider fashion to be frivolous, rather as 'an indication of deeper phenomena':[27] the future belonged to societies that were prepared 'to break with their traditions'. The Orient was static, but then only recently has the Occident been characterized by movement, which rather contradicts his notion that cultures differed in this respect over the long term. Braudel is scarcely consistent on this issue since the recourse to fashion is also the result of 'material progress'.[28] One example is the way the silk merchants of Lyons exploited 'the tyranny of French fashion' in the eighteenth century by employing 'silk illustrators' who changed the patterns every year, too quickly for the Italians to copy.[29] By this time silk production had been present in Sicily and Andalusia for almost seven hundred years, spreading in the sixteenth century, together with the mulberry, to Tuscany, Veneto, and down the Rhône Valley. Genoa and Venice had also long imported raw silk from the Near East as well as cotton in the form of yarn or raw bales. Not only the materials but also the techniques came from the so-called 'static' East. The subject of fashion is obviously related not only to change but also to luxury, in which context it will be treated at greater length in chapter 9.

In other ways too Braudel is in two minds on the subject of change. He argues convincingly for the rapid spread of American crops, such as tobacco, throughout the world, as happened with other consumables such as coffee, tea, and cocoa. Nevertheless, the static east is continuously contrasted with the dynamic west, the implication being that the innovations required for capitalism could not develop outside Europe. Braudel posits an opposition between changing societies and static ones.[30] The dichotomy is totally unacceptable; rhythms of change certainly vary and have become increasingly rapid. But the idea of an unchanging society (objectively, whatever the actors may think) seems to me out of the

---

[25] Braudel 1981: 314.   [26] Braudel 1981: 316.   [27] Braudel 1981: 323.
[28] Braudel 1981: 324.   [29] As Poni (2001a and b) had pointed out.
[30] Braudel 1981: 430, 435.

question, as I have argued especially for religion and for long myths;[31] even technology in simple societies has changed over time, from Neolithic to Mesolithic for example. That does not mean there might not be blockages from time to time, but never 'blocked systems' as a whole.

The notion that some societies are more prepared than others to change may be correct for specific periods and for specific contexts but it is manifestly an error to cast all Asia in this mould. At least until the sixteenth century China was probably more 'dynamic' than Europe (supposing one could agree upon a satisfactory measure). Braudel's concept of 'civilization' and 'culture' would tend to suggest that such differences in speed of change characterized 'la longue durée'; I would place them more at the 'historical' level of 'events', pertaining to the 'conjunctural' rather than the 'civilizational'. To do otherwise seems to project back in time Europe's undoubted differences (and in some respects advantages) in the nineteenth century. In that case why should we not equally be prepared to do the same for the convergences of societies in the twentieth and twenty-first? The argument has already been made for Japan that her earlier 'feudalism' enabled her more easily to develop 'capitalism'. Should not the same argument be applied to China, Korea, Malaysia, and a host of others?

Yet he nevertheless comes out with the notion that elsewhere there are 'static, inward-looking', that is, poor, civilizations. Only the west is distinguished by uninterrupted change. 'In the West', he writes, 'everything was constantly changing'.[32] He sees this as a long-standing feature. For example, furniture varied country by country, witness to a 'broad economic and cultural movement carrying Europe towards what it itself christened the Enlightenment, progress'.[33] And a few lines later: 'If it is established for Europe, the richest civilization and the one most ready to change, it will apply *a fortiori* to the rest'. While it is true that Europe may have been more ready to change in recent times (some would say after the Industrial Revolution, others would insist on the Renaissance), there is no evidence that Europe was more likely to change in earlier periods. Yet this formulation of Braudel's, whatever qualifications he introduces elsewhere, whatever contradictory evidence he produces, rests on a contrast between dynamic Europe and 'static' Asia that he regards as long-standing if not permanent. The west has appropriated the notion of change and adaptability for itself.

For Braudel capitalism pertains to the urban sphere, from which it spread to the countryside. Rural economies he looks upon as stagnant unless spurred on from the outside. He asks if western towns would have

---

[31] Goody and Gandah 2002.   [32] Braudel 1981: 293.   [33] Braudel 1981: 294.

been able to subsist if the 'absurd Chinese-type tillage had been the rule instead of the exception'[34] – that tillage for rice production was carried out with hand tools rather than the plough. However this 'absurdity' of course was the mark of a very intensive, very 'advanced' agriculture that allowed higher population densities and larger towns than in Europe, partly because it did not devote space to the larger domestic livestock needed to pull the ploughs. Indeed it is perverse to wonder whether western towns could 'subsist under such conditions', for these were so different.[35] He sees capitalism as reaching the countryside when agriculture is linked to exports, when crops are grown for cash. That constituted an 'invasion'.[36] But his notion neglects the fact that rural producers already build up their 'capital' by investing in terracing, in irrigation, and in many other ways. Or in Europe through increasing their herds, which were the very model for 'capital'. But for him the notion of capitalist is tied up with the investment of money that more than reproduces itself, rather than with labour or productive techniques. Here too Europe was considered unique. While he recognizes the dynamic nature of crafts in India and China, he comments that they never produced the 'high quality' of tools that marked Europe. In China, human labour was perhaps too plentiful,[37] a common but fallacious thought.[38] In any case the rice agriculture of the south demanded more intensive techniques of planting and transplanting than cereal cultivation in the north; it was not simply that mechanization was 'blocked by cheap labour'.[39] Tools were introduced. The wheelbarrow was Chinese; the bridle probably Mongol (pace Lynn White[40]). Water-mills were certainly not confined to Europe; windmills may have come from China or Iran. The Chinese were also far ahead in the production of iron and the use of coal, though Braudel refers to the country's 'stagnation after the thirteenth century', especially with regard to the use of coke.[41] His comment is that earlier 'the Chinese advance is hard to explain'.[42] But that is surely the case only if one is looking at the world from a nineteenth-century eurocentric standpoint.

One of the problems that according to Braudel held back China was that it did not possess 'a complicated monetary system' required for production and exchange;[43] only 'medieval Europe finally perfected its money', curiously because these societies had to exchange with one another and with the Muslim world. This perfection envisaged in Europe was due to the growth of towns and of capitalism, as well as 'the conquest

---

[34] Braudel 1981: 338.   [35] Braudel 1981: 338.   [36] Braudel 1984: 288.
[37] Braudel 1984: 304.   [38] Hobson 2004: 201ff.   [39] Braudel 1981: 339.
[40] White 1962.   [41] Braudel 1981: 375.   [42] Braudel 1981: 376.
[43] Braudel 1981: 440.

of the high seas' which produced 'a world supremacy that lasted for centuries'.[44] Europe, faced with a Muslim challenge, produced a perfect monetary system; the other parts of Eurasia 'represented intermediate stages half-way towards an active and complete monetary life'.[45] That claim to uniqueness was puzzling in some ways because 'the maritime civilizations had always known about each other', at least in Eurasia. The Mediterranean and the Indian Ocean formed 'a single stretch of sea', the 'route to the Indies', which had earlier included a connection between the two, known as Nechao's Canal in Suez, but later filled up. However, Egypt always provided a point of communication between east and west. So they should have been exchanging information about making silk cloth or about printing as well as the goods themselves. Nevertheless it was the conquest of the high seas that supposedly gave Europe an advantage. Long-distance trade, large-scale commercial capitalism, he importantly observes, depended on the ability to speak a common 'language of world trade', inducing 'constructive change' and rapid accumulation. In other words this trade involved exchange. Despite the trend towards equality, reciprocity, and change, Europe nevertheless has to be distinguished in his view from 'the half-way economies' of Asia. So that, despite his comparative aims, Braudel consistently seeks to explore the east in relation to the west's advantages, which he sees as long-standing, often as cultural, quasi-permanent. As a good historian he is constantly led into contradictions and inconsistencies. Unchanging India used precious metals and experienced 'an enormous burst of industrialization' with regard to cotton in the sixteenth century but the economy was marked by 'monetary chaos'.[46] Equally China can only be understood 'in the context of the primitive neighbouring economies'[47] which account for both 'the backwardness of China itself' and 'at the same time a certain strength of its "dominant" monetary system'. That strength, it should be noted, included the invention of paper money long before the west had any paper at all, though even in China it was only used extensively in the fourteenth century. The contradictions abound. Despite China's 'backwardness' under the Ming (1368–1644), 'a monetary and capitalist economy was coming to life, developing and extending its interests and services', leading to the rush on the Chinese coalmines in 1596.[48] Those developments must qualify its backwardness and make it difficult to take Braudel's word, as he asks us to (but inconsistently), that 'in monetary matters China was more primitive and less sophisticated than India',[49] which as we have seen had 'monetary chaos'. But what about Europe? The latter continent is said to

---

[44] Braudel 1981: 402.   [45] Braudel 1981: 448.   [46] Braudel 1981: 450.
[47] Braudel 1981: 452.   [48] Braudel 1981: 454.   [49] Braudel 1981: 457.

'stand alone'. Nevertheless Braudel admits that 'these [monetary] operations were not confined to Europe' but were 'extended and introduced over the whole world like a vast net thrown over the wealth of other continents'. With the import of American treasures, 'Europe was beginning to devour, to digest the world', so that 'all the currencies of the world were enmeshed in the same net'. That advantage was not new; indeed 'a long period of pressure after the thirteenth century' 'raised the level of its material life'[50] as a result of 'a hunger to conquer the world', 'a hunger for gold' or spices, accompanied by a growth in utilitarian knowledge. But Europe needed that gold because it had so little by way of manufactured goods to give to the east in return for its 'luxuries', which became more and more available to the middle classes. If China was indeed backward, as Braudel claims, why was it that precious metals were leaving the western circuits for Asia?[51] It clearly was not only Europe that had 'a hunger for gold'. The east knew what it wanted and how to get it by peaceful means, namely, by trade.

Towns and the economy

The core of Braudel's analysis is centred upon towns and cities, discussed in chapter 8, which he compares to electric transformers, constantly recharging human life. Once again, they have obviously constituted a world-wide phenomenon ever since the Bronze Age, but Europe is held to be different. However he asserts that 'a town is always a town' and is characterized by 'an ever-changing division of labour'; there is also an ever-changing population since towns have to recruit inhabitants because of their failure to reproduce themselves.[52] He writes of the self-consciousness of towns resulting from the need for secure walls (and the dangers that artillery in the west brought from the fifteenth century[53]), of urban communication and of the hierarchies among the towns themselves. However, despite a recognition of these common features, that does not stop him (or for that matter Goitein on the Near East[54]) from following Max Weber in drawing a distinction between the western town with its 'freedoms' and the static Asian cities without them. Obviously there were differences but these authors locate them on the ideological level because they are interested in the teleological result, the advent of capitalism. His main thrust therefore has to do with 'the originality of Western towns', as we saw in chapter 4. They displayed, he argues, 'an unparalleled freedom'[55] developing in opposition to the state and ruling

---

[50] Braudel 1981: 415.   [51] Braudel 1981: 462.   [52] Braudel 1981: 490.
[53] Braudel 1981: 497.   [54] Goitein 1967.   [55] Braudel 1981: 510.

'autocratically' over the surrounding countryside. As a result their evolution was 'turbulent' compared with the static nature of cities in other
parts of the world; change was encouraged. But in fact the Asian city was
equally turbulent and far from static, as recent research (for example, in
Damascus and Cairo) shows.

After the decay of the urban framework of the Roman empire which
we discussed in chapter 3, western towns revived in the eleventh century by which time there had already been 'a rise in rural vigour'[56] said
to bring into the towns both nobles and churchmen; that marked 'the
beginning of the continent's rise to eminence'.[57] That revival was possible because of the improving economy and the growing use of money.
'Merchants, craft guilds, industries, long-distance trade and banks were
quick to appear there, as well as a certain kind of bourgeoisie and some
sort of capitalism.'[58] In Italy and Germany towns outgrew the state, form-
ing 'city-states'. 'The miracle of the West', it is said, was that when towns
arose anew they displayed great autonomy. On the basis of this 'liberty',
'a distinctive civilization' was built up. The towns organized taxation,
invented public loans, organized industry and accountancy, becoming
the scene of 'class struggles' and 'the focus for patriotism'.[59] They experienced the development of bourgeois society, which according to the
economist Sombart was characterized by a new state of mind appearing in Florence at the end of the fourteenth century.[60] 'A new state of
mind was established, broadly that of an early, still faltering, Western
capitalism' accomplished in 'the art both of getting rich and of living'.
Its characteristics also included 'gambling and risk'; 'the merchant . . .
calculated his expenditure according to his returns'.[61] Of course, all merchants had to do that, otherwise they would not survive. They also had
to calculate risks, which made them particularly committed to games of
chance and gambling, as in China.

Braudel sees the key to capitalism as lying in the development of towns,
which in Europe encouraged 'freedom' and provided a centre for rural
artisanal activity. Despite phases of 'capitalist' activity, he claims, China
never succeeded either in providing the necessary freedom or in attract-
ing the rural artisans. His argument requires two contrasting models of
urban–rural relationships, the independent and self-sufficient town with
a countryside that serves its needs (the western model) and a town that is
the home of officialdom, parasitical and dependent on the more dynamic
countryside – the eastern model. However, the opposition is inadequate
because China's towns were also centres of activity, for academics, literati,

---

[56] Braudel 1981: 510.   [57] Braudel 1981: 479.   [58] Braudel 1981: 511.
[59] Braudel 1981: 512.   [60] Sombart 1930.   [61] Braudel 1981: 514.

and merchants as well as administrators. Secondly, to exclude the country from 'capitalist' activity is to restrict the definition of such activity in a questionable way; that took place in Europe and the Chinese countryside was the home to a vigorous regime and great achievements which required the investment of considerable capital. Indeed it is now obvious from contemporary China that the country had most of the requirements for 'modernization'.

While he praises the particular 'freedom' of European towns, Braudel produces a developmental scheme that runs from classical towns, open to and equal with the surrounding countryside, in which 'industry was rudimentary',[62] to the 'closed city' of the medieval period, populated by peasants who had freed themselves from one servitude to be subjected to another, and finally to the 'subjugated towns of early modern times'.[63] However, the state everywhere 'disciplined the towns', the Hapsburgs and German princes just as much as the Popes and the Medicis. 'Except in the Netherlands and England, obedience was imposed.' Given the fact that the two latter countries had centralized monarchies and that the 'free' city states of the medieval period in Germany and Italy are now listed as 'subjugated', the concept of the 'free' western town needs to be qualified. That does not prevent Braudel, like Weber and Marx before him, from claiming a dramatic contrast with the 'imperial towns' of the east. In Islam we find some towns of a similar kind to the west but these are described as 'marginal' and short-lived like Cordoba or Oran, though that marginality is open to doubt; indeed even Braudel refers to Ceuta in north Africa as an urban republic. In 'distant' Asia, imperial cities were 'enormous, parasitical, soft and luxurious'. 'The usual pattern was the huge city under the rule of a prince or a Caliph: a Baghdad or a Cairo.'[64] They were 'incapable of taking over the artisanal trades from the countryside', not because of the nature of authority itself but because 'society was prematurely fixed, crystallized in a certain mould' (thus always returning to the question of cultural change and stasis). In India the problem lay with the castes, in China with the clans. In China, he claims, there was no authority to represent the town against state or countryside; 'the rural areas were the real heart of living, active and thinking China'. However, it is clear that government officials certainly represented the towns, where they lived, as well as the countryside and that much activity took place in those urban centres. Moreover, the notion that caste and clan impeded the progress of towns follows Weber's analysis that these institutions inhibited the development of capitalism because they were collective rather than encouraging individualism. The

---

[62] Braudel 1981: 515.   [63] Braudel 1981: 519.   [64] Braudel 1981: 524.

theme is certainly overstated by Braudel especially as he sees merchant dynasties as an essential element in the accumulation of capital.[65] But in any case Indian towns contained important populations of Jains and Parsis who were often marginal to the caste system and very important for commerce. What is really problematic in his work and that of other westerners is the characterization of the eastern and by contrast the western towns.[66]

The notion of freedom associated with the town has two aspects. Wherever it occurred, country dwellers moving to the towns entered an environment that contained less restraints than the closer one they had left. But in particular societies, there is also the question of how far towns were constrained by wider political authorities. Obviously in city-states, whether in Europe or in western Asia, the towns as such were not tightly controlled, although mercantile activity might be restricted; but the restrictions were not imposed by an external authority, as in some larger state systems. By the nineteenth century western towns were firmly part of such a nation state. It is clear that the degree of 'freedom' of towns varied in different societies at different times and it may possibly be the case that in the later west this was in general greater than elsewhere. European societies certainly had 'villes franches' which were partially 'freed' from government taxation with the aim of encouraging commerce. In the east too some towns, especially ports, were less controlled than others. Braudel does not definitively demonstrate that pre-industrial towns in other parts of the world were in general less free and more static. Indeed many others seem just as 'turbulent' as European ones, in some cases more so.

That towns in the east and west should have run parallel courses in this respect is quite understandable. Urbanization, writes Braudel, is 'the sign of modern man'.[67] If so, modernity began a long way back, at least in the Bronze Age, though it has been becoming more modern ever since. As Braudel often insists, no town was an island; it did not stand alone but was part of a much wider set of relationships, necessarily so as one of its frequent characteristics was long-distance trade. And such trade involved a plurality of partners from different 'civilizations' who exchanged not only 'material products' but ways of creating them, a process that was marked by the transfer of ideas. On the basis of the assumption that such exchange was taking place, which seems obvious enough, we can

---

[65] Goody 1996: 138.

[66] However, capitalist activity also took place in the villages, especially when the latter provide water power for the mills and labour power to man them, as so frequently in the nineteenth century in southern France or in the eastern United States.

[67] Braudel 1981: 556.

account not simply for 'distinctive' civilizations but for the parallelism between them, such as the emergence of towns throughout Eurasia, with the creation of a bourgeoisie and of roughly parallel kinds of artistic development (though parallel evolution is of course possible). This happens both with painting and literature, as well as with religion. Christianity travels from the Near East to Europe and to Asia. So too does Islam. Buddhism goes from India to China and Japan as well as marginally to the Near East. The movements of these great religious ideologies would not have been possible unless there was some common ground in which this could happen, especially regarding urbanization.[68]

As discussed above, Braudel's general view of eastern towns was that they are 'enormous, parasitical, soft and luxurious';[69] they were the residences of officials and nobles rather than the property of the guilds or merchants. In reality western towns also provided residences for nobles and officials and were not *owned* by guilds or merchants. It is not easy to see the difference. Towns became somewhat 'freer' in parts of the west but many would dispute the absence of wider governmental control other than in 'city-states'. 'Freedom' was seen as critical to the effective role (indeed often to the emergence) of a 'bourgeoisie', intrinsic to the changes needed for the development of capitalism; the bourgeois is usually considered by western scholars as a uniquely European feature, like the incessant change that Wallerstein considers as the key to the 'spirit of capitalism'. Braudel admits that at times the Chinese state 'nodded' at the end of the sixteenth century, allowing the emergence of a bourgeoisie 'with a taste for business enterprise'.[70] In China the state nods; in the west the growth of the bourgeoisie is deemed natural. Meanwhile the various features he calls attention to in the 'free markets' of the west, that is, organized industry, guilds, long-distance trade, bills of exchange, trading companies, accountancy,[71] all these were also present in China and India, as recent historians like Pomeranz and Habib have pointed out.[72] India too had a complex system of trade that involved money-changing, equivalent to that in the west and including *hundi* or bills of exchange. 'Since the fourteenth century, India had possessed a monetary-economy of some vitality, which was soon on the way towards a certain capitalism.'[73] Braudel appears to contradict early remarks about

---

[68] However, the problem with the interactionist explanation of social evolution is that it neglects the parallel developments in the comparatively isolated New World which also achieved its urban civilization. While interaction is important, we also have to consider explanation in terms of the logic of internal developments. That certainly occurred in some commercial as in some artistic activities.

[69] Braudel 1981: 524.   [70] Braudel 1981: 524.   [71] Braudel 1981: 512.

[72] Pomeranz 2000; Habib 1990.   [73] Braudel 1984: 124.

its chaotic monetary system, for this 'certain capitalism' is recognized to be a 'genuine capitalism'[74] – with 'wholesalers, the rentiers of trade, and their thousands of auxiliaries – the commission agents, brokers, money-changers and bankers. As for the techniques, possibilities or guarantees of exchange, any of these groups of merchants would stand comparison with its western equivalents.' Not only were these features present in towns but they appeared *before* the rebirth of towns in eleventh-century Europe. Nevertheless Braudel still sees something lacking. For, in his view these did not constitute 'a distinctive civilization', a notion that is essential to his idea of the European genesis of capitalism, of true capitalism with its 'mighty networks' as distinct from the more widespread 'micro-capitalism'.[75]

There is some confusion here. 'Mighty networks' of the kind to which Braudel refers arrived only with industrial capitalism, though trade came well before. But he has throughout emphasized developments between the fifteenth and eighteenth centuries, which are presumably 'micro-capitalist'. This is when the question of the 'free worlds' of towns was relevant in the generation of 'real capitalism'. The problem is that while he sees capitalist activity as present in many earlier societies, he feels the need to express Europe's dominance in the nineteenth century in terms of the quality of its capitalism, that is, real capitalism, and then search teleologically for distinguishing factors in its formation, a procedure which leads him to a variety of contradictions. But in terms of pre-existing conditions which might have led to 'true capitalism' in the west, the whole of Eurasia seems roughly the same, even if the terms are used to distinguish east and west. Towns were everywhere present but 'real' towns existed only in the west; only there did 'freedom' win the day, a freedom that was seen as necessary to mercantile endeavour and to the advancement of production.

If one understands a generalized capitalism, as Braudel does, to be a feature of all towns and their commerce, then the argument about the uniqueness of the west loses much of its force. Later towns and their activities developed out of earlier ones in all their various facets, that is, not only commercial and manufacturing, but also administrative and educational, all relating to the uses of literacy and subject to a process of social development (or social 'evolution'). For it was the towns that were the literate centres, including for the production of literature, of written religion, and of textual knowledge, the last of which made an important contribution to the emergence of industrial capitalism in its various successive forms assisting as it did the process of invention, of

---

[74] Braudel 1984: 486.   [75] Braudel 1981: 562.

product development, and of exchange. The town was much more than a centre for merchants and their commerce, essential as they were to its economic well-being.

Finance capitalism

Let me turn more specifically to Braudel's discussion of the development of capitalism. We have seen earlier in the chapter how he separates the 'material life' underlying the market economy from the world of commerce and that again from the world of finance, 'the favoured domain of capitalism'.[76] In this hierarchical and chronological ordering of capitalism, it is at the third level of finance capitalism that he perceives Europe as taking the lead, indeed as being unique. We have seen the contradictions in Braudel's position regarding Europe and the rest of Eurasia. Sometimes they are considered equal, but at other times he suggests that Europe had an advantage well before the Industrial Revolution. In fact that seems to be his more general stance. He talks of a European capitalism that differs from market activity itself in that it occupied the 'commanding position at the pinnacle of the trading community'. Capitalism elsewhere seems in his eyes to be more restricted. Full or true capitalism was 'invariably borne along by a general context greater than itself, on whose shoulders it was carried upwards and onwards'.[77] Part of the general context was long-distance trade which was 'an unrivalled machine for the rapid reproduction and increase of capital',[78] and one the economist Dobb saw as critical to the creation of a merchant bourgeoisie.[79] In other words capitalism was always concerned not simply with money and credit but with finance, with money that reproduces itself.[80]

Braudel associates an emerging finance capitalism with the fair, which he views as a purely European phenomenon: 'progress forward in the sixteenth century must have been achieved from *above*, under the impact of the top-level circulation of money and credit, from one fair to another'.[81] The fairs and markets provided ways of financing exchange and settling accounts, and were of course active much earlier and elsewhere. Fairs were obviously very important in the west, not only for the sale of goods but for the financial transactions that resulted, as in Champagne. However they also existed in the east. Treaties between the Sultan of Egypt and Venice or Florence even lay down 'a kind of law for the

---

[76] Braudel 1981: 24.   [77] Braudel 1984: 374.
[78] Braudel 1984: 405.   [79] Dobb 1954.
[80] Despite this trend, much of the early wealth of Europe went into religious activity rather than into earthly investment.
[81] Braudel 1982: 135.

fairs' 'not unlike the regulations governing fairs in the West'.[82] Trading in the Near East was as vigorous as elsewhere. Muslim cities 'had more markets . . . than any city in the West'.[83] Special quarters were reserved for foreign merchants in Alexandria and Syria, as was the case in Venice. In Aleppo and Istanbul, too, khans or hostelries existed for European nationalities as well as for traders from the east. Fairs were also important elsewhere in the world. In India they were often combined with pilgrimages; in the Near East the annual pilgrimage to Mecca coincided with the biggest fair in Islam. In Indonesia the Chinese were present at similar fairs and their long-distance traffic 'was in no way inferior to the European equivalent'.[84] In China itself fairs were said to be 'closely supervised', being controlled by a 'ubiquitous, efficient and bureaucratic government'; nevertheless 'markets were comparatively free'. These fairs were often linked to the festivals at Buddhist or Taoist temples.[85] So in the sixteenth century, Braudel concludes contrary to his other statements, 'the populated regions of the world, faced with the demands of numbers, seem to us to be quite close to each other, on terms of equality or nearly so'.[86]

This equality extends to the fact that, in the sphere of trade, change was constantly taking place in the east as much as in the west. Urban and commercial life were always developing. The question of convergence was not simply a matter of numbers but of the parallel social evolution of the economy, of communication as with other spheres of cultural activity. The gap with the west only appeared relatively late in time but nevertheless constitutes 'the essential problem of the history of the modern world'. Will that gap be really important in another fifty years and if not, how 'essential' was it? But for Braudel the real take-off for Europe came during the Age of Enlightenment, after 1720. He argues that 'The two outstanding features of Western development were first the establishment of the higher mechanism of trade, then in the eighteenth century, the proliferation of ways and means.'[87] In China however, he claims, 'the imperial administration blocked any attempts to create an economic hierarchy' above the lowest level of shops and markets. Following the general European view, it was Islam and Japan that most resembled Europe. In all this he says little about production, only finance. However, in fact all mercantile and manufacturing activity, whether in China or elsewhere, required a combination of production and distribution, both of them requiring considerable finance. Braudel acknowledges that what the Europeans found when they arrived in the east was large-scale trade and cannot be properly

[82] Braudel 1982: 128.   [83] Braudel 1982: 129.   [84] Braudel 1982: 130.
[85] Braudel 1982: 131.   [86] Braudel 1982: 134.   [87] Braudel 1982: 136.

described in terms of peddling, as Leur had claimed.[88] It was much more important than that word implies. Many traders were contracted to large shareholders; the *commenda* (a maritime partnership) existed in the east as it did in the Mediterranean.[89] Eastern merchants who included Persians and Armenians visited Venice and were certainly trading on similar terms.[90] It is of course true that production, distribution, and finance become more complex over time, in Europe as elsewhere, but Braudel wants to make a categorical distinction between finance capitalism and other forms, which does not seem altogether satisfactory.

As we have seen, according to Braudel, 'true capitalism' only really developed in Europe, and possibly in Japan. The reasons for that restricted growth were political and 'historical' rather than economic and social. They related to the conditions under which over the long term great bourgeois families could accumulate wealth within dynasties, the reasons for which went far back in history. In the conclusion of his second volume, he criticizes both Weber and Sombart for considering that an explanation of capitalism 'had to have something to do with the structural superiority of the western "mind"'.[91] What would have happened, he asks, if Chinese junks *had* sailed round the Cape in 1419, roughly eighty years before de Gama? However the use of the word 'junks' seems to represent a certain ambivalence with regard to those countries which had junks rather than ships. The fact has to be faced, he argues, that 'capitalism succeeded in Europe, made a beginning in Japan and failed in almost everywhere else' – or failed to reach completion.[92] What does he mean by failure? The reference to the singularity of Japan may have been valid when Braudel was writing. By the time the book had been translated into English, the situation in the east had changed significantly with the emergence of the Asian Tigers, and indeed the widespread extension of the economies even in mainland China and India.

Braudel in fact recognized the vitality of Chinese long-distance trade in sixteenth-century Fukien when this thriving economy is contrasted with the 'stagnation' of the interior. So 'a certain form of Chinese capitalism . . . could only reach its true dimensions if it escaped from the rigid controls of the Chinese mainland'.[93] Because 'in China, the chief obstacle was the state with its close-knit bureaucracy'.[94] The government in theory owned all land (though private land-ownership went back to the Han), and 'even the nobility depended on the goodwill of the state'. Every town was patrolled. Only mandarins 'were above the law'. The state had the right to mint coinage – 'accumulation could only be achieved by the

---

[88] Leur 1955.   [89] Constable 1994: 67ff.   [90] Braudel 1984: 124.
[91] Braudel 1984: 581.   [92] Braudel 1984: 581–2.   [93] Braudel 1984: 582.
[94] Braudel 1984: 586.

state'. Indeed merchants might be demonized by the literati for an outward display of wealth. While China had a flourishing market economy, at the upper levels the state controlled all, 'So there could be no capitalism, except within certain clearly-defined groups.'[95] Many of those limitations were certainly not confined to China and marked even the 'progressive' societies of Europe. Nor is the intervention of the state necessarily harmful to the growth of the economy. In Japan and especially in contemporary (as in earlier) China, the state has played an important role in developing the economy.

Economically east and west may have been more or less equals, and here his analysis represents a great advance on that of many earlier 'world historians', including Marx and Weber. Politically, however, there was something lacking. 'Despotic' is an adjective that he uses for the Chinese, Indian, and Turkish cases, but never with regard to European states, which are 'absolutist'. Merchants existed in the east but were never 'free' in the same sense as their European counterparts; again the word 'freedom' comes up only in the context of the inhabitants of Europe. Nor is it only used of the merchants. His western bias comes out very clearly in statements such as 'the only free or quasi-free peasants were to be found in the heart of the West'.[96] As with 'despotic' the distinction is categorical, raising problems we have remarked upon in chapter 4; in some societies peasants are seen as free, in others they are not. And freedom is also believed to be a characteristic of the position of western merchants, unlike the situation of eastern ones, whether in towns and in the country at large. But recent research on the Asian city, for example by Rowe[97] in China or Gillion in India,[98] seems to contradict his Weberian claim, as does Ho Ping-ti's work on 'commercial capitalism' among salt-merchants in eighteenth century China[99] or Chin-heong Ng's study of the Amoy network on the coast, as well as Chan[100] on mandarins and merchants. Merchants had more room to operate than he recognizes; and the literati were certainly not all bureaucrats.[101] Country and town were more differentiated than Braudel suggests; although many scholars have written of 'the gentry' as a group, others have written of peasant revolts.[102] What I would regard as a mistaken account in Braudel of the social structure of these countries goes hand in hand with a correct appreciation of their economic situation.

However he accepts that there was a bourgeoisie ('after a fashion') under the Ming, as well as a 'colonial capitalism' in the East Indies. But he claims the power of the state was not checked by the presence of a

---

[95] Braudel 1984: 589.   [96] Braudel 1984b: 40.   [97] Rowe 1984.
[98] Gillion 1968.   [99] Ho Ping-ti 1954.   [100] Chan 1977.
[101] See Ching-Tzu Wu 1973.   [102] For example, Chesneaux 1976.

feudal regime as in Japan.[103] In that country one finds a kind of 'anarchy', like medieval Europe, bustling with 'liberties'. In Japan the regime was not totalitarian, as he claims was the case in China, but rather 'feudal'. 'So [in Japan] everything conspired [e.g. in the trappings of a regular Stock Exchange] to produce a kind of early capitalism',[104] emerging from a market economy with the development of long-distance trade. Equally in India and the East Indies, 'All the typical features of Europe at the same time were present: capital, merchandise, brokers, wholesale merchants, banking, the instruments of business, even the artisanal proletariat, even the workshops very similar to manufactories, . . . even domestic working for merchants handled by special brokers . . . and even, lastly, long-distance trade.'[105] But this 'high tension trading' was only present in certain places, not generalized throughout the society. One wonders, along with Pomeranz, if that is ever true of large units, or even of Britain.

In Braudel's account (as for most western scholars) feudalism 'prepared the way for capitalism'. In my view, that notion simply reflects the European chronology and is without any causal significance. But for Braudel, under the feudal dispensation merchant families were condemned to be second-class citizens and had to fight against that status, condemned to practise thrift, thus initiating the move to capitalism. India is said to have lacked such families, as did China and Islam. One needed a developed market economy for capitalism but the latter only emerges in a certain kind of society which 'had created a favourable environment from far back in time'.[106] These societies all had the kind of hierarchies and dynasties which encouraged the accumulation of wealth. Were such families in fact absent from China, India, and Islam? That is not credible, as we see from the account of Ahmedebad and of many families in the Near East. Such merchant families existed and accumulated wealth. Braudel excludes that possibility because he excludes the possibility of 'true capitalism' developing elsewhere. The cultural genes were against it. The origins of capitalism were laid down in the distant origins of cultures. In other words, as already noted, political or 'historical' factors were more significant than economic or social ones, certainly than religious ones.

Like the west, other societies too have maintained a certain coherence over time; this is Braudel's notion of 'culture' which seems to suggest that life has always been as it is, unchanging; anyhow in the east. China

---

[103] Although China was identified by the Communist Party in 1928 as having had a semi-feudal, semi-colonial regime (Brook 1999: 134ff.), feudalism in China was associated with the idea of 'parcelized sovereignty', seeing it as a universal pre-capitalist phase.
[104] Braudel 1984: 592.   [105] Braudel 1984: 585.   [106] Braudel 1984: 600.

always had its mandarins, India its caste system, Turkey its *sipahis*.[107] He claims that 'The social order steadily and monotonously reproduced itself in accordance with basic economic necessities'; culture (or civilization) continues over time, especially because of religion, and somehow 'fills gaps in the social fabric'.[108] Europe however was 'more mobile', and more open to change, a feature that again seems to be attributed to 'culture' or perhaps to its 'mentality'. It is true in fact that in many spheres change certainly seems to be more rapid since the Industrial Revolution but to push this capacity right back in cultural time seems an ahistorical approach that skips over the evidence.

Braudel recognizes the earlier parallelism in the developments of trade and finance elsewhere, for example with Islam. 'Throughout Islam there were craft guilds and the changes they underwent (the use of the master-craftsmen, home-working, and craft-making outside the towns) resemble what was to happen in Europe too closely to have been the result of anything but economic logic.'[109] There was parallel social evolution at work as well as interaction. Although China attempted to forbid foreign trade for a limited period, partly for strategic reasons, there continued to be an enormous internal market. 'The merchants and bankers of Shansi province went all over China.' Others travelled abroad. 'Another Chinese network originated in the south coast (especially in Fukien) and reached to Japan and the East Indies, building up a Chinese overseas economy which for many years resembled a form of colonial expansion.'[110] India's foreign trade too extended widely well before the advent of European ships; her bankers were present 'in large numbers' in Isfahan, Istanbul, Astrakhan, and even in Moscow. The opening-up of the Atlantic trade made an important difference but trade was already very active in Eurasia. Nor was it basically different in the east than in the west.

Those traders developed once again the strong contacts with Europe that had existed before the collapse of the Roman Empire, and which had institutionalized an 'early capitalism'. Europe opened up again after the collapse of that Empire. From the end of the first millennium CE, Venice built up a merchant fleet and navy for its trade with the eastern Mediterranean, with Asia, mainly the Muslim Near East, to which trade came from China. Venice developed both trade and a navy. The Arsenal where the ships were built was founded around 1100 but only grew with the construction of the New Arsenal around 1300. 'Arsenal' was an Arabic word and similar construction sites existed throughout the Mediterranean, including Turkey, in obvious competition with one another. For

[107] Braudel 1984b: 61.   [108] Braudel 1984b: 86.   [109] Braudel 1982: 559.
[110] Braudel 1984: 153.

the next 300 years Venice produced the best fighting ships available, especially the light galleys (*galea sottile*) supplemented by a smaller number of larger ones (*galea grossa*). The Arsenal acquired the monopoly of building for the state. The number of ships built there was large, providing a fleet that was larger than any in the western world, with 100 light galleys plus 12 great ones, which is why the Venetian contribution was so important at the battle of Lepanto against the Turks in 1571. This Arsenal, and similar enterprises in the east as well, demonstrate that features we now tend to view as a product of the Industrial Revolution were in fact present much earlier, and not only in Europe.

To build those ships, the Arsenal was organized for continuous production with 'one of the biggest concentrations of workers in the world at that time',[111] some 2,000 to 3000 employees. Starting from about 1360, the workforce was distinguished hierarchically, with a professional elite being paid a salary, the rest on a weekly basis, largely employed through master-craftsmen in a manner that gave them considerable 'freedom'. It has been described by Zan as a 'hybrid organization', 'modern and pre-modern at the same time, whereby working relations are already internalized [to the organization] according to a capitalist mode of production, though labour itself is not totally under control'.[112] That situation clearly presented problems of coordination and management. All large-scale operations employing a numerous work force do so, requiring a hierarchy, specialization, forecasting, a reckoning of costs, and varied organizational skills. In early modern Europe, these features were especially associated with arsenals which were primary among factory-type enterprises.[113] The point to be made is not that we see the emergence of 'management' in Venice before the appearance of what has been called the 'visible hand' in the twentieth-century United States[114] but that with the complexity of industrial activity, effectively beginning with the Bronze Age, we see the gradual emergence of skills along with the growth of collective production. As far as Venice was concerned, it should be emphasized that any establishment building numbers of ships, especially large vessels, whether in Turkey, in India or in China, would have to face problems of this kind. No-one 'invented' management, though they elaborated the practice under increasingly complex processes of production. As we have seen in chapter 4, there was nothing particularly unique in Venice's Arsenal, which was a function more of the activity than the culture.

That was part of the history of Europe's development of 'true capitalism', often seen as going back to earlier advantage, to earlier inequalities.

---

[111] Zan 2004: 149.   [112] Zan 2004: 149.   [113] Concina 1987.   [114] Chandler 1977.

Writing of his proposal to consider society by 'sets' or 'sectors', Braudel
claims that the overall social situation is easier to observe in Europe,
'which was so much ahead of the rest of the world' and where 'a rapidly
developing economy often seems to have dominated other sectors after
about the eleventh or twelfth century, and even more markedly after the
sixteenth'.[115] The eleventh century refers to the developments in trade,
in towns, in 'feudalism', following *l'an mille*, the new millennium.[116] The
sixteenth century refers above all to the activities of 'the great merchant
companies' of Holland and England who created monopolistic positions
in some northern parts of the globe. And it was in the sixteenth century that 'a new class' evolved, a 'bourgeoisie emerging from the background of trade'[117] which was climbing 'by its own efforts to the highest
place in contemporary society'. They only survived as capitalists for a few
generations; later they became *grands bourgeois* attached to the humanist
culture of the Renaissance, foreshadowing the Enlightenment[118] which
directed its 'revolutionary ideology' against 'the privileges of a leisured
aristocratic class'.[119] Hence, it was 'within a complex of conflicting forces
that economic expansion took place between the Middle Ages and the
eighteenth century, bringing with it capitalism'.[120] Outside Europe the
situation was different, since the state 'had been imposing its intolerable
pressures for centuries'.[121] It was only in Europe in the fifteenth century that the government embarked upon 'a determined expansion' and
created the first 'modern state'. Elsewhere the old rules obtained. 'Only
Europe was innovating in politics (and not in politics alone).'[122] That is a
strong eurocentric claim and one that diminishes political developments
in other areas; it relies more on the voices of commentators (political
philosophers) rather than on the empirical analysis of actual political systems.

Braudel's argument admits of lesser capitalist developments elsewhere
but there was always something special about Europe that produced 'true
capitalism'. He writes of the economy and indeed of social developments
generally as having 'a tendency to be synchronized throughout Europe',
which did not happen elsewhere (though the size of the unit has to be
taken into account).[123] But given the very close (reciprocal) relations that
Europe had with the Near East, how could these other developments
not be 'synchronized'?[124] And if this was the case with the Near East,

[115] Braudel 1984: 460.   [116] Duby 1996.   [117] Braudel 1984: 478.
[118] Braudel 1984: 487.   [119] Braudel 1984: 504.   [120] Braudel 1984: 461.
[121] Braudel 1982: 514.   [122] Braudel 1982: 515.   [123] Braudel 1984: 477.
[124] Peter Burke points out that Braudel argues that population rose and fell in early modern
    Europe at more or less the same time as in China, Japan, and India, which suggests the
    possibility of a measure of synchronicity in other fields.

why not the rest of Asia? His view, which sometimes disregarded the reciprocity of trade, was that basically they lacked a certain historical and political factor. In other words, the more distant past, perhaps the culture, made capitalism inevitable in Europe but impossible elsewhere. This is related to a general problem in his theoretical approach. Firstly he makes a firm distinction between the layers of the economy. Such a division does have a certain heuristic value, but it results in too severe a separation of full capitalism and the market. The market economy almost appears as 'natural';[125] only in certain places was it accompanied 'by an overarching economy which seizes these humble activities from above, redirects them and holds them in its mercy'. Full capitalism then becomes European.

Secondly Braudel believes in cycles (repetitive movements) not simply as analytic instruments but as causal factors, which emphasize his commitment to continuity, to repetition, to 'culture'. He writes of one historian denying the role of a Kondratieff cycle, that is, repetitive movements in history of standard duration. Always questioning his own premises, he asks: 'Is it possible to believe that human history obeys all-commanding rhythms which ordinary logic cannot explain? I am inclined to answer yes.'[126] I myself would place more reliance on logic, and say quite definitely no. In any case it is not clear how a cyclical view fits with the developmental one he elsewhere follows.

His general argument about development is that 'capitalism has been *potentially* visible since the dawn of history'.[127] What weight should one give to 'potentially' here? In Europe he sees the rise of towns as perhaps the first indicator of potentiality turning to possibility. Already in the thirteenth century, commercial and industrial developments were taking place, including banking. Contrary to many scholars, as we have seen, Braudel is prepared to see capitalism in earlier and other economies. However, very few areas favoured the reproduction of capital necessary for 'true' capitalism. He is led to perceive full capitalism not as rational but almost as 'the irrational behaviour of speculation'.[128] For western capitalism was different: in the long run it created 'a new art of living, new ways of thinking',[129] almost a new civilization, not at the time of the Protestant Reformation but already with the Catholic Renaissance. Thirteenth-century Florence was 'a capitalist city',[130] so too were other towns such as Venice, but because of exchange rather than production. In eighteenth-century Europe it was trade rather than industry or agriculture that made money on a large scale, but of course one had to have something to trade; that was where the profits were.[131]

---

[125] Braudel 1984: 38.   [126] Braudel 1984: 618.   [127] Braudel 1984: 620.
[128] Braudel 1984: 577.   [129] Braudel 1984: 578.   [130] Braudel 1984: 578.
[131] Braudel 1984: 428.

In Braudel's eyes, to participate at this most inclusive level of (European) capitalism, in what was not always a straightforwardly competitive activity (but sometimes monopolistic), took a capitalist working with large sums of money.[132] Even the development of monopolies was not, as Lenin claimed, characteristic of the last 'imperialistic' phase of capitalism, appearing in much earlier ones. But in the past monopoly 'only occupied a narrow platform of economic life'.[133] However one of capitalism's characteristics was that it could move the action from one sector to another at a moment's notice.[134] Here Braudel is clearly thinking of finance capitalism, including dealings in stocks and shares, which he sees as the top of the economic tree. On the other hand much trade involved a measure of flexibility in cargoes and destinations. Certainly as industry and exchange show, new finance, and more complex finance, was required. But in this development the production and distribution of goods became increasingly important.

The timing of capitalism

When did this type of real 'capitalism' put in an appearance in Europe? Some historians would select as the beginning of capitalism in Europe the opening up of the western Mediterranean by Venice's trade with the east which had gathered momentum by the new millennium. Blocking this advance was the fact that all Europe suffered a great setback with the Black Death of the fourteenth century. England only began fully to recover from that plague towards the end of the fifteenth. At that time, in response to the demographic revival, yeoman farmers, gentleman sheep breeders, urban cloth manufacturers, and merchant adventurers produced what has been described as a social and economic revolution. The export of raw wool gave way to that of woven cloth manufactured at home, which was mainly accomplished by cottage producers, then shipped to Europe. By the time Henry VII came to the throne, the Merchant Adventurers, an association of London cloth exporters, was controlling the London–Antwerp market (formerly Bruges), and replaced in economic importance the Staplers who dealt in raw wool. By 1496 they had become a chartered organization exercising a legal monopoly. As a consequence of this growth, flocks increased, enclosures proliferated, Italian bankers flocked to London. Landowners assumed a different role in economic life. The change was stimulated by the growth in trade first in the raw material for textiles, then in the textiles themselves, rather than in the agricultural production of food. That trade in textiles to Flanders, Holland, and thence to Italy was of fundamental importance to the recovery

---

[132] Braudel 1984: 432.   [133] Braudel 1984: 239.   [134] Braudel 1984: 433.

of Europe since it produced goods needed by the east and at the same time encouraged the import of eastern textiles to Europe, especially silk, then cotton. The continent later adapted their manufacture to local conditions in an effort at import substitution and initiated what has been called the Industrial Revolution.

Many would place the economic advance of Europe as a later event. For Braudel the European economy was the matrix of true capitalism, but the timing is different, developing quite early. In the first cities of Europe, every feature of latter-day capitalism seems to have developed in embryo.[135] These city-states were 'modern forms', 'ahead of their time'. The beginning of the first European world-economy appeared around 1200, with the reoccupation of the Mediterranean by the ships and merchants of Italy, primarily Venice.[136] Braudel argues that the Crusades were a great stimulus to achieving this outcome. Only after the Crusades of the fourteenth century did Italy really develop as a commercial centre. Those campaigns led to walled towns separating country from city, the creation of which was stimulated by contacts with Islam and Byzantium. For example, the rise of Amalfi in south-western Italy has been explained by the town's privileged contact with the Islamic world, where other 'city-states' were to be found.

The development of finances was obviously critical to 'finance capitalism'. It has been said that one of the few features of the economy that did not go back to classical times was the idea of the national debt. The debt lay at the centre of a 'financial revolution' in Britain which served to attract capital, especially for overseas commerce. For capitalism was always found in that section of the economy that sought to participate in the more active aspects of international trade:[137] 'Capital laughed at frontiers.'[138] As we have seen, Braudel's concentration on credit, exchange, and finance as the major characteristics of advanced capitalism leads him to play down production, even the Industrial Revolution, the machine age itself, though he does devote the penultimate chapter of his massive work to that process. He suggests somewhat tentatively that industrial production in Europe multiplied at least five times between 1600 and 1800, that is, largely before the so-called Revolution itself, a proposition we return to in Wrigley's discussion.[139] Much of this large-scale production was launched with the aid of subsidies and monopolies, a situation that only changed with the machine age, and hence was tied like the national debt to the activities of the nation state (though it is based paradoxically on

---

[135] Braudel 1984: 91.
[136] Braudel 1984: 93 (the Commercial Revolution, Lopez called it in 1971).
[137] Braudel 1984: 554.   [138] Braudel 1984: 528.   [139] Braudel 1984: 181.

international commerce). But increased production was of course important in sponsoring a consumer culture. That is partly recognized when the fact that goods could be made more cheaply in the north is described as 'the victory of the proletarian', leading to the powerful rise of Amsterdam and other Protestant countries.[140]

It needs to be added that for Braudel the Industrial Revolution was more than a question only of the increase in savings rates, of investment in technology, but rather 'an overall and indivisible process'.[141] That complexity he claims makes it difficult to transfer capitalism to other parts of the world. In order to take part in this process the contemporary Third World as a whole will have 'to break down the existing international order', whereas earlier it was possible only 'at the heart' of 'an open world-economy', namely in Europe. The mechanization associated with that Revolution he sees as starting in Europe possibly in the thirteenth and fourteenth centuries where its real forerunner may have been the German mining industry for which the dependence on machines was so well illustrated in the work of Agricola. Italy followed. It had a demographic revolution, developed the first 'territorial states' (in the early fifteenth century) and in the Milan area had an agricultural revolution developing irrigation and 'high farming' before that occurred in England and Holland. Indeed Milan might well have gone further ahead along the road to capitalism had it had an external market. However England, which lagged behind the French in the sixteenth century, also had access to coal as an energy source which permitted larger factories to supply a larger market (overseas more often than internal) and to innovate in production. However innovation was in no sense confined to the west, which adopted many features from the east, where mechanization and industrialization had already begun and where, in many areas, agriculture was very advanced.

In sum, Braudel shows himself to be in two minds about the timing of capitalism, and indeed whether we are referring to production itself or to the finance involved in making and exchanging goods. About the timing, capitalism is widespread but 'true capitalism' is specific to the later west, even if its roots go much further back in its history. His uncertainty reflects divergences among western historians more generally. Marx originally claimed the thirteenth century in Europe as the beginning of capitalism, whereas Wallerstein follows his later line in opting for the sixteenth. Nef saw the Industrial Revolution in England beginning in the sixteenth century when industrialization was 'endemic' throughout the continent. Some, such as Charles Wilson and Eric Hobsbawm, see

---

[140] Braudel 1982: 570.   [141] Braudel 1984: 539.

it beginning by the restoration of the British monarchy of 1660. In the more usual view the eighteenth century is the locus of the capitalism of the Industrial Revolution, the critical factor being the coming of the machine age, the development of technology which Marx saw as so important, especially for the cotton industry with its mass production and extensive commerce.

The timing of the onset of European advantage is thus subject to major disagreements among economic historians. So too is its location, both being linked. In a recent account, the economic geographer, Wrigley,[142] argues that by the beginning of the nineteenth century England was significantly different from its continental neighbours, wealthier, growing more rapidly, more heavily urbanized and far less dependent upon agriculture. Using national income accounting techniques, and referring to Rostow's notion of a take-off between 1783 and 1802, growth before 1830, the railway age, seems to have been slow, despite the aggregate performance of the economy as a whole. Wrigley therefore concludes that the divergence of England occurred much earlier than is often supposed and that it must have been well clear of its rivals by 1700. This advantage he argues was not due to the Industrial Revolution, since only slow surges of growth occurred from 1760, but was based upon a larger advance in the preceding century or two. This growth derived from the success in expanding the possibilities inherent in what he calls an advanced 'organic economy', in which material artefacts were made from animal or vegetable materials[143] (which also provided the energy) to an inorganic one (that is, based on coal and fossil fuels).

That anglo-centred view does not go undisputed. According to de Vries and van der Woude, it was the Dutch that developed the first 'modern' (capitalist) economy during the Golden Age between the mid-sixteenth century and c.1680. Not only commerce and industry but agriculture too was involved in dynamic expansion. Rapid urban growth took place as well as a transformation of the occupational structure that anticipated England by some 150 years,[144] a process that was assisted by an excellent transport infrastructure (mainly by water) and by cheap energy (mainly from peat, 'inorganic'). At the end of the seventeenth century, a period of stagnation set in, since a modern economy, they argue, is not necessarily self-sustaining. Wrigley however assumes that in England growth was exponential and that a dramatic divergence occurred when an organic-based economy shifted to an inorganic one.

In these nationalistic accounts first the Dutch, then the British, developed advanced 'organic' economies which were hardly self-sustaining as

---

[142] Wrigley 2004.   [143] Wrigley 2004: 23–4.   [144] Wrigley 2004: 62.

far as growth was concerned, then shifted to exploit the inorganic. However such economies were not the first in Europe to make such a move towards mechanization as we see from the history of the silk production in Lucca, nor yet of factory organization in the manufacture of ships and guns in the arsenals of the Mediterranean; in other words, Italy had preceded them in this and other ways. Moreover, like China and the Near East, it had employed water power for energy that was not subject to the same organic restraints as the burning of wood. The use of water in paper-making, for example, gave the rainier Europe an advantage over the Near East that led to more efficient production of paper which then began to be exported to rather than imported from that area. However, China also made use of water power and of fossil fuels (in blast furnaces) long before England and Europe; and features of the inorganic economy were already in place elsewhere. Or to put it in other terms, capitalism was already well entrenched, as was mechanization and even industrialization. As for the intensification of agriculture in 'pre-industrial' Holland and England, parallel events had occurred in Italy and, as Pomeranz discusses,[145] in other specific areas outside Europe, reminding us that we should beware of the use of aggregate growth based upon national political units (as Wrigley warns us for Britain or England) but rather refer to specific regions and, one should add, to specific times, since these varied considerably. The prosperous mezzogiorno of the Islamic and Norman periods became the backward Italy of the mafia in later ones. When the countries of the North Atlantic seaboard burst upon the scene, they did so on the basis of the export of 'organic' textiles, of wool and then woollen cloth, from Britain to Flanders or to the north of France and then to Italy. They developed a coastal trade around the North Sea and eventually into the Mediterranean, which is where the main action was taking place at the time.

Such oscillation between regions is not only a function of the law of diminishing returns as formulated by Riccardo. Agricultural economies do not exist in isolation, not at least since the Bronze Age when developments in that sphere were stimulated by the growth of towns and of commerce which in turn encouraged agriculture. Oscillations occurred for a variety of factors, but while growth was not sustainable in the shorter term, in the longer it was. Oscillation also took place between individual industrial economies, where the dominance of English growth gave way to Germany and then to the US, each exploiting particular advantages. Now the same is happening with China. Competition and advantage are the names of the game.

[145] Pomeranz 2000.

What is common among most western historians, including those like Weber and Braudel who study the problem comparatively, is that even after considering data from different societies, all end up where they started, seeing Europe as the 'real' home of capitalism, well before the Great Divergence. That is understandable if the situation under consideration is Europe in the nineteenth century, which undoubtedly had a comparative advantage. But to push that advantage back into the early modern and medieval periods is to discount the many achievements, in the economy, in technology, in learning, and in communication, which those other societies had undoubtedly achieved, including in the earlier stages of 'capitalism'. The result is to appropriate the whole nature and spirit of capitalism (or in Braudel's case 'true' capitalism) and to claim it uniquely for the west, or even for one component of the west, England or Holland.

In the conclusion to chapter 4, I discussed the merits of the concept of the 'tributary states' as applying throughout Eurasia and of providing for a continuous development from the Urban Revolution of the Bronze Age. We need to look at the economy growing over that five thousand years. I referred to the development of urban civilizations, the increase in the production of goods and ideas and therefore of mercantile capitalism. Of course, there were incremental developments in all of these fields, the rhythm of which was hastened by changes in communication, leading up to the electronic media. Of these developments, the increased industrialization characterizing late eighteenth-century Britain was of the utmost significance for the future. But industrialization, mechanization and mass-production developed, slowly at first, in other parts of Eurasia, in China with textiles, ceramics, and paper, in India with cotton, later taken up in Europe and the Near East, to which were added the production of weapons of destruction, mass-produced in factories organized on modern lines (involving private as well as state capital), in foundries and arsenals throughout the region. That is the kind of long-term developmental scheme we need to be considering for Eurasia.

If we doubt the relevance of a specifically European sequencing of Antiquity, feudalism, capitalism, we arrive at the notion of a long-term, sometimes rapid, sometimes slow, development of urban cultures through the Bronze Age to the Iron Age, to the efflorescence of classical cultures and the Mediterranean, but also in China and elsewhere, a collapse in western Europe, slow but continuous increase in China, the gradual renewal of towns in the west and their constant communication with the east, with the consequential growth of mercantile activity and of urban cultures. Those mercantile cultures developed a diversification of their products, the mechanization of their methods of production, leading to mass-production and mass exports and imports. But all that process can be described without adopting the nineteenth-century notion of the emergence of capitalism as a specific stage in the development of world society, and we can dispense with the supposed sequence of periods of production leading to it that are confined to Europe. Such an account avoids European periodization and its assumptions of long-term superiority.

The discussion of Braudel therefore leads us to ask whether we really need the concept of capitalism, which always seems to push the analysis in a eurocentric direction. In his account he is in fact talking about widespread mercantile activity and its concomitants, which eventually came to dominate the society. That often involves re-investing profits in the means of transport (ships) or production (looms) but the process also occurs even in many agricultural societies. The phase of so-called finance capitalism is surely an extension of this activity. Can we not therefore dispense with this pejorative term drawn from nineteenth-century Britain and recognize the element of continuity in the market and in bourgeois activities from the Bronze Age until modern times?

Part Three

Three institutions and values

8   The theft of institutions: towns, and universities

There is a widespread belief in the west that European towns differ substantially from eastern towns especially in the factors that create 'capitalism', most notably expressed by Max Weber. This distinction is supposed to stem from the specific circumstances of European life after the end of Antiquity, more specifically from the political and economic conditions characteristic of feudalism (which saw the rise of the 'commune' in northern Italy). Linked to this is the commonly held idea that higher education started with the founding of universities in western Europe beginning with Bologna in the eleventh century.[1] The same constellation that is seen to have given rise to European towns has, in this view, generated the momentum required for the qualitative leap that distinguishes European intellectual life after the first centuries of the Middle Ages. According to the medievalist, Jacques Le Goff, western Christian Europe at the turn of the twelfth and thirteenth century saw the virtually simultaneous birth of the town and the universities, though he is more interested in intellectuals as individuals rather than universities as institutions. He writes: 'the most conclusive aspect of our model of the medieval intellectual is his connection with the town'.[2] Both are seen are being particularly western and as developing modernity. Both suppositions are highly questionable and illustrate the concerted efforts of European scholars to maintain a highly eurocentric position even in the face of strong evidence that pleads for a different interpretation.

Towns

Let us take towns first. In discussing the Middle Ages, many historians have concentrated their analysis on the rural sector and on feudal relationships. As Hilton has remarked, that is especially true of Marxist

---

[1] See for example Haskins's study (1923: 7), where universities are seen as being part of 'the renaissance of the twelfth century', stimulated by Arabic learning, though Salerno is traced to the middle of the eleventh century – the 'earliest university of medieval Europe'.
[2] Le Goff 1993: xiv.

writers.[3] Towns were largely relegated to the background, and regarded as relatively unimportant to feudal developments, at least in the early stages. They resurface in European history simultaneously with the first steps towards capitalism, mirroring the progression from agrarian to industrial societies. Other writers such as Anderson have drawn attention to the 'urban enclaves' in the High Middle Ages, refusing to divorce them from the surrounding agrarian leaven.

In the west the 'corporate urban communities undoubtedly represented a vanguard force in the total medieval economy'.[4] In the extreme west of the Roman Empire, the towns had suffered drastically from its dissolution. Anderson minimizes the extent of urban collapse and draws attention to the fact that many municipios continued, in northern Italy for example. Later, in the new millennium, there was the growth of other centres, the majority of which 'were in origin promoted or protected by feudal lords'.[5] They soon gained 'a relative autonomy' throwing up a new patrician stratum and exploiting the conflict between noble and ecclesiastical power, as between Guelf and Gibelline in Italy. That meant a 'parcellized sovereignty', a split between aristocratic and clerical forces from which the bourgeoisie was held to profit, leaving them more scope to become the dominant party in the town's governance. In the east however the towns had continued, so too did the burghers; lords of the land were not needed as their promoters in the same way as in the west, though the role of religious centres and ecclesiastical towns was always important.

The classical city did not vanish with the collapse of Rome and 'with an urban population, monumental buildings, games, and a highly literate upper class, continued in at least the provincial capitals of western and southern Asia Minor, in Syria, Arabia, Palestine and Egypt right up to the Arab invasions, and in the areas under Arab rule beyond that'.[6] By the seventh century, Italy and even Byzantium 'look very different from the contemporary (and by this time Arab) Near East, where there is much more evidence of continued economic complexity and prosperity'.[7] In the west, the situation had changed radically. In Britain skills such as the use of the potter's wheel, and building with bricks and mortar disappeared; schools vanished from what towns remained; gymnasia went out of use; the complexity of Roman economic life was no more. The church and country lords became much more central to life generally, especially where 'cities ceased to have schools', literacy was low and restricted to 'a few leading families'; higher literary culture was

---

[3] Hilton 1976.   [4] Anderson 1974a: 192.   [5] Anderson 1974a: 190.
[6] Liebeschuetz 2000: 207.   [7] Ward-Perkins 2000: 360.

left to private tutors and fitfully to the church. However, in the east a literary culture continued to flourish together with Christianity and other cults throughout the sixth century. By the seventh, even in the east, a shortage of books was experienced at Constantinople, and learning was increasingly restricted to the literate clergy and to the capital itself.[8]

Looking at the reconstitution of towns in the later Middle Ages, Marx considered the European city as unique in its contribution to capitalism. It is part and parcel of his acceptance of the eurocentric genealogy of the development of capitalism through feudalism from Antiquity. According to Hobsbawm, Marx was not primarily interested in the internal dynamics of pre-capitalist systems 'except in so far as they explained the preconditions of capitalism'.[9] In *Formen* he elaborates his notion of why 'labour' and 'capital' could not arise in pre-capitalist formations other than feudalism. Why was it that only feudalism is thought to allow factors of production to emerge without interference? The answer must surely lie in the definitions of labour and capital adopted, definitions that necessarily excluded them from other types of society. In other words the answer to the enquiry was predetermined by the nature of the question. Many European scholars, pre-occupied with the achievements of their societies in the nineteenth century, set themselves similar teleological questions which precluded the analysis of other types of society in their own right, or even in an 'objective' comparative perspective. In Marx's case 'there is the implication that European feudalism is *unique*, for no other form has produced the medieval city, which is crucial to the Marxian theory of the evolution of capitalism'.[10] So the nature of earlier cities is judged on the basis of who came out top in the nineteenth-century economy. However, any general or genuine uniqueness the 'European city' may have had (and this remains a substantive question) is not necessarily linked to the growth of capitalism. Indeed Braudel sees one form of (mercantile) capitalism as characterizing all cities everywhere; for him it is only the financial form that is unique to the west (again a conclusion I have questioned in chapter 7).

Since Antiquity the main towns of the northern shores of the Mediterranean had been supplied by sea with wheat coming from Sicily, Egypt, north Africa, and the Black Sea. Trade across the Mediterranean in other commodities such as oil and ceramics was also important. Later, however, there arose a difference between the towns of east and west. The medieval towns of Europe (apart from Istanbul) were of much reduced dimensions and activity, and we have to wait until the nineteenth century

Liebeschuetz 2000: 210–11.   [9] Hobsbawm 1964: 43.   [10] Hobsbawm 1964: 43.

for London or Paris to match the size of imperial Rome.[11] Because of this decrease in size and activity the supply problems no longer involved the same level of exchange.

The life of towns only began to revive when trade began again in the Mediterranean, and commerce with the east returned. Venice played an important part but was not alone among Italian towns. A fundamental role in opening trade was played by the towns around Amalfi, southwest of the southern city of Naples. Amalfi was not the only port to be involved in trade with the South and hence with the 'Saracens', who were 'almost perennially present in the Tyrhennia arc throughout the ninth century'.[12] Skinner suggests that the founder of Gaeta, Dolcibili, was a merchant, who had made his fortune trading with the Muslims; at one point he 'unleashed a group of Arabs near Salerno to counter a move of the Pope'.[13]

The Near East generally did not only contribute to the quickening of trade in western Europe. Their influences can be discerned in the organization and layout of towns as well as in architectural developments in the period preceding the Renaissance, both directly and as a consequence of commercial interaction between east and west, and the affluence this brought to western towns. The territory of the Amalfi area was harsh; towns were built on river valleys running down to the sea. But the rocky promontories were easy to defend, which was important when the Arab raids came thick and furious. It was perhaps these Arab raids that led to the indigenes of Amalfi and neighbouring Gaeta both breaking away from the rule of the Duchy of Naples. That relationship affected both architecture and art in special ways:

The composite houses in the hill towns of Amalfi were places of spatial differentiation and decorative elaboration, characteristics that set them apart from contemporary buildings in Italy and from simpler and more austere dwellings of the early Middle Ages. The complex characters of the houses are inseparable from the act of *mercatantia* because the financial resources of the community were channelled into creating these lavish environments. As a viable site of expenditure, housing not only surpassed the basic requirements of shelter but entered the realm of artistic expression and ostentation.

While the existence and splendour of such buildings depended on the profits of *mercatantia*, their specific forms also represented the commercial experiences of the Amalfitans. With their composite layouts and intricate webs of ornaments, the Amalfi houses coincide with North African architectural and ornamental lexicons that appeared in prominent secular and religious settings alike. Many related North African works of art were located in coastal cities such Mahdiyya and Tunis, the commercial centres familiar to generations of Amalfitan merchants.

---

[11] Geraci and Marin 2003: 577–8.   [12] Skinner 1995: 32.   [13] Skinner 1995: 31.

From the eleventh century through the thirteenth, these towns were precisely where *regnicoli* [local inhabitants] sold items such as lumber, grain, and textiles in exchange for gold, leather, and ceramics.

Facilitating the reception of North African idioms was the presence of Muslims in the *Regno* itself and a long-standing though fragmented tradition of Islamic art production there. Some of the ornament used in North Africa would not have seemed unusual to elite Amalfitans because it was closely related to small-scale works made in the kingdom. As with baths and bathing, it is likely that the sophisticated housing paradigm that emphasized courtyards, differentiation of space, and decorative display was part of a broader culture of affluence in this part of the Mediterranean basin, one that transcended differences in faith. In this way the Amalfitans resemble well-to-do Constantinopolitans of the twelfth century, whose awareness and appreciation of Islamic painting led them to emulate such works in the capital.[14]

Architectural options of Islamic inspiration included the direct integration of objects produced outside of Europe. One of the main imports from North Africa and the Near East was glazed ceramics, 'one of the first widely available commodities in southern Italy that embellished the domestic environment'.[15] But such objects were often used in fragments as *tesserae* or even whole as *bacini* to incorporate into church designs, especially in Ravello where they provide evidence of the tastes and experiences of Amalfi merchants.

Architecture in Ravello was of the south, a 'generalized Mediterranean culture'. But it also contains some elements from the north. Northern influences made themselves felt in the south when the Parisian basin conquered the south of France and in Italy, the Normans taking Sicily from the Arabs and giving way first to the Hohenzellern dynasty and then to the Anjou from central France. Gothic art had started to come in with its pointed archways as well as with heraldry.[16] Gothic arches were probably Arabic in origin; in any case there was a strong influence coming from the east in urban architecture, especially in towns like Venice.

However, despite the multiple influences of eastern towns on the west, and the similarities between the two urban structures, many scholars in the west have seen Asiatic towns as being structurally different from later (post-eleventh-century) European ones in ways that are supposed to have made it possible for the latter to develop capitalism and the former not. Islamic towns, albeit communicating and exchanging with European ones, are said to partake of this difference. So too Asian cities, according to the sociologist Max Weber. But their arguments always started from the standpoint of later European achievements which they needed to

[14] Caskey 2004: 113–14.   [15] Caskey 2004: 164.   [16] Caskey 2004: 165.

explain. More recently that position has come under much criticism. For example, the Arabist, Hourani, writes: 'Scholars of the preceding generations tended to adopt the idea (ultimately derived from the works of Max Weber) that towns in the full sense of the word only existed in European countries because it was only in Europe that one found an "urban community" enjoying at least a partial autonomy under an administration directed by elected authorities.' Eastern towns were therefore not 'real' towns.[17] However modern scholars of Islam discern certain common features between the two,[18] as one would expect with urbanization and mercantile activity, and would reverse this judgement. That is also true of India[19] and China.[20]

But the western notion of uniqueness was not to be given up without a struggle. The growing power of the new western towns is seen by Anderson to be based on 'the parcellization of sovereignty peculiar to the feudal mode in Europe [hence unique] and that distinguished it fundamentally from the Oriental States with their larger towns'. The most mature western form was the commune, expressive of the feudal unity of town and country because it was 'a confederation founded . . . by an oath of reciprocal loyalty between equals, the *conjuratio*'.[21] That view of the difference is one in which he follows Marx, Weber, Braudel, and many others. The freedom of the 'community of equals' was restricted to a narrow elite but 'the germinal novelty of the institution derived from the self-government of autonomous towns', especially in Lombardy when the overlordship of episcopal rulers was overthrown. In England the towns were always dependent in some degree, for they were 'an absolutely central economic and cultural component of the feudal order'.[22] Anderson continues: 'it was on these dual foundations of impressive agrarian progress and urban vitality that the startling aesthetic and intellectual monuments of the High Middle Ages were raised, the great cathedrals (one critical achievement was Gothic architecture) and the first universities'.[23] However even in the Ancient Near East some towns had a relative autonomy (especially the city-states). In Europe, northern Italy was atypical. Other towns in Flanders and the Rhineland existed 'under charters of autonomy from feudal suzerains'. Also, Anderson's assessment overlooks the urban (and rural) achievements in both the aesthetic and the intellectual spheres elsewhere, for example under Islam in Granada or Cordoba, achievements

[17] Hourani 1990: my translation, quoted Denoix 2000: 329.
[18] Denoix 2000.   [19] Gillion 1968.   [20] Rowe 1984.
[21] In fact in Islam, for example in Syria in Crusading times, authority was constantly being divided between the caliph, the Imam or prince of the faithful, and the sultan and his various emirs, themselves capable of taking power.
[22] Anderson 1974a: 195.   [23] Anderson 1974a: 195.

in architecture and in learning which were built on rather different foundations.

The notion of 'parcellized sovereignty', so important for most analysts to the emergence of the town proper, and with it to the development of modernity, is intrinsic to Anderson's idea that feudalism was a necessary precursor of capitalism because:

1. It permitted 'the growth of autonomous towns in the interstitial spaces between disparate lordships'.[24] However, we have seen, towns in the east required no such permission; in fact they grew up throughout Eurasia following the Urban Revolution of the Bronze Age; and were intrinsic to the political economy. Some were more autonomous than others. So too with the autonomy of the church which he describes as 'separate and universal'. But all written religions in fact maintained a partial independence of the polity as a result of their organization and their property-holding.

2. The estates system led to medieval parliaments. However, moots and consultative assemblies were hardly restricted to Europe: some form of consultation, and often representation, was a widespread feature of governments in many parts of the world. So too was a division into estates, 'stände' in Weberian terminology.

3. Divided sovereignty was a precondition for the freedom of townspeople as well as of towns. But 'freedom' was not limited to the urban inhabitants of western Europe; all towns had a modicum of autonomy, of anonymity and therefore of 'freedom'.

The freedom of medieval towns is paradigmatic of eurocentric claims and deserves to be considered in greater depth. Anderson elsewhere quotes the German saying, *Die Stadt macht frei*, the town makes one free. But that remark applies to towns wherever they are found, for they inevitably provide their citizens with a measure of anonymity. Are towns in general also freer politically? Many of them gain a measure of freedom because of the nature of the activities that take place there, manufacturing, money-lending, law, medicine, administration, and commerce. But as Southall observes 'the creation of the city involved a sharp rise in inequality',[25] which I would rather put down to the increased economic differentiation the use of the plough (as well as irrigation) brought about. In this sense the city always 'exploits' the countryside, takes its surplus in order to live and work. In any case, apart from north Italy, few European towns were free of all constraints of political or religious overlordship. Elsewhere so-called 'free towns' were accorded certain financial liberties by the suzerain. In general the towns of western

[24] Anderson 1974b: 418.   [25] Southall 1998: 14.

Europe were more similar to the 'Asiatic city' than most scholars have supposed.

In a wide-ranging book on the city (1998) Southall too, though accepting Marx's distinction between eastern and western towns, observes that '[d]espite the great diversity of cities in time and space, there is a demonstrable thread of continuity through their dialectical transformations from earliest beginnings till today, as they have played an ever greater part in human life'.[26] Despite the continuities he sees, he is compelled 'to carve up this mass of time and space into manageable, communicable portions, although every dissection violates reality'.[27] For this purpose he chooses 'the modes of production adumbrated by Marx' which from my standpoint do not 'minimize distortion' as he suggests but aggravate it. He then accepts the division between Asiatic and European without really analysing it.

In considering the city, Southall does not altogether limit it to post-Bronze Age society. He recognizes the urbanization of the Yoruba in West Africa, which has been called an 'agro-city', and he acknowledges the growth of small-scale cities at Catal Hüyük and Hacilar Anatolia, in Jericho (Palestine) as in Jarmo in the foothills of the Tigris, as well as some in the New World and South-east Asia.[28] Nevertheless in general terms the development of the city is associated with the Bronze Age. However he does try to set off Asian cities (to which he devotes a long chapter of some 125 pages) from European ones, partly on the basis of the division, made by Hsu, into the key civilizational factors of caste, class, and club. Looking at cities in this way neglects the obvious similarities (to which Southall in fact calls attention) in size of population, density, organization, specialisms, educational establishments, markets, hospitals, temples, commerce, crafts, banking, and guilds. On all these dimensions there is little to distinguish the towns in the east and the west before the nineteenth century.

Universities

A claim that runs parallel with the alleged uniqueness of European towns refers to the nature of higher education, deemed to differ fundamentally from its predecessors and non-European contemporaries. Indeed Le Goff treats them in the same breath.[29] The notion of European academic singularity is dependent on the idea that only here did towns develop along lines which alone can lead to capitalism, secularization, modernity. Here,

[26] Southall 1998: 4.   [27] Southall 1998: 1.   [28] Southall 1998: 18.
[29] Le Goff 1993.

and only here, in the growing autonomy of the urban world, in the economic and trade interests of an emergent, uniquely European social class which fuelled a concern with the natural world, can we find the premises for the emergence of universities and of science corresponding to the progress towards modernity.

However, this position is hard to defend when we consider other countries and other times; the evidence suggests that post-Antiquity Europe experienced a period of comparative intellectual bareness which was overcome partly due to external contributions. Higher education obviously existed in Greece in the form of the Academy and the Lyceum. It even continued in the former Roman empire:

Schools can be traced at Alexandria, Antioch, Athens, Beirut, Constantinople, and Gaza; they were in effect the universities of the ancient world. They varied in character and importance: at Alexandria Aristotle was one of the main topics of study; the chief subject at Beirut was law. The need for such institutions was created by a vast increase in the Roman civil service in the fourth century. The government required administrators of liberal education and good prose style, as the emperor Constantius stated explicitly in 357 in an edict preserved in the Theodosian code.[30] (14.1.1.)

With the exception of Athens, closed by Justinian in 529, all these were schools in Asia or Africa. The fact that in the Christian sphere such institutions were closed down by Justinian shows what a dominant religion can do by way of limiting the spread of knowledge, although the nature of written religions meant that something had to be salvaged. Christianity certainly closed down earlier institutions of higher education. But the church inevitably required its own form of schooling, even though there were problems at the higher level, certainly with classical learning, obviously pagan.

By the latter part of the sixth century the decline of learning and culture was serious. The imperial university at Constantinople, refounded by Theodosius II c. 425, and a new clerical academy under the direction of the patriarchate, were the only major educational institutions in the main part of the empire; the school at Alexandria continued, but rather in isolation. The exhausted condition of the empire did nothing to encourage learning, and before any recovery could take place matters were made worse by the religious controversy over icon-worship. For some three centuries there is little record of education and the study of the classics. The iconoclasts were not finally defeated until 843, when a church council formally restored the traditional practices of image worship. Very few manuscripts of any kind remain from this period, and there is little external evidence about classical studies.[31]

---

[30] Reynolds and Wilson 1974: 45.   [31] Reynolds and Wilson 1974: 47–8.

Until the late third century, the east and west of the Roman empire had had a common culture, with almost identical mosaics being found a thousand miles apart.[32] Then the west dropped the use of Greek and for many reasons the gulf grew wider. There, large tracts of Roman territory passed into 'barbarian' control in the fifth century and Italy by its end became an Ostrogothic kingdom. At first schools continued to flourish but war threatened their existence and the Lombard invasion of 568 struck the final blow, 'leaving monasteries as virtually the sole institutions providing basic literacy'.[33] Even the areas of North Africa invaded by the Arian Vandals in 429, who dispatched their fleet from Carthage to control Corsica, Sardinia, and the Balearics, fared better. At first uninterested in education, they subsequently permitted Latin schools in Carthage which continued to teach until the capture of the town by the Arabs in 698.

Egypt and much of the Near East had been Christian before the Arab conquest but eastern Christianity had not been so affected by the collapse of the western Roman empire and of its economy. Cities persisted and even the conquests of the Arabs did not disrupt life in the same way as the 'barbarian' invasions and internal weakness produced in the north. Indeed the Arabs were far from 'barbarians', being the heirs to the complex cultures of south-west Arabia and to the land of Sheba, as well as being converts to a written religion on a par with Judaism and Christianity, creeds with which many of the inhabitants were already acquainted. They were also the inheritors of a distinguished tradition of poetry through living on the fringes of the great civilizations of the Near East.[34] While everywhere there were periods of decline, by and large the south and east of the Mediterranean continued to be hosts to large urban centres with something of a parallel city and commercial life to classical Greece and Rome. The relative absence of artistic culture was probably due more to the interdictions of the dominant Abrahamistic religions than it was to any more general problem.

So in the east some learning continued. What we also have to take into account is a rather neglected chapter in the history of transmission: the significance of the translation of Greek texts into Oriental languages. 'At some point during late Antiquity Greek texts began to be translated into Syriac, activity being centred in the towns of Nisibis and Edessa.'[35] Not only biblical works but Aristotle and Theophrastus and poetry were translated. Greek learning, which vanished almost without a trace in western Europe, survived in translation; Latin however continued sporadically until revived in the Renaissance.[36] Both Latin and Greek assisted in the

---

[32] Browning 2000: 872.   [33] Browning 2000: 873.   [34] Conrad 2000.
[35] Reynolds and Wilson 1974: 48.   [36] Reynolds and Wilson 1974.

relative continuity of schools in the east after the Arab conquest, including Byzantium. In that town,

The Bardas university was founded under favourable conditions, and was probably the centre of a lively group of scholars concerned to recover and disseminate classical texts of many different kinds . . . Classical learning and education continued in the eleventh century much as before . . . The philosophical school, which also gave instruction in grammar, rhetoric and literary subjects, was under the direction of Michael Psellus (1017–78), much the most versatile man of his generation, who distinguished himself as civil servant, senior adviser to several emperors, historian, and academic philosopher. His literary output attests his wide reading of the classics, but his intellectual interests were rather more in philosophy, and his eminence as a lecturer and teacher led to a renewed interest in Plato and to a lesser extent Aristotle.[37]

It was in the east that classical tradition continued, both in terms of the works of Greek as well as Roman authors and with regard to the organization of educational establishments. Whilst this did not happen seamlessly, the interruptions in the acquisition and dissemination of knowledge known by the east were less far-reaching than the long-term near-erasure of education and learning in the west. The eleventh-century school where Psellus taught had been established long before:

In 863 the assistant emperor Bardas revived the imperial university, which had disappeared in the turmoil of the preceding centuries, by founding a school in the capital under the direction of Leo, a philosopher and mathematician of distinction; other professors appointed at the same time were Theodore the geometrician, Theodegius the astronomer, and Cometas the literary scholar; the last of these may have specialized in rhetoric and Atticism, but he also prepared a recension of Homer.[38]

However it remained active even after further political disturbances briefly interrupted its activity:

The fortunes of the school were not entirely favourable. For reasons which seem to have been political rather than intellectual, the school's teachers fell into disfavour at the court, and Psellus himself had to retire to a monastery for a time; but he returned to important positions in due course, and it is likely that the school continued its work.

From the time of its foundation the Badras university went through various transformations, such as the specialization of fields of knowledge, which bring it into close proximity with modern ideas of higher learning:

The major change of this epoch consisted of a reorganization of the imperial university; whether this was provoked by a decline in the institution in the form that Bardas had given it is unknown, but the new arrangement included the setting

---

[37] Reynolds and Wilson 1974: 54, 60.   [38] Reynolds and Wilson 1974: 51.

up of a faculty of law and another of philosophy. The changes were made under the aegis of the emperor Constantine IX Monomachus in 1045. The law School does not concern us here, except to note that its foundation antedates by some years that of the famous faculty at Bologna, from which modern law faculties [in Europe] ultimately derive their origin.[39]

So eastern models may have been instrumental in the formation of academia as we know it.

In western Europe, the discontinuity with classical learning, especially in Greek, was more pronounced in cathedral and monastic schools that revived some scholarly activity and which preceded the formation of what have been seen as the first universities in Bologna and elsewhere in the eleventh and twelfth centuries. That represented the re-establishment of higher education after the decline of western learning, following the disappearance of the Roman Empire in the west. With the new institutions, knowledge, including some scientific knowledge, began to accumulate and circulate more rapidly in the west than in the east. It was part of the revival after the decline, a presence after absence, that resulted in its own rebirth, epitomized in Botticelli's painting of the *Birth of Venus*. Before that the levels of knowledge had been in favour of the east as we see in the difference in library holdings which was staggering, largely because of the east's use of abundant paper rather than scarce animal skins or papyrus.[40]

Apart from Bologna, the medieval school at Salerno in southern Italy has been described by Kristeller as 'rightly famous as the earliest university of medieval Europe'.[41] It specialized in practical medicine, conducting dissections on animals. Its renown in medicine is first reliably recorded from 985 and there is no evidence that it existed before the middle of the tenth century. Significantly it continued to be in touch with the (Greek) east. One of the earliest authors associated with Salerno was Constantine 'the African', who became a monk at Monte Cassino and is thought of as

the first translator and introducer of Arabic science in the occident. The declamations of Renaissance humanists and of modern nationalists should not blind us against the historical fact that in the eleventh and twelfth centuries Arabian science was definitely superior to occidental science, including early Salernitan medicine, and that the translation of Arabic material meant a definite progress in available knowledge. The same is true for the translations of Greek works from the Arabic, for the simple reason that at that time the Arabs possessed many more works of Greek scientific literature than the Latins, and that in their commentaries and independent works they had made definite contributions to the ancient Greek heritage.[42]

[39] Reynolds and Wilson 1974: 54, 60.   [40] See Djebar 2005: 22–3.
[41] Kristeller 1945: 138.   [42] Kristeller 1945: 152.

All did not depend upon Arabic translation. A number of works attributed to Hippocrates, Galen, and others were available in Latin versions. Nevertheless Constantine's translations were more important becoming the basis for medical instruction 'for a long time'.[43] Arabic influence seems to begin with Constantine after which there was less scholasticism and less magic in the Salernitan literature of the later tenth century.[44] After that the curriculum became 'increasingly theoretical'[45] and was probably transferred to Paris.

We have seen that the foundation of the Bolognan university and of other establishments of higher education in Europe was preceded by the Byzantium Badras university in the east. A similar discussion has arisen concerning how far the renewal of these institutions of higher learning was dependent upon outside stimulus from Islam, which inherited the schools and library of Alexandria and a large number of classical texts ('Ancient science') or whether the renewal of learning was due to the internal development of humanism leading to the Renaissance. Let us first consider the situation in Islam which has recently been reviewed by Makdisi in *The rise of colleges* (1981).

Muslim education

It was in the east that the teaching of grammar and rhetoric continued. In the west, as I have argued, cities and their schools frequently went into decline. There were of course ambivalences about allowing classical education to carry on both under Christianity and under Islam; Justinian took strong measures against 'pagan' culture. But the persistence of the Greek language in the east meant that the classics were more readily available, including to the Arabs when they arrived in the seventh century. Islam then created a worldwide religious space that stretched from southern Spain to northern China, to India and to South-east Asia, enabling information and inventions to travel easily throughout Eurasia. And it was through the Arabs that many classical and other texts were transmitted to the west, paving the way for the revival of learning in the west. Philosophy continued to flourish at Athens and at Alexandria after the collapse of the Roman Empire. In the latter town the Museum 'functioned as a University with the accent on research'.[46]

However, despite the various schools that remained active outside Europe even after the fall of Rome, the university was a form of social organization only produced in the Christian west according to Makdisi in the second half of the twelfth century.[47] The universities in Europe

[43] Kristeller 1945: 153.   [44] Kristeller 1945: 155.   [45] Kristeller 1945: 159.
[46] Childe 1964: 254.   [47] Makdisi 1981: 224.

were a 'new product',[48] completely separate from the Greek academies of Athens or Alexandria and utterly foreign to Islamic experience. Higher education in the west, Makdisi argues, was not a product of the Greco-Roman world nor did it originate in the cathedral or monastic schools which preceded it; it differed from them in organization and in its studies.[49] Moreover, according to him, it owes nothing to Islam, which did not have the abstract concept of a corporation; only physical persons could be endowed with legal personality. In addition, European universities drew their privileges from the Pope or the King, and scholars could reside away from home where they were not citizens (as in Islam).

However, Makdisi's point-blank rejection of the impact Islamic practices had upon Europe seems to neglect the fact that the rise of the universities was accompanied by a revival of learning between 1100 and 1200 when an influx of knowledge arrived from what had been Muslim Sicily (until 1091) but mainly through Arab Spain. Moreover although the universities were said to be different from the madrasas which had been established throughout the Muslim world in the tenth and eleventh centuries, there were 'significant parallels between the system of education in Islam and that of the Christian West'.[50] In fact, some scholars have claimed that the medieval university owed much to the collegiate institution of Arab education.[51] If this has been disputed, the college 'as an eleemosynary, charitable foundation was quite definitely native to Islam',[52] based on the Islamic waqf. Paris was the first western city where a college was established in 1138 by a pilgrim returning from Jerusalem; it was founded, probably copying a madrasa, as a house of scholars, created by an individual without a royal charter. So too was Balliol in Oxford before it became a corporation. We have already noted that Makdisi acknowledges the similarities between eastern and western colleges and the potential influence Islamic institutions may have had on their younger European counterparts. Nevertheless he is insistent that European universities as corporations had no equivalent, and that it is through their unique nature that modern education and science developed. The nature of the distinction between university and college is brought out by the fact that one got a hybrid institution, the college-university (as at Yale). The university was a guild, originally a corporation of masters issuing warrants (degrees), the college was a charitable trust for poor students attending the university.[53]

Needham, too, considers universities as being one institution that made the difference in the west's overcoming its backwardness in science,

---

[48] Makdisi 1981: 225.   [49] Rushdall 1936.   [50] Makdisi 1981: 224.
[51] Ribera 1928: I, 227–359.   [52] Makdisi 1981: 225.   [53] Makdisi 1981: 233.

making way for the rise of 'modern science'. But Elvin has queried the view that such institutions were absent in China, asserting that schools of higher education did exist.[54] However, while universities were institutes of higher education, not all higher education took place in universities, though the difference is certainly shaded. Institutes of higher education and learning had existed in the Ancient Near East at temple 'research institutes', in the Classical world, in ancient Persia, and virtually wherever higher literacy was installed. Like towns, universities were only European from a very narrow point of view, strongly tinged by teleology. Their existence as corporations was important in the long run but did not mean that institutions of higher learning could not function in other fashions, even though the European variety has been largely (but not universally) adopted in the modern world.

The institution that has created most controversy is the Islamic madrasa, thought of as having taken over the libraries (*dār al-'ilm*) of early Islam in a Sunni effort to bring teaching back to legal orthodoxy. The madrasas consequently concentrated upon religious education and have therefore been compared unfavourably with European schools, but many aspects of their instruction and curricula had parallels there. In any case, although madrasas were largely concerned with religious education, 'foreign sciences' (derived from Greek, Persian, Indian, and Chinese scholarship) were learned elsewhere, at libraries, courts, and at medical institutions. Moreover, European universities certainly concentrated initially upon religion and in this respect the medical concentration at Salerno and the legal studies at Bologna were unusual.

In Islam learning seems initially to have been financed privately by individual philanthropists. But institutions of learning themselves were brought into existence only after the formalization of charity by the law of waqf, of charitable foundations which were perpetual and established on a large scale in the tenth century.[55] The founding of *masjid* (mosques), where the learning of Islam began, started earlier, at least in the eighth century; the teaching of religion was endowed as a charitable foundation.

In the tenth century, Badr of Baghdad developed a new type of institution, a *masjid-khan* (inn) complex for out-of-town students. This was a prelude to the innovation of the madrasa by Nizam al-Mulk, an innovation which referred in the first place to its legal status rather than the curricula, though that was also affected; the Nizamiya itself was founded in Baghdad in 1067 CE. But neither Badr nor Nizam (both politicians) were in fact founders of these institutions, which developed gradually out of earlier schools. These were set up to encourage Sunni orthodoxy in the

---

[54] Elvin 2004.   [55] Makdisi 1981: 28.

face of the Shi'ite spread, the invasions of the Crusaders and the general need to establish Islam and its law.

Makdisi denies the status of university to the madrasa, since the latter did not form a corporation but only a charitable trust; Islam never followed the west in inventing the corporation which he regards as the great new form of perpetuity of the fourteenth century. The form of perpetuating he argues was more flexible in the west, leading to a more liberal interpretation of mortmain and, partly at least, a divergence between the two civilizations. Nevertheless the corresponding elements were many, which he lists as follows:

(1) the waqf and the charitable trust, . . . *especially* the founder establishing his charitable institution by an act of his own will without the mediation of either the central government, or the church.

(2) the madrasa and the college based on the law of the waqf or charitable trust, with their foundationers of graduates and undergraduates . . . and other corresponding elements of those institutions, inter alia, the founder's works, his freedom of choice and its limitation, the charitable object and the undeclared motives, the overseeing visitors and the beneficiaries;

(3) the will of the sovereign in creating universities in western Islam, Christian Spain and southern Italy;

(4) the development of two dialectics, one legal, the other speculative;

(5) disputation at the core of legal and theological studies;

(6) the unique status of the mudarris-professor of law in the madrasa and the professor of law in the universities of southern Europe, beginning with Bologna;

(7) the dars iftitahi and the inceptio;

(8) the mu'id and the repetitor;

(9) the shahid and the notary . . .

(10) the khadim and the student-servitor;

(11) the lectio and the two sets of three identical meanings of qara'a and legere;

(12) the ta'liqa and the reportatio;

(13) the summae . . .

(14) the craze for verification . . .

(15) the subordination of the literary arts to the three superior faculties, law, theology and medicine, brought on by a single-minded concentration on the dialectic and the disputation.'[56]

So although not a university (which he sees as a critical difference between east and west), he speaks of the east as having later 'borrowed the university system complete with Islamic elements'.[57] Earlier the borrowing may have been in the other direction, anyhow in terms of teaching. Leaving aside the corporation and the governance by masters, higher education existed in both areas. All this discussion, however, works on

[56] Makdisi 1981: 287–8.   [57] Makdisi 1981: 291.

the basis of a rather narrow conception of the university. Clearly Islam did have important institutions of higher learning for religious and legal education from an early period. Whether or not these stimulated western Europe is a moot question but there were clear parallels as there were in other advanced written cultures. But perhaps more importantly, in Islam these institutions were more or less exclusively devoted to religious studies, whereas in Europe, although religion initially dominated, other subjects were allowed to grow up within the university domain. Gradually forms of secular knowledge became increasingly important. In Islam such forms of learning had to take place elsewhere.

It is obvious that any literate culture must have schools in which to instruct the young in reading and writing, an institution in which they are taken from their 'natural' environment, looking after the cattle, guarding the younger children or fetching water in the case of the young girls, and instead confined by the limited space of a school room or place of worship where they sit in front of a master (or mistress) to learn not only to write but to remember what is contained in books (and sometimes what is contained in life). Inevitably the schools are divided into those that teach primary knowledge, which with religious schools may be confined to learning the Catechism in Christianity[58] and in Islam may be the learning by heart of the Qu'ran, the uncreated word of God. At the same time, some pupils who show themselves as particularly talented may be wanted as future masters or as administrators (since literacy is now part of society) and will be encouraged to pursue further studies. Indeed some pupils may be drawn in this direction by their own curiosity. So that a desire and a need for some form of 'higher education' became widespread in literate cultures. This would take a variety of shapes, from personal instruction to community organization, so it is not surprising that something of this kind should have been reported from China,[59] Persia,[60] Islam as well as in the ancient world.[61] It had existed in the Ancient Near East. Temple 'research institutes' in Babylon continued to operate in the Hellenistic period.[62] Childe also writes of the University of Gondēshāpur, a largely Nestorian town of doctors in Sassanian Iran (530–580), captured by the Arabs, and of the later renewal of medical and other knowledge under the Khalifs of Baghdad (750–900). This institution was critical for the continuation of the study of medicine, always privileged, among the Arabs where this form of 'ancient science' was preserved and expanded in hospital and medical schools (*maristan*) that were not subject to the restrictions of forms of religious knowledge.[63]

[58] Furet and Ozouf 1977.   [59] Elvin 2004.   [60] Childe 1964.
[61] Reynolds and Wilson 1974: 47–8.   [62] Childe 1964: 255.   [63] Makdisi 1981: 27.

For there was always a dichotomy in Islamic sciences between the 'religious' and 'the foreign' or 'ancient'. This division has led to a misunderstanding of the role of the madrasa which were Islam's institutions of higher learning. But these and their ancillary schools only looked after 'religious science'. How was it that 'foreign science', 'the sciences of the Ancestors', also flourished? Initially because there was an interplay between the traditionalist forms of the madrasa and the rationalist forms represented by the *dār al-ʿilm*, which were eventually absorbed by the former. The main obstacle for the continued pursuit of non-religious studies in endowed schools was the Islamic waqf which excluded everything pagan from the curriculum. This however did not altogether exclude the 'foreign sciences' from intellectual life in Islamic societies. They were represented in the libraries 'where Greek works were preserved, and disputations took place on rationalist subjects'[64] but that study had to be pursued privately. Thus there was access to the 'ancient sciences', which was encouraged at certain times and places, 'in spite of the traditionalist opposition, the periodic prohibitions, and autos-da-fé'. But the dichotomy in the sciences was matched by one in the institutions of learning; Islamic sciences were taught in the mosque whilst secular teaching and learning were largely confined to the private sphere.

But let us look not at origins so much as parallels of which there are many between Islam and Christian learning. Indeed in many ways it may have been Islamic methods that preceded the founding of the first European University at Bologna, teaching law, as did the Badras school in Byzantium. The *sic et non* (central to the work of the scholastics like Aquinas), the *questiones disputatae*, the *reportio*, and the legal dialectic could have their earlier Islamic parallels.[65] As Montgomery Watt remarks of Islamic influence on Europe (contra von Grunebaum): 'Because Europe was reacting against Islam, it belittled the influence of the Saracens and exaggerated its dependence on its Greek and Roman heritage. So today, an important task for our Western Europeans, as we move into the era of the one world, is to correct this false emphasis and to acknowledge fully our debt to the Arab and Islam world.'[66] That debt occurred not only in the 'natural sciences'[67] but also in the organization of learning, that is, in the institutions and in the curricula, despite the predominance of religious teaching in the madrasa and the segregation of 'ancient' (that is, modern) and religious sciences, which made the formal teaching of secular knowledge so much more difficult in Islam.

---

[64] Makdisi 1981:78.   [65] Makdisi 1981: 224.   [66] Watt 1972: 84.
[67] For a brief account, see Djebar 2005.

Humanism

In the west the history of education is bound up with the secularization of teaching, the loosening if not the freedom from religious control. This move depended in important ways on the advent of 'humanism' and the promotion of the 'pagan' authors of Greece and Rome, the revival of classical learning, which was partly due to Arab influence. In this section I want to turn to discuss 'humanism' in an educational context, its contribution to the growth of secularism, so important in the modern world, and to the part played by Islam in that movement in Europe, slightly ambiguously even before the recent 'fundamentalism'.

Despite the growth in manufacture and in trade, to look upon the Middle Ages as a progressive phase in a world-wide context (as distinct from post-collapse Europe) is to neglect the decline of literate culture as well as of urban society and its associated activities. The fall of Rome entailed a loss of literacy and literate activity which had been critical to the rapid development of post-Bronze Age societies. Secular learning developed again with the coming of humanism and eventually of the Renaissance which saw a rebirth. That was true not only of classical learning and other spheres such as architecture, but of systems of knowledge more generally. As Needham decisively demonstrates in respect of botany,[68] in the early Middle Ages there was a falling off in the general domain of scientific knowledge that accompanied a decline in urban society and its earlier schools, as well as the decrease of trade in the Mediterranean and elsewhere. The economic situation began to be reversed with the opening up of trade with the east after the first shock of the Arab conquest, but initially education revived firmly in ecclesiastical hands, excluding much of 'ancient science' as 'pagan'. That was to change with the development of communication, spatially with the east, chronologically with classical cultures, neither of them Christian.

Knowledge, education, and the arts are not of course only linked to the economy. Of great importance in Christianity, as in Islam, but not in China which had avoided domination by a single creed or hegemonic 'world religion' with important consequences for the question of humanism, was the control that religion exercised in these spheres. For religious authorities controlled education and dominated the arts, at least at the 'higher' levels. Following Judaic injunctions, Islam forbade figurative representation (including drama) over many centuries, down to today in some places. Christianity began with similar doubts but eventually permitted such activities, although until the Renaissance effectively only in

[68] Needham 1986a.

the service of religion. Earlier there was little secular drama, painting or even 'fiction'.[69] The Abrahamistic religion saw education as a branch of faith and reserved teaching largely for their own personnel.

When did the world religions give up this stranglehold over learning and teaching (which also determined the spread of religious schools)? In China, there was no hegemonic religion, apart from the emperor and ancestor worship. In Europe the process of liberation had its tentative roots in the humanist activity of the twelfth to fifteenth centuries, much influenced by Islam. In Islam the struggle between tradition and other forms of teaching was a key to understanding. It was the former that overcame the latter, especially at Baghdad (the cultural centre of Islam) and during the great Inquisition, leading to the triumph of the law and the madrasa where it was taught. The teaching of 'ancient science', as we have seen, was relegated to the private world of the individual teacher. However, far from being a negligible aspect of a religiously dominated tradition, this undercurrent of secular, 'foreign' science and knowledge erupted periodically during Islam's own humanist phases, and generally contributed to the preservation of scientific knowledge and habits of enquiry which were made available at various times to awakening Europe.

Humanism did not deny religious belief, except in some extreme forms. But it did confine its relevance and therefore drew to some extent on traditions of scepticism and agnosticism which, I have argued, are found widely in human societies.[70] In Europe, such traditions were boosted not only by humanism but later by the Reformation, which to some extent freed Europe from existing dogmas – or anyhow showed the way. Until then, the teaching of reading and writing was very firmly in the hands of the Catholic Church at all levels. The Reformation necessarily broke that monopoly, although many teachers were still clergymen and religious aims were not abandoned, just confined to a more restricted 'spiritual' sphere. This development was an important aspect of modernization, because advanced scientific enquiry, and thought generally, implied the secularization of nature so that questions could range freely in all relevant spheres, especially in institutions of higher education.

In Europe these institutions were called universities, which arose in the twelfth century. That development was part of a general revival of education in western Europe, where literacy had so badly declined. Western historians have often seen these universities as the virtual initiators of higher education, related to the independent, indigenous birth of humanism, but they were still clearly tied to the church and to the training of 'clerks', as was the case with the madrasas in Islam. However they were

---

[69] See Goody 1997.   [70] Goody 1998: chapter 11.

of great significance in Europe and for its modernization, especially when they developed a more humanistic perspective and abandoned some of their religious roles.

From the mid-fifteenth century, education itself was obviously enormously helped by the development of printing, the mechanization of writing. Printing assisted Protestantism in making the Bible more widely available. But it also helped the advance of secularism and of science by diffusing new ideas and new information. Block printing on wood arrived from China between 1250 and 1350. Paper-making came through Arab Spain in the twelfth century. About 1440 printing with moveable type, already used in the east, was developed in Mainz in Germany and the complex process of production, shifting from copyists to metal workers, spread rapidly, to Italy by 1467, to Hungary, Poland in the 1470s, and to Scandinavia by 1483. By 1500 the presses of Europe had already produced some 6,000,000 books and the continent became a much more 'learned' place, many early works being reprinted as well as much new information, assisting the project of the Italian Renaissance.

It was on the basis of the rebirth of the study of classical literature at the time of the early Renaissance in northern Italy during the fourteenth century that Europe claimed the virtues of human civilization for itself under the rubric of 'humanism'. Classical studies had been taught by educators known as early as the late fifteenth century as *umanisti*, professors or students of classical literature. The word derived from *studia humanitatis*, the equivalent significantly of the Greek *paideia*, consisting of grammar, poetry, rhetoric, history, and moral philosophy, only part of which was relevant to religious education in Christian and Islamic circles. However *humanitas* also had a wider moral significance and meant 'the development of human virtue in all its forms, to its fullest extent', that is, not only such qualities as are associated with the modern word *humanity* – 'understanding, benevolence, compassion, mercy – but also such more aggressive characteristics as fortitude, judgement, providence, eloquence, and love of honour'.[71] In other words, the positive features of humanity itself became attributed to the European Renaissance. Thus the concept took on three main meanings: (1) the return to previous written knowledge, in the case of Europe, of the classical period, (2) the development of human potential and virtues to the highest degree, and (3) the word also refers to times when religion played a relatively restricted part in intellectual activities and thus looked ahead to what today would often be seen as a desirable, 'modern' state of affairs, the triumph of secularism in most contexts, increasing free enquiry in intellectual activities.

[71] Grudin 1997: 665.

Humanism involved not only the revival of classical learning, which the Italian poet Petrarch (1304–74) saw as compatible with Christian spirituality, but also a concern with knowledge about the real world as well as the encouragement, it is claimed, of 'individualism', deemed positive for humanity; 'virtues' which are discussed in chapter 9. In addition to learning and 'virtues', there was an attempt to revive Roman institutions, the Republic itself, the crowning of the laureate, the Latin epic (as well as vernacular *canzoniere*), indeed poetry itself was now established as a 'serious and noble pursuit' (it had been downplayed in Islam as well). In fact, the name 'humanism' has been attached to other civilizations, to other periods and other places. According to Zafrani,[72] Islam itself experienced humanistic phases in the Magreb during which non-theological studies were developed, and scientific and secular knowledge was allowed a freer hand. After all Islam was a culture that sometimes reluctantly, sometimes enthusiastically, transmitted 'pagan' Greek ideas as well as Islamic ones, by means of schools of higher education, madrasas and academies. However, the major moves to secularization in schools happened later than in Christian Europe.

But secularization was also problematic in Islam where although a high valuation was placed on learning, that was largely the religious sciences. For 'in a very real sense, learning *is* worship'.[73] Moreover learning was subordinate to religious prescription, hence the very late introduction of the printing press which Islam rejected on the grounds that neither the Prophet's words nor his language should be reproduced by mechanical means. Thus despite the great achievements made by Islam in other traditional fields, that made change in the field of education not impossible but difficult. In Turkey, for example, it was only after their defeat at the hands of the Russians between 1768 and 1774, resulting in the loss of the Crimea, that the need for a drastic reform in education was acknowledged.

The leaders of the ulema, the doctors of Holy Law were therefore asked, and agreed, to authorize two basic changes. The first was to accept infidel teachers and give them Muslim pupils, an innovation of staggering magnitude in a civilization that for more than a millennium had been accustomed to despise the other infidels and barbarians as having nothing of any value to contribute, except perhaps themselves as raw material.[74]

That innovation came relatively late, although there were of course periods in Islam that have been called 'humanistic'.

---

[72] Zafrani 1994.   [73] Berkey 1992: 5.   [74] Lewis 2002: 24.

Similar phases were found in other cultures. Fernandez-Armesto has seen 'what in a western context would be called "humanism" in seventeenth-century Japan and Russia', in the first case associated with the Buddhist monk Keichu (1640–1701) who was a pioneer in the recovery of the authentic texts of the Manyoshu, poetic Shinto works of the eighth century CE. In Russia in 1648 the clerical brotherhood known as the Zealots of Piety persuaded the Tsar to banish the vulgarities of popular culture from court. Both were humanistic in the sense of advocating a return to the purity of earlier texts,[75] a religious reform for the benefit of the common people.

In Europe, too, humanism was not a one-off but a recurrent tendency. Some, such as Southern, have described twelfth-century England as 'humanistic',[76] referring largely to the renewal of interest in classical Antiquity (which had also occurred in the Carolingian period), a renewal that like the later one was also promoted by contact with Islamic learning. But what is absent in Southern's classic discussion is any treatment of possible external influences; to him all seems to be considered as internal invention. That is a highly eurocentric position. In many parts of Europe, there was considerable communication with Islamic cultures.[77] Sicily, which had been part of Muslim 'Ifriqua', was conquered by the Normans in the eleventh century, but still had a court that copied earlier Muslim ways. The king spoke Arabic and kept a harem as well as being a patron of Islamic literature and learning. He had the works of Aristotle and Averrhoes translated and distributed to European institutions. Italian vernacular literature is also said to have been born in Sicily while Arabic translations were copied by converted Christians such as the medical texts of Constantine.[78] However, more important as a link than Sicily was medieval Spain. There Christians and Muslims lived side by side, the former being known in the south as Mozarabs, and followed a Muslim style of living, even to the extent of harems and circumcision. When Toledo was captured by the Christians, the conquered and converted Muslims were then known as the Mudejars and during the twelfth century, that city became important as a centre for the dissemination of Arabic science and learning throughout Europe. Under the direction of Alphonso the Wise, Archbishop Raymond began the translation of Arab works into Spanish, and later into Latin, with the help of Mudejars and Jews, including the whole encyclopaedia of Aristotle, with commentary, as well as works by Euclid, Ptolemy, Galen, and Hippocrates.[79] Earlier, as governor of the reconquered town of Murcia, Alphonso had a school especially built for

[75] Fernandez-Armesto 1995: 279.   [76] Southern 1970.   [77] Asin 1926: 239.
[78] Asin 1926: 242.   [79] Asin 1926: 244–5.

Muhammad al-Riquat where Muslims, Jews, and Christians were taught together. Later in Seville he founded a general Latin and Arabic college at which Muslims taught medicine and science side by side with Christian professors, described as an 'interdenominational University'.[80]

It was, as Asin pointed out, an Asian culture of 'undeniable superiority'[81] that influenced Europe of that period, an influence that has been traced by him even in the great work of Dante, *The Divine Comedy*, specifically in the legends of the *hadith* about the experience of the ascension of Mohamed and the nocturnal journey to Jerusalem (*Miraj*), from which the author draws out parallels with Dante's journey to Heaven and Hell. Christian interest in Mohamed went back much further and very early on a Mozarab Christian writer (possibly Eulogius of Cordoba, d. 859 CE) actually produced a biography of Mohamed; in 1143 Robert of Reading, Archdeacon of Pamplona, also made a Latin translation of the Qu'ran. Knowledge of Islam and its mythology was therefore available. In fact, Dante's teacher, Brunetto Latini, was sent as ambassador of Florence to the court of Alphonso the Wise (1221–84) in 1260 where he would have had some exposure to that learning. Alphonso fought the Moors but nevertheless acquired Muslim learning in astronomy and philosophy. At his court the ambassador would have become acquainted with much of the literary work from Spain, so that this contact may well have led to Dante being influenced by these ideas. Indeed it has been claimed that the poet's philosophical system derived not directly from Arab philosophers themselves but from the Illuministic Mystics founded by Ibn Masarra of Cordoba (and especially from Ibn Arabi) whose ideas were transmitted to Augustinian scholastics such as Dun Scotus, Roger Bacon, and Raymond Lull.

The development of humanism was greatly assisted by the Muslim interest in the works of Aristotle who stressed the importance of studying human kind ('reality'), as distinct from faith.[82] The end of the Middle Ages saw the *reductio artis ad theologiam*, 'the reducing of everything to theological argument', as inadequate for the new situation in Europe, especially in Italy where commerce had become increasingly important, where the towns expanded and where culture and society were changing. The new education required for commerce and the bourgeoisie had its origin in the schools set up in the free cities from the late thirteenth century to cater to the needs of the urban population, rejecting the medieval tradition, and in the Renaissance turning more and more to the classical learning, much assisted by Arab translations, that developed from the

---

[80] Asin 1926: 254.   [81] Asin 1926: 244.
[82] See Peters 1968, Walzer 1962, Gutas 1998.

fourteenth to the seventeenth century. It is therefore paradoxical that the New Learning in Europe was much influenced not only in the institutions of higher education but in their move towards secularism by contact with a religious culture which also preserved secularized 'ancient science', the 'pagan' tradition of classics. But of course it also developed its own search for classical texts in Europe as well as making contact with the Greek scholarship of the Christian east at Constantinople.

For it is significant that the Renaissance and the humanist movement itself was given a great boost when an Orthodox delegation arrived from Constantinople for the interchurch council in Ferrara and Florence in 1439, seeking help against the Turkish advance. In Florence the delegation was hosted by Cosimo de Medici who was greatly impressed by the Platonic learning of the Greeks. As a result he founded the Platonic Academy which had such an influence on European learning. Leading the delegation was George Gemistus Plethon (c. 1355–1450/2), a Byzantine scholar who had studied at the Ottoman court at Adrianopolis. He introduced not only Plato but the geographer Strabo whose works helped to change European notions of space. Other scholars connected with the Academy were George of Trebizond (1395–1484), Basil Bessarion (1403–72) also of Trebizond, and Theodore Gaza, all scholars obviously coming from towns in Asia. Thus the whole movement towards humanism, secular learning, and the Renaissance gained great strength from the east and, indirectly, from cultures that were dominantly religious.

To conclude, institutions of higher education certainly differed in the west, but only relatively recently in a significant way for secular learning. In essence they were not limited to the west, nor did it have a special type that led the way to 'capitalism'. That is teleological history.

In discussing the problem of the university in the European Middle Ages, Le Goff has written 'In the beginning there were the towns. The Western medieval intellectual was born with them.'[83] This did not happen in the so-called Carolingian renascence but only in the twelfth century. But towns, intellectuals, and universities were not limited to the west, nor were the institutions fundamentally different, although they later became so. The question of universities like the question of towns is a technical matter and should be treated as such. In what respects do they differ from other institutions of higher education elsewhere? Instead it has been turned into a categorical matter where high value has been placed upon the categories. That is not the way the story of the past should be written.

---

[83] Le Goff 1993: 5.

9 The appropriation of values: humanism, democracy, and individualism

In an earlier chapter, I explained how classicists had claimed for the European Antiquity of Greece and Rome the very origin of democracy, freedom, and other values. Equally at a later period the notion of humanism and of humanistic studies was appropriated by the Occident for its own particular history. The claim was exaggerated and overlooked the question of representation, of liberties, of human values in other communities. But it is one that, even more shrilly today, the west has continued to make, arrogating to itself the effective monopoly of these virtues. One of the most disturbing myths of the west is that the values of our 'Judeo-Christian' civilization have to be distinguished from the east in general and from Islam in particular. For Islam has the same roots as Judaism and Christianity as well as many of the same values. Forms of representation existed in most societies, especially in tribal regimes, though not 'democratic' by most contemporary electoral standards. However, western democracy has hijacked many of the values that certainly existed in other societies, humanism and the triad individualism, equality, freedom, as well as the notion of charity that has been seen as a particularly Christian virtue. However there is no general agreement on what constitutes a virtuous life in the west, so this treatment will necessarily appear somewhat scrappy. I have selected some of the more prominent, talked-about qualities claimed by the west. Nevertheless, all of these western ideas about its own uniqueness need qualifying very radically.

In considering the virtues claimed by the west, 'rationality' should clearly be included. I do not do so here because I have treated the subject at length in *The east in the west* (1996); so too have many others. Some writers have seen eastern societies as lacking rationality altogether, an idea challenged (for Africa) in Evans-Pritchard's *Witchcraft, oracles and magic among the Azande* (1937). Others have sought to distinguish a western form of rationality from an earlier one, as has been done in the case of capitalism. Differences of course exist especially as I have argued between the 'logic' developed by literate societies, often of a formal academic kind, and the processes of sequential reasoning in purely oral cultures. Nevertheless the idea that the west alone has rationality or can reason logically is totally unacceptable as an account of the present or the past state of affairs.

Humanism

Nevertheless, the Whig notion of history assumes a constant progress not only in rationality but in the practice and values of human life, tending towards the emergence of more 'humanistic' goals and achievements. Living standards, technology, and science have made a constant move forward, a 'progress'. And it is commonly thought that a similar shift can be found in values. The sociologist Norbert Elias, as we have seen, writes of the emergence of the 'Civilizing process' at the time of the European Renaissance; he is discussing certain values in respect of which any vectorial movement seems more questionable.

First of all, what do we understand by humanism? We use the term in a number of ways, sometimes for the 'humanity of Christ', sometimes for the secular religion of humanity, at others for the work of those Renaissance scholars who devoted their energies to the study of the Greek and Roman classics, in other words to the 'pagan' as distinct from the Christian tradition which had long tried to set them aside. Today the term tends to refer to 'human values', which almost come to be defined as human rights and sometimes to secular rather than religious approaches as well as to the separation between political and religious power and authority. These rights are often taken for granted but certainly need to be defined (what humans, at what period, in what context? If they are rights, who has the correlative duties?).

Humanism and secularization

Europeans often trace a number of what they deem central contemporary values back not only to Antiquity but more recently to the Enlightenment of the eighteenth century. Those values are held to include tolerance,[1] hence plurality of belief, and secularism. Secularism is considered as a key to intellectual development since it freed thinking about the universe from the limitations of church dogma. One goal of modernization has been the separation of the sphere of the church from that of intellectual

---

[1] Free-thinkers like Bayle in the 1680s took China as an example of religious tolerance. Locke and Leibnitz and William Temple were equally impressed. Voltaire too praised their tolerance and saw the honour and welfare of the inhabitants as protected by the law applied throughout the empire. He attributed the reasonable nature of their government to the absence of theocratic rule (Blue 1999: 64, 89).

activity more generally, science (in the broad sense of knowledge) on the one hand and theology on the other, which parallels the separation on the political level between church and state. Secularization is interpreted not as the abandonment of religious belief but as the confinement of 'religion' to its 'proper' sphere. God is not dead but lives in his own place, the City of God. Indeed Petrarch, one of the leaders of the Italian Renaissance, saw the revival of Antiquity as reinforcing the Christian message, but for many it meant the secularization of many spheres of social activity.

What defines that proper sphere is a matter of dispute and the criteria are constantly changing. Christ declared that his followers should render unto Caesar what belonged to him. That injunction has not prevented many Christians from insisting that politics should be conducted according to Christian principles and in the same spirit. With the fall of Rome the Roman Empire became the Holy Roman Empire; the Pope and Catholic beliefs were a dominant factor in the politics of many states. With the coming of the Reformation Henry VIII was still King by the Grace of God and as a result was also the Defender of the Faith, as his descendants have remained to this day. There are even a number of contemporary European politicians who wish to define Europe as a Christian continent and so to identify polity and religion, as is common in Islam.

That aspect of the Enlightenment, the emphasis on a secular world view, was undoubtedly good for science. Think of Galileo during the Renaissance. Think of Huxley's debates with the Bishop Wilberforce about Darwinism in the mid-nineteenth century. However, not all Europe, not all individuals, were equally affected by that movement. Many people remained committed to what the secularists thought of as fundamentalist ideas. Secularism was not doing away with God but seeing him occupy less and less social and intellectual space. It was accompanied by the disestablishment of many churches, by the confiscation of church property, by the secularization of religious schools, by the decrease of church attendance, by the diminishing use of prayer. But in most politicians, most rulers, most countries still make a bow towards the dominant religion, even if that is becoming increasingly formulaic.

We would never have reached a situation where an Enlightenment in this sense had to take place, had we not been converted to a single, dominant, monotheistic religion. In Europe that religion tried to regulate the people's way of life in a very radical manner. In every village a costly church was erected, a custodian appointed, services held, births, marriages, and deaths celebrated. Villagers attended on Sundays and listened to long sermons putting forward religious themes, values, rights. There was little enough space for the secular.

Contrast the situation in earlier China. The religious tradition had no dominant player. Greater plurality obtained. Indeed Confucianism, while no stranger to morality, pursued a secular approach, rejecting supernatural explanations. It provided an alternative set of beliefs to ancestor worship, to local shrines, to Buddhism. With this plurality, an Enlightenment encouraging the freedom of secularization was hardly needed. Science pursued its course steadily and came into minimal conflict with religious beliefs. It did not seem to have experienced the same radical shifts as in Europe or the Near East under monotheistic regimes. Under neo-Confucianism, for example, plurality and secularization already existed in some considerable measure, sufficiently to allow the development of science and of alternative views. The parallels between China and Renaissance humanism are impressive, including the emphasis on ethics and literature, the recourse to the classics, the interest in editing texts, the belief that a general 'humane' education is better than a specialist training as an administrator.[2]

Indeed, a great deal of work in scientific fields was carried out in China, as Needham has shown in his magisterial series (discussed in chapter 5).[3] Elvin suggests that the somewhat secular attitude characteristic of China is later accentuated and that the mindset of the elite shows a similar move towards a disenchantment of the world in late imperial China, that is, there was 'a trend towards seeing fewer dragons and miracles, not unlike the disenchantment that began to spread across the Europe of the Enlightenment'.[4] It has also been claimed that a belief in Buddhism has some of the same consequences because of its qualified rejection of the supernatural. Those features were not simply the result of European influence.

Of course, even the monotheistic traditions allowed some science and technology to develop, just as polytheism hindered some. Here too we need a grid rather than a categorical opposition. That was especially true with Islam, despite the reported words of Caliph Omar, who declared 'if what is written [in the remaining books in the Library of Alexandria] agrees with the Book of God, they are not required, if it disagrees, they are not desired. Destroy them therefore.'[5] Nevertheless the traditions of enquiry in Greece were built upon and considerable achievements were recorded. In Europe many areas were influenced by Islamic scholarship, especially medicine, mathematics, and astronomy, which helped towards a kind of early Renaissance. The main Italian Renaissance itself also saw a move towards secularization, what Weber called the disenchantment

[2] I owe this final comment to Peter Burke.
[3] Needham 1954-.   [4] Elvin 2004: xi.   [5] Barnes 2002: 74.

of the world, especially in the arts. Following classical precedents in the Renaissance the plastic arts and the theatre freed themselves from many earlier restraints, so that non-religious themes predominated. Music too developed its secular forms at the level of high culture.

It is in the sense of secular that the word 'humanism' has sometimes been used to characterize particular periods in other, non-Christian traditions. Zafrani speaks of phases of 'humanism' in the Islamic cultures of Andalusia and the Near East, when scholars did not devote their entire attention to religious matters but also enquired into the 'sciences' and the 'arts'. He sees the same happening from time to time under Judaism. These periods again did not involve the rejection of religious beliefs but rather their containment to a more limited sphere.

However, even today, humanism has not carried all before it. There is no one-way path from the Enlightenment. While many early leaders of recently independent states were secular, that situation has ceased to be the case; in India for example, and certainly in the Near East, secular regimes have been 'changed' or threatened. Secularism has been dealt a blow in the Near East by external interference that threatens local religion. Egypt has had its difficulties with the Muslim Brotherhood, as have other countries with various Islamic groups. To some extent this movement is a rejection of humanism, a shift towards fundamentalism, partly to compensate for political threats. Nevertheless it has to be taken seriously, in Chechnya, in Ireland, in the Philippines, in Gujarat and in many other places where religious affiliation has become of central importance in a wider social and political context. Indeed the west also continues to export many thousands of missionaries to all parts of the globe, some of whom strongly resist post-Enlightenment thinking, in relation not only to secularization in general but to doctrines of evolution, monogenesis, the use of contraception, abortion, and in many other ways. Such resistance marks a percentage of the population of even the most advanced capitalist countries.

Humanism, human values, and westernization: rhetoric and practice

In the last chapter I have discussed the contribution of humanism to the education process, mainly in a European context. But we also need to look not only at a specific period but at the way in which the concept has been identified with the west as a 'human value'. It is clear that humanism, either as respect for 'human values' or as a commitment to the secular, is no recent invention of 'modern' or western societies. Human values obviously vary according to the humanity involved, but some values are widespread, for example, the notions of distributive justice, of reciprocity, of peaceful co-existence, of fertility, of well-being, even of some form of representation in government or in other hierarchies of authority, of which 'democracy', as interpreted in the west, is one variety. Modern societies are also held to be more scientific, secular, in their attitudes but as the anthropologist Malinowski pointed out,[6] a 'scientific', technological, or pragmatic approach to the world is widespread and may co-exist with religious attitudes, that is, with an approach involving a belief in the supernatural (in the definition of E. B. Tylor). Even in oral cultures we find a degree of agnosticism. In literate societies that scepticism may achieve written expression as a doctrine but is also present in oral cultures as one element of their world view, as I have tried to demonstrate with the various versions I have recorded of the long Bagre recitation of the LoDagaa of northern Ghana.[7] Even in so-called traditional societies, not everyone believes everything; indeed many myths incorporate a measure of disbelief.

But the whole notion of European colonial rule in many parts of the world was bound up with the 'humanizing' mission of educational programmes, often in the hands of religious bodies who had genuine educational goals but saw their role as one of Christianizing the population, of getting rid of local practices and introducing European standards. In this project the teaching of the classics often played an important part at the secondary level; it was always the classics of European Antiquity, perceived as allies to Christianity (as Petrarch insisted) and as inculcating a lifestyle centred on humanistic values. These efforts met with a considerable measure of success. Some of the finest European teachers in certain select secondary schools were trained in the classics at the same time as being committed to Christianity. They encouraged their best pupils to follow in their footsteps and it is significant that, leading up to Independence in 1947 when a university was established in the West African state of Ghana, the first of the colonial territories in Africa to receive its independence, the initial Department to be completely Africanized in personnel was the Department of Classics. Its head went on not only to translate Greek texts into his native language but to become the first Ghanaian head of the university and subsequently head of the UN University in Tokyo. Such was the power provided by the classics and by the 'humanities'!

With the disappearance of colonialism some politicians have associated the emergence of 'humanism' with the process of globalization which is also seen as one of westernization. One widespread contribution to such

---

[6] Malinowski 1948.   [7] Goody 1972b.

an outcome has been the world-wide movement for Independence after the Second World War. Many of the early leaders of the new nations were of a secular bent – well-educated individuals such as Nehru in India, Nkrumah in Ghana (the first of the new leaders of sub-Saharan Africa), Kenyatta in Kenya, Nyerere in Tanzania, Nassar in Egypt. They opposed the Western colonial powers and won their independence (their 'freedom'), adopting their opponents' value-laden slogans in the process of so doing. I well remember a demonstration in the early 1950s in the town of Bobo-Diolassou in the French colonial territory of Upper Volta (now Burkina Faso) where an orderly mass of African workers surrounded by French police were demonstrating, carrying banners proclaiming 'Liberté, Egalité, Fraternité'.

These movements were supported by the western powers and by the United Nations in the name of liberty and democracy, the expression of the will of the people. Commentators and politicians tend to see the values associated with them, such as respect for human dignity, as being imported to communities that previously lacked them. At the same time these outside bodies, like everybody else, often fail to live up to their own proclaimed standards. For example the USA was also interested in promoting its own agenda which was partly dictated by its enormous consumption of oil and by its desire to protect its 'way of life', 'capitalism', against possible Soviet expansion, even if the latter was achieved by majority rule. The Near East in particular suffered from this Cold War and the help given to 'non-democratic' regimes that supported some of these aims. In the course of containing communism and of securing its oil, one commentator writes, 'The USA spared no efforts to back, promote and even impose regimes in the domain of Islam which were thoroughly corrupt and contrary to all the democratic and liberal values in defence of which the USA claims to act.'[8] In other words there was a gross discrepancy between the rhetorically proclaimed value of democracy and the actual policy pursued.

We are constantly faced by declarations of universal 'humanistic' values by politicians and individuals alike, and yet their constant breach in specific situations. Take two contemporary examples. Laid down in the Geneva Convention are strict rules about the treatment of combatants and civilians captured in war. Recently the US and allied forces that invaded Afghanistan and Iraq transported a number of prisoners to Guantanamo Bay in Cuba where the US has an extra-territorial base and where they have been kept in frightening conditions. Following the declaration that these captives of varied nationalities could not be considered

[8] Saikal 2003: 67.

prisoners-of-war and that the Cuban base was not US territory, the inmates have been denied full international rights or indeed even rights under US law. In other words they were denied 'freedom', the access to lawyers, and their 'human rights' generally, a situation subsequently condemned by the UN.[9] A similar contradiction took place with the capture of Saddam Hussein on 13 December 2003 after he had been caught hiding 'like a rat', according to one coalition spokesman. Despite earlier protests at their prisoners being displayed on television, held to be contrary to the Geneva convention, pictures showed the former ruler, who as the commander-in-chief was entitled to be treated as a prisoner of war, having his hair searched for lice and his mouth being given a detailed inspection, no doubt for hidden objects. Such pictures undoubtedly breached the Geneva convention regarding the public humiliation of prisoners.

The second instance has to do with the recent bombing of Tikrit (and other towns) in response to the death of American soldiers in the neighbourhood, some months after President Bush had announced the end of hostilities. Such collective punishment, of the kind often carried out by Israeli troops in Palestinian communities under their control, is exactly what the Allies protested and acted against during the Second World War when the German forces took collective action against villages and communities after they had come under attack, for example, at the Ardeantine caves in Italy or in the village of Oradour in France. Those actions were considered to be war-crimes and led to international punishment.

In sum, the west has laid claims to a set of values centring around the concept of humanism and humane behaviour. While there have undoubtedly been some changes over time that could be so characterized, all societies have standards of what they regard as humane. Sometimes these are phrased in universalistic terms, such as 'thou shalt not kill'. But such statements are often rhetorical and apply only to certain groups, not to the 'other', the enemy, the terrorist, the traitor. That is very clear in wartime where such widespread values are often suppressed or upturned, despite the best efforts of bodies like the International Red Cross to ensure their maintenance in the contemporary world.

Democracy

One of the main features of newly 'emergent humanisms' is 'democracy' which has been closely tied to the notions of 'freedom', 'equality', civic

---

I have to admit that having had these rights largely respected when I was a prisoner of war of the Fascists in Italy and of the Nazis in Germany, I feel strongly on this issue. Obviously in those countries worse things happened to political prisoners.

participation, and 'human rights'. Clearly as far as representative government goes, there has been some general movement towards a new participation in many parts of the world over recent centuries. But that movement needs to be seen in perspective. Early groups certainly had much direct participation. Today matters have become more complex. Greater participation in voting is accompanied by less practical participation in other areas because the government in which humans are participating has become more complex, more remote, and embracing more people. That means greater professionalization of politicians and less direct representation.

A wider problem arises when democracy today is viewed as a universal value of which the contemporary western world is the primary custodian and the only model. But is it? Let me begin by suggesting that democratic procedures have to be viewed contextually, in relation to specific institutions. I have heard members of the contemporary work-force argue that there is no democracy in the workplace. Certainly there is only a limited amount in the institutions of learning. But compare the contemporary workplace with that existing under conditions of simple agriculture. My Ghanaian friend whom I took to visit a local factory in England saw women standing in line over a workbench, punching a 'clock' on entering and leaving the workplace. 'Are they slaves?' he asked me in his own language. His own labour in the fields was of a much 'freer' kind, that did not involve relationships of authority.

In Ancient Greece, the concept of democracy referred to 'the rule of the people', and stood in opposition to autocracy or even 'tyranny'. The will of the people was determined by elections, but they were limited to 'free' males, excluding slaves, women, and resident strangers. So in the political context democracy in Europe has in the past also been frequently restricted. Today, in what is seen as 'full democracy', every man and woman has a single vote and the elections take place at regular, arbitrary, intervals. There is an 'individualization' of representation, although research shows that husband and wife tend to vote the same way but no longer as a household or lineage. In this form the practice of democracy is new. In Britain, voting was only widened in 1832 to include male householders, while women did not achieve the vote until after the First World War, in France much later. Even in the USA, supposedly the epitome of modern democracy in the eyes of de Tocqueville, George Washington advocated confining participation in elections to white 'gentlemen', that is, to land owners and college graduates. In each case there was earlier a severely restricted franchise. The use of the ballot box and of the selection it entails is dependent on the view that the choice is free and unencumbered; the French left at first rejected female suffrage on the grounds that women would be too prone to vote as the clergy told them.

Even now there are some technical problems about the interpretation of choice, as was remarked in the US election in Florida in November 2000, as well as about the question of what a majority consists of, for instance, simple or overall, by number of votes or by number of units (states). Secondly the matter is further complicated by the problem of coercion, whether by the offer of pre-election bribes as in eighteenth-century England, or by post-election rewards, the extent to which promises of future benefits are part of the process itself. Differential access to publicity because of political control of the radio (as in Russia) or economic control by means of finance (as in USA) can also limit the optimal scope of freedom of choice.

In the west, electoral democracy is now seen not simply as one among a number of alternative modes of representation, but is regarded as a form of government suitable for introduction in all places and at all times.[10] In that sense it has taken the form of a universalized value. The object of the contemporary western powers has been to promote democracy and to do away with regimes such as those in the USSR or in Yugoslavia that did not meet the criteria, although those regimes objected that political freedom of choice was not the only value to be considered. At Independence in Africa, the colonial rulers insisted on handing over power to elected governments, according to what in British terms was labelled the Westminster model, in order to ensure popular consent. In fact these forms of government did not persist, as I have mentioned, partly because people voted along 'tribal' or sectarian lines. They were followed by one-party rule, deemed essential by the rulers to consolidate the new state, and then by military coups as the only way to change a one-party regime. For many a new state, the main political problem has not been the shift towards democracy but that of establishing a central government over a territory that had none before. That remains very difficult where the state includes groups defined by primordial characteristics, tribal or religious, which may inhibit the establishment of a 'party' government in the western sense but does not exclude those groups themselves from having their own representative ('democratic') procedures.

Israel was a partial exception to this sequence (as too were India and Malaysia). It is lauded as the only democratic state in the Near East,

---

[10] One of my interlocutors in Alexandria objected to the description of democracy as a form of representation, claiming it was 'a form of culture'. However, even where electoral procedures are used in the political sphere, they rarely obtain in other contexts, such as employment or the family.

though that form of government has done nothing to inhibit its enormous accumulation of armaments and soldiery to defend itself and to threaten others; this small country has twelve divisions, one of the largest airforces in the world, and the nuclear weapons that are forbidden to or frowned upon in other powers. Nor does it inhibit the frequent selection of former soldiers to lead a civilian government (as in the USA), nor yet prevent atrocities as in the Arab village of Deir Yasin, in the camps of Sabra and Shatilla in the Lebanon, or more recently in Jenin on the West Bank. Nevertheless by placing it in the category 'democratic', it is automatically contrasted with the 'corrupt', authoritarian government of the Palestinians who like most other Arabs are considered never to have known 'true democracy'.

Such an unambiguous preference for one form of government regardless of context is new. In Ancient Greece, in Rome too, over time there were major changes in regime, which shifted between 'democracy' and 'tyranny', or between a republic and an empire, just as has happened in Africa since Independence. Even in Europe, there was no widely held view until the eighteenth century, and even later, that democracy was the only acceptable form of government. There were shifts of various kinds, not necessarily of a violent nature. Force was sometimes used. Radical changes in forms of government have been denied for earlier social formations. Rebellion occurred but not revolution; that is, people rebelled in order to change the incumbents but not the socio-political system itself.[11] The validity of that statement is not always clear. In many such societies, there were shifts in the mode of government as well as of representatives. It is true that the overthrow of the entire system according to a prepared plan was rare in earlier societies, especially in pre-literate ones. But there has often been some oscillation not only within centralized regimes, but between them and those tribal ones that are described as segmentary, or between the location of power at the centre or at the periphery. Change in the nature of government was characteristic of earlier regimes, when 'democracy' was only one of the possibilities.

When we speak of democratic procedures, we think of the ways in which the opinion of people should be formally taken into account. There are many ways of doing this. In the west, the electorate are consulted by secret (usually written) ballot every four, five, or six years. The number is arbitrary. It is a compromise between testing the opinions of the *demos* and pursuing a consistent policy over a given period. Some have argued that the public should be consulted more frequently, especially on major issues like a declaration of war, which in Britain does not even require a vote of

[11] Gluckman 1955.

Parliament because of the fiction of the royal prerogative (yet the adoption of the Euro does!). It is difficult to argue that we live in a democracy (i.e., under the rule of the people) when governments can decide a major course of action such as war against the will of the majority. On the other hand, should we be ruled by constant referenda and opinion polls? Or does chaos lie in that direction? It could be argued that democracy is only really ensured by the ability to recall representatives when they cease to represent, so that the will of a people could throw out a government about to engage in war against the wishes of a majority of the country. If this 'true democratic' possibility had been available, a number of European governments would have been toppled at the outset of the invasion of Iraq.

However it could also be argued that some social programmes require a longer period to inaugurate than four or five years and that a regime should therefore be chosen for a more extended period. That was frequently the claim in post-Independence Africa, for example, when some elected governments turned themselves into one-party regimes. Of course there is nothing to stop a government from being elected for a number of successive occasions to enable it to carry out a more extensive programme, but what if the electors themselves 'choose' a government to be selected for a long term or indeed permanently?

Modern democracy does present a number of problems even for democrats. Hitler was elected by the German people and proceeded to turn the regime into a dictatorship. Communist parties, too, may have been elected in the first place but have had no hesitation in setting up 'a dictatorship of the proletariat'. What is an elected dictatorship? It is a regime that has postponed or abandoned 'normal' elections and suppressed the opposition, though it may make use of referenda. But what if it has done so with the consent or choice of the majority? The problem for democrats is that one-party regimes and similar systems do not allow for electoral change.

Another problem is that the proponents of democracy allow no system other than their chosen procedures to count as 'the rule of the people'. But such consultation could involve choosing a leader by acclamation rather than by vote. Even voting procedures may be thought to represent the will of God rather than of the people, as in elections in the Vatican or in Cambridge colleges where the votes for a Pope or a Master are recorded in the chapel. The choice between political parties, which are implied by an electoral system, has not met with great success in much of Africa where tribal and local loyalties are of greater relevance. Nor in other parts of the world, such as Iraq, where 'fundamental' religious beliefs or linguistic identifications are involved.

If the term 'democracy' refers to the kind of recurrent electoral procedure developed most prominently in Europe in the nineteenth century, it constitutes only one possible form of representation. Most political regimes of whatever kind have some mode of representation. It is perhaps possible to visualize in the abstract an authoritarian regime that is completely autocratic, but if it does not in some way take into account the wishes of the people, its days are likely to be numbered, even under what are called dictatorships or despotisms. For example, it has been remarked that in early China neither the Ch'in nor Wang Mang probably deserved their reputation for despotism; there were a number of checks and balances. The classical texts themselves formed a check on government, as with the writings of Confucius, referred to in chapter 4. And as a result the literati often found themselves in opposition to the current regime.[12]

There are a number of situations in which modern states have not seen democracy as universally appropriate, even in politics. In some parts of the USA, until recently the black population had no right to vote in a country where everyone else had an entitlement. Nationally this substantial minority was eventually given the vote. Had they been in a majority, it is doubtful if the white population would have voluntarily agreed to this. The country would have remained an apartheid regime as in earlier South Africa.

In Palestine, towards the end of the British mandate, the government proposed a single-state solution to the Jewish-Arab question and tried to establish an assembly based on democratic principles. The Jewish population rejected this offer since they were in a minority. Later on, when most of the Arabs had left or been driven out in the territory of newly formed Israel, they established a 'democracy' with reduced rights for those Muslims who remained; today those who had left have been refused 'the right of return', a right that the Jews themselves had loudly proclaimed but which in the present case would threaten their 'democratic' majority. In religiously, 'racially', or ethnically divided states, one 'man', one vote is not necessarily an acceptable solution; the principle of one man, one vote may lead to a permanent majority or even to 'ethnic' cleansing, as in Cyprus. Where full democracy is attempted under these conditions, it may create a struggle for increased demographic reproduction in order to gain a majority, as many Protestants in Northern Ireland believe to be the case with the Catholics.

Is democracy, for example, the answer for contemporary Iraq? It could be argued that with heavily divided religious and ethnic communities, one should opt for 'power sharing', as was recently done in Northern

---

[12] Nylan 1999: 70, 80ff.

Ireland, so that there is no permanent majority of one group (the Shia or the Protestant) over another but rather a 'consociational democracy', a very different institution. In Ancient Greece, the vote was limited to citizens. The notion of citizenship, often associated with liberal and even revolutionary regimes, may in practice involve the exclusion of a large category of non-citizens. 'Civus Romanus sum' implies that there are residents of the same territory that do not share equal rights, like Turkish immigrants in Germany until recently, or any immigrant or indeed sojourner in Switzerland or in India who is unable to purchase land or house. Citizenship is an excluding as well as an including concept.

But even within the notion of citizenship, the semi-permanent attachment of the majority, to a specific religious group for example, may mean the effective exclusion of similar, less numerous groups on a long-term basis. In order to counter a relatively permanent imbalance which virtually excludes the short-term changing of votes on which 'full democracy' depends, there may, as we have seen, be a resort to power-sharing to ensure representation (and thus social 'order' or acquiescence). Another 'quasi-democratic' technique is 'positive discrimination' which gives additional privileges, perhaps in a national assembly, perhaps in training, to certain underprivileged minority groups. This procedure has been accepted for blacks in the USA, for women elsewhere under certain 'electoral' arrangements, but the first example on a national scale known to me was its introduction for 'scheduled castes' in the Indian constitution of 1947 which was largely written by Dr Ambedkar, himself by origin belonging to an untouchable caste and who felt that his community would not receive 'fair' treatment under a Hindu government controlled by other castes.

Despite these problems, today's climate has seen democracy become a highly value-laden concept considered to have universal applicability. But while democracy is held in great regard rhetorically and looked upon (mistakenly) as the invention of European cultures, the practice is somewhat different. Even the reference has changed. Whereas originally it meant the rule of the people, the meaning has narrowed and it now refers quite specifically to regimes where parliaments are elected every four or five years by universal secret ballot. Even so, the notion has become questioned under some circumstances. Not all elections are considered 'democratic' by the west. Under Arafat, the Palestinians had an elected leader who offered to submit himself to re-election. On 24 June 2003 President Bush of the United States suggested a peace plan for the Middle East, the first item of which was that the Palestinians should elect a new leader because Arafat was tainted with terrorism. So too of course was the former Israeli Prime Minister, Begin, and some would argue Sharon as well. One may hope for different leaders in a foreign country, but to demand the 'democratic' replacement of elected politicians as a condition of negotiation (as in the case of Hamas) is arrogant in the extreme, not democracy at all but the expression of the dictatorial demands of a dominant world power who regards interference in the running of other countries as a legitimate aspect of its foreign policy. In the recent past such a policy has openly supported dictators rather than democratically chosen leaders and even today has little difficulty in allying itself to the strongly centralized monarchy of Saudi Arabia or to the military rulers of post-coup Pakistan.

One major excuse for invading Iraq was that the regime was undemocratic, indeed a brutal dictatorship. There does not exist any international agreement on the nature of the kind of government a country must adopt. Before the Second World War the governments of both Germany and Italy came into power as the result of democratic elections. That was not true of Spain, but the Allies made no attempt to depose Franco after the war, even though he came into office as the result of a fascist military coup and a bloody civil war. So did many of the governments of Africa, some in South America and elsewhere (Fiji, for example). On the other hand, the presence of a democratic government in the Caribbean island of Grenada did not prevent it being invaded by the USA, even though it was a Commonwealth territory associated with its closest ally.

The 'democracy' that exists at home is rarely applied on a world scale. Electoral practice operates very differently in decision-making at an international level. In the General Assembly of the United Nations, delegates are chosen by governments and each has a single vote irrespective of the number of inhabitants – one government, rather than one person, one vote. The eighteen-member Security Council is elected by the Assembly, with the exception of five permanent members, the victor nations in the Second World War, each of whom has a veto. It is a 'legal' system created by the victors. In that Council, majority decisions do not count because of the veto. In any case the dominating powers, and specifically the one superpower, may use their resources, military, economic, cultural, to put pressure on others to vote the way they wish, using methods that would be condemned within a national parliament. In a recent instance the representatives of a number of European countries, including Bulgaria and Romania, sent a letter to the White House approving the US line in Iraq. These representatives apparently meet regularly in Washington where they are 'advised' by an American official who has worked in intelligence. It was he who wrote the letter on behalf of the states who were at the same time candidates for NATO, for which they have to be approved by the US government.[13] The decision to offer support was made without any consultation of their own people, who would almost certainly have objected. The same is true of Prime Minister Blair of Britain who felt no obligation to consult the electorate on the war in Iraq, since he had decided his position was the right one, whatever others might think. That was also Bush's position. Moreover those who take an alternative line are not only condemned, that is to be expected. But sanctions of various kinds may be taken against them. It was intimated that if other nations did not take part in the war against Iraq, they would have no say in post-war decisions which were clearly to be made not by the UN but by the superpower and its allies. Russia, France, and China were to have no future access to Iraqi contracts or to its oil (as they had done under Saddam Hussein), whose disposition would be in the hands of the victors. 'Law' was the product of war.

Such discriminatory measures hardly respect the legitimate right and freedom to choose between alternative courses of action, which is basic to democracy and to the rule of the people. Indeed we are left with the rule of force. On a more domestic level those measures did not await the end of the war. A discussion on the news programme CNN[14] raised the possibility that the US should give up drinking French wines (in favour of Australian, a country whose government was giving its support to the war in Iraq), and predicted also that the sales of Mercedes cars would also decline. Even the names of dissident countries were sometimes taboo: on some menus 'French fries' became 'freedom fries', freedom being associated with participation in the war. The dominant position of the US in the cinema, on TV, in the world media generally, ensured that its situation was constantly explained in its own terms. There do seem to be arguments of a democratic kind in favour of restricting the ownership and control of mass media, to limiting the role of money (as well as of arms) in influencing the people's choice. But the world-wide electronic media can hardly be restrained in this way. Nevertheless democracy rests on the notion of effective 'freedom of choice'. Money and monopolies clearly affect that freedom when on an international level voting may be influenced by loans or gifts and nationally when candidates are chosen from those who can afford the publicity or the price of drinks to offer to the voters. In general the international situation differs substantially from the national; the democratic system is contextually applied. A former secretary of the United Nations recently remarked in an article entitled 'The United States against the rest of the World' that 'the most important argument can be summarized in a formula inspired by

---

[13] *Herald Tribune* 20/02/03.   [14] *Herald Tribune* 20/02/03.

the philosopher Pascal. "Democracy within the United States; authoritarianism outside".[15] At an international level, democratic powers do not respect democratic procedures.

The notion that democracy only emerged as a feature of modern, indeed western, societies is a gross simplification as is the attribution of its origin to the Greek city-states. Obviously Greece provided a partial model. But many early political systems, including very simple ones, embodied consultative procedures designed to determine the will of the people. In a general sense the 'value' of democracy, though sometimes held in abeyance, was frequently, if not always, present in earlier societies and specifically emerged in the context of opposition to authoritarian rule. What the modern world did was to institutionalize a certain form of election (choice) – initially for certain political reasons because the people were required to contribute actively to national expenditure in the form of taxes. It was to raise that money that parliament had to be called. General taxation was hardly possible without some form of representation, as the American colonies effectively proclaimed. The particular forms so lauded in the west are, however, not always the most effective to secure adequate representation; the promotion of the Westminster model did not prove a universal panacea even at a national level. Internationally, there is a long way to go before electoral procedures are accepted rather than imposed by force or by other sanctions.

Individualism, equality, freedom

Associated with democracy are three values which form a triad in European thinking and are often proposed as the exclusively European causes – or effects – of exclusively European developments in the arts, the sciences, and the economy. They are constantly on call throughout the humanities, in literary criticism for example, in the discussion of the rise of the novel and of autobiography as the paradigmatic genre of individualism, to mention just a few instances.[16] Individualism has also been claimed by the west as contributing to the entrepreneurship deemed central to capitalism. As we discuss in the next chapter, individualism involves a certain freedom of personal choice (as distinct from collective responsibilities), which comes to the fore in contemporary questions of marriage and the nuclear family, and is again held to be particularly European. Freedom of this kind is often equated with the irrelevance of family ties in the choice of partners. But total freedom from family ties is not what actors experience, for they soon create alternative bonds. Children may depart

[15] *Unità* 22/04/03.   [16] Watt 1957.

relatively early from their natal household, but shortly after they do so, they establish strong links with others, a lover, a spouse, and eventually with their own children; at the same time they maintain ties over distance (interrupted by visits and frequent communication by letters, telephone, and e-mail) with their parents and with their siblings. Indeed it has been suggested by Laslett and others that in Europe fission of this kind may even strengthen closer attachments within the conjugal family as distinct from wider ties of kinship. That view of stronger attachments in the west within the conjugal family does not appear to be altogether consistent with the notion of the ('free') isolated individual making his way against the world, in the manner of Robinson Crusoe or other mythical heroes of the continent, such as Faustus. The ideological inconsistency becomes totally apparent in the notion that our economy is created by individual entrepreneurs. For that is far from the reality. In fact, family firms still play a very important role even today.[17]

That triad of values, individualism, freedom, equality, is not confined to Europe. It has recently been pointed out[18] that equality and freedom together with love are fundamental features of the ethical teaching of Islam, as is a concern for the individual. Equality Yalman sees as a 'fundamental aspect' of the 'culture of Islam'. Certainly it is 'translated' into practice in the notion of open access to opportunities for people and the absence of a religious group (a priesthood) with privileged access to divine truths. This 'value' does not mean there is no inequality among Islamic peoples. 'In practice, inferiority and superiority are as much a part of daily Islamic experience as any other.'[19]

Yalman draws the contrasts between a highly idealized formula relating equality and love in Islam on the one hand, and hierarchy and renunciation in India on the other. But ideology and practice are often very different. As mentioned above, Yalman recognizes that equality has not always been achieved by Islamic states and, on the other hand, he quotes a comment noting that even in the rigid caste societies of India, dominated by a supposedly permanent hierarchy, the presence of *bhakti* means that the ranking may be modified and those who have fallen from twice-born status may be brought to a higher condition.[20] Equally, love is a feature of Indian as well as of Muslim society and is not confined to one or the other; he refers to the great Hindu traditions of sexual love, for instance, of the gopis for Krishna, and he might well have mentioned love in the body of Sanskrit poetry. So that similarity constitutes a 'point of profound contact in Hindu and Muslim devotionalism', and he goes on to claim

---

[17] Goody 1996a: 192ff.   [18] Yalman 2001.
[19] Yalman 2001: 271.   [20] Hopkins 1966; Yalman 2001: 277.

that in the Hindu case, like equality, love is a minor theme of a great civilization, as we shall discuss in the next chapter.[21] How far removed this assessment is from the usual European prejudices about these societies (and their views regarding equality and love)! What Yalman shows is as it were a Hegelian interpenetration of opposites, the practice of both societies displaying features that run against not only the stereotypes of outsiders but to some extent their own dominant ideologies.

So we need to modify the stark contrast regarding equality (and fraternal love) in these ideologies by taking into account the similar features that accompany them in practice. Compared to Africa, which has experienced a different developmental trajectory involving less social differentiation, both the Islamic society of Turkey and the Hindu society of India are representative of the post-Bronze Age cultures of Eurasia all of which are heavily stratified, literate, and for the most part based on unequal access to valuable land and other resources, as well as upon military prowess. However, the inequalities in those forms of stratification may be qualified by written religious ideologies. Islam does something to loosen and even oppose the secular stratification; there is the encouragement of charity (an aspect of fraternal love) from the better-off, occasionally a revolt of the poor, even if no effective redistribution occurs. Indeed charity of this individual kind may be said to reinforce the status quo. In India the secular hierarchy is supported by the religious ideology, but not unambiguously since, rather than the political-military rulers, it is the literate priesthood who conducts the religious rites, who are considered to stand at the top of the hierarchy. The secular rulers follow. The same is broadly true in Islam, though they do not have a priesthood as such, only a group of men learned in the sacred text. And learning is said to be more important than political power.[22]

In India too the class divide is modified by charity, as in Islam, by acts of giving, as when in a Congress-dominated village in Gujarat, I saw the harijan, formerly the untouchables, queuing up to obtain the whey left-over from the yoghurt-making activities of the 'peasant' Patels. More significant however are those aspects of religion, *bhakti* and Krishna-worship, that display positive egalitarian characteristics. And there has always been some outright opposition to the hierarchy of others, especially in the long tradition of Indian atheistic thought which included Dalit (untouchable) resistance to the caste system where they found themselves at the bottom of the pile. That opposition was typified in Pune by the counter-activities in the nineteenth century of Mahatma Phule, a low-caste flower merchant, who founded a girls' primary school, and later by

---

[21] Yalman 2001: 277.   [22] Berkey 1992: 4.

the work of Dr Ambekhar, leader of the harijan under Mahatma Gandhi, who drafted the Indian constitution to include the positive discrimination we have mentioned but eventually led his group away from Hinduism and into Buddhism. Both Buddhism and Jainism had grown out of Hinduism but rejected the caste system. That is why Ambedkhar could successfully lead the former untouchables back to Buddhism, to an Indian religion which had little following in that country and therefore fewer internal political implications.

The notion of equality was certainly not confined to Europe but was present in Hindu society, even if not always prominent in Brahman religious thought, just as the practice and to some extent the ideology of hierarchy existed in Islam. These contrary tendencies of equality and hierarchy are mirrors of each other within each society; the beliefs may display contrasting aspects, but considered in a wider frame both trends are present not only in both societies but in Christianity as well. How and why? Because these societies, being dependent upon advanced agriculture and its commercial and artisanal concomitants, are heavily stratified from a socio-economic point of view as well as having political and religious-educational stratification in relation to the use of the written word and to the holy scriptures more generally. But such stratification is often seen as contrary to what are virtually pan-human notions of equality among humans (e.g. among siblings, among brothers and sisters) which run as a counter-current in hierarchical societies and are based on the idea of distributive justice. From the standpoint of the family, equality is associated with relations between siblings ('all men are brothers') or between partners, rather than between parents and children (prototypically fathers and sons, as with Oedipus).[23] One set involves inequality, the other equality, and both are built into social relationships from the family outwards. Both involve love, one set fraternal or sororal as well as 'sexual' love, which is between equals, a lateral relationship. The other relates to parental love and its complement, which is hierarchical, between unequals. The imposition of hierarchy by the father or parent is countered by claims to equality on behalf of the brother or sibling. These claims may dominate the lifestyles of a person or of a community, or they may constitute a distant point of reference that does little to prevent one continuing to act in a rapacious or consumerist manner. We are well acquainted with these contradictions in ideological and practical behaviour from our own daily lives, as when we decry the pollution that cars make to the environment and jump into our Nissan to go down to the supermarket (which we decry as having taken over the small, personalized shops).

[23] See Mitchell 2003.

Like equality, the notion of freedom[24] was widespread in human societies. It is a concept that depends upon context and is not confined to
the west. The Englishman, Sir Adolphus Slade, who served as an officer
under the Ottoman Navy in the 1820s, wrote: 'Hitherto the Osmanly
has enjoyed by custom some of the dearest privileges of the freemen, for
which Christian nations have so long struggled.' He paid a very limited
land-tax, no tithes, needed no passport, encountered neither customs nor
police . . . 'from the lowest origins he might aspire without presumption
to the rank of pasha'. He compares this freedom, 'this capacity of realis-
ing the wildest wishes', to the achievements of the French revolution.[25]
There are many practical significances in this situation. You could make a
slave a Muslim, but you could not make a Muslim a slave. Equally a new
convert, as for example an Albanian boy taken to Istanbul as a devirsne,
could rise to the highest offices in the land, bar that of Sultan.

Yalman explains how the notion of freedom is connected to that of
equality. The 'high ideals of Islam', he notes,

do turn around the principle that there are no privileged persons in Islam, or rather
that a person's worth depends upon the morality of his/her intentions, behaviour
and piety. This may lead to the gates of heaven, but even in the worldly kingdoms,
all people, once converted to the belief of Islam – i.e., having 'surrendered' (*teslim*)
to the will of God – must be given an equal chance to rise in society. Hence
the promise of Islam, for instance, to Black Muslims in America and oppressed
peoples elsewhere?[26]

As we have seen, while the major 'virtues' of individualism, equality, and
freedom are often seen as basically European, as part of the continent's
cultural heritage that enabled it to move forward to modernization before
the rest of the world, this idea is built on shaky foundations. 'The freedom
of subjects to pursue their understanding' has long been seen as a feature
of modern capitalism. But, as Wallerstein points out,[27] the absence of
constraints may mean the opposite, that is, 'the elimination of guarantees for reproduction', setting aside rights derived from heritage, leaving
it uncertain how great the difference is between 'capitalism' and past systems.[28] In different forms these attributes are found in other societies, no
only advanced literate ones, although there the ideologies are inevitably
more explicit. Nevertheless, ideologically Europeans try to appropriate

---

[24] But freedom is even more complex than described. Caroline Humphries has recentl
analysed Russian concepts of freedom in the post-Communist era as compared with th
west. There are two concepts that can be used to translate the English word, *slobude* an
valya. The first refers to the freedom to pursue political goals, the second to the freedor
to pursue personal ones.
[25] Quoted in Yalman 2001: 271.   [26] Yalman 2001: 271.
[27] Wallerstein 1999: 16.   [28] Wallerstein 1999: 16–17.

for themselves the positive aspects of these notions, which also have their negative features, fraternity involving the strife between brothers, and love, the hatred that may follow the end of intimacy. The apparently straightforward virtues are in fact more complex than is often thought, especially that of fraternity (fraternal love) which, through charity, tends to modify the hierarchical inequalities of state systems.

Charity and ambivalence regarding luxury

One central aspect not so much of humanism, but of humanity or human values is the notion of charity. St Paul proclaimed that the great virtues were 'faith, hope and charity and the greatest of these is charity'. The Latin *caritas* has been translated both as charity and as love, love for one's fellow human beings; the sexual aspect of love I discuss in the following chapter. Charity is a virtue that was extended above all to one's fellow Christians and sometimes said to be uniquely associated with Christianity. But in fact all the major written religions solicited support and needed to attract funds for charitable purposes, for the maintenance of buildings of worship, as well as for the personnel required to staff the institution. So it was inevitable that they sought to acquire wealth, especially from the richer members of society. If an individual had an excess of wealth, it should be given for God's work (or for the Buddha or other agency). At the same time, poverty was in principle praiseworthy. The rich man had difficulties entering the kingdom of Heaven (unless he gave away his goods). The poor man had far fewer problems; he or she was a worthy recipient of charity, of gifts made ultimately by the rich but mediated by the church. So charity was never a purely Christian virtue. It is found in equal measure among Muslims, among Hindus, among Parsis, Jains, and Buddhists. For Muslims, charity was a sacred duty, one of the five pillars of Wisdom. In West Africa, personal charity was exercised every Friday when *saddaqa* was given to the poor or to the worthy. In Mediterranean lands, where there was greater 'class' differentiation and a different system of land holding, more substantial charitable gifts (*waqf*) were donated either to support a mosque and its associated institutions, a hospital, a caravanserai, a market, a madrasa (college) or else to a family trust to aid those in need. Similar provisions were made in all other world (written) religions where giving to a beggar or to a monk was a mark of merit. Building almshouses and supplying food as well as shelter for the poor were important gifts an individual could make, possibly cancelling out earlier misdeeds.

In this way, both the poor and the church were provided for. Indeed in Christianity poverty was claimed to be a holy state in itself. That is not to say that in these cultures there was no striving for riches, for luxury. Indeed in some self-justifying accounts, the rich are seen as necessary to help support the poor, just as rich nations are necessary to support the less well-off. But the priesthood, the princes of the church, were as engaged in luxury behaviour and in acquiring luxury objects as anyone else. However, there was always a degree of ambivalence about the very existence of such luxury, with not only religious doctrines but philosophers like Mencius too, proclaiming that luxury was unnecessary to human life as well as being harmful and in some cases positively evil. Yet it was certainly the aim of the powerful, whether in ecclesiastical or in lay society, whether merchant, farmer, or professional, to accumulate wealth in order to be able to behave in a special way. The two trends were therefore at odds, producing ambivalence in many, which was resolved for some by the practice of asceticism, by the negation and even destruction of luxurious objects, as in the notable case of St Francis of Assisi. In his youth Francis was devoted to gaiety, to chivalry, to ostentatious prodigality. Illness turned his attention to another dimension of life. Devoting himself to poverty, he took a vow never to refuse alms to a beggar. However, he abandoned his inheritance and wore only a single brown tunic of coarse woollen cloth, tied with a hempen cord. The saint subsequently founded the Franciscan order which, like others, was based on the three vows of poverty, chastity, and obedience. Of these, poverty was the most important (inviting charity) and the order repudiated all idea of owning property.

The widespread ambivalence regarding luxury and riches was rarely manifested in such an extreme form. But the very nature of charity depends, to a considerable extent, on the realization that what is small change to the better-off, living in comparative luxury, is an essential to the poor. Both the heightened consumption that luxury implies and on the other hand its absence, indeed poverty, are aspects of differentiation in the economy, the emergence of the rich and poor, that occurred in so marked a manner with the Bronze Age, when the relative economic 'egalitarianism' of earlier societies was shattered by the new productive techniques that enabled one man with a plough to produce so much more than another, to make one man richer, another poorer.[29] In other words both charity and an ambivalence towards luxury, as well as poverty and riches, were to a large extent products of the Bronze Age changes and were mainly lacking in the hoe agricultural societies

[29] I do not mean to suggest that there was no poverty in other types of society, but it was of a different order.

of Africa, not altogether absent but less explicitly subjects of ideological elaboration.

While luxury behaviour like charity is an aspect of all stratified societies, it is also a dynamic one. It changes over time for both external and internal reasons. By external I refer to the market forces and to productive techniques, that, for instance, turned sugar from being a luxury into an item of mass consumption. Since the upper elements in society define themselves by means of luxuries, they have now to seek new items to serve as markers of difference, items which others cannot acquire because of their rarity or expense. In *The Structures of Everyday Life*, Braudel observes that we always need to distinguish the condition of the minority, 'the privileged, whom we may regard as living in luxury', from that of the majority.[30] However, the distinguishing features are frequently changing. 'Sugar was, for example, a luxury before the sixteenth century; paper was still a luxury in the closing years of the seventeenth, so were alcohol and the first "aperitifs" at the time of Catherine of Medici, or the swansdown beds and silver cups of the Russian boyars before Peter the Great.' Oranges were a luxury in England in the Stuart period and later, being especially prized at Christmas time. All that changed as the luxuries of the better-off became universal necessities, and production for the elite moved to mass consumption.

However, changes in luxury goods may also occur internally as the result of fashion. Braudel saw fashion as making its appearance in Europe about 1350 with the move to short, light tunics although it only really became powerful around 1700 when fashion 'began to influence everything'.[31] But only among the upper class; villagers continued in their old unchanging ways, which was the pattern, according to him, of the civilizations in the east.

That theme of change is a favourite of some Eurocentric historians who see the west as 'inventing invention'.[32] That statement is of course nonsense, as we see from Needham's great work on China discussed in chapter 5. So too is Braudel's more nuanced claim. The problem of change, not only in luxury behaviour but more generally, is intrinsic to western perceptions of eastern societies. Capitalism requires change; tradition stasis. However, all societies change at different speeds in different contexts. I have argued that in earlier religious systems, many cults tend to display a built-in obsolescence, being addressed to the God that Failed.[33] Eventually they are seen not to work, so that the search for new solutions

---

[30] Braudel 1981 [1979]: 183.   [31] Braudel 1981: 317.
[32] Landes 1999; Goody 2004.   [33] Goody 1957.

to human difficulties was an essential feature of those societies. A characteristic result is the turn-over of shrines; the old are set aside as failing to deliver, new ones are born. Perhaps this process should be considered as outside the realm of fashion, also a matter of change but one that exists at a more trivial level. But that level too one finds in oral cultures like that of the LoDagaa of northern Ghana. Songs and tunes for the xylophone change frequently even in rituals, so too, at least at present, do the dances and the cotton dresses women wear to perform them. Such behaviour is very close to fashion, especially in the use of imported cloth.

The role of fashion and luxury in promoting capitalism was a theme of the German economist Sombart among others, as we saw in chapter 7. This role was not unique to Europe but widely promoted by the increased economic activity of post-Bronze-Age societies. The rapidity of change increased over time. Just as the increase in the volume of trade and of commerce and its products has been an important feature of modern life, so too has the increase in shifting fashion. Braudel, we have seen, puts the beginning of that increase around 1700. That date refers to the growth of fashion at the French court under Louis XIV (1638–1715). Louis insisted that his nobles reside at Versailles for at least part of the year and it was in that context of their leisured existence that regular changes of fashion in dress were established. The French court started to invite silk-manufacturers from the southern town of Lyon to visit every six months to discuss future designs. It was not the appearance of change, of new fashion, that was remarkable but the way that rapid change was regularly established; the effects this had on industrialized production were remarkable. In France the speed of change in the design of silk clothing for the aristocracy was so fast that it led to the demise of the manufacture of silk in the Italian town of Bologna, up to then the great producer of silk cloth, in the eighteenth century; the Italian industry could not keep up.[34] That process rivalled, and set the pattern for, today's annual fashion shows in Paris, Milan, New York, London, and other capitals, shows that are market places for the costumes of the rich (women in this case) but which also set the terms for production for the masses who with modern socio-economic developments have now been drawn in to the frequent dictates of 'la mode', although on a less luxurious scale.

There was certainly an increase in the speed of turn-over of fashion and luxury goods in Europe, as well as in the number of participants, along with the development of industrial production and a mass consumer

---

[34] Poni 2001a and b.

market. That shift was not due to some inherent willingness to change that distinguished Europe, to some different 'mentality', but rather to the nature of the market and the productive processes. So that with regard to the claim that fashion was uniquely European, Braudel was quite wrong. Falsifying his notion of changing and unchanging societies, Elvin records that in China fashion in women's clothing was known as a 'trend of the times', found in Shanghai in the later seventeenth century.[35] I suspect that, at a lower pace, we could trace it earlier and probably everywhere.

Fashion in clothing was initially one way for the rich to maintain their explicit status markers, as was luxury more generally. As in many other post-Bronze-Age societies, clothing was often dictated by class; in some parts there were sumptuary laws that limited certain products to certain groups in the hierarchy, in others differences were of a more informal kind. Silk for example was forbidden to the citizens of Paris by Henry IV.[36] But with the development of manufacture and of exchange both national and international, the growth in numbers and prestige of those involved, the bourgeoisie, made it increasingly difficult to maintain these restrictions, in Europe and elsewhere. The lower made every effort to adopt the behaviour of the upper, especially when the acquisition of riches threatened existing status categories. Interestingly, sumptuary laws were eased in China at approximately the same time as in Europe when in both regions the rising bourgeoisie could no longer be held back, parallel changes which were no doubt the result of external trade and internal 'evolution'. After that time, fashion and 'taste' rather than law took over the role of distinguishing the elite and the whole process became more flexible but more complex. Nevertheless, the virtue of giving charity (to the poor), the ambivalence about luxury (for the rich), the use of clothing for distinguishing status and of laws to protect that, the role of fashion, while these vary, they are not unique to one culture in Eurasia but are found in all the major urbanized societies.

In conclusion, many Europeans see themselves as being heirs to the humanism of the Enlightenment, as well as to the French, American, and even English Revolutions, which supposedly led to new societies, to different ways of life. One aspect of this new, enlightened life was modern democracy. Europe also laid claim to values which, seen as invented by that continent at a rhetorical (and in particular at a textual) level, were considered as of universal applicability, but in practice are treated contextually and contingently. The gap between these stated goals (values) and actual practice can be very great; while the east are largely seen as lacking

[35] Elvin 2004: xi.   [36] Braudel 1981: 311.

them altogether. In fact, human values, and in that sense humanism, are found throughout human societies, not always in the same form but often recognizably comparable. Certainly the triad of individualism, equality, and freedom is not to be uniquely associated with modern democracy nor with the modern west; like charity they are found distributed much more widely.

10   Stolen love: European claims to the emotions

Not only have certain much prized institutions and values been claimed by Europe as unique to itself, but the same has happened even with some emotions, particularly that of love.[1] Some forms of love, sometimes the idea of love itself, have been seen as a purely western phenomenon. This idea is especially strong among many medieval historians, such as Duby, who have created a tradition which claims that 'romantic love' had its birth in the troubadour society of twelfth-century Europe. Modern historians of the family have used the notion of the uniqueness of love relationships to account for certain features of domestic life connected with the demographic transition from larger to smaller families and with the role of the conjugal family in the growth of capitalism. Some sociologists have seen it as a key to modernization, especially the modernization of the affectual life. Others more generally have considered it to be linked to their religion – an attribute of Christianity and of Christian charity ('love thy neighbour') where love is interpreted as fraternal love. It has been a general assumption of many European scholars, including psychologists like Person who saw the idea as spreading throughout western culture with the 'increasing emphasis on individuality as a primary value'.[2] Love, romantic love, is frequently believed to go hand in hand with individualism, with freedom (of choice of partner, as distinct from arranged marriage), and with modernization in general. I am not concerned primarily with why Europeans have made this ethnocentric claim.[3] But I am critical of the claim's validity.

In this chapter I have followed Europeans (especially Hollywood) in treating romantic love as something which differs from love in general

---

This chapter is dependent upon the chapters I have written for collections made by Louisa Passerini, notably 'Love, lust and literacy', reprinted in *Food and Love* (J. Goody), 1998, and 'Love and religion: comparative comments', to appear in L. Passerini (ed.) forthcoming, Berghan Books, Oxford. In addition there are references to the subject in *Islam in Europe*, Polity Press, 2003, as well as in a paper I wrote for C. Trillo San José (ed.), *Mujeres, familia y linaje en la edad media*, 2004.
Person 1991: 386.   [3] Passerini 1999.

and which is seen very much as something the west alone has. I do not think this proposition is correct, for reasons that will become clear, nor do I think that 'romantic' love is to be distinguished, except in detail, from love more generally. In other words it is by and large an invention of the west to distinguish the cultures of that continent from the rest of the world.

Let us begin with the widespread proposal that, in writing about courtly love, the troubadours of the twelfth century were the first to introduce the idea and practice of romantic love. This assumption was central, for example, to the historian de Rougemont's study of love in Europe.[4] Love is seen in similar developmental terms by the sociologist Norbert Elias. What 'we call "love"', 'that transformation of pleasure, that shade of feeling, that sublimation and refinement of the affects'[5] comes into being, he claims, in the feudal society of the troubadours and is expressed in 'lyric poetry'. He sees those texts, indeed the whole genre, as representing 'genuine feelings' and, in the words of the medievalist C. S. Lewis, as an indicator of a 'new state of affairs'.[6] That we find here a poetic genre new to Christian Europe, there can be little doubt. But there is no evidence of new feelings in general, unless we mean by that new forms of expressing those feelings; even here the newness of expression applies only to Christian Europe, not to an overall change in man's consciousness. As we will see, there were many expressions of love, even romantic love, outside Europe. The claim that it arose for the first time in feudal Europe is quite unsustainable.[7]

A similar theme was recently taken up by the distinguished medieval historian, Georges Duby. He too thought that 'twelfth-century Europe discovered love'.[8] But he does not see the troubadours of Aquitaine as being the only agents. Songs of the same kind were sung in Paris, by Abelard, for example, who acts 'as a troubadour'.[9] Such activity also appeared at the Anglo-Norman courts under the Plantagenet Henry II which constituted 'the most productive workshops of literacy creation' and gave birth to the legend of Tristan and Isolde.[10] Changes in the orientation of love he regards as related to the 'feminization of Christianity' and to the new role of the younger sons of knights who had benefited from the increasing wealth of that period.

The kind of love (la fin d'amor) expressed in these troubadour poems involves a measure of absence and distance, often social distance as

---

[4] de Rougemont 1956.   [5] Elias 1982: 328.
[6] Lewis 1936: 11.   [7] See Goody 1998.
[8] Duby's writings on love include *Que sait-on de l'amour en France en XIIe siècle?* (1988) and *A propos de l'amour que l'on dit courtois* (1988).
[9] Duby 1996: 61, 66.   [10] Duby 1996: 73, 68.

between a courtier and the wife of his lord. Not only men but women too (*troubaritz*) composed love poems; one of the most famous of these women poets was Na Castelosa from the Auvergne, wife of Turc de Meyonne, who wrote addressing one Armand of Bréon. The opening of one of her poems began (in French translation):

> *Vouz avez laissé passer un bien long temps*
> *Depuis que vous m'avez quitté.*
> You have let a long time pass
> Since you left me.

The loved one has so often departed, or is unobtainable, that this distance, physical or social, is seen as a general characteristic of courtly love.

However, this form of love poetry is hardly unique in sentiment, though perhaps in specifics. The ancient historian, Keith Hopkins, found love poems in Ancient Egypt written between sister and brother, where they were permitted partners.[11] In China as early as the ninth to seventh centuries BCE we find love poetry anthologized in *The Book of Songs*. In the middle of the sixth century a court poet, Hsu Ling, put together a whole collection of love poems which he called *New Songs from a Jade Terrace*, consisting largely of poetry belonging to the aristocratic court tradition of southern China. The 'Palace Style Poetry' took on a standardized rhetorical form that bristled with conventions. One of those was that 'the woman's lover must be absent from the love scenario'.[12] As we will discuss later, distance was intrinsic to the whole nature of both letter-writing and love poetry. In Japan too, during the Heian period (794–1185 CE), the country was known to the Chinese as the 'court of queens', and their women dominated the literary scene. In courting a future spouse for an aristocratic family, the young man sent love poems to the girl and she replied in kind. Once married, the women often passed their time writing poetry and engaging in competitions, one of which involved the hanging of poems on paper strips at the Spring Cherry Blossom Festival, an act that had both religious and secular implications.[13] The art of letter-writing was the most important for gallantry and for 'courtoisie'.[14] Love-letters were especially valued; unlike the situation in the Christian west (at least in a religious context), love was not a sin but a celebration. Books of sexual education (literally, images of different positions) were often written by monks and hidden in the trousseaux of young girls. However, in a later period when the military virtues were much prized, love and sex were treated in a more puritanical fashion. That

---

[11] Hopkins 1980.   [12] Birrell 1995: 8.
[13] See *La Culture des Fleurs* French edition, Le Seuil, 1994, p. 496.
[14] Beurdeley 1973:14.

alternation between puritanism and celebration in the public attitudes to love was associated not only with the military but with religion too. Indeed one might view the troubadour period as being a European manifestation of just such a process, following the restraint enjoined by earlier Christianity.

China and Japan are not the only extra-European cultures which have known and cultivated love poetry; we find the literary expression of love in the Hebrew Bible in the *Song of songs* (which undoubtedly exerted an influence upon Christian Europe, where it was, however, often interpreted allegorically, as in other such traditions, as if the genre was unworthy of serious attention in its literal form) and also in a considerable body of ancient Sanskritic poetry in India.[15] A more immediate model for the poetry of the troubadours, and well known in twelfth century Europe, lay in the works of Ovid, who lived in Rome at the time of the Emperor Augustus. For him, however, love is said to be 'frankly sensual' and extramarital; in Rougemont's view 'there is little or no trace of the romantic affection of later times'.[16] However, that author neglects the various similarities. In both traditions love was often extra-marital; moreover among the troubadours there was certainly an undercurrent of sexuality, just as in Ovid there is more than a trace of romance.

In a comprehensive study of the medieval Latin love lyric and the rise of the European form (1965), Dronke concludes, contrary to Lewis, that there was no 'new feeling' in the twelfth century,

(i)   'that "the new feeling" of *amour courtois* is at least as old as Egypt of the second millennium B.C., and might indeed occur at any time or place: that it is, as Professor Marrou suspected, 'un secteur du coeur, un des aspects éternels de l'homme';

(ii) that the feeling of *amour courtois* is not confined to courtly or chivalric society, but is reflected in even the earliest recorded popular verse of Europe (which almost certainly had a long oral tradition behind it);

(iii) that researches into European courtly poetry should therefore be concerned with the variety of sophisticated and learned *development* of *courtois* themes, not with seeking specific origins for the themes themselves. For if the mirage of the sudden new feeling is done away with, the particular problems of literary history undoubtedly remain.'[17]

I would agree wholeheartedly with Dronke that we are dealing with 'a mirage' seen in European terms, though I would emphasize the role that

---

[15] Brough 1968.   [16] Parry 1960: 4.
[17] Dronke 1965 I: ix. The reference to Marrou is RMAL, iii (1947), 189. The phrase 'the new feeling' is used by C. S. Lewis, *The Allegory of Love*, p. 12.

this mirage has played in world history. At the same time I would have my doubts about oral societies that I have expressed elsewhere;[18] the love-lyric seems almost to require written composition.

But while Latin poetry may have served as a precedent for the troubadours of Languedoc, specific sources and influences were closer at hand in the shape of the strong Islamic tradition of love poetry which was to be found in Arabic-speaking Spain and Sicily. The most plausible explanation for the difference between Ovid and later work in this field was 'that the troubadours were influenced by the culture of Muslim Spain'.[19] During the period of the 'petty courts' (taifas), before the advent in 1086 of the puritanical Almoravids who were Berbers from Africa, Muslims and Christians in Andalusia lived side by side practically on an equal footing. The Muslim courts of Andalusia were part of the same tradition as those of the rest of Spain which were also important centres for the writing and recitation of love poetry. Representative of this tradition was the well-known poet, Ibn Hazm, who wrote The Ring of the Dove (1022), a poem about the art of love (sometimes interpreted allegorically). There was of course much love poetry written throughout the Muslim world, influencing even peripheral areas such as Somalia in the Horn of Africa. But in southern Spain the tradition was especially strong not only among men but among women too. One of the most prominent of the latter was Wallada, a Caliph's daughter, who held a literary salon at Cordoba. There were other females too who wrote poetry displaying 'a surprising freedom in their expression and fulfilment in their feelings of love'.[20] In Andalucia even some Jewish women were moved to write love poetry in the same mode.

Interaction with Christian states was easy and frequent and the poets themselves were often the mediums of communication. 'A set of wandering poets came into existence, who passed from one court to another',[21] much as developed a century later in France. In Sicily poets from the north used to frequent the Norman court of Roger II and then that of Frederick II (1194–1256) at Palermo, which was strongly oriented towards Arabic culture, in order to learn about local artistic activities.[22] The members of the Sicilian school used their vernacular rather than Provençal for the language of love poetry and are credited with the invention of two major poetic forms in Italy, the canzone and the sonnet.

In fact Muslim and Jewish women participated in activities which European tradition seems to have regarded as incompatible with the culture of gender inequality (which would make them incapable of experiencing

---

[18] Goody 1998: 119.   [19] Parry 1960:1.   [20] Viguera 1994: 709.
[21] Parry 1960: 8.   [22] Asin 1926.

romantic love, except perhaps in a religious context). As well the unde-niable influence of Muslim Europe upon its Christian neighbours poses a serious threat to the idea that romantic love was somehow sponta-neously invented in the knightly courts of Europe. In order to rescue an indigenous European origin for love (along with other components of what are seen as 'modern' family life), some scholars have implied that the prominent role of women in Andalucia drew its strength from the older roots of the country, from the population (Visigothic, Iberic) that had been in place before the Muslim invasions. A similar view has been taken of other features of Andalucian family life and was particularly popular during the Fascist period in Spain when there was a tendency to downplay the Islamic contribution to its social life as well as to Europe more generally. That tendency was counteracted by Guichard's pioneer-ing contribution to the history of the area in his book, *Structures sociales 'orientales' et 'occidentales'*[23] and by the subsequent research of Spanish scholars in Andalucia. But it is also the case that on a wider canvas there has been a new insight into the position of women under Islam. West-erners are today often overwhelmed by the images of women wearing the veil, by the knowledge that marriage is polygynous and that schooling for females has not always been encouraged. These views persist in popular consciousness, political discourse, and even academic argument despite the fact that recent research opens more nuanced perspectives upon these matters, and reveal a deeper resemblance between European and Muslim attitudes and practices in the Mediterranean than is often allowed for. In the Mediterranean region the use of the veil depends upon social status, as it did in Renaissance Italy or in Victorian Europe. Apart from princely harems, plural marriage is in fact confined to a small minority of unions at any one time, less than 5 per cent, where it usually occurs in special circumstances, for example, to provide an heir. In this polygyny has its resemblances to the kind of serial marriage in which Henry VIII notably engaged, save that the non-favoured wife is not dismissed (divorced). Other practices akin to polygyny such as concubinage and extra-marital liaisons are common among European populations. In any case polygyny certainly does not prevent the development of personal and individualized sentiments, including love. As we see from the story of Jacob's marriage as well as a senior wife there is always a 'favourite' ('Sarah') to whom the husband may be romantically attached. As for education, Qur'anic schools (for males) were not the only way of becoming educated; tutors sometimes from within the family, gave private lessons to women. But the exclusion of women from school did influence the life choices of many

[23] Guichard 1997.

in Islam, as it did until recently in Judaism and for many in Christian Europe.[24]

As this discussion shows, the argument over the origin of troubadour poetry ran parallel to a more general dispute over the nature of Andalucian and Islamic society. Is the position of women (which affects their participation in love relationships) to be attributed to European roots, or instead to Muslim outsiders? Under Islam, women have generally been free to come to markets, both as buyers and sellers. In Turkey, they often appeared in law courts. From Ghana and elsewhere they undertook the arduous pilgrimage to Mecca. As I have remarked, Guichard suggests that we need to apply a class analysis to the situation. Women in upper groups were often restricted whereas women in the entertainment business were very free. These latter were singers, dancers, musicians, poets, who were sometimes subject to gift-exchange between courts, even between Muslim and Christian rulers. That exchange seems to illustrate the structural similarities in the two traditions as well as the channels for the communication of ideas about poetry and love. Indeed the boundaries between the courts and territories of different religious persuasions were often quite porous.

It is this fact that has recently led some scholars to consider more profoundly the question of Muslim influence on troubadour poetry. It has been argued that the themes are similar in many respects as are the metrical forms. We have seen that poets travelled from one region to another, often under a kind of informal protection.[25] If so, the likelihood of what was for western Europe an innovative form of literature having been stimulated by contact with Islam seems high. On the levels both of prosody and content it has been said that 'there are no precursors of troubadour lyrics in the west but convincing analogues in theme, imagery, and verse form occur earlier with Hispanic-Arab poetry'.[26] In his work on European–Arab relations in the Middle Ages, the historian Daniel comments that:

On the whole, it seems undeniable that courtly poetry in Arabic, often trivial, yet ranged much more widely in theme and treatment than troubadour verse. If the latter had not a special position in European literary history, it might be well regarded as no more than a provincial and decadent offshoot of the court poets of Spain . . . If, however, European concepts of courtly love derive from the petty courts of the taifas [which appeared when the Caliphate collapsed in 1031], the

---

[4] Although Muslim women were excluded from formal instruction in most madrasas, they nevertheless sometimes received a religious education, as Berkey discusses (1992: 161ff.).

[5] Asin 1926.   [26] Nykl 1946.

whole romantic tradition in European literature owes an almost disproportionate debt to eleventh-century Spain.[27]

Even Nelli, the French historian of the troubadours and of the Cathars, sees the romantic tradition, the refraining from intimate sexual acts, and the man's subordination to the lady as deriving partly from Arabian sources as well as from Byzantium and elsewhere. 'All Nelli's possibilities', remarks Daniel, 'suggest the ambiguity or multiplicity of the origin of European romanticism.' How different that is from the conclusions of the influential English literary medievalist, C. S. Lewis, who wrote of the troubadours that they

> in the eleventh century, discovered or invented, or were the first to express, that romantic species of passion which English poets were still writing about in the nineteenth . . . and they erected impassable barriers between us and the classical past or the Oriental present. Compared with this revolution the Renaissance is a mere ripple on the surface of literature.[28]

The idea that it was the troubadours who, for the first time, made love 'not a sin but a virtue'[29] may be correct for medieval Europe; it is certainly unsustainable from a world perspective and illustrates the narrowness of a literary viewpoint confined to western literature. One interesting element, noted by Roux, is that Provençal poetry not only elaborated on the physical beauty of women in a theocratic age but, for the first time in Europe, excluded any reference either to salvation or to the supernatural and the marvellous,[30] bringing to birth a new humanism, by which he refers to a secular approach to life and which he sees as integrating the feudal ethic with 'relationships of love'. As we have argued, under Islam too people experienced similar periods, in Europe and elsewhere. So too did other major traditions. The secular, in love as in other matters, was no monopoly of Europe, though it was true that the Renaissance saw its extension into many spheres. But in any case the exclusion of religious and supernatural reference among the troubadours argues in favour of the influence of poets and scholars coming from a different tradition who knew what they had to exclude. Such influence is not surprising, given the fact that Provençal was linguistically close to the Catalan of northern Spain and that the Cathars, for example, thought nothing of crossing that frontier, their communities existing in Spain as well as in 'France'.[31]

It may be that in Christian Europe the expansion of love had to take place in a secular context, outside the religious sphere, because of the restraints that the latter imposed. That was not everywhere the case:

---

[27] Daniel 1975: 105–6.   [28] Lewis 1936: 4.   [29] Roux 2004: 166.
[30] Roux 2004: 166–7.   [31] Weis 2001.

humanism in the secular sense was not a prerequisite for the development or expression of feelings of love. The subject was of wide interest in the Muslim world both in secular and in religious contexts. The emphasis on the latter was especially marked in Sufism. One Sufi master writes, 'I am neither Christian, Jew nor Muslim . . . love is my religion'.[32] In fact secular and religious love were very much intertwined. In an interesting contribution, which I take up in detail because of its links with previous chapters, the anthropologist, Yalman, writes:

The interest in love as a social doctrine can be said to arise with the mystic *tarikats* very early in Islam. There is much talk of the heart: love in this sense is a dangerous, even subversive, doctrine. Thus are the *tarikats* regarded to this day in many places. The love of men for God, and for each other, has a Dionysian quality difficult for authorities to control. Such irrepressible and all-consuming love is expressed in highly emotive rituals – the passion plays of the Shi'a, or the ritual chanting (*dhikr*) of the various dervish orders, or the *sema* (whirling ritual) of the Mevlevis, and, in all cases, it is reported that the effect of the communal ritual is the submerging of the individual in an 'ocean of love' in his group. The degree to which the Middle East, at least, was susceptible to such ideas can be understood from the fact that Divine love (*tasăvvŭj*) is the largest and most persistent subject in the poetry and music of the Ottoman, Persian, and indeed Mughal Empires. The stream ran deep and wide for many centuries. It is in full flood still. The entire and vast corpus of major poets such as Yunus Emre and Mevlana Celaleddin Rumi, Sadi, Hafiz, and many others is about Divine love. Behind the divine spirituality one senses the powerful imagery of love as a metaphor for human relations. Again, the insistence is on communal mystic experience. Individual mystic experience and ecstasy is said to belong properly to Christians.

The metaphor of love, the love of men for God and for each other, has certain political implications. It denies, of course, the machine-like quality that well-run societies sometimes come to exhibit. Love as a consuming passion would set aside formalities and would undermine social barriers. It would erode the privileges of those small, closed groups that often run the important institutions of society, and would insist that hierarchical structures, built up with such care and dependent upon people keeping their places and doing their duties, be brought down. It would insist that men be equal to each other, that they dissolve the barriers separating them and unite with one another in a sense of community and identity and become one with each other and with God.[33]

A most remarkable example of the ecstasy of love, associating the divine and the earthly, was the homosexual relationship of the great poet Rumi for the wandering Shems. But a similar association, in this case heterosexual, occurs in the very influential work of the Andalucian Sufi poet, Ibn Arabi (CE 1165, Murcia–1240, Damascus). He was studying the

---

[32] Zafrani 1986: 159.   [33] Yalman 2001: 272.

prophetic tradition in Mecca with Ibn Rustan of Isfahan when he me
the latter's virginal daughter, Nizam; she was 'a slim maiden with a capt
vating look, who filled our meetings with grace . . . If it were not for suc
souls, prone to wicked thoughts and intentions, I could describe in deta
all the virtues God has given her, comparable to a fertile orchard.' H
work on 'The Interpretation of Desires' is dedicated to Nizam (Harmony
and he later explains that all the expressions used in his verse (expres
sions appropriate to love poetry) allude to her and at the same time to
spiritual reality.[34] The relationship has been compared to that betwee
Dante and Beatrice; indeed a claim has been made for his direct influenc
on the Florentine poet. While the association of secular and divine lov
is particularly strong in Islam, it also existed in Christianity; nevertheles
in Islam one finds a separation in certain forms of poetry and in the a
of the Mughal and other courts, but without any absolute distinction.

As we know from Caroline Bynum's studies of medieval women mys
tics,[35] sometimes the two aspects of love, the spiritual and the ser
sual, become very much intertwined. The thirteenth-century mystic
Hadewijch, wrote of her union with Christ, 'after that he came himse
to me, took me entirely in his arms and pressed me to him; and all m
members felt his in full felicity . . .'[36] This concern with the flesh is linke
to the idea that Christ had a human as well as a divine nature, the invisibl
God made visible as embodied in the doctrine of incarnation. As in othe
major religions, in Christianity the boundary between the earthly love c
man/woman and the spiritual love of God (and God for mankind) is ofte
blurred. The same word is used for both emotions, and romantic love, a
in the *Song of songs* or in *The ring of the dove*, may be given an allegorica
spiritual significance since love is often seen as an intrinsic part of a com
plex of religious ideas and practices. The love of God (given and received)
the love of man, the love of women, all are drawn together by the use c
this one word, which implies a common element but a variety of forms
The Hebrew Bible also uses the same word for the love of God, of fello
men or of fellow women. Hence the rabbis could interpret the appar
ently erotic *Song of songs* as the love of God for Israel, an interpretatio
that Christians later transfer into the love of Christ for his people. Tha
book was only included in the canon because rabbi Aqivah (first centur
CE) decided to read it allegorically; there is nothing in the text itself t
suggest such an interpretation.[37] The first three chapters of Hosea sho

---

[34] See V. Cantarino 1977, R. Nicholson 1921, Ibn Arabi 1996.
[35] Bynum 1987.   [36] Hart, quoted J. Soskice 1996: 38.
[37] I am grateful to Jessica Bloom for this comment, to Andrew Macintosh, and to th
writings of Prof. N. O. Yalman.

the same identification, some later Protestants would say confusion. However there does seem to be a difference in Hebrew between love ('*ahebh*) and desire (*shawq*). When God curses Eve, he says that her 'desire' (*shawq*) shall be for Adam, not that she shall 'love' ('*ahebh*) him.

This identification of love for a woman and for one's country or for one's God was common in the Old Testament, and continued later. In the writing of the Jew, Ibn Gabirol (*c.*1021–*c.*1057), much influenced by Islamic models, the love poetry also contains an element of cosmic love, of the privileged relation between Israel and her God. Zafrani writes of 'compositions du reste ambiguës, qu'elles soient liturgiques ou profanes, dont on ne peut dire s'il s'agit d'amour mystique, ou de la relation avec un être plus proche, le disciple ou l'ami' ('ambiguous compositions, whether liturgical or profane, of which one cannot say if they refer to mystical love, or to the relation to someone nearer, the disciple or the friend').[38] Note that while Arab poetry was often profane, even erotic,[39] Jewish poetry in the Maghreb was always mainly religious, although it had its other side. The great Jewish philosopher, Maimonides, vigorously denounced the use of poetry. Secular verse was not always respectable, especially song, often sung by slave-girls and accompanied by the drinking of wine.[40]

In some branches of European Christianity, the two forms of love, even if given the same name, are in many contexts diametrically opposed. In the Roman Catholic church, priests are forbidden married love (as well as of course as unmarried intercourse), whereas they are enjoined to enter into the mutual love of God as well as into eternal amity (fraternity), to all mankind and indeed to all God's creation. However, quite apart from the merit that Catholicism awards to the celibacy of both males and females, doubts or qualifications about love, even married love, are part of Christian beliefs, in the story of Adam and Eve and embodied in the words of Christ and of his disciple Paul. The opposition becomes particularly acute in the dualistic versions of the Christian faith, approaching the Manichean, where a sharp line is drawn between this world and the next, between the evil and earthly on the one hand and the good and spiritual on the other. To be a 'perfect' among the Cathars of the twelfth century – and all had to aim for this – carnal love has to be renounced as one of the things of this world that is completely antithetical to the spiritual, to God, to the religious life. As a result they renounced the world, the flesh, and the devil. That path of renunciation affects even the Christian laity. Towards the end of his life, Tolstoi's new religion of love led to the abandonment of his family, and to a renouncing of earthly ties, including the love of his wife and thirteen children. Here the shift was not so much between

[38] Zafrani 1986: 109.   [39] Zafrani 1986: 134.   [40] Zafrani 1986: 136.

earthly and divine love, as between carnal and fraternal love. The Greeks distinguished the two main forms of spiritual and earthly love as *eros* (that is erotic, sexual) and *agape* (fraternal or social). In Christianity these were the same terminologically and the ideas often blurred, but there were certainly contexts in which a distinction was drawn. The troubadours dealt with earthly love. But so did some trends in the love poetry of Sanskrit India, of early China and in Islam. And while the poetry of the Jews of the Maghreb was largely religious, the *Song of songs* points to a distinctly secular element (albeit often interpreted allegorically). What we find in most of these traditions, over the long term, is some alternation in emphasis between the religious (and puritanical) elements and the secular (more expressive) ones. The contemporaries of the troubadour poets, from the same regions of southern France, were the Cathars who placed secular love firmly within a puritanical religious frame, certainly for the 'perfects', the spiritual leaders among them. Ambiguity was to be found not only in alternation over time but in contemporary differences in belief.

Let us extend this discussion to the realm of sex, because while love and sex cannot be identified, neither in most cases can they be separated. True, we have 'platonic love', love of fellow man or woman, love of God, even self-love. But in the majority of cases 'making love' with another is an aspect of love, and that love is essentially earthly and generally secular.

The duality between good and evil remains, but in Islam legitimate sex falls on the opposite side of the divide compared with the Cathars. However, some ambivalence exists very widely in human societies and extends to variations in behaviour that surrounds love; in some societies sex is forbidden between close kin (as in Christianity), in others broadly encouraged (as in Islam). Islam seems to be one religion which does not normally put a strong regulatory hand on human sexuality, indeed one of the *hadith*, the traditional tales associated with the life of Mohammed declares that every time a man has lawful sexual intercourse he undertakes a work of charity.[41] But ambivalence is nevertheless present; among Arabs the ritually appropriate remark in initiating sex relations with one's wife was: 'I seek refuge in God from the accursed Satan; in the name of God the beneficent, the merciful.'[42] For while intercourse could imply carrying out the service of God, the total situation is more complicated, since Islam too harks back to the story of the fall of man which displays an obvious aspect of ambivalence about sex. The fall attaches to male sexuality, but an Adam requires an Eve, so that there is something here of the same doubt about sex and love we have elsewhere found in the Bagre recitation

---

[41] 'On the authority of Abu Dharr.'   [42] Goode 1963: 141.

of the LoDagaa,[43] although in each case unions approved by God seem to be opposed to Satan's variety.

Those committed to the notion of the European discovery of romantic love by the troubadours have often discerned a similarly exclusive development of certain attitudes towards sexuality and marriage. For example, Elias, whose work we have examined in chapter 6, treats sexuality in a section headed 'changes of attitude towards relations between the sexes'.[44] In accordance with his general view of the 'history of manners', he begins by claiming that 'the feeling of shame surrounding human sexual relations changed considerably in the process of civilization'.[45] The evidence for that progression he derives from the nineteenth-century comments on Erasmus's *Colloquies* published in the sixteenth century; that work expresses 'a different standard of shame' from the later period, a difference that is part of the civilizing process since in the later period 'even among adults, everything pertaining to sexual life is concealed to a high degree and dismissed behind the scenes'.[46] Shame about the sexual act is seen as part of the civilizing process of Renaissance Europe. I myself would regard it as relating to a much wider ambivalence.

He perceives a similar progression towards monogamous marriage which the Church had proclaimed much early on in its history. 'But marriage takes on this strict form as a social institution binding on both sexes only at a later stage, when drives and impulses come under firmer and stricter control. For only then are extramarital relationships for men really ostracised socially, or at least subject to absolute secrecy.'[47] This seems a highly dubious assertion that perhaps held for the Victorian period in Britain but by no means everywhere even in Europe. Yet he firmly pursues the question in trying to establish his thesis: 'in the course of the civilising process the sexual drive, like many others, is subjected to ever stricter control and transformation'.[48] It may have been possible to make this statement in the 1930s (though I myself have many doubts), but after the 1960s it is hardly correct to claim a progression to 'ever stricter controls'. Women have experienced some liberation in this as in other spheres; men too are not more 'straight-laced' than in Victorian times. Indeed, in this respect, Victorian England has to be looked upon as a special case of inhibition.

Qualms about earthly love do not begin with written religions, though some have argued from the story of Adam and Eve, so widely proclaimed

---

[3] Goody and Gandah 2002: 15.   [44] Elias 1982: 138 ff.
[5] A note refers to comments by Ginsberg, Montaigne, and Freud about social influences on behaviour but which give no support whatsoever to the idea of a progression in notions of shame.
[6] Elias 1982: 146.   [47] Elias 1982: 150.   [48] Elias 1982: 149.

on the facades of Romanesque churches, that it is the Judaeo-Christian tradition (as it is so often called, erroneously omitting Islam from their company) that confers feelings of guilt on the sexual act, a guilt that God forced upon the first humans whose breach of his taboo meant they were excluded from Paradise. Indian religion too, though much more explicit about the sexual act in temple sculpture, not only encourages its renunciation in other ways but sees that act as 'polluting', as bringing dirt or impurity, at least spiritual, upon the participants. We see a similar ambivalence in accounts of human procreation in the Bagre myth of the LoDagaa, an oral culture.[49] In one version the first man and woman have sex but display great reticence about admitting the fact to God, who was the Creator in a different way. Sexuality is virtually always a private act; and this mingling of fluids has its dangers as well as its blessings.

While it is the troubadours (but not the Cathars who as Manichaeans were wary of carnal love) who have so often been credited with the European invention of love, as we have seen other writers considered the development of that sentiment (at least in its fraternal form) as rooted in Christianity itself, in the notion of 'charity' (*caritas*) and in the injunction to love one's neighbour, brother, or another. No explanation is offered of how Christianity, with similar roots and sacred texts to Judaism and Islam, should have developed independently in this way. In fact all the great world religions, born of the Bronze Age with its radical socio-economic differences in the form of 'classes', made some provision for the charitable support of their co-religionists at least. That was included in the role of the Islamic *waqf* as well as of similar institutions among Parsis, Jains, Buddhists, and others. Meanwhile the injunction 'love thy neighbour' was part of the inevitable universalism of the literate world religions which did not remain 'tribal' but aimed to convert people from other groups.[50] In any case the injunction was in practice often limited in its application, even among members of the same persuasion. This is an area in which, more than most, we need to distinguish rhetoric and ideology from practice. Despite the assertions of its apologists, in this respect it is difficult to see Christianity as having had a particularly important influence on people's sentiments.

Not only is love alleged to be European – a highly questionable thesis – but for a much later period too, historians and sociologists have seen the supposed fact of love (at least of the romantic variety) being European as one reason for the emergence in that continent of a truly modern society, a modernization that is linked to the advent of capitalism, considered to be another European invention. The theme lies behind

[49] Goody and Gandah 2002: 15.   [50] See Goody 1986.

ome distinguished contributions in the field of historical demography.
is not love but 'family', too, that is at stake in these confrontations.
their work on English parish registers of births and deaths since the
.eformation, Peter Laslett and his colleagues of the Cambridge Group
nowed that households in England had never been of the 'extended'
ariety since mean household size (MHS) numbered only around 4.7
om the sixteenth century.[51] They saw the small household as linked to
ne nuclear family, the presence of which was deemed one of the factors
ehind the modernization and the capitalism of the west. Sociologists like
alcott Parsons pointed to the affinity between industrial capitalism and
ne small family that allowed for the mobility of labour and eliminated
xpenditure on wider kinship obligations. Historians of the family saw
ne 'nuclear family', based on romantic love, as providing the conjugal
ove (through the free choice of spouse) and the parental love (care for
hildren) that produced the motivation for bettering oneself in a com-
etitive environment. Indeed, England, it was argued, did not need to
wait capitalism to adopt this type of household; it was already in place,
nlike the situation in many other parts of the world who did not share
his (west) European pattern.[52]

A recent study of *The household and the making of history* by Mary Hart-
nan (2004), which claims to offer 'a subversive view of the western past',
tates that 'a unique late marriage pattern, discovered in the 1960s but
riginating in the Middle Ages, explains the continuing puzzle of why
vestern Europe was the site of changes . . . that gave rise to the modern
vorld'. There is nothing new about this Malthusian-type claim, which has
long history, involving the linking of demographic facts and ethical or
ocial 'progress'. Factually we do not doubt the existence in Europe of an
nusually late marriage age for men and women, which some have seen
s encouraging 'love', but the conclusion that these arrangements were
esponsible for the modern world seems exaggerated and highly specula-
ve and once again teleologically based on a position of later advantage,
vithout any thought of comparison.

These claims for the uniqueness of the European family also present
roblems from the standpoint of the wider study of kinship. China for
xample was thought to be quite different with its so-called 'extended'
ouseholds (which turn out to be confined largely to the better-off who
ave always lived in larger households than the poor). At an early confer-
nce organized by the Cambridge Group,[53] I offered evidence to show
hat even in societies with kin-groups of considerable size (e.g. clans), the

---

[51] Laslett and Wall 1972.   [52] Laslett and Wall 1972; Hajnal 1965.
[53] The proceedings of which were published in 1972 (Laslett and Wall, eds.).

existential household (as distinct from the houseful, the dwelling group) was usually small, based on a reproductive and economic unit[54] not all that different in size from that recorded by Laslett for Europe. While I recognized the validity of the concept of the European marriage pattern,[55] the sharp division into European and non-European types was far too radical and categorical, ignoring the many similarities between eastern and western practices, at least as far as the major post-Bronze Age societies were concerned. For that opposition neglected the common features associated with the presence of the dowry and 'the woman's property complex'.[56] Indeed, these considerations led one to question even Hajnal's later refinement of the problem relating to mean household size in west and east,[57] in which he proposes not so much differences in size as differences in the process of household formation.

Apart from the size of the household, there have been two broad trends regarding the evolution of the 'family' in anthropological quarters. The first, mainly appearing in speculations of nineteenth-century writers, looked for a shift from hordes to tribes to families, involving a change from larger to smaller units. That move was reflected in those historical accounts which looked for larger (but mainly unanalyzed) units, for example 'the extended family' in earlier societies and smaller ones ('the nuclear family') in later, modern ones. However, 'extended' families always have 'elementary families' at their core; in part at least, the contrast is therefore mistaken. The second trend represents another anthropological view, derived from the examination of recent field material rather than from speculations about an unknown past, and embodied in particular in the thesis of the Polish anthropologist, Bronislaw Malinowski, in his monograph, *The family among the Australian aborigines*,[58] where he showed that even the most 'primitive' of existing societies, the so-called 'hordes' were organized on the basis of small conjugal groups. Thus, in relation to these units, there was no shift from 'horde' or 'tribe' to 'family'; both could exist together side by side. While larger kinship groups tended to disappear over historical time, especially in urban societies, the family and its interlocking personnel remained critical actors in the field of social relationships. That seems to me basically the position taken by most of the major social theorists in this field, not only Malinowski, Radcliffe-Brown, and Lévi-Strauss, but by Evans-Pritchard and Fortes who followed them, whatever emphasis they may have given, following Durkheim and Gifford, to the much wider lineage.[59]

---

[54] Goody 1972.   [55] Hajnal 1982.   [56] See Goody 1976.
[57] Hajnal 1982; Goody 1996b.   [58] Malinowski 1913.
[59] For a critical comment, see Goody, 1984.

Accepting this wide prevalence if not universality of the smaller family, can we envisage a unit that does not work on the basis of (sexual) 'love' for the spouse (or spouses) and (non-sexual) 'love' for the children? The first does not necessarily involve partner-choice. It did not in eighteenth-century Europe, at least among propertied families. But we can appreciate how central that form of love is for ideologically oriented historians of modernity because it implies *freedom* of choice as well as *individualism*, seen as essentially western values. It also implies close relations between the partners (though more frequently broken by divorce) and it implies equally close (but more fragile) ties between parents and children, leading not only to a heavy investment in the training of the young but later on to the decision to go for smaller families (quality rather than quantity), a process that is known as the demographic transition. Smaller households, smaller families, hence more intense relationships between parents and children, and between the parents themselves, in other words parental love and conjugal love. Optimally such a family was initiated by the choice of the partners themselves, not by an arranged marriage (which again was less common among the poor where property and status were hardly significant issues).

Whilst there are various ways of establishing a union of which arranged marriages and 'free choice', romance, represent possibilities, few societies see these as stark alternatives.[60] Certainly arranged marriages, antipathetic as they may be to modern Europeans, do not preclude the growth of very affectionate relations after marriage has taken place; in this case sex precedes love. And if the union does not prove compatible, then many societies permit the recourse to divorce after which 'free choice' is much more likely to be an important feature in a further marriage. If we recall that throughout history human cultures have reproduced themselves through sexual unions, each of which has involved the selection of partners (not necessarily by themselves alone, others are frequently involved, rules apply), then the claim that only in the west does this involve love, or at least romantic love, seems to smack of hubris. And indeed there is a minor counter-current in the west that has long recognized something special in man–woman relationships in the east, whether expressed in the language of flowers which at the beginning of the nineteenth century was thought to have been invented in the harems of Turkey, in tales such as that of Scheherazade, in the eroticism embodied in the miniatures of Mughal court paintings, or in the erotic albums used to tempt or instruct Japanese brides and so sought after in late nineteenth-century Europe.

See Hufton 1995.

In fact that giving of flowers, accompanied by various significations, has long existed in the major societies of Asia.

In extreme cases this conjunction of males and females has been attributed to lust rather than to love, especially in polygynous societies. This dichotomy is wrong and relationships, at least comparable to what we call love, are to be found even in the simple non-literate cultures of Africa, such as the LoDagaa of northern Ghana,[61] although a significant factor in many a first marriage was the wishes of parents.

However, although I regard love as being present in African cultures, oral 'literature' fails to elaborate the sentiment in the way found in the major societies of Europe and Asia. Note that all these societies are literate and our evidence for twelfth-century France and those other societies is essentially textual. Literacy means that the presentation of love takes a special form. In the first place, one does not employ writing except when one is communicating at a distance (unless you are a school teacher with a class, a blackboard, and a piece of chalk). So the written communicative act is very different from those that involve a face-to-face audience, as in purely oral cultures. Written love poetry is essentially a matter of communicating with someone who has gone away, has been left behind, or is 'distant' (perhaps socially) in some other way, a characteristic that has already been noted of troubadour poetry but can equally be found in Chinese verse, as I have argued earlier in this chapter. Secondly, the composition of poetry or prose in writing involves a process of reflection that is again different from speech itself. There is a reflexivity about what one is writing that encourages an elaboration of the expression of sentiment that one rarely finds in purely oral cultures. Consequently the poetry of love is likely to be more elaborate in literate societies and more so at certain times than at others. We do not imply for one moment that an identical notion of 'love' is to be found in all societies, nor, above all, that 'romantic love' is everywhere the main method of seeking a spouse. Nevertheless that form of relationship is certainly not the unique prerogative of the west nor of the modern. Nor, it should be said, is the 'congruent love' recently sponsored by the sociologist Giddens as post-romantic and characteristic of 'modern' society[62] and as the evolutionary successor to 'romantic love'.

The contrary view about the previous absence of love and of choice was part and parcel of the idea that early societies were organized on collective rather than on an individual basis. That notion, which gave rise to that of 'primitive communism', was partly supported by the presence of larger kin groups (clans or kindreds) but failed to take account of

[61] Goody 1998: 113ff.   [62] Giddens 1991.

the ways that these groups were always divided into 'nested segments' ('segmentary lineages', for example) which acted on their own account. At their base was often a 'minimal lineage' around which clustered an elementary or perhaps more complex family. Equally, land tenure was virtually never communal in the manner implied by that phrase; small groups had more or less exclusive rights to the produce of a farm, and usually to the outcome of a hunt, though these activities could sometimes take more communal forms.

What is a notable factor in this discussion of the expression of love (especially romantic) is that most (but not all) systems outside Europe encourage an early age for such unions. Girls get married soon after puberty and are sometimes betrothed beforehand, either through particular arrangements or through the kinship system, for example in Islam to the father's brother's daughter, though a degree of choice is often allowed. Arrangements of this kind may be made partly to be sure of a partner, partly to provide a suitable one (a 'match'), partly (where contraceptive techniques are limited) to avoid the birth of children not considered legitimate under current norms. When this happens we do not find long periods of adolescence in which sex is postponed, when sexual partners are being sought, and where the final prospects are 'distant'. It is in that postponed search that 'romantic love' is frequently elaborated and expressed, that unsatisfied longings abound. Nevertheless, even at an early age prospective partners may become submerged in each other's personality and readily go off to live in a strange household. In these circumstances, it is love (not often expressed) that is apparent rather than lust.

There is an important difference between the expression of an emotion and its existence. As I have suggested, it is elaborated in the written word, characteristically in love-letters, which are found widely in literate cultures. But the emotion is present much more widely, even if the forms are different. It really does rule the world, not only the continent of Europe.

Finally, the associated claim that love is uniquely European has also had a number of political implications being bound up not only with the development of capitalism but also being used in the service of imperialism. There is a palace in Mérida in Yucatan, the decoration of which portrays helmeted and armoured conquistadores towering over vanquished savages, with an inscription that proclaims the conquering power of love. That emotion, fraternal rather than sexual, had been claimed by the imperialist conquerors from Europe. Love literally conquers all in the hands of the invading military.

11   Last words

In this book I have been concerned with the way that Europe has stolen the history of the East by imposing its own versions of time (largely Christian) and of space on the rest of the Eurasian world. We can perhaps claim that a world history demands a single reckoning of time and space which Europe has provided. But my special problem has been with the attempts at periodization that historians have made, dividing historical time into Antiquity, Feudalism, the Renaissance followed by Capitalism; this development is seen as leading from one to the other in a unique transformation until the dominance of the known world by Europe in the nineteenth century, following the Industrial Revolution that is considered to have begun in England. Here the question of imposing concepts has very different, teleological, implications.

Colonial or world domination in any form carries a considerable danger as well as possible benefits for intellectual work, not so much in the sciences as in the humanities where the 'truth' criteria are less clear-cut. In the present case the west assumes a superiority (which it has obviously displayed in some spheres since the nineteenth century) and projects that superiority back in time, creating a teleological history. The problem for the rest of the world is that such beliefs are used to justify the way 'others' are treated, since those others are often seen as static, as being unable to change themselves, certainly without help from outside. But history teaches us that any superiority is a temporary factor and that we also have to look for alternation. Already the enormous country of China seems to be taking a leading role in the economy, which can be the basis of educational, military, and cultural power, as earlier it was in Europe and then in the USA, and earlier still in China itself. This latest shift has been carried out by a communist government, without much deliberate help from the west.

In this study I have been trying to lay out the way in which the domination of the world by Europe since its expansion in the sixteenth century but above all since its leading position in the world's economy through to the industrialization of the nineteenth century, resulted in the domination of accounts of the world's history. I call the alternative an anthropo-archaeological approach to modern history. It starts from the work of the prehistorian Gordon Childe who described the Bronze Age as the Urban Revolution, the onset of 'civilization' in the literal sense. The Bronze Age began in the Ancient Near East, spreading eastwards to India and China, south to Egypt and west to the Aegean. It consisted of the introduction of mechanized agriculture, in the shape of the cattle-drawn plough, the large-scale control of water, the development of the wheel and of a variety of urban crafts, including the invention of writing, probably connected with the expansion of mercantile activity. This specialization in towns obviously required an increase in productivity to enable artisans and others to escape from primary agricultural production, and at the same time it encouraged vast differences in land-holdings between 'classes', since one was no longer confined to produce with the hoe but with the help of the plough could cultivate much more territory. The plough is simply an inverted hoe, mechanized by being drawn by animal transport, but which represents a great advance in productivity.

The Bronze Age was initially an Asian-based 'civilization' which long preceded the European Renaissance linked by Elias to the civilizing process. I want to enquire historically how it was that the comparative unity of the Bronze Age then was considered to break up into a European and an Asiatic branch, with the former thought of as opposing a dynamic continent characterized by the growth of capitalism and the latter marked by stasis, by despotism and by what Marx called 'Asiatic exceptionalism', based upon different 'modes of production'.

The split had to begin somewhere. Where did it start? There is a general agreement that the Minoan situation (and necessarily the Egyptian) belonged to the Bronze Age, with its early written tradition. The split was seen as coming in Europe first with Archaic Greek, then Roman, Antiquity, which was held to be fundamentally different from what went on before and that however took place partly in Asia, with Homer's story and the Ionian philosophers. I argue that this idea of difference, of divergence was produced largely by Europeans, either in the Renaissance which they saw as the rebirth of classical Antiquity (through humanism) or in the eighteenth and nineteenth centuries when the economy of the Industrial Revolution in Europe gave that continent a distinct economic advantage over the rest of the world (an advantage that had begun with the learning, the economy, and the guns and sails of the Renaissance). In other words, there was a strong element of teleology behind the European claim that its tradition distinguished itself in earlier times when its subsequent superiority was seen as having its origin.

But how far in fact did Antiquity itself distinguish the period as a separate phase? The classical historian, Moses Finley, saw Ancient Greece as inventing democracy, the rule of the people. That is a theme close to the hearts of contemporary politicians, of Bush and Blair, who see it as characteristic of our Judaeo-Christian civilization (from which Islam is excluded, although it was plainly the third member), as a gift Europe can now export to the rest of the world. There is little doubt that Athens was one of the first to institutionalize the direct popular, written, vote and that this was seen to distinguish that polity from the monarchical regimes of Persia and other Asian states, though the preliterate kingdom of Dahomey took a vote by means of dropping stones in a container. As a city-state, Athens was small enough to operate by direct representation. Nevertheless the city state and its democracy did not exist only there. That form of government was present in the city states of Phoenicia, of present-day Lebanon, especially in Tyre which was the mother city of the Phoenician colony of Carthage. Not only had Phoenicia developed the vowel-less alphabet used to write down the Bible as well as other Arabic and other Semitic works, but they also had a form of democracy by which representatives (*sufrafetes*) were chosen not every few years but every year, thus ensuring a close link between public opinion and government. But Carthage has been written out of world, or at any rate, European history. It was African, not European; it was Semitic, not Aryan, Indo-European; and its libraries were dispersed, partly as the result of the Roman conquest, so we hear much less of its accomplishments.

But it was not only Phoenicia. Even monarchical systems in Asia might have democratic governments in their constituent towns. While in the vicinity of many centralized governments, that is, kingdoms, we find peoples with very different systems of acephalous, representative government, described by Ibn Khaldun for the Bedouin and for Fortes and Evans-Pritchard for Africa more generally. Antiquity was not the only source for the model of democratic rule.

Finley also celebrates Antiquity as having invented 'art'. Obviously it invented Greek art, very important in Europe and indeed in world history. But there is no way that it invented art per se. The round columns of Greece for instance came from Egypt; that country and Assyria were both of great importance in the development of visual forms, but in any case many other countries, apart from the west, were of significance in the artistic fields. The apparent world-wide authority of the west in this sphere is very much connected with the nineteenth-century dominance of Europe, and through Europe of the world. But the problem comes when

Antiquity is viewed as a direct but necessary stage of world development on the way to western capitalism.

In the European view, Antiquity is not only a period but a type of society, unique to that continent. It was necessary for them to establish Antiquity as a distinct phase of development because the collapse of the Roman Empire was eventually followed by the rise of another period, namely feudalism, which was also seen as unique to the west and whose contradictions gave rise to the subsequent emergence of capitalism in the west. The concept of Antiquity has been elaborated by European classicists to account for the singularity of the traditions coming down from Greece and Rome. While those societies certainly differed from other ancient cultures, just as they differed from earlier Archaic Greece and Rome, radical attempts were made to distinguish them from others not so much on the basis of the economy as of the political system and the ideology – for example, democracy and freedom found in Europe as distinct from tyranny and despotism supposedly prevalent in Asia. Whatever the case with these prestigious attributes, what is quite clear is that knowledge systems were considerably advanced in the classical world by the technologies of the intellect, by the adoption of the alphabet; its widespread use extended the possibilities of the written word, first invented in Mesopotamia and Egypt, subsequently moving towards a phonetic alphabet in Syria (Ugarit) and then in mainland Greece. The Greek alphabet was of course unique in its representation of vowels, and highly influential for later Europe. But it was close to the Phoenician and the consequences of the relatively minor difference, and of differences with other forms of writing, were not as radical as many, including Watt and myself, had supposed.

Other scholars have used Christianity in a similar way to point to Europe's singularity. But Christianity was one of a trilogy of West Asian religions, using related myths and scriptures, embracing similar values and codes. There was little specifically European about it, with the main early ideologues coming from the Near East, or, in the case of Augustine, from North Africa. It was a thoroughly intercontinental Mediterranean creed, with an Old Testament of a partly nomadic, Semitic background of parched deserts and fertile oases.

The critical point in the history of the modern world has been not the search for the singularity of early Europe but the abandonment of the prehistorian's perspective, epitomized by Gordon Childe in *What appened in history*, a view that stresses the broad unity of Bronze Age civilizations across Europe and Asia. This unity, fractured by the western notion of a purely European Antiquity (who else had it?), was based on the development of many artisanal crafts, including that of writing itself. Early writing was associated, *inter alia*, with religious scriptures, placing instruction in the hands of the priesthood (the teachers were priests), the growth of temple as well as of palace complexes, and the development of the religious body into what the ancient historian, Oppenheim, called 'a great organisation'. The notion of an independent European Antiquity breaks with this broad unity, proclaims a phase in the history of the world that is unique to Europe and in the minds of its protagonists prefigures the development of modernity and of capitalism in that continent. There is little at the economic level to justify this exceptionalism. Iron came to be used instead of bronze throughout these civilizations, with many implications of a 'democratic' kind (iron was more widely available and more serviceable than bronze) for warfare, for farming, for crafts, and also for the development of 'machinery', though for this purpose wood remained the dominant material until the nineteenth century. Some societies undoubtedly developed faster than others. In the ancient world, Greece took the lead in forms of urban construction, temples, schools, domestic buildings in towns such as Ephesus, as well as in the production not only of written knowledge and of literature but of the arts more generally, although depending in many spheres on Near Eastern precedents (the famed column, for instance) and rivalled in others by distant India and China. However, the problem of Antiquity becomes especially acute, both for the present and for the past, when European scholars attribute the prestigious origin of a form of government (democracy), of values like freedom, of individualism, even of 'rationality', to this historical period, and hence to Europe rather than elsewhere.

The economy has not been selected as major factor of this difference except for the description of Greece and Rome as slave societies that has been used 'paradoxically' to strengthen the notion of Antiquity, by contrast, as 'inventing' freedom. It is said to have invented not only freedom but democracy and individualism. I have suggested that the claim has been greatly exaggerated, as has the unique role of slavery. Achievements in literature, science, and the arts are quite outstanding, but should be seen as extensions of the Bronze Age cultures of the region, as Bernal has argued. The attempt to distinguish these as societies of quite another type follows the Greeks' own desire to set Europe apart from Asia as well as that of subsequent western scholars to boost their own lineage.

It may well be that, as the partial result of the alphabet, the abundance of the literary sources themselves has created the overall impression of a different 'mentality' and way of life. In moving from prehistory to history, the actors begin to speak for themselves through a written language. One is no longer confined to the interpretation of predominantly material data, but one has to take into account the 'spiritual', the verbal (recorded in writing); one is forced to take into account how the Greeks thought of themselves (which one cannot do for the Phoenicians in the same way because they left so little writing behind them). That means giving greater weight to their opinions of themselves and of others, as well as raising the consequent danger of accepting their self-evaluation as the 'truth'. Their values become our judgements. We accept (and even extend) their appropriation of democracy, of freedom, and of other 'virtues'. Greece differed only in degree from Phoenicia and Carthage which have been largely written out of the script. The small city-states that existed in both areas could arrange more flexible systems of government than larger units, although at times they too acquired, even chose, tyrants. But other types of society employed democratic procedures and there is no way that Greece or Europe can be considered as the inventors of popular consultation, although it may have developed a written one. Nor yet of freedom. Was it with tongue-in-cheek that Finley saw the emergence of the concept of freedom in Greece in opposition to slavery? In fact many communities living on the margins of great states, or any centralized polity, deliberately rejected centralized authority (for example, the Robin Hoods of all around the globe) while some, for other reasons altogether, organized themselves in different, 'acephalous', ways. The peoples of the margins, of the deserts, of the woods, and of the hills would always provide a different model for government than the centralized peoples of the plains.

The exclusion of Phoenicia, pre-empting the later exclusion of the rest of Asia and the east, is an index of the fragility of the concept of a unique European Antiquity, since to many contemporaries its colony, Carthage, was clearly the rival to Rome and Greece. For later Europeans it has never been seen as having left behind a similar literary heritage, but that may well be because of the deliberate destruction or dispersal of its libraries by Romans and others, or because of the ephemeral nature of papyrus. Some have interpreted this exclusion as a matter of 'Aryan' Europeans disregarding the influence of Semitic Asians or Africans on major developments, which is certainly one possibility. But we should treat gingerly the claim of Bernal and more recently of Hobson that such exclusion arose from nineteenth-century anti-Semitism or imperialism; these features belong to the wider category of ethnocentrism that goes back much further in time, being part of the inevitable process of defining identity though that itself is variable in strength at particular periods and particular places).

Just as Antiquity is seen to have no counterparts elsewhere, so in most accounts feudalism too was confined to the west. Some have doubted this restriction – Kowalewski for India, Coulbourn for other areas, but in the kind of evolutionary schema that Marx laid out or implicitly accepted, Antiquity necessarily preceded European feudalism, just as the latter was essential for European capitalism. The contradictions inherent in one phase led to their resolution in the next. The assertion of uniqueness was appealing to many western medievalists; even though they were not committed to the explicit unilinear arguments of Marx, nevertheless the European trajectory was considered unique. So of course it was, but in what respects and in respect of what? Was it dependent land-tenure, was it decentralized government? What is needed in respect of both these features is an analytic grid against which the variations can be plotted. By itself the assertion that 'we are different' can provide little useful basis for analysis or enquiry. We need to know which of its 'unique' factors was essential to the growth of the 'modern' world.

For, associated with this view of Marx and others, is the notion of feudalism as a 'progressive phase' in world history, heading towards the 'ultimate' development of 'capitalism'. It is not easy to see it as such in the west of Europe, where the collapse of urban settlement was extensive. So too were the activities connected with the towns, some urban crafts, education, literary activity, knowledge systems, art, and theatre. Of course, matters gradually improved; a 'rebirth' there had to be, if only because of mercantile exchange. There were some changes in the rural domain, which has received most attention. But towns did not start to revive in the west until about the eleventh century, monastic schools somewhat earlier, the economy about the same time, most of the arts and intellectual life, too, really with the early universities though the real recovery did not come until the justly named Renaissance. When the European economy did eventually revive, it was largely dependent on the Italian trade with the eastern Mediterranean, a region that had never experienced the same devastation as the west. There towns continued to flourish, trading with the further east. Intellectual life as well as trade, too, owed a great deal to the Muslim east and south before the fourteenth century, based not only on translations from the Greek but on their own contributions (as well as on those of the Jews) in medicine, astronomy, mathematics, and other spheres. India and China too played their part in this revival, for the band of Islamic societies stretched right across the whole of Asia, from southern Spain to the frontiers of China. More particularly there was the eastern origin of many plants, trees, and flowers (oranges, tea, and chrysanthemums), as well as the innovations that Francis Bacon saw as central to modern society, the compass, paper and gunpowder, not to speak of the eastern origin of the printing press and of the manufacture, indeed industrialization, of porcelain and of silk and cotton textiles. Little of this achievement makes early feudalism look a particularly progressive period in European or world history; in the west progress was often exogenous in character, though that is not at all how many European scholars see the question. For them Europe had been set on a self-sufficient, self-made course in Antiquity which led inevitably through feudalism, to colonial and commercial expansion, and then to industrial capitalism. But that is teleological history that excluded other social formations from these developments, seeing them as imprisoned in static, despotic states built on irrigation and immense towns. Whereas the west had rain-fed agriculture (in general much less productive) and smaller towns.

These non-European towns are often denied the description of 'having a bourgeoisie'; they were different, according to Weber, even though they displayed many of the same kinds and levels of achievement as in the west, in particular, in domestic and in 'cultural' life, as well as in commerce and in manufactures. Chapter 6 analyzed the study of the sociologist Elias of the sociogenesis of 'civilization' which concentrated solely upon the post-Renaissance west. The whole notion of 'civilized' (urbanized, polite) behaviour which was so marked in China over many centuries is neglected. In this case Europe has stolen the idea and actuality of the civilization process. But how civilized was the west before it acquired paper from the Arabs, and through them from China? A better balance between the civilizations is achieved by Fernandez-Armesto in his book *Millennium*,[1] which begins with Heian Japan and treats the major Eurasian societies as being on a similar level.

Obviously important movements, manufacturing, commercial, intellectual, artistic, took place at the time of the European Renaissance. But so too other revivals have taken place in written cultures in Eurasia, perhaps less spectacularly, as a result both of internal developments and of reciprocal interaction. For Europe, these changes have been chronicled by the historian Braudel who makes a determined effort to consider comparative data, setting aside for example Weber's attribution of importance to the Protestant ethic (chapter 7) which has for so long been a stand-by of European explanations of their achievements (but less comforting to Italian and other Catholics). He points to the extensive market activity that characterized the east well before the west; mercantile capitalism flourished later in Europe, and was never confined to one continent or the other. But 'finance capitalism' he sees as the critical western contribution to 'true capitalism'. It is the case that industrial capitalism, with its expensive manufacturing plants, required greatly increased capital; so

---

[1] Fernandez-Armesto 1995.

too did the national economy. But the basis for this expansion was already present in the banking and financial reforms that emerged in Italy in relation to the rise in Mediterranean trade with the east. That development produced similar institutions that already existed or were soon to develop in the major trading centres of Asia.

The same case can be made for industrialization. Here too there was a spectacular development in the Industrial Revolution in Britain and the west. But once again, the bases were to be found earlier and elsewhere. The major Bronze Age economies gave rise to some large-scale manufacturing enterprises, especially for textiles, and mostly run by the state. In Mesopotamia woollen cloth was manufactured in what the archaeologist, Wooley, called 'factories'. His Soviet counterpart, Diakonoff, protested that they were only workshops, following Marx in reserving the term 'factory' for later capitalist (or proto-capitalist) production. In India, under the Mughals, *kharkhanas* were again state-organized institutions employing workers under one large roof to engage in the large-scale production of cotton cloth. China is an even more clear-cut case of an early form of industrialization. Ledderose has written of the extensive production of ceramics ('china') shipped in large quantities to the west and how it was marked by modular (mass) production techniques with a complex division of labour of an Adam Smithian kind. The manufacture of ceramics in China has been described as industrial, making use of a complex division of labour, of modular production and a factory-type organization. Equally, while silk textiles were largely woven in a domestic context before being acquired by the state through taxation, paper which was used so widely after its development around the beginning of the Common Era was also made by an 'industrial' process. That was mechanical too, since paper was produced using the water-mill, the prototype of the later factories ('mills') used in the west for textile manufacture, and employing in addition to human labour the energy derived from flowing streams and rivers, providing a cheaper writing material than local silk or than the skins (parchment) and imported papyrus of Europe, the latter expensively brought in from Egypt, since by the new process paper could be made anywhere out of local materials. Paper manufacture spread throughout the Muslim world and eventually reached western Europe in time for the printing revolution, coming first to Italy from Sicily. The presence of this cheap locally manufactured, mass-produced material for writing meant that even without printing the circulation of information and ideas was considerably more rapid and extensive in the east than in the west.

The notion of 'Asiatic exceptionalism' that characterized so much of historians' teleological thinking about the past, overwhelmed as they are by the development of 'modernity' and 'industrial capitalism' in the west, blinds them to the many similarities that existed. In a recent book Brotton has written of the Renaissance Bazaar and the contribution made by Turkey and the Near East generally to that period. We could also think of the contribution made by Islam in Spain to earlier 'renascences', mathematical, medical, literary (for example, to troubadour poetry and to narrative fiction), to Platonic studies and to the ideas of Dante. However, there is a further step that we need to take, to consider the idea that such rebirths were not a purely European phenomenon. Theoretically, every literate society can resurrect knowledge that has been forgotten or deliberately set aside. In Europe following the classical period, the Christian church had been involved in setting aside a great deal of classical learning, stigmatized as pagan, as forbidden or as redundant to their beliefs, not only in the fields of the arts (viz., sculpture, theatre, and secular painting), but also in science (e.g. medicine). The severity was such that when the rebirth came, it was more marked in Europe than elsewhere, and indeed the pace of the recovery in intellectual matters was more rapid under the impact of printing and paper as well as with the renewal of extensive commerce, especially with the east.

The problem about seeing the Renaissance as a revival or even continuation of classical life is this – although Roman buildings continued to affect the life of the church in many ways, both as models and as structures, and Latin continued to be used by Christians in the west, the coming of that religion and the collapse of the Empire had led to a sharp break. I have spoken of the disappearance of literacy, of schools, of urban crafts, possibly even of Christianity in Britain. There was also the wider disappearance of Greek and Roman art, especially sculpture and the theatre, because of the ideological adoption of Semitic iconoclasm, putting limits on representation. I am aware this did not continue in the same form in a Catholic religious context, but in a lay, secular one it effectively did until the early Renaissance. Europe had a lot to throw aside until the expression of secularism once again became possible. That made conceivable the rebirth of a secular theatre, giving rise to the work of the Paduan secretary, Albertino Mussato, whose tragedy of *Ecerinis* (1329), local tyrant, was written in Latin verse modelled on that of Seneca. But it was still a long way (250 years) to the vernacular plays of Marlowe and Shakespeare in English, of Racine and Corneille in French.

In other words, in many spheres there was a significant break with antiquity in post-Roman times, a break which *required* a rebirth, a Renaissance in the west – but not in the east where there had been no such formidable gap in urban culture. Indeed it was the east which helped to restore the west, not only commercially but in the arts and sciences as well. There was the influence of Islam in Andalucia, on Brunetto Latini (Dante's teacher) for example, the influence of Arabic numerals whose use in the west was spread by Pope Sylvester II. But take the example of medicine. Its study in the west had fallen behind, partly because of a ban on dissection, on cutting up the human body, partly throught an absence of medical texts, by Galen for example. These latter were brought back into western medicine by the many translations by the Muslim world, through Constantine the African at Monte Cassino (near the medical school of Salerno) and by others around Montpellier. The problem is that if we see medicine as based simply on a revival of classical scholarship, we tend to exclude the fact that this scholarship, and important Muslim additions, came to us by an indirect route.

It was the east, which had not experienced the decline of the western Roman empire, that stimulated the Renaissance, since it did not go through the same disastrous collapse of 'culture' as western Europe and remained a focus of trade and cultural transfer when initially the Italian towns, especially Venice, renewed the links which were to prove so important. Throughout Asia, the east did not need the same rebirth since it did not have the same death. That is why China remained ahead of the west in science until the sixteenth century, in the economy (according to Bray and others) until the end of the eighteenth. It neither had the extensive material collapse nor did it have in the same way a restrictive, hegemonic religion. Despite the assertions of many writers, it developed an active mercantile urban culture even before Europe. Weber, Pirenne, Braudel, and others concentrate on what they think was different about towns in Asia. These arguments were teleologically based and very dubious. Look for instance at the culture of flowers and of food, which I have discussed in detail in other contexts. Each of these developments preceded those in post-classical Europe. The development of connoisseurship and of interest in the 'antique' in this sense was roughly contemporary with Europe. So too with theatre (*kabuki* in Japan, for example) and the realistic novel, though later than classical achievements. This is completely understandable if we abandon the idea of Asiatic (and indeed of European) exceptionalism and think rather in terms of roughly parallel developments since the Urban Revolution, varying of course in tempo and in content, that occurred throughout Eurasia, based upon similar processes of social evolution and broadly reciprocal exchange relationships. Trade required such contacts that involved not merely the exchange of material goods but of information, including information about techniques and ideas.

Again we need to consider the intellectual developments of the Renaissance that we speak of as the scientific revolution. This was not of course the beginning of science. Joseph Needham edited a series of extremely important volumes on Chinese achievements in which he concludes that science was more advanced in that vast country until the sixteenth century. At that time paper and printing had recently come into Europe which permitted the much faster circulation of information (like computers later on). Thus Needham sees the west as taking over and as introducing a science based upon the testing of mathematically formed hypotheses. He called this 'modern science' and linked it to the coming of capitalism, the bourgeoisie, and the Renaissance. However, it has been suggested that the testing was influenced by Arab alchemists while mathematics came originally from a large number of sources. Moreover, Needham's suggestion involves the particular developmental hypothesis that I have been criticizing. My preference is for more regular evolutionary change rather than for a sudden revolution of a putative kind. 'Modern science' should be more closely linked to earlier science, and developments in the west seen as more continuous with China than Needham finally proposes.

Equally Elias for 'civilization' and Braudel for 'true capitalism' have abrogated critical parts of the developmental process to the west. The same has been done for institutions more generally, especially the town and the university. I discuss the combined problem in chapter 8 and find that the uniqueness argument has been greatly overdone, especially with the towns. There is some indication that the university in western Europe managed to throw off religious bonds and to secularize learning earlier than, say, the madrasas of Islam, but China never had that problem with higher education as it escaped the embrace of a hegemonic creed with its own vision of the world. Undoubtedly there were special features of both these institutions in the west but the claim that Europe invented the type most conducive to capitalism seems to contradict the long-standing parallelism between east and west. This parallelism has not prevented Europeans from attributing to themselves a variety of virtues (chapter 9) which they consider to have helped them, rather than others, to achieve modernization. It started (at least as far as the written evidence goes) with the Greeks. As we have seen, they often defined themselves as democratic in permitting the people to choose their government (at least all the people except slaves, women and metics), while the states of Asia practised 'tyranny'. It is a similar story with individualism. That feature long existed in many of these groups; the notion of the 'collective' primitive, of 'primitive communism' as a type of society, is unacceptable, even though in some societies certain rights to resources might be held in common.

Emotions, too, have been appropriated by the west. The most clear-cut case is that of love, which some Europeans have claimed as being invented by twelfth-century troubadours, others as an intrinsic feature of Christianity, like charity; for some, too, it characterizes the European, even the English, family, and for others the modern, western world. All these claims are equally unsustainable. If Hollywood has marketed 'romantic love', it did not invent it. Nor did the English, nor the Christians, nor the moderns, while the troubadours of Provence and Aquitaine had a great deal of help from their Arabo-Spanish neighbours who were heirs to a long and important tradition of secular (and religious) love poetry from the Near East, going back to at least the *Song of songs*. While it is interesting to enquire what led Europeans to make claims for the unique development of certain virtues and emotions, the proofs of that uniqueness are lacking and could only emerge from a systematic comparison at a cross-cultural level.

Let me return to Childe's notion of the Urban Revolution of the Bronze Age which was clearly connected with L. H. Morgan's concept of civilization and the culture of cities as presented in *Ancient Society*[2] as well as with more general sources. One great advantage of this notion is that it does not privilege the west but describes a common historical development that took place in the Ancient Near East, reaching Egypt and the Aegean, in India and China. The resulting cultural affinity between the main urban civilizations of Eurasia at this period runs up against the notion of a radical discontinuity or difference that is the basis of some of the major and most influential socio-historical accounts of world development. According to the dominant European view, looking back in the nineteenth century from a standpoint of the undoubted achievements following the Industrial Revolution, historians and sociologists (and to some extent anthropologists) felt they had to account for the differences. So the west was seen as passing through a number of stages of development from ancient society, to feudalism, to capitalism. The east on the other hand was marked by what Marx saw as 'Asiatic exceptionalism', characterized by hydraulic agriculture and despotic government, in contrast to the west, especially Europe, which was rain-fed and consultative. That is not just a Marxist argument; it was held in a different form by Weber and by many historians, and versions of it have been put forward by the sociologist, M. Mann,[3] and by others who are wedded to a commitment to long-term European advantage – eurocentric historians the geographer Blaut calls them. Those versions take many forms; for example, there is the highly influential account given by Malthus for the failures of China to control her population because she did not have the internalized restraints of the west, a view bearing some resemblances to Weber's idea of the role

[2] Morgan 1877.   [3] Mann 1986.

of the Protestant ethic in the birth of capitalism, the nature of restraint being widely taken up by the demographic-historians of the Cambridge Group under the leadership of Peter Laslett, and indeed that was likewise proposed by Freud and Elias.

Certainly there were broad differences in the sequencing of social life in the west and east. In the west of Europe, the fall of the classical empires meant a partial decay of urban civilization, some disappearance of towns, and the increased importance of the countryside and its rulers, leading eventually to 'feudalism'. In the European account of the process this stage is often seen as a 'progressive' move in terms of world history, resulting in the birth of a new kind of town, beginning with the communes of North Italy, sheltering their freedom-loving bourgeoisie, their autonomous governments and displaying the various features that made them the forerunners of capitalism and modernization. But the sequence also goes back to earlier views of Asia as 'despotic' in contrast to 'democratic' Greece (though it also had its tyrants, just as Asia had its democrats). Europe certainly had theirs.

The notion of Asiatic exceptionalism has recently come under fire. It has been implicitly criticized among others by Eric Wolf in his work on *Europe and the people without history*[4] where he suggested that the authority systems of both the east and the west, despotic or democratic, should be seen as variants one of another, of the 'tributary state', with the east sometimes being more centralized than the west. The implications for the later development of capitalism have been firmly criticized by a new generation of European scholars who have rejected or modified the notion of European advantage before the Industrial Revolution and whose work I have discussed in a recent book entitled *Capitalism and modernisation: the great debate*.[5] But little attempt has so far been made to link up these new perspectives on post-classical history with the earlier work on the similarities of development in Eurasia that emerges from the archaeological background. If there was a broad unity in terms of 'civilization' at the time of the Bronze Age, how did that 'exceptionalism' in the east and the corresponding uniqueness of the west subsequently emerge? Did it ever emerge at all? Was the disappearance of towns (and the prevalence of 'feudalism') ever anything but a particular western European episode in world history? Because around the Mediterranean, towns, especially as ports or 'ports-of-trade', continued to have a vigorous life in Constantinople, Damascus, Aleppo, Baghdad, Alexandria, and elsewhere. And of course further east as well. Some time later, Venice recaptured the spirit and activity of its Roman past and vigorously entered into a profitable exchange with the

---

[4] Wolf 1982.   [5] Goody 2004.

east. If we look at the more or less continuous history of towns in Asia we get a very different picture of world history rather than by concentrating on the decay of urban culture and on the rural mode of production (leading to 'feudalism') in western Europe. That could even be seen as a question of European rather than Asiatic exceptionalism. Outside that continent towns and ports did not disappear to be reborn as forerunners of capitalist enterprise; they continued to flourish throughout Asia and formed the nodes of exchange, manufacture, education, learning, and other specialist activity that pointed towards later developments. While the new towns of western Europe undoubtedly had some singular features of their own, they were hardly unique in the way that Weber and Braudel[6] posited. Wherever they were found, towns were involved in early mercantile ('capitalist') action, in India, in China, in the Near East. They were centres of specialist activities, of written culture, of commerce, of manufacture, and of consumption of various degrees of complexity carried out by merchants, artisans, and other bourgeois elements. Indeed while advanced industrial capitalism was developed in the west, it is a travesty of world history to see its early growth as being unique to that continent. The usual criteria of advanced capitalism are industrialization and high finance (Braudel) or extensive commerce (Marx, Wallerstein). With mass production under industrial conditions, finance had necessarily to have a greater role and exchange became more intensive, but neither were new European features of the economy. Nor was industrialization. It has been argued convincingly that industrialization marked some of the early manufacturing processes especially of China. Within Europe the industrial production of textiles certainly did not begin with the English cotton industry in the middle of the eighteenth century. It had already started in Italy in the eleventh with the reeling of silk which gave that country's industry a very considerable comparative advantage.[7] Those processes were developed in competition with the silk imported from China and the Near East, manufactured eventually by water-driven machines, the plans for which were probably imported as well as the raw materials.

We need to query many of these old myths and take another look at the supposed discontinuity with the Bronze Age between ancient societies, Antiquity and feudalism. Elsewhere the history of urbanization displays a very different profile. Urban cultures, with their elements of 'luxury' and learning, continued to develop and change from those earlier times. The case of prepared food[8] and indeed of luxury products more generally such as domesticated flowers[9] helps us to do just this. What is especially

[6] Braudel 1981.   [7] Poni 2001a and 2001b.   [8] Goody 1982.   [9] Goody 1993.

interesting about the development of *hautes cuisines* is the fact that they have appeared in all the major civilizations in Eurasia in what can be seen in very broad terms as roughly the same period. One can trace the emergence of a literature of connoisseurship in China, at roughly the same epoch as its emergence in Europe.[10] Complex cuisine came earlier in the former, but not if we count the ancient world in the eastern Mediterranean. Similar statements could be made about developments in many of the arts, including the complete rejection of forms of figurative representation (icons) that we find at certain times and certain places in all the major (i.e. written) world religions.

If we were to take seriously those accounts of world development which see the east as static, the west as dynamic, over the long term – and even Braudel takes this line in his great synthesis on *Civilization and capitalism 15th to 18th century*, this parallelism would seem surprising. Or again if one subscribes to the doctrines of 'Asiatic exceptionalism' or 'Oriental despotism', which would appear to inhibit this development of urban tastes, because urban they largely were.

It is true that after the fall of the Roman Empire, or perhaps after the Muslim dominance of the Mediterranean, there was a decline of commerce and the decay of urban culture in the west,[11] partly linked to the coming of Christianity[12] where, for example, property was given to the Church rather than to the municipality. But the consequent stress on rural life, giving rise to the notion of feudalism, was a largely western phenomenon which cannot, should not, be seen as a necessary phase of the history of either world or European development.

Elsewhere the urban civilization of the Bronze Age continued to produce an increasingly wider range of artisanal and manufactured objects, a wider set of trading networks, a greater development of mercantile culture. One step led to another in what Childe saw as 'social evolution'. Eventually the west caught up again after the revival of trade and the growth of towns that Pirenne speaks of in the eleventh century. That took place mainly because of the return of exchange with the Near East where urban mercantile culture had never disappeared, a return in which the role of Venice and other Italian centres was critical.[13] Elsewhere trade networks had continued to extend from the Bronze Age onwards, in

---

[10] Clunas 1991 and Brook 1998.
[11] This question has been usefully discussed by Hodges and Whitehouse (1983) who have attempted to modify the Pirenne thesis regarding the disruption of that trade (1939) with the aid of archaeological evidence.
[12] Speiser (1985) has argued the point in reference to some urban centres in the Byzantine world.
[13] Lane 1973.

Ceylon,[14] in South-East Asia,[15] in the Near East,[16] the Indian Ocean.[17] Eventually Christian Europe caught up with the 'modernizing' process, often by borrowing from the east, for example, with printing, paper, silk weaving, the compass and gun powder, foods such as citrus and sugar, many species of flowers; they later developed, though did not originate, the process of industrial manufacture (as well as the manufacture of ships and armaments – the arsenal was particularly important in the development of industry and its production processes[18]) in the course of which they gained an impressive comparative advantage. No sooner had it done so than advanced industrial activity began to spread to other parts of the world, especially among the metropolitan powers and in those places where the urban cultures of the Bronze Age had been most developed (as well as in some others as a result of migration).

While these processes of 'modernization' have proceeded more rapidly in some major societies in Eurasia than in others, the overall movement has been widespread. Archaeologists are used to dealing with general transitions of this kind, taking place in the same sequence but at different times, for example, the shift from the Mesolithic to the Neolithic. They tend to look for explanations, when they give them, in terms either of external communication or else of structural similarities arising internally from a parallel initial situation.[19] Anthropologists on the other hand often resort to vague indications of cultural change and historians to 'mentalities'. In my view this latter is dangerous territory for these scholars, and even more dangerous for the archaeologist who has less data to build on. Explanation based on culture or on mentalities may be misleading if it leads automatically to conceiving difference, which may well be temporary, in a permanent frame. Some developments we have considered have run parallel courses over the long term in various post Bronze Age cultures, even if at somewhat different speeds. This process has not been a question of globalization as often understood, that is westernization today. Rather, it represents the growth of urban, bourgeois societies, which have been developing continually ever since the times of which Childe was writing, partly by interacting and exchanging with each other, partly by a kind of internal 'logic'. For these were merchant cultures, engaged in creating products and services which they would exchange with their own urban population, with the local countryside but also with other towns

[14] Perera 1951, 1952a and b.
[15] Sabloff and Lamberg-Karlovsky 1975; Leur 1955; Melink-Roelofsz 1962, 1970.
[16] Goitein 1967.   [17] Casson 1989, for the Periplus.   [18] Zan 2004.
[19] See G. Stein, The organizational dynamics of complexity in Greater Mesopotamia, Stein and Rothman 1994, pp. 11–22.

elsewhere. They developed new products, improving upon the old, and they extended the range of their contacts.

In essence the towns were 'ports of trade', to use an expression of Karl Polanyi (but in a somewhat different way). They were making goods, providing services, and from time to time improving those products, increasing their range and their clientele, rarely standing still. They were engaged in manufacture and trade to earn a living, which meant they had to make greater profits (or at least break even), not make a loss, in order to pay for a greater range of imports. They were therefore in continuous transition. Merchants, notes Southall,[20] were the 'essential midwives to the capitalist mode of production, magnified and transformed into industrialists and financiers'. Following Weber, he sees this process as emerging in the feudal mode, although merchants have been an essential component of all towns and cities everywhere.[21] 'Cities were the creation of merchants, which they struggled to defend against the state, creation of kings and nobles.' They were 'always the centres of innovation' especially, Southall claims, in feudal times, though that is something to be disputed. They were the centres too of class conflict, a 'theatre of perpetual social war of relentless cruelty' but at the same time scenes of great artistic activity.[22]

These activities should be seen as the roots of 'capitalism', at least of mercantile capitalism. Or perhaps of 'the sprouts of capitalism' as they have been designated by some Chinese scholars. At this level, there is no problem about the origin of capitalism or more importantly the growth of urban cultures in all their many socio-cultural forms, including the arts. About which, the great leap in our thinking comes when we realize that, whatever has taken place regarding the mass media of recent times, the west was not the inventor of these arts, of literature (the novel for example), of the theatre or of painting and sculpture, much less of a special set of values that permitted modernization to occur there and nowhere else. These activities have been developing throughout the urban societies of the Eurasian continent (and elsewhere), sometimes one society taking the lead, sometimes another. But early in the Middle Ages, the west fell dramatically behind, partly because of the break with the classical past, partly because of the deliberate rejection of representation (anyhow secular) by early Christianity and the Abrahamic religion.

I have spoken above of the broad base of mercantile capitalism; that base seems obvious enough given the extent of early merchant activities in Asia and the export of Indian cotton to the East Indian islands (Indonesia) and to South-east Asia (Indo-China), as well as the export of Chinese bronzes, silks, and porcelain throughout those regions. Compared to western Europe and even to the Mediterranean, in earlier times the Far East was a hive of mercantile activity. According to Bray, China remained the greatest economic power in the world until the end of the eighteenth century.[23] What about manufacture, and even industry, which are rightly seen as the key features of modern capitalism? Such widespread exchange in East Asia already involved manufacturing. Ceramics were not the only product that was subject to large-scale techniques. In India as in China textiles were produced predominantly on a domestic basis, often organized by merchants by means of putting-out systems and cottage industries similar to proto-industrial Europe.[24] But there were also large factory-type institutions.[25] In China a more impressive example was the important paper industry. That situation reflects the fact that, throughout the major societies of Asia, urban cultures had experienced a more or less continuous development over the long term beginning with those of the Bronze Age. There were interruptions, due to ecological, economic, military, and even religious factors – invasions of 'barbarians', disruption of commerce, failures of government, the prohibition of printing. But overall urban cultures developed in complexity over the centuries, in relation to production, exchange, distribution, finance as well as to material, artistic and intellectual life, in the arts, in education, in commerce, and manufacture. However, most western historians, looking back teleologically after the Industrial Revolution, have overlooked these parallel developments and tried to account for later advantage in terms of imagined earlier ones. The relative unity of the Bronze Age was disregarded and they posited the emergence of Antiquity in Europe and nowhere else. For most authors that uniqueness was also true of feudalism and again of capitalism which is the point from which they started their search. In this way, the broad continuity of post-Bronze Age societies has been disastrously fractured by a concentration on European experience alone, a concentration by scholars and public alike that has led to the theft of history.

To affect a valid comparison would involve using not predetermined categories of the kind Antiquity, feudalism, capitalism, but abandoning these concepts to construct a sociological grid laying out the possible variations of what is being compared. That is notably lacking from most historical discourse in the west. Instead historians have simply claimed desirable and 'progressive' features for themselves. They have stolen history by imposing their categories and sequences on the rest of the world.

---

[23] Bray 2000: 1.   [24] Bray 1997.   [25] Goody 1996b: 187.

The problem of the theft of history and of the social sciences also affects other humanities. In recent years, scholars have also taken steps to make their disciplines more comparative, more relevant to the rest of the world. But these measures are grossly inadequate to the task. Literature has become 'comparative literature' but the range of comparison is usually limited to a few European sources; the east is ignored, oral cultures unconsidered. The field of cultural studies, both in its British and its American variants, is chaotic. The textual base of the latter is virtually exclusively western writings, usually philosophers, often French, who comment upon life without offering much data except their own internal reflections or comments upon other philosophers, all representative of modern, urban societies. The level of generality of such comments is such that one has no real need of information to enter into the conversation.

In conclusion, this has been a book not so much about world history as about the way that European scholars have perceived it. The problem comes in trying to explain the background of the comparative advantage Europe achieved. Searching back in history almost inevitably invites a teleological bias, whether implicit or explicit. In looking at what led to one's own 'modernization', one makes judgements about other people, their lack of the Protestant ethic, of the entrepreneurial spirit, of the ability to change, that is thought to have made this difference.

A fundamental difficulty in that history is the way that the later advantage of Europe has been specified. If that continent is seen as developing a unique form of the economy, something called 'capitalism', then one is justified in tracing back its roots, to 'absolutism', to 'feudalism', to Antiquity, even to seeing it as the result of a cluster of unparalleled institutions, virtues and emotions, even religion. But supposing the development of human society from the Bronze Age is regarded in different terms, as an ongoing elaboration of urban and mercantile culture without any sharp breaks involving categorical distinctions of the kind suggested by the use of the term 'capitalist'. In his magisterial survey, Braudel in fact adopts the position that such activity is found throughout the range of society with which he is dealing, in Asia as in Europe. However, he reserves the concept of 'true capitalism' for the modern west, just as Needham does with 'modern science' as contrasted with 'science'. But if 'capitalism' is seen as characterizing all these societies, its uniqueness inevitably disappears and so too does the problem of explanation. One is left with explaining increasing intensity, with elaboration rather than categorical change. Indeed the situation might be clarified by the abandonment of the term 'capitalism' altogether, since its use will always tend to suggest some kind of long-term, privileged position for the west. So why not phrase the discussion for the advantage of the west in modern times in terms of the intensification of economic and other activities within the long-term framework of urban and mercantile developments, a framework that would allow for periods of more or less intense activity and would take full account of the negative as well as the positive aspects of the 'civilizing process'? Of course, this sequence needs cutting up, periodizing from time to time, but we can speak of the increasing scope of industrialization, even of an Industrial Revolution, without denying the beginnings of this process to Asian or other societies, without regarding it as a purely European development.

References

Adams, R. M. 1966 *The evolution of urban society: early Mesopotamia and prehispanic Mexico*. Chicago: Aldine

Ágoston, G. 2005 *Guns for the Sultan: military power and the weapons industry in the Ottoman Empire*. Cambridge: Cambridge University Press

Amory, P. 1977 *People and identity in Ostrogothic Italy, 489–554*. Cambridge: Cambridge University Press

Amstutz, G. 1998 Shin Buddhism and Protestant analogies with Christianity in the west. *Comparative Studies in Society and History* 40: 724–47

Anderson, P. 1974a *Passages from Antiquity to feudalism*. London: Verso
    1974b *Lineages of the absolutist state*. London: Verso

Arizzoli-Clémental, P. 1996 *The textile museum, Lyons*. Paris: Paribas

Asin, P. M. 1926 *Islam and the Divine Comedy*. London: J. Murray

Astour, M. C. 1967 *Hellenosemitica*. Leiden: Brill

Bacon, F. 1632 *The essays, or counsels, civil and moral*. London: John Haviland

Baechler, J., Hall, J. A., and Mann, M. (eds.) 1988 *Europe and the rise of capitalism*. Oxford: Blackwell

Barnard, A. 2004 Mutual aid and the foraging mode of thought: re-reading Kropotkin on the Khoisan. *Social Evolution and History* 3 (1): 3–21

Barnes, R. 2002 Cloistered bookworms in the chicken-coop of the muses: the ancient library of Alexandria. In R. MacLeod (ed.), *The Library of Alexandria: centre of learning in the ancient world*. Cairo: American University Press

Barth, F. 1961 *Nomads of South Persia*. Boston: Little, Brown, & Co.

Barthélemy, D. 1996 The 'feudal revolution'. *Past and Present* 152: 196–205

Bayly, C. 1981 *Rulers, townsmen and bazaars: northern Indian society in the age of British expansion 1770–1870*. Cambridge: Cambridge University Press
    2004 *The birth of the modern world 1780–1914*. Oxford: Oxford University Press

Beloch, J. 1894 Die Phoeniker am aegaeischen Meer. *Rheinisches Museum für Philologie* 49: 111–32

Berkey, J. 1992 *The transmission of knowledge in medieval Cairo: a social history of Islamic education*. Princeton, New Jersey: Princeton University Press

Berlin, I. 1958 *Two concepts of liberty* (Inaugural lecture). Oxford: Clarendon Press

Bernal, M. 1987 *Black Athena: the Afroasiatic roots of classical civilization*. Vol. I: *The fabrication of Ancient Greece 1785–1985*. London: Free Association Books

1990 *Cadmean letters: the transmission of the alphabet to the Aegean and further west before 1400 B.C.* Winona Lake, IN: Eisenbrauns

1991 *Black Athena: the archaeological and documentary evidence.* London: Free Association Books

2001 *Black Athena Writes Back: Martin Bernal Responds to his Critics,* ed. D. C. Moore London: Duke University Press

Bernier, F. 1989 [1671] *Travels in the Mughal empire, AD 1656–68.* Columbia, Missouri: South Asia Books

Beurdeley, C. and M. 1973 L'amour courtois. In *Le Chant d'Oreiller: l'art d'aimer au Japan.* Fribourg, Switzerland: Office du Livre

Bietak, M. 1996 *Avaris, the capital of the Hyksos.* London: British Museum

2000 Minoan paintings at Arquis/Egypt. In S. Sherratt, ed., *Proceedings of the First International Symposium: The Wall Paintings of Thera.* Athens: Thera Foundation

Bion, W. R. 1963 *Elements of psychoanalysis.* London: Heinemann

1970 *Attention and interpretation: a scientific approach to insight in psycho-analysis and groups.* London: Tavistock

Birrell, A. 1995 *Chinese love poetry: new songs from a jade terrace – a medieval anthology.* Harmondsworth: Penguin Classics

Blaut, J. M. 1993 *The colonizer's model of the world: geographical diffusionism and eurocentric history.* New York: The Guilford Press

2000 *Eight eurocentric historians.* New York: The Guilford Press

Bloch, Marc 1961 *Feudal society,* trans. L. A. Manyon. London: Routledge and Kegan Paul

Bloch, Maurice (ed.) 1975 *Political language and oratory in traditional society.* New York: Academic Press

Bloom, J. M. 2001 *Paper before print: the history and impact of paper on the Islamic world.* New Haven: Yale University Press

Blue, G. 1999 Capitalism and the writing of modern history in China. In T. Brook and G. Blue (eds.), *China and historical capitalism.* Cambridge: Cambridge University Press

1999 China and Western social thought in the modern period. In T. Brook and G. Blue (eds.) *China and historical capitalism.* Cambridge: Cambridge University Press

Boas, F. 1904 The folk-lore of the Eskimo. *Journal of American Folk-Lore.* 17 1–13

Bodin, J. 1576 *Les six livres de la republique.* Paris: Chez Iacques du Pays

Bohannan, P. J. and Dalton, G. (eds.) 1962 *Markets in Africa.* Evanston, IL Northwestern University Press

Bonnassie, P. 1991 *From slavery to feudalism in south-western Europe.* Cambridge Cambridge University Press

Boserup, E. 1970 *Woman's role in economic development.* London: Allen & Unwin

Bovill, E. W. 1933 *Caravans of the old Sahara: an introduction to the history of the Western Sudan.* London: Oxford University Press

Braudel, F. 1949 *Méditerrané et le monde Méditerranéen à l'époque de Phillipe I* Paris: Colin

Braudel, F. (cont.)[1979] 1981–4 *Civilization and capitalism, 15th–18th century. The structures of everyday life.* Vol. I. London: Phoenix Press
1981–4b *Civilization and capitalism, 15th–18th century. The wheels of commerce.* Vol. II. London: Phoenix Press
1981–4c *Civilization and capitalism, 15th–18th century. The perspective of the world.* Vol. III. London: Phoenix Press
Bray, F. 1997 *Technology and gender: fabrics of power in late imperial China.* Berkeley: University of California Press
2000 *Technology and society in Ming China (1368–1644).* Washington, DC: American Historical Society
Briant, P. 2005 'History of the Persian Empire, 550–330 BC'. In J. Curtis and N. Tallis (eds.) *Forgotten empire: the world of ancient Persia.* London: British Museum
Brodbeck, M. (ed.) 1968 *Readings in the philosophy of the social sciences.* London: Macmillan
Brook, T. 1998 *The confusions of pleasure: commerce and culture in Ming China.* Berkeley: University of California Press
Brook, T. and G. Blue (eds.) 1999 *China and historical capitalism.* Cambridge: Cambridge University Press
Brotton, J. 2002 *The Renaissance bazaar: from the silk road to Michelangelo.* Oxford: Oxford University Press
Brough, J. 1968 *Poems from the Sanskrit.* Harmondsworth: Penguin
Browning, J. 1979 *Palmyra.* London: Chatto & Windus
Browning, R. 2000 Education in the Roman empire. *The Cambridge Ancient History,* vol. XIV. Cambridge: Cambridge University Press
Burke, P. 1998. *The European Renaissance: centres and peripheries.* Oxford: Blackwell
Burkhardt, J. 1990 *The civilisation of the Renaissance in Italy.* New York: Penguin
Buruma, I. and Margalit, A. 2004 Seeds of revolution. *The New York Review of Books* 51: 4
Butterfield, H. 1949 *Origins of modern science 1300–1800.* London: G. Bell
Bynum, C. 1987 *Holy feast and holy fast: religious significance of food to mediaeval women.* Berkeley: University of California Press
Cabanès, Dr. 1954 *La vie intime.* Paris: Albin Michel
Cahen, C. 1992 Iqta. *Encyclopaedia of Islam.* Leiden: Brill 1988–91
Cai Hua 2001 *A society without fathers or husbands: the Na of China.* New York: Zone Books
Cameron, A. 2000 Vandals and Byzantine Africa. *The Cambridge Ancient History,* vol. XIV. Cambridge: Cambridge University Press
Cantarino, V. 1977 *Casidas de amor profano y mistico.* Mexico: Porrúa
Capellanus, A. 1960 [1186] *The art of courtly love,* ed. J. J. Parry. New York: Columbia University Press
Cardini, P. 2000 *Breve Storia di Prato.* Sienna: Pacini
Cartledge, R. 1983 Trade and politics revisited. In *Trade in the ancient Economy,* eds. P. Garnsey, K. Hopkins, and C. R. Whittaker. London: Hogarth Press

Caskey, J. 2004 *Art as patronage in the medieval Mediterranean: merchant customs in the region of Amalfi*. Cambridge: Cambridge University Press

Casson, L. 1989 *The Periplus Maris Erythraei: text with introduction, translation, and commentary*. Princeton: Princeton University Press

Castoriadis, C. 1991 The Greek polis and the creation of democracy. In D. A. Curtis (ed.), *The Castoriadis reader*. Oxford: Blackwell

Cesares, A. M. 2002 La logique de la domination esclavagiste: vieux chrétiens et neo-convertis dans la Grenade espagnole des temps moderne. *Cahiers de le Méditerranée. L'Eslavage en Méditeranée à l'epoque moderne*, 219–40

Chan, W. K. K. 1977 *Merchants, mandarins, and modern enterprise in late Ch'ing China*. Cambridge, MA: Harvard University Press

Chandler, A. D. 1977 *The visible hand: the managerial revolution in American business*. Cambridge, MA: Harvard University Press

Chang, K. C. (ed.) 1977 *Food in Chinese culture – anthropological and historical perspectives*. New Haven: Yale University Press

Chartier, R. 2003 Emmanuel Le Roy Ladurie Daniel Gordon and 'The second death of Norbert Elias'. In E. Dunning and S. J. Mennell (eds.), *Norbert Elias* (vol. IV). London: Sage Publications

Chase-Dunn, C. and Hall, T. D. 1997 *Rise and demise: comparing world systems*. Oxford: Westview Press

Chayanov, A. V. 1966 *The theory of peasant economy*. Madison: The University of Wisconsin Press

Chesneaux, J. 1972 *La Révolte des Tai-Ping 1851–1864: prologue de la révolution chinoise*. Paris
1976 *Le Mouvement paysan chinois. 1840–1949*. Paris: Seuil

Childe, G. [1942] 1964 *What happened in history*. Harmondsworth: Penguin Books
1951 *Social evolution*. London: Watts

Ching-Tzu Wu 1973 *The scholars*. Beijing: Foreign Languages Press

Cipolla, C. 1965 *Guns, sails and empires: technological innovation and the early phases of European expansion 1400–1700*. New York: Minerva Press

Clark, G. D. 1961 *World prehistory: an outline*. Cambridge: Cambridge University Press
1977 *World prehistory in new perspective*. Cambridge: Cambridge University Press

Clone, R. (ed.) *The story of time and space*. Greenwich: National Maritime Museum

Clunas, C. 1991 *Superfluous things: material culture and social status in early modern China*. Cambridge: Polity Press

Cohen, E. E. 1992 *Athenian economy and society: a banking perspective*. Princeton, N J: Princeton University Press.

Cohen, M. J. 2004 Writs of passage in Late Imperial China: the documentation of partial misunderstandings in Minong, Taiwan. In M. Zelin and J. K. Ocko and R. Gardella, *Contract and property in Early Modern China*. Stanford, CA Stanford University Press

Concina, E. 1984 *Arsenale della repubblica di Venezia*. Milan: Electa
1987 *Arsenali e città nell'occidente europeo*. Rome: La Nuova Italia Scientifica

Confucius 1996 [*c.* 500 BCE.] *The great learning. The doctrine of the mean.* Beijing: Sinolingua

Conrad, L. I. 2000 The Arabs. *The Cambridge Ancient History,* vol. XIV. Cambridge: Cambridge University Press

Constable, O. R. 1994 *Trade and traders in Muslim Spain: the commercial realignment of the Iberian Peninsula, 900–1500.* Cambridge: Cambridge University Press

Coquéry-Vidrovich, C. 1978 Research on an African mode of production. In D. Seddon (ed.), *Relations of production* (translated from the French, 1969). *Pensée* 144: 61–78. London

Cormack, R. 2000 The visual arts. *The Cambridge Ancient History,* vol. XIV. Cambridge: Cambridge University Press

Coulbourn, R. (ed.) 1956 *Feudalism in history.* Princeton, NJ: Princeton University Press

Crane, N. 2003 *Mercator: the man who mapped the planet.* London: Phoenix

Curtis, J. and Tallis, N. (eds.) 2005 *Forgotten empire: the world of ancient Persia.* London: British Museum

Daniel, G. 1943 *The three ages: an essay on archaeological method.* Cambridge: Cambridge University Press

Daniel, N. 1975 *The Arabs and medieval Europe.* London: Longman

Davies, J. K. 1978 *Democracy and classical Greece.* Sussex: Harvester

Davies, W. V. and Schofield, L. (eds.) 1995 *Egypt, the Aegean, and the Levant.* London: British Museum

Denoix, S. 2000 Unique modèle ou types divers? La structure des villes du monde arabo-musulman à l'époque médiévale, ed. C. Nicolet *et al. Mégapoles méditerranéenes: géographie urbaine rétrospective.* Paris: Maisonneuve et Larose

Djebar, A. 2005 *L'âge d'or des sciences arabes.* Paris: Le Pommier

Dobb, M. 1954 *Studies in the development of capitalism.* London: Routledge

Dronke, R. 1965 *Medieval Latin and the rise of the European love-lyric* (2 vols.). Oxford: Clarendon Press

Duby, G. 1996 *Féodalité.* Paris: Gallimard

Dumont, L. 1970 [1966] *Homo hierarchicus: the caste system and its implications.* Chicago: Chicago University Press

Durkheim, E. 1893 *De la division du travail social: étude sur l'organisation des sociétés supérieures.* Paris: Alcan
    1947 [1st French edn 1912, 1st English trans. 1915] *The elementary forms of the religious life.* Glencoe, II.: Free Press

Dürr, H.-P. 1988 *Der Mythos vom Zivilisationsprozess.* Frankfurt am Main: Suhrkamp Verlag

Edler de Roover, F. 1993 *La sete Lucchesi* (Italian trans. from German 1950. *Die Seidenstadt Lucca.* Basle: CIBA.) Lucca

Eisenstein, E. L. 1979 *The printing press as an agent of change: communications and cultural transformations in early modern Europe.* Cambridge: Cambridge University Press

Elias, N. 1994a [1939] *The civilizing process* (trans. E. Jephcott). Oxford: Blackwell
    1994b *Reflections on a life.* Cambridge: Polity Press

Elvin, M. 1973 *The pattern of the Chinese past.* London: Eyre Methuen
    2004 Ave atque vale. In Needham, *Science and civilization in China,* Pt 2, vol.
    VII. Cambridge: Cambridge University Press
Evans, A. 1921–35 *The palace of Minos at Knossos.* 4 vols. London: Macmillan
Evans-Pritchard, E. E. 1937 *Witchcraft, oracles and magic among the Azande.*
    Oxford: Clarendon Press
    1940 *The Nuer.* Oxford: Clarendon Press
Fantar, M. H. 1995 *Carthage: la cité punique.* Paris: CNRS
Faure, D. 1989 The lineage as business company: patronage versus law in the
    development of Chinese business. *The Second Conference of Modern Chinese
    Economic History,* 5–7 January, The Institute of Economics, Academia Sinica,
    Taipei
Fay, M. A. 1997 Women and waqf: property, power and the domain of gender in
    eighteenth-century Egypt. In M. C. Zilfi (ed.) *Women in the Ottoman empire:
    Middle Eastern women in the early modern era.* Leiden: Brill
Fernandez-Armesto, F. 1995 *Millennium: a history of our last thousand years.*
    London: Black Swan
Fevrier, M., P.-A. Fixot, G. Goudineau, and N. Kruta 1980 *Histoire de la France
    urbaine. Des origines à la fin du IXe siècle. Période traitée: la Gaule de VIIe au
    IXe siècle.* Paris: Seuil
Finley, M. I. (ed.) 1960 *Slavery in classical antiquity.* Cambridge: W. Heffer
    1970 *Early Greece: the Bronze and Archaic ages.* London: Chatto & Windus
    1973 *The ancient economy.* London: Chatto & Windus
    1981 *Economy and society in ancient Greece.* ed. B. D. Shaw & R. P. Saller.
    London: Chatto & Windus
    1985 *Democracy ancient and modern.* London: Hogarth
Firth, R. 1959 *Social changes in Tikopia: re-study of a Polynesian community after a
    generation.* New York: Macmillan
Flannery, K. 1972 The cultural evolution of civilizations. *Annual Review of Ecology
    and Systematics* 3: 399–426
Fortes, M. and Evans-Pritchard, E. E. 1940 *African political systems.* London:
    Oxford University Press
Fowden, G. 2002 Elefantiasi del tardantica (Review of the *Cambridge Ancient
    History,* vol. XIV). *Journal of Roman Archaeology* 15: 681–6
Frank A. G. 1998 *ReOrient: global economy in the Asian age.* Berkeley: University
    of California Press
Freud, S. 1961 [1927] *The future of an illusion. Civilization and its discontents,* ed.
    J. Strachey. Standard Edition, vol. XXI (1927–31). London: Hogarth
    1964 *New introductory lectures on psycho-analysis and other works.* Trans. and ed.
    J. Strachey, Standard edition, vol. XXII (1932–6). London: Hogarth
    1964 [1933] *Why war?* Letter to Einstein. In Standard edition vol. xxii (1932–
    6). London: Hogarth
Furet, F. and Ozouf, J. 1977 *Lire et écrire, l'alphabétisation des français de Calvin à
    Jules Ferry.* Paris: Minuit
Garnsey, P., Hopkins, K., and Whittaker, C. R. (eds.)1983 *Trade in the ancient
    economy.* London: Chatto & Windus
Geertz, C. *et al.* (eds.) 1979 *Meaning and order in Moroccan society.* New York
    Cambridge University Press

Gellner, E. 1994 The mightier pen: the double standards of inside-out colonial-ism. *Encounters with nationalism*. Oxford: Blackwell (reprinted from *Times Literary Supplement*, 19 February 1998)

Geraci, G. and Marin, B. 2003 L'approvisionnement alimentaire urbain. In B. Marin and C. Virlouvet (eds.) *Nourire les cités de Mediterranée: antiquité – temps moderne*. Paris: M. M. S. H.

Ghosh, A. 1992 *In an antique land*. New York: Vintage Books

Giddens, A. 1991. *Modernity and self-identity: self and society in the late modern age*. Cambridge: Polity Press

Gillion, K. L. 1968 *Ahmedabad: a study in Indian urban history*. Berkeley, CA: California University Press

Gilson, E. 1999 *La Philosophie au Moyen Age* (2nd edition). Paris: Payot

Gledhill, J. and Larsen, M. 1952 The Polanyi paradigm and a dynamic analysis of archaic states. In C. Renfrew *et al.*, *Theory and explanation in archaeology*. New York: Academic Press

Glick, T. F. 1996 *Irrigation and hydraulic technology: medieval Spain and its legacy*. Aldershot: Variorum

Gluckman, M. 1955 *The judicial process among the Barotse of Northern Rhodesia*. Manchester: Manchester University Press

1965 *Custom and conflict in Africa*. Oxford: Blackwell

1965 *The ideas in Barotse jurisprudences*. New Haven: Yale University Press

Godelier, M. 1978. The concept of the 'Asian mode of production' and Marxist models of social evolution. In D. Seddon (ed.), *Relations of production: Marxist approaches to economic anthropology*. London: Cass

2004 *Métamorphoses de la parenté*. Paris: Fayard

Goitein, S. D. 1967 *A Mediterranean society, the Jewish communities of the Arab world as portrayed in the documents of the Cairo Geniza*. Vol. I. Berkeley: University of California Press

1999 *A Mediterranean society. An abridgement in one volume*. Berkeley: University of California Press

Goode, W. 1963 *World revolution and family patterns*. New York: The Free Press

Goodman, M. 2004 *Jews in a Graeco-Roman world*. Oxford: Oxford University Press

Goody, J. 1957 Anomie in Ashanti? *Africa* 27: 75–104

1962 *Death, property and the ancestors*. Stanford, CA: Stanford University Press (reprinted 2004, London: Routledge)

1968 The social organization of time. In *The encyclopaedia of the social sciences*. New York: Macmillan.

1971 *Technology, tradition and the state in Africa*. London: Oxford University Press

1972a The evolution of the family. In P. Laslett and R. Wall (eds.), *Household and family in past times*. Cambridge: Cambridge University Press

1972b *The myth of the Bagre*. Oxford: Clarendon

1976 *Production and reproduction: a comparative study of the domestic domain*. Cambridge: Cambridge University Press

1977 *The domestication of the savage mind*. Cambridge: Cambridge University Press

Goody, J. (*cont.*)1982 *Cooking, cuisine and class: a study in comparative sociology.* Cambridge: Cambridge University Press
1984 Under the lineage's shadow. *Proceedings of the British Academy* 70: 189–208.
1986 *The logic of writing and the organisation of society.* Cambridge: Cambridge University Press
1987 *The interface between the written and the oral.* Cambridge: Cambridge University Press
1993 *The culture of flowers.* Cambridge: Cambridge University Press
1996a *The east in the west.* Cambridge: Cambridge University Press
1996b Comparing family systems in Europe and Asia: are there different sets of rules? *Population and Development Review* 22: 1–20
1997 *Representations and contradictions.* Oxford: Blackwell
1998 *Food and love.* London: Verso
2003a The Bagre and the story of my life. *Cambridge Anthropology* 23, 3, 81–9
2003b *Islam in Europe.* Cambridge: Polity Press
2004 *Capitalism and modernity: the great debate.* Cambridge: Polity Press
Goody, J. and Watt, I. 1963 The consequences of literacy. *Comparative Studies in Society and History* 5: 304–45
Goody, J. and Tambiah, S. 1973 *Bridewealth and dowry.* Cambridge: Cambridge University Press
Goody, J. and Gandah, S. W. D. K. 1980 *Une récitation du Bagre.* Paris: Colin
2002 *The third Bagre: a myth revisited.* Durham, NC: Carolina Academic Press
Gordon, D. 1994 *Citizens without sovereignty: equality and sociability in French thought, 1670–1789.* Princeton: Princeton University Press
Gough, K. 1981 *Rural society in Southeast India.* Cambridge: Cambridge University Press
Griaule, M. 1948 *Conversations with Ogotommeli.* Paris: Fayard. (English trans 1965 London: Oxford University Press)
Greenberg, J. 1963 The languages of Africa. (Supplement to *International Journal of American Linguistics* 29)
Grudin R. 1997 Humanism. In *Encyclopaedia Britannica* (15th edition). Chicago: Chicago University Press
Guichard, P. 1977 *Structures occidentales et structures orientales.* Paris: Mouton
Gurukkal, R. and Whittaker, D. 2001 In search of Muziris. *Roman Archeology* 14: 235–350
Gutas, D. 1998 *Greek thought, Arabic culture.* London: Routledge
Guthrie, D. J. and Hartley, F. 1997 Medicine and surgery before 1800. In *Encyclopaedia Britannica* (15th edn) 23: 775–83. Chicago: Chicago University Press
Habib, I. 1990 Merchant communities in precolonial India. In J. D. Tracy (ed.) *The rise of merchant empires.* Cambridge: Cambridge University Press
Hajnal, J. 1965 European marriage patterns in perspective. In D. V. Glass and D. E. C. Eversley (eds.), *Population in History.* London: Aldine
1982 Two kinds of pre-industrial household formation systems. *Population and Development Review* 8: 449–94
Halbwachs, M. 1925 *Le Cadres sociaux de la mémoire.* Paris: F. Alcan

Hart, K. 1982 *The political economy of West African agriculture*. Cambridge: Cambridge University Press
 2000 *Money in an unequal world*. New York: Texere
Hart, Mother Columba (trans.) 1980 *Hadewijch: the complete works*. London: Paulist Press
Haskins, C. H. 1923 *The rise of universities*. New York: Henry Holt
Hill, P. 1970 *Studies in rural capitalism in West Africa*. Cambridge: Cambridge University Press
Hilton, R. (ed.) 1976 *The transition from feudalism to capitalism*. London: NLB
Hobsbawm, E. J. 1959 *Primitive rebels*. Manchester: Manchester University Press
 1964 *The age of revolution. 1789–1848*. New York: Mentor
 1965 *Pre-capitalist economic formations*. New York: International Publishing
 1972 *Bandits*. Harmondsworth: Penguin
Hobson, J. M. 2004 *The eastern origins of western Civilisation*. Cambridge: Cambridge University Press
Hodges, R. and Whitehouse, D. 1983 *Mohammed, Charlemagne and the origins of Europe*. London: Duckworth
Hodgkin, L. 2005 *A history of mathematics: from Mesopotamia to modernity*. Oxford: Oxford University Press
Ho Ping-ti 1962 *The ladder of success in Imperial China; aspects of social mobility, 1368–1911*. New York: Columbia University Press
Hopkins, T. J. 1966 The social teaching of the *Bhagavata Purana*. In *Krishna: myths, rites and attitudes*, ed. M. Singer. Honolulu: East–West Center
Hopkins, K. 1980 Brother–sister marriage in Roman Egypt. *Comparative Studies in Society and History* 22: 303–54.
 1983 Introduction to P. Garnsey, K. Hopkins, and C. R. Whittaker (eds.), *Trade in the ancient economy*. London: Chatto & Windus
Hourani, A 1990 L'oeuvre d'André Raymond. *Revue des Mondes Musulmans et de la Méditerranée* 55–6, 18–27.
Howard, D. 2000 *Venice and the East: the impact of the Islamic world on European architecture 1100–1500*. New Haven: Yale University Press
Hsu-Ling 1982 [534–5] *New songs from a jade terrace*. A. Birrel (ed.). New York: Penguin
Hufton, O. 1995 *The prospect before her: a history of women in Western Europe*, vol. I, *1500–1800*. London: Harper Collins
Huntington, S. P. 1991 *The clash of civilizations and the remaking of world order*. New York: Simon & Schuster 1996
Ibn Arabi 1996 *L'interprète des desirs*. Paris: Albin Michel
Ibn Khaldûn 1967[1377] *Al-Muqaddimah*. Beirut: UNESCO
Ibn Hazm 1981 [c. 1022] *The ring of the dove. A treatise on the art and practice of Arab love*. New York: AMS Press
Inalcik, H. with D. Quataert 1994 *An economic and social history of the Ottoman empire, 1300–1914*. Cambridge: Cambridge University Press
Jackson, A. and A. Jaffes (eds.) 2004 *Encounters: the meeting of Asia and Europe 1500–1800*. London: V&A Publications
Jacquart, D. 2005 *L'Épopée de la science arabe*, Paris: Gallimard
Jayyussi, S. K. (ed.), 1992 *The legacy of Muslim Spain*. Leiden: Brill

Jidejian, N. 1991 *Tyre through the ages*. Beirut: Librarie Orièntale
1996 *Sidon à travers les ages*. Beirut: Librarie Orièntale
2000 *Byblos through the Ages*. Beirut: Librarie Orièntale
Jones, E. L. 1987 *The European miracle: environments, economies and geopolitics in the history of Europe and Asia*. Cambridge: Cambridge University Press
Kant, I. 1998 [1784] Ideas on a universal history from a cosmopolitan point of view. In J. Rundell and S. Mennell (eds.), *Classical readings in culture and civilization*. London: Routledge
Keenan, J. G. 2000 Egypt. *The Cambridge Ancient History*, vol. XIV. Cambridge: Cambridge University Press
Kennedy, P. 1989 *The rise and fall of the great powers: economic change and military conflict from 1500 to 2000*. New York: Vintage Books
Krause, K. 1992 *Arms and the state: patterns of military production and trade*. Cambridge: Cambridge University Press
Kristeller, P. O. 1945 The School of Salerno: its development and its contribution to the history of learning. *Bulletin of the History of Medicine* 17: 138–94
Kroeber, A. L. 1976 *Handbook of the Indians of California*. New York: Dover Publications
Lancel, S. 1997 *Carthage: a history*. Oxford: Blackwell
Landes, D. 1999 *The wealth and poverty of nations: why some nations are so rich and some so poor*. London: Abacus
Lane, R. C. 1973 *Venice: a maritime republic*. Baltimore: Johns Hopkins University Press
Lantz, J. R. 1981 Romantic love in the pre-modern period: a sociological commentary. *Journal of Social History* 15: 349–70
Laslett, P. 1971. *The world we have lost: England before the industrial age*. New York: Scribners
and Wall, R. (eds.) 1972 *Household and family in past times*. Cambridge: Cambridge University Press
Latour, B. 2000 Derrida dreams about Le Shuttle. Reviews of E. Durian-Smith, *Bridging divides: the Channel tunnel and English legal identity in the New Europe*, Berkeley. *The Times Higher Education Supplement* 2/6/2000: 31
Ledderose, L. 2000 *Ten thousand things: module and mass production in Chinese art*. Princeton: Princeton University Press
Lee, J. Z. and Wang Feng, *One quarter of humanity. Malthusian mythology and Chinese realities, 1700–2000*. Cambridge, MA: Harvard University Press.
Le Goff, J. 1993 *Intellectuals in the middle ages*. London: Blackwell
Lenin, V. I. 1962. The awakening of Asia. In *Collected works*. Moscow: Foreign Language Press
Letts, M. 1926 *Bruges and its past*. London: Berry
Leur, J. C. van 1955 *Indonesian trade and society: essays in Asian social and economic history*. The Hague: W. van Hoeve
Lewis, B. 1973 *Islam in history: ideas, men and events in the Middle East*. London Alcove
2002 *What went wrong? Western impact and Middle Eastern response*. London Orion House

Lewis, C. S. 1936 *The allegory of love: a study in medieval tradition*. Oxford: Clarendon Press

Liebeschuetz, J. H. W. G. 2000 Administration and politics in the cities of the fifth to the mid seventh century: 425–40. *The Cambridge Ancient History, vol.* XIV. Cambridge: Cambridge University Press

Lloyd, G. E. R. 1979 *Magic, reason and experience: studies in the origin and development of Greek science*. Cambridge: Cambridge University Press

  2004 *Ancient worlds, modern reflections: philosophical perspectives on Greek and Chinese science and culture*. Oxford: Oxford University Press

Lopez, R. 1971 *The commercial revolution of the middle ages, 950–1350*. Englewood Cliffs: Prentice Hall

Love, J. R. 1991 *Antiquity and capitalism: Max Weber and the sociological foundations of Roman civilization*. London: Routledge

Maalouf, A. 1984 *The crusades through Arab eyes*. London: Al Saqi Books

Macfarlane, A. 1978. *The origins of English individualism: the family, property and social transition*. Oxford: Blackwell

Macfarlane, A. and Martin G. 2002 *The glass bathyscape*. London: Profile Books

Machiavelli, N. 1996 [1532] *The prince* (trans. S. J. Millner). London: Phoenix Books

Maine, H. S. 1965 [1861] *Ancient law*. London: Everyman Library

Makdisi, G. 1979 An Islamic element in the early Spanish University. In *Islam: past influences and present challenges*. Edinburgh: Edinburgh University Press

  1981 *The rise of colleges: illustrations of learning in Islam and the west*. Edinburgh: Edinburgh University Press

Malinowski, B. 1913 *The family among the Australian aborigines*. London: Hodder & Stoughton

  1947 *Crime and custom in savage society*. London: Kegan Paul

  1948 *Magic, science and religion and other essays* (ed. R. Redfield). Boston: Beacon Press

Mann, M. 1986 *The sources of social power*. Vol. I: *A history of power from the beginning to A.D. 1760*. Cambridge: Cambridge University Press

Marx, K. 1964 *Pre-capitalist economic formations* (intro. E. Hobsbawm). New York: International Publishers

  1973 *Grundrisse*. London: Penguin

  1976 *Capital*. London: Penguin

Marx, K. and Engels, F. 1969 *Selected Works*, Vol. I. Moscow: Progress Publishers

Matar, N. 1999 *Turks, Moors and Englishmen in the age of discovery*. New York: Columbia University Press

McCormick, M. 2001 *Origins of the European economy: communications and culture A.D. 300–900*. Cambridge: Cambridge University Press

McMullen, I. J. 1999 *Idealism, protest, and the tale of Genji: the Confucianism of Kumazawa Banzan 1619–91*. Oxford: Clarendon Press

Meier, C. 1990 *The Greek discovery of politics* (trans. David McLintock). Cambridge, MA: Harvard University Press

Meilink-Roelofsz, H. A. P. 1962 *Asian trade and European influence in the Indonesian archipelago between 1500 and about 1630*. The Hague: Nijhoff

  1970 Asian trade and Islam in the Malay-Indonesian archipelago. In D. S. Richards (ed.), *Islam and the trade of Asia*. Oxford: B. Cassirer

Mennell, S. 1985 *All manners of food: eating and taste in England and France from the Middle Ages to the present.* Oxford: Blackwell

Mennell, S. and Goudsblom, J. 1997 Civilizing process – myth or reality? A comment on Duerr's critique of Elias. *Comparative Studies in Society and History* 39: 729–733

Meriwether, K. L. 1997 Women and waqf revisited: the case of Aleppo 1770– 1840. In M. C. Zilfi (ed.), *Women in the Ottoman empire: Middle Eastern women in the early modern era.* Leiden: Brill

Miller, J. 1969 *The spice trade of the Roman empire.* Oxford: Clarendon Press

Millett, P. 1983 Maritime loans and the structure of credit in fourth-century Athens. In P. Garnsey, K. Hopkins, and C. R. Whittaker (eds.), *Trade in the ancient economy.* London: Chatto & Windus

Mintz, S. and Wolf, E. 1950 An analysis of ritual co-parenthood (compadrazgo). *Southwestern Journal of Anthropology.* 341–67

Mitchell, J. 2003 *Siblings.* Cambridge: Polity Press

Montesquieu, C. S., 1914 *The spirit of laws.* London: G. Bell & Sons. (French original 1748 *L'Esprit des lois*)

Morgan, L. H. 1877 *Ancient society.* New York: Henry Holt

Mossé, C. 1983 The 'world of the emporium' in the private speeches of Demosthenes. In P. Garnsey, K. Hopkins, and C. R. Whittaker (eds.), *Trade in the ancient economy.* London: Chatto & Windus

Mundy, M. W. 1988. The family, inheritance and Islam: a re-examination of the sociology of *farā'id* law. In A. al-Azmeh (ed.), *Social and historical contexts of Islamic law.* London: Routledge

2004. Ownership or office? A debate in Islamic Hanafite jurisprudence over the nature of the military 'fief', from the Mamluks to the Ottomans. In A. Pottage and M. Mundy (eds.), *Law, Anthropology and the constitution of the social: making persons and things.* Cambridge: Cambridge University Press

Murasaki, S. 1955 [11 c.] *The tale of Genji* (trans. A. Waley). New York: Anchor Books

Murdock, G. P. 1967 Ethnographic atlas: a summary. *Ethnology* 6, 109–236

Nafissi, M. 2004 Class, embeddedness, and the modernity of ancient Athens. *Comparative Studies in Society and History* 46: 378–410

Nakosteen, M. 1964 *History of the Islamic origins of western education, A.D. 800– 1350.* Boulder, Colorado: University of Colorado Press

Needham, J. (ed.) 1954- *Science and civilization in China.* Cambridge: Cambridge University Press

1965 *Time and eastern man.* London: Royal Anthropological Institute

1970 *Clerks and craftsman in China and the west.* Cambridge: Cambridge University Press

(ed.) 1986a *Biology and biological technology, pt. 1: Botany*, vol. VI, *of Science and civilization in China.* Cambridge: Cambridge University Press.

(ed.) 1986b *Military technology; the gunpowder epic, pt. 7, Chemistry and chemical technology*, vol. V, *Science and civilization in China.* Cambridge: Cambridge University Press.

2004 General conclusions and reflections. *Science and civilization in China, P 2*, vol VII. Cambridge: Cambridge University Press

Nef, J. U. 1958 *Cultural foundation of industrial civilization*. Cambridge: Cambridge University Press

Ng, Chin-keong 1983 *Trade and society in China: the Amoy network on the China coast, 1683–1735*. Singapore: Singapore University Press

Nicholson, R. 1921 *Studies in Islamic mysticism*. Cambridge: Cambridge University Press

Nykl, A. R. 1931 *Abū Muammad, 'Alā ibn Hazm al-Andalusā: a book containing the Risāla known as the dove's neck-ring about love and lovers*. Paris: Geuthner

Nylan, M. 1999 Calligraphy, the sacred text and test of culture. In C. Y. Liu *et al.*, *Character and context in Chinese calligraphy*. The Art Museum, Princeton University, NJ

Ong, W. 1974 *Ramus, method and the decay of dialogue*. New York: Octagon Books

Oppenheim, A. L. 1964 *Ancient Mesopotamia*. Chicago: Chicago University Press

Osborne, R. 1996 *Greece in the making 1200–479 BC*. London: Routledge

Parker, G. 1988 *The military revolution: military innovations and the rise of the west, 1500–1800*. Cambridge: Cambridge University Press

Parry, J. J. (ed.) 1960 [1184?] *Andreas Capellanus: the art of courtly love*. New York: Columbia University Press

Parsons, T. 1937 *The structure of social action*. New York: McGraw-Hill

Pasinli, A. 1996 *Istanbul archaeological museums*. Istanbul: A Turizm Yayinlari

Passerini, L. 1999 *Europe in love, love in Europe: imagination and politics in Britain between the wars*. London: I. B. Tauris

Passerini, L. Ellena and A. C. T. Geppert (eds.), forthcoming *New dangerous liaisons*. Oxford: Berghahn

Perera, B. J. 1951 The foreign trade and commerce of ancient Ceylon. I: the ports of ancient Ceylon. *Ceylon Historical Journal* 1: 109–19

1952a The foreign trade and commerce of ancient Ceylon. II: ancient Ceylon and its trade with India. *Ceylon Historical Journal* 1: 192–204

1952b The foreign trade and commerce of ancient Ceylon. III: ancient Ceylon's trade with the empires of the eastern and western worlds. *Ceylon Historical Journal* 1: 301–20

Person, E. S. 1991 Romantic love: at the intersection of the psyche and the cultural unconscious. *Journal of the American Psychoanalytic Association* 39 (supplement): 383–411

Peters, F. E. 1968 *Aristotle and the Arabs: the Aristotelian tradition in Islam*. New York: New York University Press

Petit, P. 1997 Greek and Roman civilizations. In *Encyclopaedia Britannica* (15th edition) 20: 2205

Pirenne, H. 1939 *Mohammed and Charlemagne* (trans. B. Miall). London: Allen & Unwin

Polanyi, K. 1947 Our obsolete market mentality. *Commentary* 3: 2

1957 The economy as instituted process. In K. Polanyi, C. Arensberg, and H. Pearson (eds.), *Trade and markets in the early empires*. New York: Free Press

1957 *The great transformation: the political and economic origins of our time*. Boston: Beacon Press

Polybius. 1889 *The histories of Polybius* (trans. E. Shuckburgh). London: Macmillan

Pomeranz, K. 2000 *The great divergence: China, Europe and the making of the modern world economy*. Princeton, NJ: Princeton University Press

Poni, C. 2001a Il *network* della setta nelle città italiana in età moderna. *Iscuola Officina* [Bologna] 2: 4–11

2001b Comparing two urban industrial districts: Bologna and Lyon in the early modern period. In P. L. Porta, F. Scazzieri, and A. Skinner (eds.), *Knowledge, social institutions and the division of labour*. Cheltenham: Edwards

Radcliffe Brown, A. R. *Structure and function in primitive society*. London: Cohen and West

Rashdall, H. 1988 [1936] *The universities of Europe in the Middle Ages* (new edn). London: Oxford University Press

Rattray, R. S. 1923 *Ashanti*. London: Oxford University Press

1929 *Ashanti law and constitution*. London: Oxford University Press

Rawson, J. 1984 *Chinese ornament: the lotus and the dragon*. London: British Museum

Renfrew, C., M. J. Rowlands, and B. A. Segraves (eds.), 1982 *Theory and explanation in archaeology*. New York: Academic Press

Repp, R. C. 1986 *The Mufti of Istanbul: a study in the development of the Ottoman learned hierarchy*. London: Ithaca Press

Reynal, J. 1995 Al-Andulas et l'art roman: le fil d'une histoire. In: T. Fabre (ed.) *L'Héritage Andalou*. La Tour d'Aigues: Éditions De L'Aube

Reynolds, L. D. and Wilson, N. G. 1968 *Scribes and scholars*. London: Oxford University Press

Ribera, J. 1928 *Disertaciones y opúsculos*. 2 vols. Madrid: E. Maestre

Richards, A. I. 1950 Some types of family structure amongst the central Bantu In A. R. Radcliffe Brown and C. D. Forde (eds.) *African systems of kinship and marriage*. London: Oxford University Press

Rodinson, M. 1949 Recherches sur les documents arabs relatifs à la cuisine. *Revue études islamique*, 95–106

Rougement, D. de 1956. *Love in the western world*. New York: Princeton University Press

Roux, J. 2004 Cortesia e fin'amor, un nouvel humanism. In R. Bordes (ed. *Troubadours et Cathares: en occitanie médiévale*. Cahors: L'Hydre

Rowe, W. T. 1984 *Hankow: commerce and society in China, 1796–1889*. Stanford CA: Stanford University Press

Sabloff, J. A. and Lamberg-Karlovsky, C. C. (eds.) 1975 *Ancient civilisation an trade*. Albuquerque, NM: University of New Mexico Press

Said, E. 1995 *Orientalism*. London: Penguin Books

2003 *Freud and the non-European*. London: Verso

Saikal, A. 2003 *Islam and the west: conflict or cooperation?* London: Palgrave Macmillan

Say, J. 1829 *Cours complet d'économie politique practique*. Paris: Rapilly

Sayili, A. 1947–8 *Higher education in medieval Islam: the madrasas*. Annales d l'université de l'Ankara II: 30–69

Schapera, I. 1985 [1955] The sin of Cain. In B. Lang (ed.) *Anthropologic approaches to the Old Testament*. Philadelphia: Fortress Press

Schwartz, S. B. 1985 *Sugar plantations in the formation of Brazilian society: Bahia 1550–1835*. Cambridge: Cambridge University Press

Setton, K. M. 1991 *Venice, Austria and the Turks in the seventeenth century*. Philadelphia, PA: American Philosophical Society

Sherratt, S. (ed.) *Proceedings of the First International Symposium, the wall paintings of Thera*. Athens: Thera Foundation

Singer, C. (ed.) 1979–84 *A history of technology*. Oxford: Clarendon Press

Singer, C. 1950 Medicine. In *Chambers Encyclopaedia*, vol. IX: 212–28. London: Newnes

Skinner, P. 1995 *Family power in Southern Italy: the Duchy of Gaeta and its neighbours, 850–1139*. Cambridge: Cambridge University Press

Slicher van Bath, B. H. 1963 *The agrarian history of Western Europe A.D. 500–1850*. London: Edward Arnold

Smith, P. J. 1991 *Taxing heaven's storehouse: horses, bureaucrats, and the destruction of Sichuan tea industry, 1077–1224*, Cambridge, MA: Harvard University Press

Snodgrass, A. M. 1983 Heavy freight in Archaic Greece. In P. Garnsey, K. Hopkins, and C. R. Whittaker (eds.) *Trade in the ancient economy*. London: Chatto and Windus

Sombart, W. 1930 Capitalism. In *Encyclopaedia of the Social Sciences*, vol. III. New York: Macmillan
    1911 *The Jews and modern capitalism*. Leipzig: Dunker and Humblot (Engl. trans. 1993, London: T. F. Unwin)

Soskice, J. 1996 Sight and vision in medieval Christian thought. In *Vision in context: historical and contemporary perspectives on sight*, ed. T. Brennan and M. Jay, New York: Routledge, 29–43

Southall, A. 1998 *The city in time and space*. Cambridge: Cambridge University Press

Southern, R. W. 1970 *Medieval humanism*. New York: Harper and Row

Sovič, S. forthcoming *Western families and their Others*. MS.

Speiser, J. M. 1985 Le christianisation de la ville dans l'Antiquité tardive. *Ktema: civilisations de l'orient, de la Grèce et de Rome antiques* 10: 49–55

Steensgaard, N. 1973 *Carracks, caravans, and companies: the structural crisis in the European-Asian trade in the early seventeenth century*. Copenhagen: Studentlitteratur

Stein, G. 1994 The organizational dynamics of complexity in Greater Mesopaotamia. In *Chiefdoms and early states in the Near East, The organizational dynamics of complexity*, G. Stein, and M. S. Rothman M. S. Madison, Wisconsin: Prehistory Press

Stone, L 1977 *Family, sex and marriage in England, 1550–1800*. London: Weidenfeld and Nicolson

Strayer, J. R. 1956 Feudalism in Western Europe, in *Feudalism in History*, ed. R. Coulbourn. Princeton: Princeton University Press

Tandy, D. W. 1997 *Warriors into traders: the power of the market in early Greece*. Berkeley, CA: California University Press

Thapar, R. 1966 *A history of India*. Harmondsworth: Penguin
    2000 *History and beyond*. New Delhi: Oxford University Press

Tognetti, S. 2002 *Un industria di lussoo al servizio del grande commercio*. Florence: Olschki

Tolstoi, L. 1960 *Last diaries* (ed. L. Stilman). New York: Capricorn Books

Trevor-Roper, H. R. 1965 *The rise of Christian Europe*. London: Thames and Hudson
  1958 *Historical essays*. London: Macmillan
Tylor, E. B. 1881 *Primitive culture*. London
Valensi, L. 1993 *The birth of the despot: Venice and the sublime porte*, trans. A. Denner. Ithaca: Cornell University Press (French edition, 1987)
Vico, G. 1984 [1744]. *New science*. Ithaca: Cornell University Press
Viguera, M. 1994 Asludu li'l-ma'ālı: on the social status of Andalusi women. In S. K. Jayyusi (ed.), *The legacy of Muslim Spain*. Leiden: Brill
Villing, A. 2005 Persia and Greece. In J. Curtis, and Tallis, N. (eds.), *Forgotten empire: the world of ancient Persia*. London: British Museum.
Von Staden, H. 1992 Affinities and visions – Helen and hellenocentrism. *Isis*, 83: 578–95
Wallerstein, I. 1974 *The modern world-system*, vol. I: *Capitalist agriculture and the origins of European world-economy in the sixteenth century*. New York: Academic Press
  1999 The west, capitalism and the modern world system. In T. Brook and G. Blue (eds.), *China and historical capitalism*. Cambridge: Cambridge University Press
Walzer, R. 1962 *Greek into Arabic*. Oxford: B. Cassirer
Ward, W. A. 1971 *Egypt and the east Mediterranean world 2200–1900 BC*. Beirut: The American University of Beirut
Ward-Perkins, B. 2000 Specialised production and exchange. *The Cambridge Ancient History*, vol. XIV. Cambridge: Cambridge University Press
Watson, A. M. 1983 *Agricultural innovation in the early Islamic world: the diffusion of crops and farming techniques, 700–1100*. Cambridge: Cambridge University Press
Watt, I. P. 1957 *The rise of the novel*. London: Chatto
Watt, W. M. 1972 *The influence of Islam on medieval Europe*. Edinburgh: Edinburgh University Press
Weber, M. 1930 *The Protestant ethic and the spirit of capitalism*. London: Allen and Unwin
  1949 *The methodology of the social sciences* (trans. E. A. Shils and H. A. Finch). Glencoe, IL: The Free Press
  1968 *Economy and society. An outline of interpretive sociology*. Translated and edited by Guenther Roth and Claus Wittich. New York: Bedminster Press.
  1976 *The agrarian sociology of ancient civilizations*. London: NLB
Weis, R., 2001 *The yellow cross: the story of the last Cathars, 1290–1329*. London: Penguin
Weiss, W. M. and K. M. Westerman 1998 *The Bazaar: markets and merchants of the Islamic world*. London: Thames and Hudson
Whitby, M. 2000 The army c. 420–602. *The Cambridge ancient history*, vol. XIV. Cambridge: Cambridge University Press
White, K. D. 1970 *Roman farming*. London: Thames and Hudson
  1984 *Greek and Roman technology*. London: Thames and Hudson
White, L. 1962 *Medieval technology and social change*. Oxford: Clarendon Press

White, S. D. 1996 The 'feudal revolution'. *Past and Present* 152: 205–23

Whittaker, C. R. 2004 *Rome and its frontiers: the dynamics of empire*. London: Routledge

Wickham, C. 1984 The other transition: from the ancient world to feudalism. *Past and Present* 103: 3–36

2001 Un pas vers le Moyen Age? Permanences et mutations. In P. Ouzoulias *et al.* (eds.) *Les campagnes de la Gaule à la fin de l'antiquité*. Antibes: Editions ACDCA

Will, E. 1954 Trois quarts de siècle de recherches sur l'economie greque antique. *Annales E.S.C.* 9: 7–22

Wilson, A. 1995 Water power in north Africa and the development of the horizontal water wheel. *Journal of Roman Archeology* 8: 499–510

Wittfogel, K. 1957 *Oriental despotism*. New Haven: Yale University Press

Wolf, A. P. and Huang, C.-S. 1980 *Marriage and adoption in China, 1845–1945*. Stanford, CA: Stanford University Press

Wolf, E. R. 1982 *Europe and the people without history*. Berkeley: University of California Press

Wong, R. Bin 1999 The political economy and agrarian empire and its modern legacy. In T. Brook and G. Blue (eds.), *China and historical capitalism*. Cambridge: Cambridge University Press

Worsley, P. 1957 *The trumpet shall sound: a study of cargo cults in Melanesia*. London: MacGibbon and Kee

Wrigley, E. A. 2004 *Poverty, progress and population*. Cambridge: Cambridge University Press

Yalman, N. O. 2001 Further observations on love (or equality). In J. Warner (ed.) *Cultural horizons*. Syracuse, NY: Syracuse University Press

Zafrani, H. 1986 *Juifs d'Andalousie et du Maghreb*. Paris: Maisonneuve Larose

1994 *Los judíos del occidente musulmán: Al-Andalus y el Magreb*. Madrid: Editorial Mapfre

Zan, L. 2004 Accounting and management discourse in proto-industrial settings: the Venice Arsenal in the turn of the 16th century. *Accounting and Business Research* 34: 2, 345–78

Zilfi, M. C. 1996 Women and society in the Tulip Era, 1718–1730. Amira El Aazhary Sonbol (ed.), *Women, the family, divorce laws in Islamic history*. Syracuse, New York: Syracuse University Press

Žižek, S. 2001 A Leftist plea for 'Eurocentrism'. In *Unpacking Europe: towards a critical reading*, S. Hassan and I. Dadi (eds.). Rotterdam: NAI Publishers

Zurndorfer, H. T. 2004 Not bound to China: Étienne Balasz, Fernand Braudel and the politics of the study of Chinese history in post-war France. *Past & Present* 185: 189–221

Index

Lightning Source UK Ltd.
Milton Keynes UK
UKHW020748280421
382689UK00013B/206

9 781107 683556